Cracking the

PSAT/ NMSQT®

with 2 Practice Tests, 2019 Edition

The Staff of the Princeton Review

PrincetonReview.com

Penguin
Random
House

The Princeton Review
110 East 42nd Street, 7th Floor
New York, NY 10017
E-mail: editorialsupport@review.com

ISBN: 978-0-525-56787-5
eBook ISBN: 978-0-525-56791-2
ISSN: 1549-6120

PSAT/NMSQT is a registered trademark of the College Board and the National Merit Scholarship Corporation, which are not affiliated with, and do not endorse, this product.

The Princeton Review is not affiliated with Princeton University.

Editor: Meave Shelton
Production Editors: Kathy G. Carter and Lee Elder
Production Artist: Deborah A. Weber

Printed in the United States of America.

10 9 8 7 6 5 4 3 2 1

2019 Edition

FEB 1 2 2019

Editorial

Rob Franek, Editor-in-Chief
Mary Beth Garrick, Executive Director of Production
Craig Patches, Production Design Manager
Selena Coppock, Managing Editor
Meave Shelton, Senior Editor
Colleen Day, Editor
Sarah Litt, Editor
Aaron Riccio, Editor
Orion McBean, Associate Editor

Penguin Random House Publishing Team

Tom Russell, VP, Publisher
Alison Stoltzfus, Publishing Director
Amanda Yee, Associate Managing Editor
Ellen Reed, Production Manager
Suzanne Lee, Designer

Acknowledgments

Special thanks to Sara Kuperstein for her contributions to this edition, as well as Jonathan Chiu for his expert guidance.

Thanks also to Chris Knuth, Jim Havens, Tony Krupp, Anne Goldberg, Chris Chimera, Christina Bonvicino, and Spencer LeDoux.

The Princeton Review would also like to thank Debbie Weber, Kathy Carter, and Lee Elder for their time and attention to each page.

Special thanks to Adam Robinson, who conceived of and perfected the Joe Bloggs approach to standardized tests, and many other techniques in this book.

Contents

Get More (Free) Content

1 Go to **PrincetonReview.com/cracking.**

2 Enter the following ISBN for your book: 9780525567875.

3 Answer a few simple questions to set up an exclusive Princeton Review account. (If you already have one, you can just log in.)

4 Click the "Account Home" button, also found under "My Account" from the top toolbar. You're all set to access My Campus and your bonus content!

Need to report a potential **content** issue?

Contact **EditorialSupport@review.com.**
Include:

- full title of the book
- ISBN number
- page number

Need to report a **technical** issue?

Contact **TPRStudentTech@review.com**
and provide:

- your full name
- email address used to register the book
- full book title and ISBN
- computer OS (Mac/PC) and browser (Firefox, Safari, etc.)

The **Princeton** Review®

Once you've registered, you can...

- Take a full-length practice PSAT, SAT, and ACT

- Get valuable advice about the college application process, including tips for writing a great essay and where to apply for financial aid

- If you're still choosing between colleges, use our searchable rankings of *The Best 384 Colleges* to find out more information about your dream school

- Access printable resources, including a score conversion table, a study guide, and extra bubble sheets for the practice tests in this book

- Check to see if there have been any corrections or updates to this edition

- Get our take on any recent or pending updates to the PSAT/NMSQT

Look For These Icons Throughout The Book

 ONLINE ARTICLES

 PROVEN TECHNIQUES

 APPLIED STRATEGIES

 STUDY BREAK

 MORE GREAT BOOKS

 COLLEGE ADVISOR

Part I
Orientation

Chapter 1
What Is the PSAT/NMSQT?

The PSAT/NMSQT—from now on, we'll just call it the PSAT—is a standardized test given primarily to high school juniors to give them a "preliminary" idea of how well they could do on SAT question types. The test is also used to determine which students are eligible for National Merit Scholar recognition. This chapter will give you a general overview of the test and how it is used, along with the basics to start your preparation. First, a glimpse at the other tests in the College Board's Suite of Assessments: the PSAT 8/9 and the PSAT 10.

PSAT 8/9

Just like the SAT and PSAT, the PSAT 8/9, which is designed for eighth and ninth graders, contains a Reading Test, a Writing and Language Test, and a Math Test. The content of each subject is comparable as it consists of core areas of focus.

Psst...

There's the PSAT 8/9, the PSAT 10, and PSAT/NMSQT. But when we refer to just the plain old "PSAT" in this book, we're referring to the PSAT/NMSQT.

According to the College Board, the "Evidence-Based Reading and Writing section asks you to interpret, synthesize, and use evidence found in a wide range of sources." The bottom line: Be prepared to justify your selected answer with evidence from the passage and/or graph provided. This test is still not about making up anything, but finding the correct answer based on the text.

The College Board also claims that the "Math Test focuses in-depth on two essential areas of math: Problem Solving and Data Analysis, and Heart of Algebra." The bottom line: expect to see Algebra I and II, some Geometry, as well as questions that have charts, graphs, data tables, scatterplots, or other form of data display provided.

The Math Test is split into two sections: one in which a calculator may be used and one in which it may not be used. Even though a calculator is allowed in one section, it is up to the test taker to determine whether the calculator will be a benefit in solving a question. According to the College Board, "students who make use of structure or their ability to reason will probably finish before students who use a calculator." The bottom line: show your work and use the calculator for tedious calculations, but a calculator most likely will not be necessary to solve a majority of the questions.

All questions in the Evidence-Based Reading and Writing section are multiple choice. Most of the Math Test questions are multiple choice, with 18 percent of all Math Test questions in the grid-in, or student-produced, format. For each question answered correctly, one raw point is earned, and there is no penalty for an incorrect response or a question left blank. The bottom line: don't leave anything blank!

PSAT 10

Though this test is called the PSAT 10, it is identical to the structure of the PSAT/NMSQT in terms of both number of questions and time limits per section. The major differences are who takes the test and when: 10th-graders and schools choose a date in the spring. Additionally, this test does not qualify you for National Merit Scholarship consideration.

Just as with the SAT and the PSAT, the PSAT 10 includes an Evidence-Based Reading and Writing section and a Math Test. The Evidence-Based Reading and Writing section tests the ability to select, among the choices provided, the answer that is best evidenced in the provided passage and/or informational graphics that accompany select passages. The Math Test is divided into two sections: one in which a calculator may be used and one in which it may not be used. Even though the calculator is allowed in one section, it is up to the test taker to determine whether or not the calculator will prove necessary.

WHAT'S WITH ALL THE CHANGES?

The PSAT has gone through a massive overhaul in both its structure and format. The College Board no longer deems it necessary to memorize randomly obscure vocabulary words that are forgotten the second the test is completed.

The College Board now maintains that the best way to prepare for the test is to

- take challenging courses
- do your homework
- prepare for tests and quizzes
- ask and answer lots of questions

College admissions advisors wanted a more "well-rounded" picture of the applicant, so the College Board did its best to meet the demand. The test provides a measurement of four Evidence-Based Reading and Writing Subscores (Command of Evidence, Words in Context, Standard English Conventions, and Expression of Ideas), and three Math Subscores (Heart of Algebra, Problem Solving and Data Analysis, and Passport to Advanced Math).

In addition to the seven subscores reported, the College Board now provides two cross-test scores to offer more insight: one score for Analysis in History/Social Studies and another for Analysis in Science. Remain calm; these scores are gathered only from select questions that deal with appropriate subject matter and are not actual entire test sections. We will go into PSAT scoring in more detail later.

How Do You Pronounce PSAT/NMSQT, Anyway?
Ah, yes—first things first. Well, to be honest, we're not really sure. You can pronounce it *pee-sat-nim-squit* if you want. However, we think it's easier just to call it the PSAT.

When Is the PSAT Given?

The PSAT is officially administered twice each year, typically on a Wednesday and Saturday of the same week in October. Your school will announce the exact dates at the beginning of the school year, or you can find out at PrincetonReview.com, or the College Board at CollegeBoard.com.

Keep on Schedule
You'll officially take the PSAT in the fall of your junior year. Plan to take the SAT anytime between the winter of your junior year and the fall of your senior year.

How Do I Sign Up for the PSAT?

You don't have to do anything to sign up for the PSAT; your school will do all the work for you. Test registration fees can vary from school to school, so be sure to check with your school counselor if you have questions about how much the PSAT will cost you.

What About Students with Special Needs?

If you have a diagnosed learning difference, you will probably qualify for special accommodations on the PSAT. However, it's important that you get the process started early. The first step is to speak to your school counselor who handles learning differences. Only he or she can file the appropriate paperwork. You'll also need to gather some information (documentation of your condition) from a licensed practitioner and some other information from your school. Then your school counselor will file the application for you.

You will need to apply for accommodations only once; with that single application you'll qualify for accommodations on the PSAT, SAT, SAT Subject Tests, and AP Exams. The one exception to this rule is that if you change schools, you'll need to have a counselor at the new school refile your paperwork.

Does the PSAT Play a Role in College Admissions?

No! The PSAT plays no role in college admissions. It's really just a practice test for the SAT.

The one exception is for that very small group of students, about 4 percent of all students nationwide, whose PSAT scores qualify them for National Merit recognition. (We'll tell you more than you ever wanted to know about that in the next chapter.) Recognition as a commended scholar, semifinalist, or finalist for National Merit is a fairly impressive addition to your college admissions portfolio, and is something that you should certainly pursue if you are seriously in contention for it.

Want to know which colleges are best for you? Check out The Princeton Review's College Advisor app to build your ideal college list and find your perfect college fit! Available for free in the iOS App Store and Google Play Store.

What Happens to the Score Report from the PSAT?

Only you, your high school, and the National Merit Scholarship Corporation (which co-sponsors the PSAT) will receive copies of your score reports. They won't be sent to colleges.

WHAT DOES THE PSAT TEST?

First off, while the PSAT may have recently changed, we at The Princeton Review understand that certain fundamentals of a test always stay the same. As you begin your prep, it's useful to remember that the PSAT is not a test of aptitude, how good of a person you are, or how successful you will be in life. The PSAT simply tests how well you take the PSAT. That's it. And performing well on the PSAT is a skill that can be learned like any other. The Princeton Review was founded more than 30 years ago on this very simple idea, and—as our students' test scores show—our approach is the one that works.

All of these changes to tests that you hear could heavily influence your college admission strategy can be extremely daunting. However, remember that any standardized test is a coachable test. A beatable test. Just remember:

The PSAT doesn't measure the stuff that matters. It measures neither intelligence nor the depth and breadth of what you're learning in high school. It doesn't predict college grades as well as your high school grades do. Colleges know there is more to you as a student—and as a person—than what you do on a single test.

Who Writes the PSAT?

The PSAT is administered by Educational Testing Service (ETS) on behalf of the College Board and National Merit Scholarship Corporation. You might think that the people at ETS and the College Board are educators, professors of education, or teachers. They're not. They are people who just happen to make a living writing tests. In fact, they write hundreds of tests, for all kinds of organizations.

The folks at ETS and the College Board aren't really paid to educate; they're paid to write and administer tests. And even though you'll be paying them to take the PSAT, you're not their customer. The actual customers ETS and the College Board cater to are the colleges, which get the information they want at no cost. This means that you should take everything that the College Board says with a grain of salt and realize that its testing "advice" isn't always the best advice. (Getting testing advice from the College Board is a bit like getting baseball advice from the opposing team.)

Every test reflects the interests of the people who write it. If you know who writes the test, you will know a lot more about what kinds of answers will be considered "correct" answers on that test.

WHAT IS THE PRINCETON REVIEW?

The Princeton Review is the nation's leading test-preparation company. In just a few years, we became the nation's leader in SAT preparation, primarily because our techniques work. We offer courses and private tutoring for all of the major standardized tests, and we publish a series of books to help in your search for the right school. If you'd like more information about our programs or books, give us a call at 800-2-Review, or check out our website at PrincetonReview.com.

> **Shortcuts**
> The Princeton Review's techniques are the closest thing there is to a shortcut to the PSAT. However, there is no shortcut to learning these techniques.

HOW TO USE THIS BOOK

This book is divided into two main parts. The first three parts of the book (Chapters 1–12 and the subsequent Drill Answers and Explanations) contain both general testing strategies and question-specific problem-solving instruction. The back of the book (Chapters 13–16) contains two practice PSATs. The "Session-by-Session Study Guide" starting on page 9 will give you a plan of attack for these tests and the rest of the book. There is no single plan that will fit everyone, so be prepared to adapt to the plan and use it according to your own needs.

Practice Test 1 will give you an idea of your strengths and weaknesses, both of which can be sources of improvement. If you're already good at something, additional practice can make you great at it; if you're not so good at something, what you should do about it depends on how important it is. If the concept is one that frequently appears on the test, you should spend a lot of time on it; if it comes up only once in a while, you should spend very little time working on it and remember that it's something you should either put off until you've completed easier things or skip it entirely.

How do you know what's important? We'll tell you throughout this book, when we discuss techniques like Plugging In and so forth, but you can also get an idea of what to focus on simply by observing how this book is laid out. For example, if you're shaky on critical reading, you know you'll need to devote some time to Reading questions because there are a total of 47 such questions on the test. And if you're not so confident when it comes to geometry, don't panic: geometry questions appear only in the Advanced Math Principles chapter, which tells you that this topic isn't as much of a priority as Plugging In or Math Basics.

Time Management

To manage your PSAT preparation, make use of the study guide on the following pages. This guide will break down the seemingly daunting task of PSAT prep into bite-sized pieces we call "sessions." We have mapped out tasks for each session to be sure you get the most out of this book. Sessions will generally take between an hour or two, unless you're taking a practice test. The tests will be the first and last sessions, so you should be sure to plan to have about two and a half hours for these sessions. Most other sessions will last between an hour and two hours, so plan to take a short break in the middle, and if it looks like the session is going to exceed two hours, feel free to stop and pick up where you left off on the next day.

When You Take a Practice Test

You'll see when to take practice tests in the session outlines. Here are some guidelines for taking these tests:

- Time yourself strictly. Use a timer, watch, or stopwatch that will ring, and do not allow yourself to go over time for any section. If you try to do so at the real test, your scores will probably be canceled.
- Take a practice test in one sitting, allowing yourself breaks of no more than two minutes between sections. You need to build up your endurance for the real test, and you also need an accurate picture of how you will do.
- Always take a practice test using an answer sheet with bubbles to fill in, just as you will for the real test. For the practice tests in the book, use the answer sheets provided at the back of this book. You need to be comfortable transferring answers to the separate sheet because you will be skipping around a bit.
- Each bubble you choose should be filled in thoroughly, and no other marks should be made in the answer area.
- As you fill in the bubble for a question, check to be sure you are on the correct number on the answer sheet. If you fill in the wrong bubble on the answer sheet, it won't matter if you've worked out the problem correctly in the test booklet. All that matters to the machine scoring the test is the No. 2 pencil mark.

Session-by-Session Study Guide

Session Zero You're involved in this session right now. Finish reading the first chapter so you'll know what the test is about, why it is important for you to take, and what to expect from the rest of the book. This step probably won't take you long, so if you have a couple of hours after you complete Chapter 1, you can go on to Session One and take the first practice test.

Session One Take Practice Test 1 (in the back of this book) and score it. You'll use this result to get an idea of how many questions on each section you should attempt before guessing strategically, and the parts of the math sections you should concentrate on.

Session Two Work through Chapters 2 and 3 of the Orientation and Chapter 4, Reading Comprehension.

Session Three Read Chapter 5, Introduction to Writing and Language Strategy, along with Chapter 6, Punctuation.

Session Four Work through the Math Basics in Chapter 9 and the corresponding drills.

Session Five Work through the Math Techniques section in Chapter 10 and associated drills. Take a look at Chapter 7, Words.

Session Six Review Advanced Math Principles, Chapter 11. As you work through this chapter, be sure to apply techniques like Plugging In that you learned in Chapter 10. Since these techniques are central to doing well on the math sections, you can never practice them too much. If there's time, start Chapter 12.

Session Seven Work through the Additional Math Topics in Chapter 12. When you finish, read through Chapter 8, Questions. This will give you a good idea of how the PSAT will put together all the things you've gone over for the Writing and Language section of the test.

Session Eight Take Practice Test 2. Use the techniques you've been practicing throughout the book. Score your test and go through the explanations, focusing on where you may have missed the opportunity to use a technique and your decisions about whether you should have attempted a question or not, given your pacing goals and Personal Order of Difficulty.

Some of the terminology in the study guide may be unfamiliar to you now, but don't worry, you'll get to know it soon. Also, you'll want to refer back to this study guide at each session to keep yourself on track.

One important note: In this book, sample questions do not appear in numerical order within a chapter. For example, you might see a question 4 followed by a question 14. This is because on the PSAT, a higher question number generally indicates a higher level of difficulty—for the Math questions in particular (this is not so much the case with Reading or Writing and Language.) Chapter 3 has great advice on how to crack some of the most difficult questions.

> **…The Less to Study**
> While higher-level math may sound scary at first, stay tuned for further information from us on the most effective techniques to use on the PSAT that can, sometimes, drastically reduce the math complexity for many questions.

HOW IS THE PSAT STRUCTURED AND SCORED?

Category	PSAT/NMSQT (as of fall 2015)
Time	2 hours and 45 minutes
Components	• Evidence-Based Reading and Writing: Reading; Writing and Language • Math
Number of Questions, Time by Section	Reading: 47 Questions, 60 minutes Writing and Language: 44 Questions, 35 minutes Math: 48 Questions, 70 minutes
Important Features	• Emphasis on reasoning and a strong focus on the knowledge, skills, and understandings important to college and career readiness and success • Emphasis on the meaning of words in extended contexts and on how word choice shapes meaning, tone, and impact • Rights-only scoring (a point for a correct answer but no deduction for an incorrect answer; blank responses have no impact on score)
Score Reporting	• Scored on a scale of 320–1520 that will be the sum of the two section scores (Evidence-Based Reading and Writing and Math) that range from 160–760
Subscore Reporting	Subscores for every test, providing added insight for students, parents, educators, and counselors
Answer Choices	4 answer choices for multiple-choice questions

According to the College Board, the PSAT redesign of 2015 raised the complexity of questions across the board. For the Reading and Writing and Language Tests, this refers in part to the way in which all questions are now connected to full passages, which are themselves purportedly aligned with what introductory college courses and vocational training programs offer. This means that there will be a good amount of history- and science-based reading material. Additionally, there are no longer any fill-in-the-blank sentence completion questions or stand-alone sentence-editing questions. Instead, the PSAT tests your ability to demonstrate a full understanding of a source's ideas.

Moreover, the scope of math content focuses on a specific set of problem-solving and analytical topics, and it includes high-level content like trigonometry. You are also likely to encounter more grid-in questions, and you will face topics that are both specifically geared to test your ability to use a calculator and for which calculators are not permitted.

The Math Test is divided into two sections, one with the calculator, with 31 questions over the course of 45 minutes, and one without, with 17 questions administered in 25 minutes. Because of the tight time limit, particularly in the No Calculator section, you should work as efficiently as possible. Therefore, even if you answer a question correctly, we recommend that you review the explanations for the problems in the drills and the practice tests. You may discover techniques that help to shave seconds from your solutions. A large part of what's being tested is your ability to use the appropriate tools in a strategic fashion, and while there may be multiple ways to solve a given problem, you'll want to focus on the most efficient.

Scoring on the PSAT

The PSAT is scored on a scale of 320–1520, which is the sum of the two section scores that range from 160–760. The two sections are the Evidence-Based Reading and Writing section and the Mathematics section. Wrong answers to multiple-choice questions are not penalized, so you're advised never to leave a question blank—even if that means blindly picking a letter and bubbling it in for any uncompleted questions before time runs out.

In addition to the overall total score and the section scores, you'll find several subscores on your PSAT score report:

An **Analysis in History/Social Studies** and **Analysis in Science** cross-test score is generated based on questions from all three of the subject tests (Math included!), and these assess the cross-curricular application of the tested skills to other contexts. Relax! This doesn't mean that you have to start cramming dates and anatomy—every question can be answered from the context of a given reading passage or the data included in a table or figure. The only changes have to do with the content of the passages and questions themselves.

Additionally, the Math Test is broken into several categories, as we've done in this book. The **Heart of Algebra** subscore looks specifically at how well students understand how to handle algebraic expressions, work with a variety of algebraic equations, and relate real-world scenarios to algebraic principles. **Problem Solving and Data Analysis** focuses more on interpretation of mathematical expressions, graphical analysis, and data interpretation. Your ability to not only understand what a problem is asking, but also to represent it in your own words, will come in handy here. **Passport to Advanced Mathematics** questions showcase the higher-level math that's been added to the test, from quadratics and their graphs to the creation and translation of functions.

Finally, there is an **Additional Topics** domain that's filled with what you might consider wild-card material. Although these questions might not correlate directly to a subscore, six of these miscellaneous types will show up on the redesigned test. In the Verbal portions of the test, the **Command of Evidence** subscore measures how well you can translate and cite specific lines that back up your interpretation, while the **Relevant Words in Context** subscore ensures that you can select the best definition for how a word is used in a passage. The Writing and Language Test additionally measures **Expression of Ideas**, which deals with revising language in order to make more logical and cohesive arguments, and **Standard English Conventions**, which assesses your ability to conform to the basic rules of English structure, punctuation, and usage.

Scoring Your Practice Tests
As you can see, scoring is a little tricky. That's why we provide scoring tables to help you determine your approximate score. When we say that the score is "approximate," we mean that the score is accurate for that particular test. However, the number of questions you need to get right or wrong to earn a certain score can vary depending on the PSAT's scale from test to test. For example, if you miss 10 Math questions and get a 680 on a practice test, that does not necessarily mean that 10 missed Math questions on the actual exam will result in a 680 as well; it could be 8 questions or 12 questions.

HOW DOES THE SAT DIFFER FROM THE PSAT?

The SAT does not differ significantly from the PSAT in structure and timing! Indeed, the PSAT's Reading Test, which contains 5 fewer questions, is only 5 minutes shorter than the SAT's Reading Test. The Writing and Language Test is the same in terms of length and timing for both tests. The PSAT's Math Test has only 10 fewer total questions as compared to those of the SAT's Math Test. The tables below summarize the differences—or actually, the similarities!—of the two tests.

Here's a breakdown of how the tests differ:

	SAT	PSAT
Structure	4 (+ optional Essay) sections	4 sections
Length	3 hours (+ 50 minutes for Essay)	2 hours 45 minutes
Purpose	College admissions	NMSQT
Scoring	1600	1520

Are You Ready for the SAT?

If you want to start preparing for the SAT, pick up a copy of our *Cracking the SAT Premium,* which is chock full of content review, strategy, and realistic practice!

What Does the PSAT Score Mean for My SAT Score?

The SAT is scored on a 1600 scale, whereas the PSAT is scored on a 1520 scale. However, because the PSAT and SAT are aligned by the College Board to be scored on the same scale, your PSAT score indicates the approximate SAT score you would earn were you to have taken the SAT on that same day.

How Much Should I Prepare for the PSAT?

If you're in that very small percentage of students who are in contention for National Merit recognition, it may be worth your while to put in a good deal of time to prepare for this test. After all, your extra hard work may well put you in a better position for National Merit recognition. Otherwise, you should prepare enough so that you feel more in control of the test and have a better testing experience. (Nothing feels quite as awful as being dragged through a testing experience feeling like you don't know what you're being tested on or what to expect—except perhaps dental surgery.) The other reason to prepare for the PSAT is that it will give you some testing skills that will help you begin to prepare for the tests that actually count, namely the SAT and SAT Subject Tests.

The bottom line is this: the best reason to prepare for the PSAT is that it will help you get an early start on your preparation for the SAT.

Study

If you were getting ready to take a biology test, you'd study biology. If you were preparing for a basketball game, you'd practice basketball. So, if you're preparing for the PSAT (and eventually the SAT), study the PSAT. The PSAT can't test everything, so concentrate on learning what it *does* test.

Chapter 2
All About the National Merit Scholarships

The NMSQT part of the name PSAT/NMSQT stands for National Merit Scholarship Qualifying Test. That means that the PSAT serves as the test that will establish whether or not you are eligible for National Merit recognition. This chapter will help you figure out what that may mean for you.

WHAT IS THE NATIONAL MERIT SCHOLARSHIP PROGRAM?

You might think that the PSAT is simply a warm-up for the SAT, but the National Merit Scholarship Program makes the PSAT an important test in its own right.

The mission of National Merit Scholarship Corporation (NMSC) is to recognize and honor the academically talented students of the United States. NMSC accomplishes this mission by conducting nationwide academic scholarship programs. The enduring goals of NMSC's scholarship programs are the following:

- to promote a wider and deeper respect for learning in general and for exceptionally talented individuals in particular
- to shine a spotlight on brilliant students and encourage the pursuit of academic excellence at all levels of education
- to stimulate increased support from organizations that wish to sponsor scholarships for outstanding scholastic talent

The National Merit Scholarship Program is an academic competition for recognition and scholarships that began in 1955. High school students enter the National Merit Program by taking the Preliminary SAT/National Merit Scholarship Qualifying Test (PSAT/NMSQT) and by meeting published program entry and participation requirements.

HOW DO I QUALIFY FOR NATIONAL MERIT?

To participate in the National Merit Scholarship Program, a student must:

1. take the PSAT/NMSQT in the specified year of the high school program and **no later than** the third year in grades 9 through 12, regardless of grade classification or educational pattern;
2. be enrolled as a high school student (traditional or homeschooled), progressing normally toward graduation or completion of high school, and planning to enroll full time in college no later than the fall following completion of high school; and
3. be a citizen of the United States; or be a U.S. lawful permanent resident (or have applied for permanent residence, the application for which has not been denied) and intend to become a U.S. citizen at the earliest opportunity allowed by law.

The Index

How does your PSAT score qualify you for National Merit? The National Merit Scholarship Corporation uses a selection index, which is the sum of your Reading, Writing and Language, and Math Test scores that are each on a scale of 8–38. Those three test scores are added together and then multiplied by 2 to calculate your Selection Index score that has a range of 48–228. Qualifying scores for National Merit recognition will vary from state to state, so check with your school counselor as to what the cutoff score is that year for your particular state. For instance, if your PSAT scores were 24 Math, 22 Reading, and 30 Writing and Language, your index would be 152.

Math   +   Reading   +   Writing and Language   =   Test Scores
                                                        Total

24   +   22   +   30   =   76

National Merit Selection Index

76 × 2 = 152

The Awards and the Process

In the fall of their senior year, about 50,000 students will receive one of two letters from NMSC (National Merit Scholarship Corporation): either a Letter of Commendation or a letter stating that they have qualified as semifinalists for National Merit.

Commended Students   Roughly two-thirds of these students (about 34,000 total students each year) will receive a Letter of Commendation by virtue of their high scores on the test. This looks great on your college application, so if you have a reasonable chance of getting one, it's definitely worth your time to prepare for the PSAT. Make no mistake, though, these letters are not easy to get. They are awarded to students who score between the 95th and the mid-99th percentiles—that means to the top four to five percent in the country.

If you receive this honorable mention from NMSC, you should be extremely proud of yourself. Even though you won't continue in the process for National Merit scholarships, this commendation does make you eligible for special scholarships sponsored by certain companies and organizations, which vary in their amounts and eligibility requirements.

Semifinalists   The other third of these students—those 16,000 students who score in the upper 99th percentile in their states—will be notified that they are National Merit semifinalists. If you qualify, you'll get a letter announcing your status as a semifinalist, along with information about the requirements for qualification as a finalist. These include maintaining high grades, performing well on your SAT, and getting an endorsement from your principal.

Becoming a National Merit semifinalist is quite impressive, and if you manage it, you should certainly mention it on your college applications.

What does "scoring in the upper 99th percentile in the state" mean? It means that you're essentially competing against the other people in your state for those semifinalist positions. Since some states have higher average scores than others, this means that if you're in states like New York, New Jersey, Maryland, Connecticut, or Massachusetts, you need a higher score to qualify than if you live in other states.

Finalists   The majority of semifinalists (more than 90 percent) go on to qualify as finalists. Students who meet all of the eligibility requirements will be notified in February of their senior year that they have qualified as finalists. This means that they are now eligible for scholarship money, though it doesn't necessarily mean that they'll get any. In fact, only about half of National Merit finalists actually win scholarships through NMSC. What determines whether a student gets money or not? There is a final screening process, based on criteria that NMSC doesn't release to the public, to determine who actually gets these scholarships. 2,500 finalists earn $2,500 one-time scholarships from NMSC, and approximately 1,000 more win corporate-sponsored merit scholarships, which are typically given to children of the sponsors' employees, residents of certain communities, and students who plan to study or work in specific fields. The monetary amount of corporate-sponsored scholarships can be anywhere from $500–$10,000, and some are one-time scholarships while others are given for each year of study. Some students who meet the corporation's qualifications but aren't finalists will also earn Special Scholarships. Approximately an additional 4,000 students will be offered college-sponsored scholarships from the schools they plan to attend. These awards range from $500 to $2,000 and are renewable for four years.

Though the amounts of money may not be huge, every little bit helps. One other point to keep in mind is that while most of the scholarships through NMSC are relatively small, many universities seek out National Merit finalists because of their academic abilities and (who are we kidding?) because the universities like to brag about how many such students chose them. For this reason, a number of state schools and less elite universities offer significant scholarships to National Merit finalists and sometimes semifinalists as well. Some schools offer full tuition for National Merit finalists, including the University of Alabama, University of Central Florida, University of Kentucky, University of Mississippi, University of Nevada—Las Vegas, Baylor University, and quite a few others. Many more schools award incomplete but large scholarships to National Merit finalists and semifinalists.

Aside from the possibility of winning a scholarship, the award itself looks great in your portfolio. So if you think you are in contention for National Merit recognition, practice diligently and smartly! If not, don't sweat it too much, but prepare for the PSAT anyway because it is good practice for the SAT.

If you're willing to forego the name-brand recognition of an Ivy, a state school can be an excellent choice—and if it offers you a National Merit scholarship, the trade-off can be more than worth it. Check out our megaguide, *The Complete Book of Colleges,* for well-researched profiles of over 1,000 public and private schools.

But I'm Not a Junior in High School Yet...
If you are not yet a junior, and you're interested in National Merit, you will have to take the test again your junior year in order to qualify.

A certain number of schools give the PSAT to students in their sophomore year—and sometimes even earlier. These schools hope that earlier exposure to these tests will help their students perform better in later years. If you're not yet in your junior year, the PSAT won't count for National Merit scholarship purposes, so it's really just a trial run for you. It's still a good idea to go into the test prepared in order to feel and perform your best. After all, there's nothing more unpleasant than an unpleasant testing experience, except maybe having a tooth drilled or watching the sad downward spiral of certain pop stars.

What If I'm in a Three-Year or Other Nonstandard Course of Study?

If you're going to spend only three years in secondary school, you have two options for when to take the PSAT for National Merit purposes: you can take it either in your next-to-last year or in your last year of secondary school. However, our advice is this: if you're in any program other than a usual four-year high school, be sure to talk to your school counselor. He or she will consult with NMSC and help ensure that you take the PSAT at the right time. This is important, because not taking the PSAT at the right time can disqualify you from National Merit recognition.

What If I Miss the PSAT Administration My Junior Year?

If you aren't concerned about National Merit scholarships, there's no reason to do anything in particular—except, perhaps, to obtain a few PSAT booklets to practice with, just to see what fun you missed.

However, if you want to be eligible for National Merit recognition, then swift action on your part is required. If an emergency arises that prevents you from taking the PSAT, you should write to the National Merit Scholarship Corporation *immediately* to request alternate testing dates. If your request is received soon enough, it should be able to accommodate you. (NMSC says that this kind of request must absolutely be received by April 1 following the missed PSAT administration.) You'll also need a signature from a school official.

For More Information

If you have any questions or problems, the best person to consult is your school counselor, who can help make sure you're on the right track. If you need further help, contact your local Princeton Review office at 800-2-REVIEW or Princeton-Review.com. Or, you can contact National Merit directly:

National Merit Scholarship Corporation
1560 Sherman Avenue, Suite 200
Evanston, IL 60201-4897
(847) 866-5100
NationalMerit.org

Advice from the Experts
If you're thinking about starting the college search or have already started, our *College Insider* is a fantastic resource that covers all things college admissions. Head over to My Campus to download your copy! Instructions are on the "Get More (Free) Content" spread at the beginning of this book.

Chapter 3
General Strategies

The first step to cracking the PSAT is to know how best to approach the test. The PSAT is not like the tests you've taken in school, so you need to learn to look at it in a different way. This chapter will show test-taking strategies that immediately improve your score. Make sure you fully understand these concepts before moving on to Part II. Good luck!

BASIC PRINCIPLES OF CRACKING THE TEST

What ETS Is Good At

The folks at ETS have been writing standardized tests for more than 80 years, and they write tests for all sorts of programs. They have administered the test so many times that they know exactly how you will approach it. They know how you'll attack certain questions, what sort of mistakes you'll probably make, and even what answer you'll be most likely to pick. Freaky, isn't it?

However, ETS's strength is also a weakness. Because the test is standardized, the PSAT has to ask the same type of questions over and over again. Sure, the numbers or the words might change, but the basics don't. With enough practice, you can learn to think like the test writers. But try to use your powers for good, okay?

The PSAT Isn't School

Our job isn't to teach you math or English—leave that to your supersmart school teachers. Instead, we're going to teach you what the PSAT is and how to crack the PSAT. You'll soon see that the PSAT involves a very different skill set.

> **No Penalty for Incorrect Answers!**
> You will NOT be penalized on the PSAT for any wrong answers. This means you should always guess, even if this means choosing an answer at random.

Be warned that some of the approaches we're going to show you may seem counterintuitive or unnatural. Some of these strategies may be very different from the way you learned to approach similar questions in school, but trust us! Try tackling the problems using our techniques, and keep practicing until they become easier. You'll see a real improvement in your score.

Let's take a look at the questions.

Cracking Multiple-Choice Questions

What's the capital of Azerbaijan?

Give up?

Unless you spend your spare time studying an atlas, you may not even know that Azerbaijan is a real country, much less what its capital is. If this question came up on a test, you'd have to skip it, wouldn't you? Well, maybe not. Let's turn this question into a multiple-choice question—just like all the questions on the PSAT Reading Test and Writing and Language Test, and the majority of questions you'll find on the PSAT Math Test—and see if you can figure out the answer anyway.

1

The capital of Azerbaijan is

A) Washington, D.C.

B) Paris.

C) London.

D) Baku.

The question doesn't seem that hard anymore, does it? Of course, we made our example extremely easy. (By the way, there won't actually be any questions about geography on the PSAT.) But you'd be surprised by how many people give up on PSAT questions that aren't much more difficult than this one just because they don't know the correct answer right off the top of their heads. "Capital of Azerbaijan? Oh, no! I've never heard of Azerbaijan!"

These students don't stop to think that they might be able to find the correct answer simply by eliminating all of the answer choices they know are wrong.

You Already Know Almost All of the Answers

All but a handful of the questions on the PSAT are multiple-choice questions, and every multiple-choice question has four answer choices. One of those choices, and only one, will be the correct answer to the question. You don't have to come up with the answer from scratch. You just have to identify it.

How will you do that?

Look for the Wrong Answers Instead of the Right Ones

Why? Because wrong answers are usually easier to find than the right ones. After all, there are more of them! Remember the question about Azerbaijan? Even though you didn't know the answer off the top of your head, you easily figured it out by eliminating the three obviously incorrect choices. You looked for wrong answers first.

In other words, you used the Process of Elimination, which we'll call POE for short. This is an extremely important concept, one we'll come back to again and again. It's one of the keys to improving your PSAT score. When you finish reading this book, you will be able to use POE to answer many questions that you may not understand.

> ### It's Not About Circling the Right Answer
> Physically marking in your test booklet what you think of certain answers can help you narrow down choices, take the best possible guess, and save time! Try using the following notations:
>
> ✔   Put a check mark next to an answer you like.
>
> ∼   Put a squiggle next to an answer you kinda like.
>
> ?   Put a question mark next to an answer you don't understand.
>
> A̶   Cross out the letter of any answer choice you KNOW is wrong.
>
> You can always come up with your own system. Just make sure you are consistent.

The great artist Michelangelo once said that when he looked at a block of marble, he could see a statue inside. All he had to do to make a sculpture was to chip away everything that wasn't part of it. You should approach difficult PSAT multiple-choice questions in the same way, by chipping away everything that's not correct. By first eliminating the most obviously incorrect choices on difficult questions, you will be able to focus your attention on the few choices that remain.

PROCESS OF ELIMINATION (POE)

There won't be many questions on the PSAT in which incorrect choices will be as easy to eliminate as they were on the Azerbaijan question. But if you read this book carefully, you'll learn how to eliminate at least one choice on almost any PSAT multiple-choice question, if not two or even three choices.

What good is it to eliminate just one or two choices on a four-choice PSAT question?

Plenty. In fact, for most students, it's an important key to earning higher scores. Here's another example:

2

The capital of Qatar is
A) Paris.
B) Dukhan.
C) Tokyo.
D) Doha.

On this question you'll almost certainly be able to eliminate two of the four choices by using POE. That means you're still not sure of the answer. You know that the capital of Qatar has to be either Doha or Dukhan, but you don't know which.

Should you skip the question and go on? Or should you guess?

Close Your Eyes and Point

There is no guessing penalty on the PSAT, so you should bubble something for every question. If you get down to two answers, just pick one of them. There's no harm in doing so.

You're going to hear a lot of mixed opinions about what you should bubble or whether you should bubble at all. Let's clear up a few misconceptions about guessing.

FALSE: Don't answer a question unless you're absolutely sure of the answer.

You will almost certainly have teachers and school counselors who tell you this. Don't listen to them! The pre-2016 PSAT penalized students for wrong answers, but the current PSAT does not. Put something down for every question: you might get a freebie.

FALSE: If you have to guess, guess (C).

This is a weird misconception, and obviously it's not true. As a general rule, if someone says something really weird-sounding about the PSAT, it's usually safest not to believe that person.

FALSE: Always pick the [fill in the blank].

Be careful with directives that tell you that this or that answer or type of answer is always right. It's much safer to learn the rules and to have a solid guessing strategy in place.

As far as guessing is concerned, we do have a small piece of advice. First and foremost, make sure of one thing:

Answer every question on the PSAT. There's no penalty.

LETTER OF THE DAY (LOTD)

Sometimes you won't be able to eliminate any answers, and other times there are questions that you won't have time to look at. For those, we have a simple solution. Pick a "letter of the day," or LOTD (from A to D), and use that letter for all the questions from which you weren't able to eliminate any choices.

This is a quick and easy way to make sure that you've bubbled everything. It also has some potential statistical advantages. If all the answers show up about one-fourth of the time and you guess the same answer every time you have to guess, you're likely to get a couple of freebies.

LOTD should absolutely be an afterthought; it's far more important and helpful to your score to eliminate answer choices. But for those questions you don't know at all, LOTD is better than full-on random guessing or no strategy at all.

PACE YOURSELF

LOTD should remind us about something very important: there's a very good chance that you won't answer every question on the test.

Think about it this way. There are 5 passages and 47 questions on the Reading Test. You have 60 minutes to complete those questions. Now, everyone knows that the Reading Test is super long and boring, and 47 questions in 60 minutes probably sounds like a ton. The great news is that you don't have to work all 47 of these questions. After all, do you think you read most effectively when you're in a huge rush? You might do better if you worked only four of the passages and LOTD'd the rest. There's nothing in the test booklet that says that you can't work at your own pace.

Let's say you do all 47 Reading questions and get half of them right. What raw score do you get from that? That's right: 23 or 24.

Now, let's say you do only three of the 10-question Reading passages and get all of them right. It's conceivable that you could because you've now got all this extra time. What kind of score would you get from this method? You bet: 30—and maybe even a little higher because you'll get a few freebies from your Letter of the Day.

In this case, and on the PSAT as a whole, slowing down can get you more points. Unless you're currently scoring in the 650+ range on the two sections, you shouldn't be working all the questions. We'll go into this in more detail in the later chapters, but for now remember this:

> Slow down, score more. You're not scored on *how many questions you do*. You're scored on *how many questions you answer correctly*. Doing fewer questions can mean more correct answers overall!

EMBRACE YOUR POOD

Embrace your what now? POOD! It stands for "Personal Order of Difficulty." One of the things that PSAT has dispensed with altogether is a strict Order of Difficulty—in other words, an arrangement of problems that puts easy ones earlier in the test than hard ones. In the absence of this Order of Difficulty (OOD), you need to be particularly vigilant about applying your *Personal* Order of Difficulty (POOD).

Think about it this way. There's someone writing the words that you're reading right now. So what happens if you are asked, *Who is the author of Cracking the PSAT?* Do you know the answer to that question? Maybe not. Do we know the answer to that question? Absolutely.

So you can't exactly say that that question is "difficult," but you can say that certain people would have an easier time answering it.

As we've begun to suggest with our Pacing, POE, and Letter of the Day strategies, The Princeton Review's strategies are all about making the test your own, to whatever extent that is possible. We call this idea POOD because we believe it is essential that you identify the questions that you find easy or hard and that you work the test in a way most suitable to your goals and strengths.

As you familiarize yourself with the rest of our strategies, keep all of this in mind. You may be surprised to find out how you perform on particular question types and sections. This test may be standardized, but the biggest improvements are usually reserved for those who can treat the test in a personalized, nonstandardized way.

Summary

o   When you don't know the right answer to a multiple-choice question, look for wrong answers instead. They're usually easier to find.

o   When you find a wrong answer choice, eliminate it. In other words, use Process of Elimination, or POE.

o   There's no penalty for wrong answers, so there's no reason NOT to guess.

o   There's bound to be at least a few questions you simply don't get to or where you're finding it difficult to eliminate even one answer choice. When this happens, use the LOTD (Letter of the Day) strategy.

o   Pace yourself. Remember, you're not scored on the number of questions you answer, but on the number of questions you answer correctly. Take it slow and steady.

o   Make the test your own. When you can work the test to suit your strengths (and use our strategies to overcome any weaknesses), you'll be on your way to a higher score.

Part II
Cracking the PSAT/NMSQT

Chapter 4
Reading Comprehension

Half of your Evidence-Based Reading and Writing score comes from the Reading Test, a 60-minute test that requires you to answer 47 questions spread out over five passages. The questions will ask you to do everything from determining the meaning of words in context, to deciding an author's purpose for providing a detail, to finding the main idea of an entire passage, to pinpointing information on a graph. Each passage ranges from 500 to 750 words and has 9 or 10 questions. Time will be tight on this test. The purpose of this chapter is to introduce you to a basic approach that will streamline how you take the test and allow you to focus on only what you need to get your points.

PSAT READING: CRACKING THE PASSAGES

Answering passage-based reading questions is exactly like taking an open-book test: all of the information that you could be asked about is right in front of you, so you never have to worry about any history, literature, or chemistry that you may (or may not) have learned in school. Of course, you will use the passage to answer the questions, but you will *not* need to read the passage from beginning to end, master all its details, and then carefully select the one choice that answers the question perfectly. What you need is a way to get in and get out of this section with as little stress and as many points as possible.

If someone asked you in what year Louis Pasteur invented pasteurization, would you read the Wikipedia entry on Pasteur from the beginning until you found the answer? Or would you quickly scan through it looking for words like "invented" and "pasteurization"—or better yet, look for the numbers that represent a year, which are easy to spot? We're sure his childhood was fascinating, but your job is to answer a specific question, not read an entire text. This is exactly how to approach passage-based reading questions on the PSAT.

Your Mission:

Process five passages and answer 9 or 10 questions for each passage (or pair of passages). Get as many points as you can.

Okay…so how do you get those points? Let's start with the instructions for the Reading Test.

DIRECTIONS

Each passage or pair of passages below is followed by a number of questions. After reading each passage or pair, choose the best answer to each question based on what is stated or implied in the passage or passages and in any accompanying graphics (such as a table or graph).

Notice that the directions clearly state the correct answer is based on "what is stated or implied in the passage." This is great news! You do not have to rely on your outside knowledge here. All ETS and the College Board care about is whether you can read a text and understand it well enough to answer some questions about it. Unlike in the Math or the Writing and Language Tests, there are no formulas to memorize, no comma rules to learn. You just need to know how to efficiently process the text, the questions, and the answer choices in order to maximize your score. A mantra you can use here: Don't think! Just read!

Another benefit of this open-book test format: you can (and should!) flip back and forth between the passage and the questions so that you are reading only what you need in order to answer a given question.

Your POOD and Your Reading Test

You will get all five of the Reading passages at the same time, so use that to your advantage. Take a quick look through the entire section and figure out the best order for you to do the passages. Depending on your target score, you may be able to temporarily skip (don't forget LOTD!) an entire passage or two, so figure out which passages are hardest, and save them for last (or for never).

How do you decide which ones to do and which ones to skip? Consider these concepts:

- **Type of passage:** You'll have one literature passage, two science passages, and two history/social studies passages. If you like to read fiction, the literature passage may be a good place for you to start. If you like to read nonfiction, the science or history/social studies might be a better starting place for you.
- **Topic of passage:** The blurb will give you some basic information about the passage that can help you decide whether to do the passage or skip it.
- **Types of questions:** Do the questions have a good number of Line References and Lead Words? Will you be able to find what you're looking for relatively quickly, or will you have to spend more time wading through the passage to find what you need?

Don't forget: On any questions or passages that you skip, always fill in your LOTD!

Basic Approach for the Reading Test

Follow these steps for every Reading passage. We'll go over these in greater detail in the next few pages.

1. **Read the Blurb**. The little blurb at the beginning of each passage may not contain a lot of information, but it can be helpful for identifying the type of passage.
2. **Select and Understand a Question**. For the most part, do the questions in order, saving the general questions for last and using your LOTD on any questions or passages you want to skip.
3. **Read What You Need.** Don't read the whole passage! Use Line References and Lead Words to find the reference for the question, and then carefully read a window of about 10–12 lines (usually about 5 or 6 lines above and below the Line Reference/Lead Word) to find the answer to the question.
4. **Predict the Correct Answer**. Your prediction should come straight from the text. Don't analyze or paraphrase. Often, you'll be able to find something in the text that you can actually underline to predict the answer.
5. **POE.** Eliminate anything that isn't consistent with your prediction. Don't necessarily try to find the right answer immediately, because there is a good chance you won't see anything that you like. If you can eliminate answers that you know are wrong, though, you'll be closer to the right answer. If you can't eliminate three answers with your prediction, use the POE criteria (which we'll talk about in a few pages.)

> ### Where the Money Is
> A reporter once asked notorious thief Willie Sutton why he robbed banks. Legend has it that his answer was, "Because that's where the money is." While reading comprehension is safer and slightly more productive than larceny, the same principle applies. Concentrate on the questions and answer choices because that's where the points are. The passage is just a place for ETS to stash facts and details. You'll find them when you need to. What's the point of memorizing all 67 pesky details about plankton if ETS asks you about only 12?

Let's see these steps in action!

A sample passage and questions appear on the next few pages. Don't start working the passage right away. In fact…you can't! The answer choices are missing. Just go ahead to page 36, where we will begin going through the steps of the Basic Approach, using the upcoming passage and questions.

SAMPLE PASSAGE AND QUESTIONS

Here is an example of what a reading comprehension passage and questions look like. We will use this passage to illustrate the reading Basic Approach throughout this chapter. You don't need to do the questions now, but you might want to paperclip this page so it's easy to flip back to later.

Questions 21–30 are based on the following passage.

The passage below is adapted from an article discussing minor Elizabethan dramatists. It focuses on the works of Thomas Heywood and Thomas Middleton, two influential playwrights of the early seventeenth century.

Thomas Heywood, of whom little is known, was one of the most prolific writers the world has ever seen. In 1598 he became an actor, or, as
Line Henslowe, who employed him, phrases it, "came
5 and hired himself to me as a covenanted servant for two years." The date of his first published drama is 1601; that of his last published work, a "General History of Women," is 1657. As early as 1633 he represents himself as having had
10 an "entire hand, or at least a main finger," in two hundred and twenty plays, of which only twenty-three were printed. "It is true," he says, "that my plays are not exposed to the world in volumes, as others are: one reason is that many of them,
15 by shifting and change of companies, have been negligently lost; others of them are still retained in the hands of some actors, who think it against their peculiar profit to have them come in print; it was also never any great ambition in me to be in
20 this kind voluminously read." It was said of him, by a contemporary, that he "not only acted every day, but also obliged himself to write a sheet every day for several years; but many of his plays being composed loosely in taverns, occasions them to
25 be so mean." Besides his labors as a playwright, he worked as translator, versifier, and general maker of books. Late in life he conceived the design of writing the lives of all the poets of the world, including his contemporaries. Had this
30 project been carried out, we should have known something about the external life of Shakespeare; for Heywood must have carried in his brain many of those facts which we of this age are most curious to know.
35 Heywood's best plays evince large observation, considerable dramatic skill, a sweet and humane

spirit, and an easy command of language. His style, indeed, is singularly simple, pure, clear, and straightforward; but it conveys the impression of
40 a mind so diffused as almost to be characterless, and incapable of flashing its thoughts through the images of imaginative passion. He is more prosaic, closer to ordinary life and character, than his contemporaries.
45 With less fluency of diction, less skill in fastening the reader's interest to his fable, harsher in versification, and generally clumsier in construction, the best plays of Thomas Middleton are still superior to Heywood's in force of
50 imagination, depth of passion, and fullness of matter. It must, however, be admitted that the sentiments which direct his powers are not so fine as Heywood's. He depresses the mind, rather than invigorates it. The eye he cast on human life
55 was not the eye of a sympathizing poet, but rather that of a sagacious cynic. His observation, though sharp, close, and vigilant, is somewhat ironic and unfeeling. His penetrating, incisive intellect cuts its way to the heart of a character as with a knife;
60 and if he lays bare its throbs of guilt and weakness, and lets you into the secrets of its organization, he conceives his whole work is performed. This criticism applies even to his tragedy of "Women Beware Women," a drama which shows a deep
65 study of the sources of human frailty, considerable skill in exhibiting the passions in their consecutive, if not in their conflicting action, and a firm hold upon character; but it lacks pathos, tenderness, and humanity; its power is out of all
70 proportion to its geniality; the characters, while they stand definitely out to the eye, are seen through no visionary medium of sentiment and fancy.

There is, indeed, no atmosphere to Middleton's
75 mind; and the hard, bald caustic peculiarity of his genius, which is unpleasingly felt in reading any one of his plays, becomes a source of painful weariness as we plod doggedly through his works. This is most powerfully felt in his tragedy of "The

80 Changeling," at once the most oppressive and impressive effort of his genius. The character of De Flores in this play has in it a strangeness such as is hardly paralleled in the whole range of the Elizabethan drama. The passions of this
85 brute imp are not human. They are such as might be conceived of as springing from the union of animal with fiendish impulses, in a nature which knew no law outside of its own lust, and was as incapable of a scruple as of a sympathy.

These are the questions for the passage. We've removed the answer choices because, for now, we just want you to see the different question types the PSAT will ask. Don't worry about answering these here. Not all of these questions will have answers. This is just to demonstrate how to read questions in the Reading Comprehension section.

21

The primary purpose of the passage is to

22

According to the information in the passage, the author most likely would agree that Heywood

23

Which choice provides the best evidence for the answer to the previous question?

24

The author's reaction to Middleton is best described as a mix of

25

According to the information in the passage, one primary difference between Heywood and Middleton is that Heywood

26

Which choice provides the best evidence for the answer to the previous question?

27

Heywood claims that all of the following are reasons that many of his plays were not published EXCEPT

28

As used in line 28, "design" most nearly means

29

As used in line 53, "fine" most nearly means

30

The information in lines 58–62 serves primarily to

Step 1: Read the Blurb

The Strategy
1. Read the Blurb

You should always begin by reading the blurb (the introductory material above the passage). The blurb gives you the title of the piece, as well as the author and the publication date. Typically the blurb won't have much more information than that, but it'll be enough to let you know whether the passage is literature, history/social studies, or science. It will also give you a sense of what the passage will be about and can help you make a POOD decision about when to do the passage.

Read the blurb at the beginning of the passage on page 33. Based on the blurb, is the passage literature, history/social studies, or science? What will the passage be about?

_____

_____

Step 2: Select and Understand a Question

The Strategy
1. Read the Blurb
2. Select and Understand a Question

Select…

Notice that the steps of the Basic Approach have you jumping straight from the blurb to the questions. There is no "Read the Passage" step. You get points for answering questions, not for reading the passage, so we're going to go straight to the questions.

On a test you take in school, you probably do the questions in order. That seems logical and straightforward. However, doing the questions in order on a Reading passage can set you up for a serious time issue. ETS and the College Board say the order of the questions "is also as natural as possible, with general questions about central ideas, themes, point of view, overall text structure, and the like coming early in the sequence, followed by more localized questions about details, words in context, evidence, and the like." So to sum it up, the general questions come first, followed by the specific questions.

That question structure works great in an English class, when you have plenty of time to read and digest the text on your own. When you're trying to get through five passages in only an hour, you don't have time for that. Instead of starting with the general questions and then answering the specific questions, we're going to flip that and do the specific questions first.

Look back at the questions on page 35.

What does the first question ask you about?

In order to answer that question, you'd have to read what part of the passage?

And what we don't want to do is read the whole passage! So skip that first question. You'll come back to it, but not until you've done the specific questions. Once you go through and answer all (or most) of the specific questions, you'll have a really good idea what the test writers think is important. You'll also have read most of the passage, so answering the general questions at the end will be easier than it would if you had started with them.

Remember we mentioned earlier that the questions are in "natural" order? Look at the Line References in the specific questions. What do you notice about them?

Yep! They're in order through the passage! So work through them as they're given, and you'll work through the passage from beginning to end. Do not get stuck on a hard question, though. If you find yourself stumped, use your LOTD and move on to the next question. You can always come back if you have time.

Based on that logic, let's skip the first question and move on to the second question.

...and Understand

Once you've selected a question, you need to make sure you understand what it's asking. Reading questions are often not in question format. Instead, they will make statements such as, "The author's primary reason for mentioning the gadfly is to," and then the answer choices will follow. Make sure that you understand the question by turning it into a question—that is, back into a sentence that ends with a question mark and begins with Who/What/Why.

22

According to the information in the passage, the author most likely would agree that Heywood

What is this question asking?

> **Rephrase the Question...**
> ...so that it asks:
> Who?
> What?
> Why?

Notice the phrase *most likely would agree that*. This phrase lets you know that the question can be rephrased as a "what" question. So for this particular question, you want to figure out "What does the author most likely think about Heywood?" Notice also the phrase *according to the information in the passage* at the start of the question. This phrase lets you know that you don't have to be psychic! You just need to find something the author actually said about Heywood, and use that information to answer the question.

Step 3: Read What You Need

The Strategy
1. Read the Blurb
2. Select and Understand a Question
3. Read What You Need

Line Reference and Lead Words

Many questions will refer you to a specific set of lines or to a particular paragraph, so you won't need to read the entire passage to answer those questions. Those are Line References. Other questions may not give you a Line Reference, but may ask about specific names, quotes, or phrases that are easy to spot in the text. We'll call those Lead Words. It's important to remember that the Line Reference or Lead Word shows you where the *question* is in the passage, but you'll have to read more than that single line in order to find the *answer* in the passage.

If you read a window of about five lines above and five lines below each Line Reference or Lead Word, you should find the information you need. It's important to note that while you do not need to read more than these 10–12 lines of text, you usually cannot get away with reading less. If you read only the lines from the Line Reference, you will very likely not find the information you need to answer the question. Read carefully! You should be able to put your finger on the particular phrase, sentence, or set of lines that answers your question. If you save the general questions that relate to the passage as a whole for last, then by the time you begin those questions, you'll have a greater understanding of the passage even if you haven't read every word of it.

5 Above, 5 Below
5 is the magic number when it comes to Line Reference questions. Read about 5 lines above the Line Reference and then about 5 lines below it to get all of the information you need in order to answer the question correctly.

> Read a window of about 5 lines above and 5 lines below
> your Line Reference to get the context for the question.

24

The author's reaction to Middleton is best described as a mix of

What are the Lead Words in this question?

What lines will you need to read to find the answer?

Once you use the Lead Words to find your window, draw a bracket around the window so that you can find it easily. The more you can get out of your brain and onto the page, the better off you'll be. Because the Lead Word is *Middleton*, skip to line 48 and start reading there. In this case, the first half of the third paragraph would be a good window.

Now it's time to read. Even though you're reading only a chunk of the text, make sure you read it carefully.

Step 4: Predict Your Answer

ETS and the College Board do their best to distract you by creating tempting—but nevertheless wrong—answers. However, if you know what you're looking for in advance, you will be less likely to fall for a trap answer. Before you even glance at the answer choices, take the time to think about what specific, stated information in your window supplies the answer to the question. Be careful not to paraphrase too far from the text or try to analyze what you're reading. Remember that what might be a good "English class" answer may lead you in the wrong direction on the PSAT! Stick with the text.

> **The Strategy**
> 1. Read the Blurb
> 2. Select and Understand a Question
> 3. Read What You Need
> 4. Predict Your Answer

As you read the window, look for specific lines or phrases that answer the question. Often what you're looking for will be in a sentence before or after the Line Reference or Lead Word, so it's crucial that you read the full window.

Once you've found text to answer the question, underline it if you can! Otherwise, jot down a prediction for the answer, sticking as close to the text as possible.

Let's keep looking at question 24, this time with the window.

24 �\[_____\]

    The author's reaction to Middleton is best described as a mix of

Here's your window from the passage. Read it and see if you can find something that answers the question. Underline your prediction if you can.

> With less fluency of diction, less skill in fastening the reader's interest to his fable, harsher in versification, and generally clumsier in construction, the best plays of Thomas Middleton are still superior to Heywood's in force of imagination, depth of passion, and fullness of matter. It must, however, be admitted that the sentiments which direct his powers are not so fine as Heywood's. He depresses the mind, rather than invigorates it. The eye he casts on human life was not the eye of a sympathizing poet, but rather that of a sagacious cynic. His observation, though sharp, close, and vigilant, is somewhat ironic and unfeeling.

Did you underline some negative terms as well as some positive ones? The passage gives you clear evidence that the author's reaction to Middleton involves both a positive and a negative judgment. The sentence *His observation, though sharp, close, and vigilant, is somewhat ironic and unfeeling* shows this ambivalence.

Step 5: Use Process of Elimination

The Strategy
1. Read the Blurb
2. Select and Understand a Question
3. Read What You Need
4. Predict Your Answer
5. Use Process of Elimination

A multiple-choice test is a cool thing because you have all the right answers on the page in front of you. All you have to do is eliminate anything that isn't correct. Sometimes, especially on Reading, it's easier to find wrong answers that aren't supported by the passage rather than trying to find the right answer that might not look the way you think it should.

Process of Elimination, or POE, involves two steps. The first step will be the question, "What can I eliminate that doesn't match—or is inconsistent with—my prediction?" For many of the easy and medium questions, this step will be enough to get down to the right answer.

24 ▬▬▬▬▬▬▬▬▬▬▬▬▬▬▬▬▬▬

The author's reaction to Middleton is best described as a mix of

Remember, on the previous page, you used the text to predict that the author reacted to Middleton with a mix of positive and negative judgment. Start by eliminating anything that does not fit that prediction.

	Keep?	Eliminate?
A) admiration for his ingenuity but criticism for his absence of warmth.		
B) disgust for his style but appreciation for his displays of tenderness.		
C) confusion about his use of diction but curiosity about his sentiments.		
D) apathy toward his ability to dishearten readers but dislike of his coldness.		

Did you eliminate (C) and (D) right away? Neither choice involves a mix of positive and negative. That was fast! Now that you're down to two answer choices that fit your prediction, use the text to get the right one. On the negative side, what's the author's criticism? Middleton *depresses* us because he is *unfeeling*. Does that better match (A), criticism, or (B), disgust? Disgust seems too extreme. If you're not sure yet, look at the positive side: What does the author like about Middleton? The *force of imagination, depth of passion, and fullness of matter*. Does that match (A), admiration, for his ingenuity? Maybe. Does that match (B), appreciation, for his displays of tenderness? Not at all. Either way you slice it, (A) is better than (B). Pick (A).

POE Criteria

On most of the easy and medium questions, you'll be able to eliminate three of the four answers simply by using your prediction. On other questions, usually the Hard questions, your prediction will help you get rid of one or two answers, and then you'll need to consider the remaining answers a little more carefully. If you're down to two answers, and they both seem to make sense, you're probably down to the right answer and the trap answer. Luckily, there are some common traps that ETS and the College Board will set for you, and knowing them can help you figure out which is the trap answer and which is the right answer. Here are a few of those traps:

Predictions and POE
Use these criteria after you have eliminated anything that doesn't match your prediction.

- **Mostly Right/Slightly Wrong**: These answers look just about perfect except for a word or two that doesn't match what's in the text.
- **Could Be True**: These answers might initially look good because they make sense or seem logical. You might be able to support these answers in an English class, but they lack the concrete support from the text to make them correct PSAT answers.
- **Deceptive Language**: These answer choices have individual words that look exactly like what you saw in the passage, but the words are put together in such a way that they don't actually say what you need them to say. Make sure you're reading carefully and not just matching words.

QUESTION TYPES AND FORMATS

Now that you know the steps of the Basic Approach, let's consider the different types of questions you'll be answering. It's not important that you can identify the question types by the names we give them. But it is extremely important that you can read a question and know how to respond. Is the question asking you WHAT the author says, WHAT the author means, WHAT a particular word means, WHAT evidence supports a point, etc.? The next section of this chapter will help you decode those question types and formats. The final section will help you make sense of questions that ask HOW or WHY an author does something. Your score will depend on your ability to figure out if a question is asking you WHAT, WHY, or HOW.

Question Types and Formats

- Detail
- Vocabulary in Context
- Infer/Imply/Suggest
- Except/Not/Least
- Paired Questions

DETAIL (*What?*)

When you see a question that contains the phrase *according to the passage* or *according to the author*, your job is fairly simple. Get to that part of the text, find the detail that tells you WHAT the passage or the author is saying, and then use POE to get rid of wrong answers. Carefully read the window and do not simply rely on your memory. The question writers are really good at tricking people who use their memories rather than their eyes.

25

According to the information in the passage, one primary difference between Heywood and Middleton is that Heywood

A) displayed a more cynical attitude toward humanity.

B) had fewer of his works published.

C) was a more disciplined writer.

D) showed less powerful creativity in his writing.

Here's How To Crack It

First, you need to go back to the text and find a *primary difference* between the two writers. Since paragraphs 1 and 2 are about Heywood only, and paragraph 4 is about Middleton only, focus on paragraph 3. Since the second half of paragraph 3 is about only Middleton, focus on the first half, which contrasts both writers. As you read that window, underline whatever is true about Heywood but not Middleton. You should notice that, compared to Middleton, Heywood has more *fluency of diction* and *skill in fastening the reader's interest to his fable*, better *versification* and *construction*, but has less *force of imagination, depth of passion, and fullness of matter*. Once you have this prediction—based completely on the text, not on your opinion and not on your memory—use POE to work through the answer choices. Choice (A) doesn't match the prediction (and actually fits Middleton, rather than Heywood), so eliminate it. Choice (B) might seem logical, but it's not in the text and does not match the prediction. Eliminate it. Choice (C) could be true because the text says he had more fluency and skill and better construction. If he's better at the technical parts of writing, it might make sense that he's a more disciplined writer. However, nothing in the text actually supports that. Watch out for answers that you might be able to justify in an essay. There has to be support in the text! Choice (C) does not have that support, and it does not match the prediction. Eliminate it. Choice (D) totally matches the prediction. Remember: Don't think—read! Put another way: Don't remember—underline!

VOCABULARY IN CONTEXT (*What?*)

Another way that ETS and the College Board will test your reading comprehension is with Vocabulary-in-Context (VIC) questions. The most important thing to remember is that these are ***IN CONTEXT!*** Gone are the days of "SAT Vocabulary" when you had to memorize lists of obscure words like *impecunious* and *perspicacious*. Now the test writers want to see that you can understand what a word means based on context. You'll see words that look familiar but may be used in ways that are a little less familiar. Do not try to answer these questions simply by defining the word in your head and looking for that definition. You have to go back to the text and look at the context for the word.

28

As used in line 28, "design" most nearly means

A) draft.

B) pattern.

C) biography.

D) intention.

Here's How To Crack It

With VIC questions, you don't need to read a full 10–12-line window. Typically a few lines before and a few lines after will give you what you need. Go to line 28 and find the word *design*. Underline it. When you read a bit before and after the word, say lines 25 through 29, the text says: *Besides his labors as a playwright, he worked as translator, versifier, and general maker of books. Late in life he conceived the design of writing the lives of all the poets of the world, including his contemporaries.* Now read the sentence and put in a different word than "design" that means the same thing. Did you use a word like "plan"? Did you use that exact word? Compare your prediction to the four answer choices, and you can quickly eliminate (A), (B), and (C).

Do not give in to the temptation to simply answer the question without looking at the text. Did you notice that at least two of the wrong answer choices do legitimately mean *design*? If you don't go back to the text, you can easily fall for such a wrong answer. But if you look at what the text actually says, VIC questions are among the easiest to answer. Don't think—just read!

Now try this one:

———————————○———————————

29

As used in line 53, "fine" most nearly means
A) dainty.
B) admirable.
C) skillful.
D) exact.

Here's How To Crack It

Here are lines 48–54: *[T]he best plays of Thomas Middleton are still superior to Heywood's in force of imagination, depth of passion, and fullness of matter. It must, however, be admitted that the sentiments which direct his powers are not so fine as Heywood's. He depresses the mind, rather than invigorates it.*

So it seems Middleton is *not so fine,* and Heywood is therefore *fine.* Great. But you don't have to guess! The sentence gives us some clues as to the meaning here: since depressing the mind is Middleton's thing, depressing the mind is apparently *not so fine.* Well, then, invigorating the mind is apparently a *fine* thing. Thinking along these lines, what's a word you could now use where you've been using *fine*? How about "good/happy/invigorating/something like that"? Does "dainty" have the same meaning? No. Does "admirable"? Maybe. Does "skillful"? That fits "good," but doesn't fit the rest. Does "exact"? That also fits good, but not the rest. So using these predictions, (A) is out, (B) seems okay, and (C) and (D) both seem weakly possible. In a situation like this, choose (B)!

———————————○———————————

INFER/IMPLY/SUGGEST (*What?*)

When you see a question that contains the word *infer, imply,* or *suggest,* be extra careful. In real life, those words often signify a question asking your opinion. You may think that the test writers want you to do some English-class-level reading between the lines. In actuality, though, they don't. It's still just a straight reading comprehension question. There may be a tiny bit of reading between the lines, so far as the answer will not be directly stated in the text as it will with a detail question, but there will still be plenty of evidence in the text to support the correct answer.

A few pages ago, we discussed this question:

24

The author's reaction to Middleton is best described as a mix of

A) admiration for his ingenuity but criticism for his absence of warmth.

B) disgust for his style but appreciation for his displays of tenderness.

C) confusion about his use of diction but curiosity about his sentiments.

D) apathy toward his ability to dishearten readers but dislike of his coldness.

Recall how we solved it by going back to the text, finding relevant evidence, predicting an answer, and then using POE to eliminate answer choices that didn't fit the prediction. If you rely on this procedure, you will improve your performance with these sorts of questions.

Inference questions can seem confusing, but remember that these are still WHAT questions. Whereas Detail questions ask WHAT the author says, Inference questions ask WHAT the author *really* says? The correct answer will have the same *meaning* as the text, even though the *words* may be different.

EXCEPT/NOT/LEAST (*What???*)

Now that you know how to answer a basic WHAT question, let's consider what changes when you get one of these three pesky words in the question stem. Consider this question stem:

27

Heywood claims that all of the following are reasons that many of his plays were not published EXCEPT

So apparently, three of the answer choices are true, and one is false. Except for that, this is a "detail" question. But now you have to be willing to find three parts of the passage that correspond to an answer choice, which you will eliminate. And you will select the lonely remaining answer choice with no support from the passage. These can be time-consuming (after all, you have to find three pieces of information in the text instead of just one), but carefully reading your window can help eliminate some choices efficiently.

Let's see how this works using the full question:

> **27**
>
> Heywood claims that all of the following are reasons that many of his plays were not published EXCEPT
>
> A) many of his plays accidentally went missing.
>
> B) Heywood lacked a strong desire for popularity.
>
> C) a number of his plays feature mean characters.
>
> D) some individuals kept the plays to prevent their publication.

Since lines 12–20 give a direct quote from Heywood explaining why his plays were not published, use that window and underline the reasons he gives.

"It is true," he says, "that my plays are not exposed to the world in volumes, as others are: one reason is that many of them, by shifting and change of companies, have been negligently lost; others of them are still retained in the hands of some actors, who think it against their peculiar profit to have them come in print; it was also never any great ambition in me to be in this kind voluminously read."

Notice that there are phrases that support (A) (*have been negligently lost*), (B) (*it was also never any great ambition in me to be in this kind voluminously read*), and (D) (*some actors…think it against their peculiar profit to have them come in print*). With support from the text, those three choices can all be eliminated, leaving (C) as the correct answer.

PAIRED QUESTIONS (BEST EVIDENCE)

Remember the full name of this section of the test? It's the PSAT Evidence-Based Reading Test. Throughout this chapter, you've been using evidence to answer all of these questions, so this next step won't come as a complete surprise. In fact, once you get a hold of the best way to manage evidence questions, you'll be glad. You can do the work for one question and get points for two.

Best Evidence: Specific Paired Questions

We discussed question 25 earlier. Here it is:

> **25**
>
> According to the information in the passage, one primary difference between Heywood and Middleton is that Heywood

The correct answer was (D): *showed less powerful creativity in his writing.* Recall that we based this answer on the part of the text that said Heywood had less *force of imagination, depth of passion, and fullness of matter.*

So now you encounter the following question:

---○---

> **26**
>
> Which choice provides the best evidence for the answer to the previous question?
>
> A) Lines 8–12 ("As early as . . . printed")
>
> B) Lines 20–25 ("It was said . . . mean")
>
> C) Lines 45–51 ("With less . . . matter")
>
> D) Lines 54–56 ("The eye . . . cynic")

Here's How to Crack It

What to do? Since the text you already used to answer question 25 (*force of imagination, depth of passion, and fullness of matter*) was in lines 49–51, simply pick (C) and move on! Buy one, get one free.

---○---

We're not kidding: specific best evidence questions are like free points. Get them all!

Best Evidence: General Paired Questions

Sometimes, though, the best evidence question follows a general question, rather than a specific one. And that general question may have no Lead Words or Line References. You might think that you have to solve the general question first by rereading the entire passage, and then answering the evidence question based on that exhaustive research. But luckily, we have a time-saving and accuracy-improving strategy for you: Parallel POE.

Using Parallel POE, you'll be able to work through the questions at the same time! When you find yourself faced with a set of paired questions, you can start with the second question (the "best evidence" question) if (1) you aren't sure where to look for the answer, or (2) the first question is a general question about the passage. Because the second question in the pair asks which lines provide the *best evidence* for the previous question, you can use those lines to help work through the answers for the previous question. Let's take a look.

Best Evidence
Not sure where to find the answer? Let the "best evidence" lines help!

22

According to the information in the passage, the author most likely would agree that Heywood

A) could have contributed more to our knowledge of influential seventeenth-century writers than he actually did.

B) was more involved in professions other than playwriting than many authorities today believe.

C) was an actor in more than two hundred plays, although only slightly more than twenty became popular productions.

D) would have been the most talented playwright of his day had he possessed more imagination and passion.

23

Which choice provides the best evidence for the answer to the previous question?

A) Lines 3–12 ("In 1598 . . . printed")

B) Lines 20–27 ("It was said . . . books")

C) Lines 27–34 ("Late . . . know")

D) Lines 37–44 ("His style . . . contemporaries")

Here's How to Crack It

Heywood is the subject of the first two paragraphs. At 44 lines, that's a pretty big window! What to do? That's where Parallel POE comes in. Notice that question 23 gives you the only possible lines for your evidence. Choice (23A) references 10 lines, (23B) references 8 lines, (23C) references 8 lines, and (23D) references 8 lines. So what would you rather do: read the entire passage hoping you might find an answer somewhere or read these tiny chunks one at a time to see if they answer the question? We hope you answered the latter!

What's great about Parallel POE is that, in the first instance, the original question does not even matter. Think for a moment about how paired questions operate. The correct answer to the first question *must* be supported by an answer to the best evidence question, and the correct answer to the best evidence question *must* support an answer to the first question. In other words, if there is a best evidence answer that doesn't support an answer to the first question, it is wrong. Period. Likewise, if there is an answer to the first question that isn't supported by a best evidence answer, it too is wrong. Period.

Let's use this to our advantage! Rather than worry about what the first question is asking and what the answer might be, just start making connections between the two answer sets. If a best evidence answer supports a first question answer, physically draw a line connecting them. You should not expect to have four connections. If you are lucky, you will have only one connection, and you will have your answer pair. Otherwise, you might have two or three connections and will then (and only then) worry about the first question. The important thing to remember is that any answer choice in the first question that isn't physically connected to a best evidence answer—and any best evidence answer that isn't connected to an answer in the first question— must be eliminated.

———————————○———————————

Let's take a look at how this first Parallel POE pass would look. (The paired questions have been arranged in two columns to help understand this, and the lines have been written out for your convenience. This does not represent what you will see on the official test.)

22. According to the information in the passage, the author most likely would agree that Heywood	23. Which choice provides the best evidence for the answer to the previous question?
A) could have contributed more to our knowledge of influential seventeenth-century writers than he actually did.	A) Lines 3–12 ("In 1598 . . . printed")
B) was more involved in professions other than playwriting than many authorities today believe.	B) Lines 20–27 ("It was said . . . books")
C) was an actor in more than two hundred plays, although only slightly more than twenty became popular productions.	C) Lines 27–34 ("Late . . . know")
D) would have been the most talented playwright of his day had he possessed more imagination and passion.	D) Lines 37–44 ("His style . . . contemporaries")

Don't worry about the question itself yet. Go straight to the best evidence lines.

• Choice (23A) says *In 1598 he became an actor, or, as Henslowe, who employed him, phrases it, "came and hired himself to me as a covenanted servant for two years." The date of his first published drama is 1601; that of his last published work, a "General History of Women," is 1657. As early as 1633 he represents himself as having had an "entire hand, or at least a main finger," in two hundred and twenty plays, of which only twenty-three were printed.* Does this evidence support any of the answer choices for question 22? Nope. So eliminate (23A) and move on.

• Choice (23B) says *It was said of him, by a contemporary, that he "not only acted every day, but also obliged himself to write a sheet every day for several years; but many of his plays being composed loosely in taverns, occasions them to be so mean." Besides his labors as a playwright, he worked as translator, versifier, and general maker of books.* Does this evidence support any of the answer choices for question 22? Choice (22B) looks possible, so draw a line physically connecting (23B) with (22B).

- Choice (23C) says *Late in life he conceived the design of writing the lives of all the poets of the world, including his contemporaries. Had this project been carried out, we should have known something about the external life of Shakespeare; for Heywood must have carried in his brain many of those facts which we of this age are most curious to know.* Does this evidence support any of the answer choices for question 22? Yes, it very strongly supports (22A), so draw a line physically connecting (23C) with (22A).

- Choice (23D) says *His style, indeed, is singularly simple, pure, clear, and straightforward; but it conveys the impression of a mind so diffused as almost to be characterless, and incapable of flashing its thoughts through the images of imaginative passion. He is more prosaic, closer to ordinary life and character, than his contemporaries.* Does this evidence support any of the answer choices for question 22? Nope. So eliminate (23D) and move on.

Look at your progress so far: (22C) and (22D) have no support from question 23, so go ahead and eliminate (22C) and (22D). No matter how good they may sound, they CANNOT be right if there is no evidence supporting them from the best evidence question.

Your work should look something like this at this point:

22. According to the information in the passage, the author most likely would agree that Heywood	23. Which choice provides the best evidence for the answer to the previous question?
A) could have contributed more to our knowledge of influential seventeenth-century writers than he actually did.	A) ~~Lines 3–12 ("In 1598 . . . printed")~~
B) ~~was more involved in professions other than playwriting than many authorities today believe.~~	B) Lines 20–27 ("It was said . . . books")
C) ~~was an actor in more than two hundred plays, although only slightly more than twenty became popular productions.~~	C) Lines 27–34 ("Late . . . know")
D) ~~would have been the most talented playwright of his day had he possessed more imagination and passion.~~	D) ~~Lines 37–44 ("His style . . . contemporaries")~~

Now you're down to a very nice 50/50 split. Go back to the question. Of the two pairs, which one best describes Heywood in a way that *the author would most likely agree with*? Your strong reaction that (23C) strongly matched (22A) is a clue that this is what the author would most likely agree with, since it's something the author actually did say. The other pair was a weaker match, with a feeling of Could Be True. Eliminate (23B), eliminate (22B), choose the remaining answer (22A) and (23C), and get two points.

On the actual test, it would be too complicated for you to draw a full table like the one above, but all you need to do is create a column to the left of the best evidence answer choices for the answers to the previous question. Basically, it should look something like this:

Q22   23. Which choice provides the best evidence for the answer to
            the previous question?

A   A) Lines 3–12 ("In 1598 . . . printed")

B   B) Lines 20–27 ("It was said . . . books")

C   C) Lines 27–34 ("Late . . . know")

D   D) Lines 37–44 ("His style . . . contemporaries")

Parallel POE
Since you can't draw a full table on the actual exam, try making notations as shown in question 22; that is, create a column to the left of the best evidence answer choices listing out the choices to the previous question.

SAMPLE PASSAGE AND QUESTIONS

Here is another example of a Reading passage and questions. We will use this passage to further illustrate the Basic Approach to let you independently practice the questions you already know how to do (Detail, Infer) and to model for you how to manage some other question types you will encounter.

Questions 19–28 are based on the following passage and supplementary material.

This passage is from Michael Greshko, "Jumping Spiders Can Think Ahead, Plan Detours." Copyright © January 2016 by National Geographic Creative.

With brains the size of a sesame seed, jumping spiders may seem like mental lightweights. But a new study shows that many
Line species plan out intricate detours to reach their
5 prey—smarts usually associated with far bigger creatures. The arachnids, already well known for their colors and elaborate mating rituals, have sharp vision and an impressive awareness of three-dimensional space. "Their vision is more
10 on par with vertebrates," says Damian Elias of the University of California, Berkeley, who wasn't involved in the new research. "And that allows them to do things that are physically impossible for other animals that size."
15 Jumping spiders of the subfamily Spartaeinae (spar-TAY-in-ay) are particularly ambitious— they eat other spiders. Researchers suspect that preying on other predators requires extra intelligence and cunning. In the 1980s and
20 1990s, Robert Jackson of New Zealand's University of Canterbury demonstrated that *Portia fimbriata*, a member of this spider-snacking subfamily, methodically plans winding detours to sneak up on prey spiders. *Portia* can
25 even find hidden prey, suggesting that the predator can visualize its prey's location and a path to get there.

But Jackson, who received funding from National Geographic's Committee for Research
30 and Exploration, and his colleague Fiona Cross were sure that *Portia* wasn't alone in its forward thinking. "There's so much attention given to *Portia*," says Cross, "but there are these other [jumping] spiders: why not
35 them?" Demonstrating in the lab that other spider species also planned detours, however,

proved challenging: Other spiders ignored the experimental walkways that *Portia* used. So Jackson and Cross decided to take advantage of
40 jumping spiders' dislike of getting wet.

Their new setup consisted of a tower on a platform surrounded by moats. From atop the tower, a famished jumping spider could see two distant boxes: one containing juicy spider
45 fragments, the other containing unappetizing leaves. To reach the box containing the meal, the spider would have to crawl down the tower and onto the platform, which also had two pillars leading to separate suspended walkways—one
50 to the food, one to the leaves. But once the spider started its descent from the tower, the researchers emptied out the boxes, preventing it from getting visual reminders of the meal's location. In their lab at Kenya's International
55 Centre for Insect Physiology and Ecology, Cross and Jackson placed individuals from 14 different Spartaeinae species in this tortuous obstacle course. "We have to hide ourselves, so that the spider isn't distracted," says Cross.
60 "They're attracted to blinking."

It turned out that each species was overwhelmingly successful at finding its way to the box containing food—despite the fact that none of the subjects could see the food mid-
65 detour, according to the study, published Tuesday in the *Journal of the Experimental Analysis of Behavior*. What's more, spiders that chose the wrong path often paused, seemingly confused. "Their expectations for what they were going to
70 weren't met," says Cross. "It wasn't part of their plan."

The finding hammers home that, like *Portia*, many related jumping spiders must have an abstract sense of the food's location and a
75 working plan for how to navigate the walkways. "A lot of times, when papers are published about a particular organism, broad generalizations are made about the group," says Berkeley's Elias.

The study authors have "done a really good
80 job of showing [planning] in this very large
group." Researchers still have a long way to go
to understand how spiders think, but for now
they're left to wonder what's going on in those
tiny little heads.
85 "What they do just astounds me," says Cross.

Figure 1

Figure 2

Species	Prey were in Box A		Prey were in Box B	
	Completed Walkway A	Completed Walkway B	Completed Walkway A	Completed Walkway B
Brettus adonis	6	0	0	5
Brettus albolimbatus	7	0	0	4
Cocalus gibbosus	5	0	0	5
Cyrba algerina	4	0	0	2
Cyrba ocellata	5	0	0	4
Cyrba simoni	4	0	1	4
Gelotia lanka	4	0	0	6
Meleon solitaria	6	0	0	6
Neobrettus nangalisagus	4	0	1	6
Portia africana	10	1	0	6
Portia albimana	3	0	0	4
Portia fimbriata	7	0	0	10
Portia labiata	10	1	0	9
Portia cf occidentalis	7	0	0	7
Portia schultzi	6	0	0	6

19

Over the course of the passage, the focus shifts from

A) a general discussion of animal behavior to specifics about a certain species.

B) an introduction of an unexpected characteristic to a discussion of an experiment testing that characteristic.

C) contradictory hypotheses to a discovery which resolved the conflict.

D) an overview of a certain animal to the specifics of that animal's eating habits.

20

Which choice best supports the claim that jumping spiders are more intelligent than their size would suggest?

A) Lines 1–3 ("With brains . . . lightweights")

B) Lines 6–9 ("The arachnids . . . space")

C) Lines 15–17 ("Jumping . . . other spiders")

D) Lines 35–37 ("Demonstrating in . . . challenging")

21

As used in line 4, "intricate" most nearly means

A) complicated.

B) obscure.

C) unfathomable.

D) confused.

22

The primary purpose of the second paragraph (lines 15–27) is to

A) refute a controversial claim.

B) describe a complicated experiment.

C) provide a specific example.

D) prove a long-disputed hypothesis.

23

It can reasonably be inferred that, compared to other jumping spiders, the *Portia* spiders

A) don't mind getting wet.

B) are more aggressive.

C) have very small brains.

D) are more thoroughly researched.

24

Which choice is an underlying assumption of the jumping spider experiment in the passage?

A) If a jumping spider can simply see food, it will recognize it as food.

B) If a jumping spider is close to water, it will avoid the path entirely.

C) If a jumping spider uses a walkway, then it must be in the *Portia* family.

D) If a jumping spider can't see its food, it will become confused.

25

Which choice provides the best evidence for the answer to the previous question?

A) Lines 37–38 ("Other spiders . . . used")

B) Lines 42–46 ("From atop . . . leaves")

C) Lines 50–54 ("But once . . . location")

D) Lines 67–68 ("What's more . . . confused")

26

As used in line 49, "suspended" most nearly means

A) hanging.

B) delayed.

C) discontinued.

D) attached.

Figure 2 best supports which claim from the passage?

A) Other spiders did not pay attention to the same walkways that *Portia* spiders used.

B) The *Portia* spider had a more accurate plan to get food than other species of jumping spider.

C) Each species of jumping spider was able to find its way to the box containing the food.

D) The spiders were distracted by the researchers' blinking.

28

Based on Figure 1, the greatest number of spiders

A) made an incorrect choice with an indirect approach.

B) made an incorrect choice with a direct approach.

C) made a correct choice with an indirect approach.

D) made a correct choice with a direct approach.

Do you recognize questions 20, 21, and 26 as Detail questions? Do you recognize question 23 as an Infer question? Try answering them on your own, using the strategies we've been discussing. So that leaves us with a few other mysterious question types. In the following pages, we will demystify them for you.

WHAT? (MAIN IDEA/GENERAL QUESTIONS)

For many of the Reading passages, the very first question will ask a general question about the passage. It might ask about the main idea or purpose of the passage, the narrative point of view, or a shift that occurs through the passage. Remember the Select a Question step? Those general questions are not good to do first because you haven't read the passage yet, but once you've answered most of the other questions, you have a good idea of the overall themes of the text.

Let's take a look at question 19:

> **19**
>
> Over the course of the passage, the focus shifts from

Because this question asks how the focus shifts *over the course of the passage,* there's no one place you can look. General questions don't have line references or lead words, so there's no way to use the text to predict an answer. It's okay, though: you've answered almost all of the questions about the passage, so you know what the main idea of the passage is. Not only that, but you also have a good sense of what the test writers found most interesting about the passage. While having this knowledge does not always help, it sure can sometimes. If there are answer choices that have nothing to do with either the questions or the answers you've seen repeatedly, you can eliminate them and instead choose the one that is consistent with those questions and answers. For this question, consider what the passage begins with (how surprisingly awesome the jumping spiders are) and then how it shifts (to experiments about the jumping spiders). Eliminate anything that's inconsistent with that shift.

Let's take a look at the answer choices:

A) a general discussion of animal behavior to specifics about a certain species.

B) an introduction of an unexpected characteristic to a discussion of an experiment testing that characteristic.

C) contradictory hypotheses to a discovery which resolved the conflict.

D) an overview of a certain animal to the specifics of that animal's eating habits.

What can you eliminate?

The first half of (A) is immediately a problem. The passage begins with a discussion of the jumping spiders, not a *general discussion of animal behavior,* so eliminate (A).

The first half of (B) is consistent with the idea that the spiders are remarkable and the second half is consistent with the experiments described in the passage. Keep (B).

Choice (C) mentions *contradictory hypotheses.* Can you find any evidence in the text of hypotheses that contradict each other? No. Eliminate (C).

The first half of (D) is consistent with the beginning of the passage describing the spider. However, the passage goes on to describe experiments about the spiders' planning abilities, not their eating habits. Eliminate (D).

Since (B) is the only answer supported by the passage, that's the correct answer.

WHY? (PURPOSE QUESTIONS)

Take a look at this question, and think about how it's different from what we've been talking about.

> 22
>
> The primary purpose of the second paragraph
> (lines 15–27) is to

Notice that it's not asking you WHAT the second paragraph says. It is asking about the purpose. The purpose for something is the reason it is there. How would you talk about that? You would explain WHY it is there, right? Yes! So when you see questions with phrases like "what is the purpose" or "the author says/does X/Y/Z in order to," just translate them into questions starting with WHY.

So question 22 is really asking WHY the author included the second paragraph. Doesn't that feel easier to deal with than the way it was originally worded? We think so too.

Begin by carefully reading the second paragraph. It begins with a statement that jumping spiders are *particularly ambitious* because they *eat other spiders.* The paragraph then goes on to explain that in order to do this, they must have *extra intelligence* and, in fact, researchers have done studies which show the spiders can *find hidden prey.* In this paragraph, the author tells the reader that this spider is unique and demonstrably intelligent. But remember, the question is asking WHY the author includes that information. If you look at the last sentence of the previous paragraph, the author says that the spiders' vision allows them to do things *physically impossible for other animals that size.* The second paragraph then continues with a description of something that supports that statement. Let's compare that prediction with the answer choices.

    A) refute a controversial claim.

    B) describe a complicated experiment.

    C) provide a specific example.

    D) prove a long-disputed hypothesis.

The author did not include the second paragraph in order to *refute* or *prove* anything, nor to *describe a complicated experiment,* so eliminate (A), (B), and (D). Choice (C) is consistent with the prediction, so choose (C)!

HOW? (STRUCTURE AND ARGUMENT QUESTIONS)

The last time someone asked you about a film you just saw, did you answer "A character was introduced, a problem emerged, possible solutions were explored and rejected, and a resolution emerged from an unexpected alliance with a former antagonist"? Doubtful. But if so, the test writers might have a job for you!

Take a look at this question, and think about how it's different from what we've been talking about.

24

Which choice is an underlying assumption of the jumping spider experiment in the passage?

Notice that this question is not asking you WHAT the author is saying, nor is it asking you WHY the author says certain things. It's asking you about an assumption in an experiment. The answers for these questions might look a little different, because they are not going to come directly from the text. However, they will still be supported by the text. Eliminate what is clearly wrong, and then look for specifics to justify keeping or eliminating the remaining answers.

    A) If a jumping spider can simply see food, it will recognize it as food.

    B) If a jumping spider is close to water, it will avoid the path entirely.

    C) If a jumping spider uses a walkway, then it must be in the *Portia* family.

    D) If a jumping spider can't see its food, it will become confused.

Notice that this is also the first question in a paired set, so you can do this question in tandem with question 25. Consider the answers to question 25 first.

    A) Lines 37–38 ("Other spiders . . . used")

    B) Lines 42–46 ("From atop . . . leaves")

    C) Lines 50–54 ("But once . . . location")

    D) Lines 67–68 ("What's more . . . confused")

The lines for (25A) say that *other spiders ignored the walkways* Portia *used.* These lines might initially seem to support (24C), so draw a line connecting those two answers.

The lines for (25B) say that from the tower, *a famished jumping spider could see two boxes,* one containing *juicy spider fragments* and the other containing *unappetizing leaves.* These lines support (24A); although the passage does not directly state that the spider will see food and recognize it as such, the passage gives specific examples that still support that claim. Draw a line connecting these two answers.

The lines for (25C) state that once the spiders headed down the tower, the researchers emptied out the boxes. Although these lines might initially seem to support (24D), make sure you read carefully. While the spider certainly can't *see the food,* there is no evidence that it *will become confused.* Eliminate (25C).

The lines for (25D) say that spiders are *seemingly confused* when they *chose the wrong path.* Although we now have confused spiders, which goes with (24D), there's no indication that they can't see their food. Eliminate (25D).

Without support from Q25, (24B) and (24D) can both be eliminated. Now look back at your remaining two answer pairs. (24A) and (25B) are solidly connected and supported by the passage. (24C) and (25A) aren't so strongly connected. While the text says that other spiders ignored the walkways, the text doesn't support the idea that *only* the jumping spiders used the walkways. Eliminate (24C) and (25A).

The correct answers are (24A) and (25B).

CHARTS AND GRAPHS

Charts, graphs, and diagrams are no longer limited to the Math Test! You will now see a variety of graphics in the Reading Test and even in the Writing and Language Test! (More on the Writing and Language Test later.) The good news is that the graphics you'll be dealing with in the Reading Test are very straightforward and do not require any computations. All you need to do is make sure you can put your pencil on the place on the graphic that proves a reason to keep or eliminate an answer choice. Let's take a look at an example.

Figure 2

Species	Prey were in Box A		Prey were in Box B	
	Completed Walkway A	Completed Walkway B	Completed Walkway A	Completed Walkway B
Brettus adonis	6	0	0	5
Brettus albolimbatus	7	0	0	4
Cocalus gibbosus	5	0	0	5
Cyrba algerina	4	0	0	2
Cyrba ocellata	5	0	0	4
Cyrba simoni	4	0	1	4
Gelotia lanka	4	0	0	6
Meleon solitaria	6	0	0	6
Neobrettus nangalisagus	4	0	1	6
Portia africana	10	1	0	6
Portia albimana	3	0	0	4
Portia fimbriata	7	0	0	10
Portia labiata	10	1	0	9
Portia cf occidentalis	7	0	0	7
Portia schultzi	6	0	0	6

Step 1: Read the graphic.

Carefully look the titles, labels, and units. In this figure, we have a list of spider species and which walkway each species chose when the prey were in either Box A or Box B.

Step 2: Read your question.

 27

Figure 2 best supports which claim from the passage?

Since the question asks you which claim from the passage is best supported by the graph, your job will be to compare all four answer choices with information from the passage and information in the graph. Make sure you can put your pencil on the data point you're using to keep or eliminate certain answers.

Step 3: Read your answers.

A) Other spiders did not pay attention to the same walkways that *Portia* spiders used.

B) The *Portia* spider had a more accurate plan to get food than other species of jumping spider.

C) Each species of jumping spider was able to find its way to the box containing the food.

D) The spiders were distracted by the researchers' blinking.

Choice (A) says that other spiders *did not pay attention to the same walkways* that the *Portia* spiders used, but the table shows very clearly that they did use the same walkways. Eliminate (A).

Choice (B) says that the *Portia* spider had a *more accurate plan* to get to the food. There is nothing in the table that indicates whether one plan is more accurate than another, so eliminate (B).

Choice (C) is supported by the table: each species was able to get to the box with the food multiple times. Keep (C).

Choice (D), while supported by the text of the passage, is irrelevant to the figure, so (D) can be eliminated.

The correct answer is (C).

DUAL PASSAGES

One of your Science or History/Social Studies passages will be a set of dual passages. There will be two shorter passages about one topic. Although the two passages will be about the same topic, there will also be differences that you'll need to pay attention to. Rather than attempting to read and understand both passages at the same time, just follow the Basic Approach and focus on one at a time.

The questions for Passage 1 will come before the questions for Passage 2, and the questions for each passage follow the order of the passage, just like single-passage questions. The questions about both passages will follow the questions for Passage 2.

Two-Passage Questions

For questions asking to compare or contrast both passages, it's helpful to consider one passage at a time rather than trying to juggle both passages at the same time. First, find the answer for the first passage (or the second passage if that one is easier) and use POE to narrow down the answer choices. Then find the answer in the other passage and use POE to arrive at the correct answer. This will save time and keep you from confusing the two passages when you're evaluating the answer choices. Always keep in mind that the same POE criteria apply, no matter how two-passage questions are presented.

- If a question is about what is supported by both passages, make sure that you find specific support in both passages, and be wary of all the usual trap answers.

- If a question is about an issue on which the authors of the two passages disagree or on how the passages relate to one another, make sure you find support in each passage for the author's particular opinion.

- If the question asks how one author would respond to the other passage, find out what was said in that other passage, and then find out exactly what the author you are asked about said on that exact topic.

The bottom line is that if you are organized and remember your basic reading comprehension strategy, you'll see that two-passage questions are no harder than single-passage questions! In the following drill, you'll have a chance to try a set of dual passages. Answers and explanations can be found in Part III.

Dual Passage Drill

Answers can be found in Part III.

Questions 38–47 are based on the following passages.

The following are modified passages that explore the design and construction of drug delivery vehicles for biomedical applications.

Passage 1

The technology of drug delivery is one of the most important in the field of medicine and biomedical engineering. The more site-specific a delivery system is, the more effective the drug it is delivering will be; the more conservative a delivered drug dosage is, the less severe the side effects will be. This is especially true of different drugs used to predominantly treat infections and cancers. A new technology called electrostatic processing, or electrospinning, accomplishes both of these goals.

Electrospinning creates biodegradable scaffolds composed of fibers ranging from nanometers to micrometers in diameter, an attribute that is intrinsically difficult to obtain from other fiber-fabrication processes. The electrospinning process begins with a polymer solution at a prescribed charge and viscosity that is pumped through a spinneret. An electric field, powered by a high voltage power supply, is applied to this spinneret so that a droplet is formed at the tip of the spinneret. This droplet morphs into the shape of a cone, in which the surface tension of the droplet is counterbalanced by the applied external electrostatic forces. Once the applied voltage is strong enough to overcome the droplet's surface tension, a fibrous jet is emitted from the cone and captured on a grounded collecting plate. The distance between the spinneret and the collecting plate is where any residual solvent in the ejected jet stream evaporates, resulting in a collection of non-woven submicron-sized fibers that, ultimately, form a highly porous scaffold. Drug delivery via these electrospun scaffolds affords ample flexibility in creating an optimal delivery vehicle for therapeutic treatment.

The chemical properties of the materials utilized as base polymers determine how stable the electrospun scaffolds are and how well they function. Both synthetic and natural materials can be used as base polymers. Between the two, natural polymers typically possess lower levels of toxicity, immunogenicity, and improved biocompatibility. In other words, natural polymers have a greater ability to perform more effectively than synthetic polymers do in the treatment of human disease. Examples of a natural base commonly used as a base for electrospun fibers include collagen and elastin. Collagen is the most prevalent protein in the extracellular matrix (ECM) of soft and hard tissues, and collagen types I, II, and III have all been utilized as the main component of electrospun scaffolds. Elastin has also been substantially utilized as a polymer in electrospinning, especially for vascular tissue engineering. Beyond the inherent advantages that natural polymers possess, the combination of natural polymers can sometimes provide a greater benefit toward constructing an ideal electrospun scaffold. For example, the combination of collagen and elastin in certain ratios has been demonstrated to produce ideally-sized fiber diameters. Thus, the potential to combine—or include—other natural polymers is tremendous in attempting to engineer a drug delivery vehicle with optimal biodegradable properties.

Passage 2

Although it has historically been the case that natural polymers were favored in the construction of electrospun fibers for drug delivery systems, there is a growing trend towards employing synthetic polymers. Synthetic polymers are used to enhance various characteristics of the drug delivery system goals. These characteristics include degradation time, mechanical properties, and cell attachment affinities. Synthetic polymers are able to improve these characteristics as they are more easily tailored to a wider range of properties such as hydrophilicity and hydrophobicity—in other

words, the desired solubility of an electrospun
80   scaffold. Because synthetic polymers can be
created in laboratories, a nearly innumerable
number of possible products that are made from
synthetic polymers can be engineered to address
any particular clinical need. The most popular of
85   these are the most hydrophobic and biodegradable
polymers such as poly(glycolide) (PGA) and
poly(lactide).
    Despite the clear benefits of synthetic
polymers when compared with natural
90   polymers, it is of the utmost importance to not
limit scientific or medical pursuit by a purist
approach. The ability to blend the variety of
synthetic polymers with the strong biocompatible
properties of natural polymers may allow
95   biomedical engineers to more precisely fine-tune
the properties of electrospun scaffolds. It is this
wide-ranging flexibility of polymer compositions
that gives electrospun scaffolds such huge
promise in medical applications, causing the
100 huge spike of research done in this space in the
last several decades. With even more to discover,
it is both likely and lucky that this interest will
continue for some time.

38

The author mentions infections and cancers
(lines 8–9) in order to

A)   provide an example of the types of diseases
     that electrospun scaffolds have cured.

B)   point out illnesses that still do not have
     effective treatments.

C)   illustrate types of medical conditions that
     are more effectively treated by precisely
     controlled internal drug delivery.

D)   demonstrate the kind of vaccines
     electrospinning technology will help to
     develop.

39

In Passage 1, the reference to "nanometers to
micrometers" (lines 13–14) serves to

A)   give a precise measurement of fibers used in
     electrospinning.

B)   further elaborate on the minuteness of
     electrospun fibers.

C)   relate the size of the fibers in electrospun
     scaffolds to that of the cells of the human
     body.

D)   inform the reader of one of the qualities of
     electrospun fibers absent in other similar
     technological approaches.

40

As used in line 30, "residual" most nearly means

A)   durable.

B)   remaining.

C)   steadfast.

D)   inhabiting.

41

In discussing the nature of natural polymers, the
author of Passage 1 suggests that

A)   they are more effective as an electrospun
     scaffold base as they may be less harmful to
     people than synthetic polymers.

B)   they are not as effective as when blended with
     synthetic polymers such as poly(glycolide)
     and poly(lactide).

C)   because they are natural materials that exist
     in the human body, the body is unable to
     reject them.

D)   collagen and elastin are effective polymer
     bases only when blended together.

In Passage 2, the connection between natural and synthetic polymers is best described in which of the following ways?

A) Researchers are increasingly using synthetic polymers more than the historically preferred natural polymers, while more attention is being paid to electrospun fiber research that combines the two types of polymers.

B) Because synthetic polymers can be created in laboratories, they are easier to work with than natural polymers.

C) Because of the importance of a purist approach, it is important to separate research conducted on differing types of base polymers.

D) Synthetic polymers are more hydrophobic when compared to natural polymers.

43

The second paragraph of Passage 2 primarily serves to

A) confirm the author's assertion that synthetic polymers are the most effective polymers for electrospinning.

B) support the purist approach to polymer research in order to preserve the impeccable methods of scientific and medical study.

C) assert that it is because there has been a huge spike in research on polymers that scientists have learned how flexible polymers are.

D) acknowledge that both types of polymers have positive attributes that, when combined, may lead to even more effective electrospun scaffolds.

44

From the information presented in Passage 2, it can be inferred that

A) history favors things from nature.

B) it is the man-made nature of synthetic polymers that accounts for their flexibility.

C) the solubility of an electrospun scaffold depends more on its hydrophilicity than its hydrophobicity.

D) synthetic polymers degrade more quickly over time than natural polymers.

The authors of both passages would most likely agree with which of the following?

A) Hydrophilicity and hydrophobicity are important factors to consider when selecting a base polymer material.

B) Differing electric charges and viscosity will result in differing constructions of electrospun scaffolding.

C) The more exact the system of drug delivery is, the more beneficial it is likely to be.

D) A blended polymer base will be more effective than a non-blended one.

46

The passages differ in that Passage 1

A) does not discuss the possibility of using multiple materials for base polymers, while Passage 2 does.

B) provides information on electrospun scaffolding construction, while Passage 2 looks to the future of electrospun scaffolding research.

C) is concerned only with drug delivery systems to address cancers, while Passage 2 aims to treat all diseases.

D) advocates that the type of polymer base used for electrospun scaffolds is unimportant, while Passage 2 advocates that the type of polymer base is important.

What is the primary difference in the tones of Passages 1 and 2?

A) Passage 1 is belligerent, while Passage 2 is enthusiastic.

B) Passage 1 biased, while Passage 2 is subjective.

C) Passage 1 is unequivocal, while Passage 2 is conciliatory.

D) Passage 1 is pessimistic, while Passage 2 is optimistic.

Summary

o   The Reading Test on the PSAT makes up 50 percent of your score on the Evidence-Based Reading and Writing section.

o   Reading questions are *not* presented in order of difficulty, but they are in chronological order. Don't be afraid to skip a hard question, and don't worry if you can't answer every question.

o   Use your POOD to pick up the points you can get, and don't forget LOTD on the rest!

o   Reading is an open-book test! Use that to your advantage by focusing only on the text you need to get each point.

o   Translate each question back into a *what* or *why* question before you start reading your window.

o   Use Line References, Lead Words, and chronology to help you find the answer in the passage. Always start reading a few lines above the Line Reference or the Lead Words and read until you have the answer.

o   Use the text to predict your answer to the question before you look at the answer choices.

o   Use POE to eliminate answers that don't match your prediction.

o   If you have more than one answer left after you eliminate anything that doesn't match your prediction, compare your remaining answers to see if any of them

  •   are mostly right/slightly wrong
  •   could be true
  •   contain deceptive language

- For Paired Sets, make sure you're following the right strategy.
  - Specific Paired Questions simply require you to follow the Basic Approach, making sure you've underlined the evidence for your prediction in the text.
  - General Paired Questions will be much more straightforward if you use Parallel POE to consider the "best evidence" in tandem with the previous question.

- For Dual Passages, do questions about the first passage first, questions about the second passage second, and dual questions last. Remember that even with dual questions, you must find support in the passages.

- Save Main Idea or General Questions until the end of the passage. POE will be much more efficient once you've completed all the other questions.

- Don't get bogged down by hard or time-consuming questions! If you find yourself stuck or running short on time, use LOTD and move on!

Chapter 5
Introduction
to Writing and
Language Strategy

CAN YOU REALLY TEST WRITING ON A MULTIPLE-CHOICE TEST?

We'd say no, but the PSAT (and a heck of a lot of other tests) seems to think the answer is yes. To that end, the PSAT is giving you 35 minutes to answer 44 multiple-choice questions that ask about a variety of grammatical and stylistic topics. If you like to read and/or write, this test may frustrate you a bit because it may seem to boil writing down to a couple of dull rules. But as you will see, we will use the next few chapters to suggest a method that keeps things simple for pro- and anti-grammarians alike.

It is worth noting also that the breakdown of the test is exactly that of the SAT. While other sections of this test may provide slightly easier or shorter versions of what is to come on the real SAT, the Writing and Language Test is a carbon copy. Even the topics tested and the difficulty levels are likely to be the same.

WHERE DID ALL THE QUESTIONS GO?

One thing that can seem a little strange about the Writing and Language section of the PSAT is that many of the questions don't have, well, questions. Instead, many of the questions look something like this:

The history of standardized testing although it may seem pretty dull, is in many ways a story about beliefs about how people learn and succeed.

1
A) NO CHANGE
B) standardized testing, although it may seem pretty dull
C) standardized testing, although it may seem, pretty dull,
D) standardized testing, although it may seem pretty dull,

How are you supposed to pick an answer when there's no question?

Well, actually, what you'll find throughout this chapter and the next two is that the PSAT gives you a *lot* of information in this list of answer choices. (The answer is (D), by the way, but stick with us for a second here.)

Look at these pairs, and you'll see just what we mean. As you read through these pairs of answer choices, think about what each question is probably testing.

1. A) could of
    B) could have
2. A) tall, dark, and handsome
    B) tall, dark and handsome
3. A) let them in
    B) let Sister Susie and Brother John in
4. A) We arrived in Paris on a Sunday. Then we took the train to Nantes. Then we took the train to Bordeaux.
    B) We arrived in Paris on a Sunday. Then we took the train to Bordeaux. Then we took the train to Nantes.

If you were able to see the differences in these answer choices, you're already more than halfway there. Now, notice how the differences in these answers can reveal the question that is lurking in the heart of each list of answer choices.

1. The difference between the word "of" and "have" means that this question is asking *Is the correct form "could of" or "could have"?*
2. The difference between having a comma after the word "dark" and not having one there means that this question is asking *How many commas does this sentence need, and where do they belong?*
3. The difference between "them" and "Sister and Susie and Brother John" means that this question is asking *Is "them" adequately specific, or do you need to refer to people by name?*
4. The difference in the order of these sentences asks *What order should the sentences be in?*

Therefore, what we have noticed in these pairs of answer choices is something that may seem fairly simple but which is essential to success on the PSAT.

THE ANSWER CHOICES ASK THE QUESTIONS

At some point, you've almost certainly had to do the English-class exercise called "peer editing." In this exercise, you are tasked with "editing" the work of one of your fellow students. But this can be really tough, because what exactly does it mean to "edit" an entire essay or paper when you aren't given any directions? It's *especially* tough when you start getting into the subtleties between whether things are *wrong* or whether they could merely be improved.

Look, for example, at these two sentences:

It was a beautiful day outside birds were singing cheerful songs.

It was a beautiful day outside; birds were singing cheerful songs.

You'd have to pick the second one in this case because the first has a grammatical error: it's a run-on sentence. Or for the non-grammarians out there, you have to break that thing up.

Now, look at these next two sentences:

> *The weather was just right, so I decided to play soccer.*

> *Just right was how I would describe the weather, so a decision of soccer-playing was made by me.*

In this case, the first sentence is obviously better than the second, but the second technically doesn't have any grammatical errors in it. The first may be *better*, but the second isn't exactly *wrong*.

What made each of these pairs of sentences relatively easy to deal with, though, was the fact that you could compare the sentences to one another. In doing so, you noted the differences between those sentences, and so you picked the *better* answer accordingly.

Let's see how this looks in a real PSAT situation.

In particular, the early history of standardized [2] tests that reveals some of the basic assumptions about what education was supposed to do.

2

A) NO CHANGE
B) tests they reveal
C) tests reveals
D) tests, which revealing

Here's How to Crack It

First, look at what's changing in the answer choices. The word *tests* remains the same in each, but what comes after it changes each time. This question, then, seems to be asking *Which words will best link the two ideas in the sentence?*

Choices (A) and (D) make the sentence incomplete, so those should be eliminated. Choice (B) creates a run-on sentence, so that should also be eliminated. It looks like only (C) appropriately links the ideas without adding new errors.

Notice how that entire process started with asking *What's changing in the answer choices?* With that question, we figured out what was being tested, and we used POE to do the rest.

Let's try another.

In many ways, a civilization's self-image can be assessed through what that civilization expects [3] their citizens to know.

3

A) NO CHANGE
B) they're citizens
C) their citizen
D) its citizens

Here's How to Crack It

As always, start with what is changing in the answer choices. It looks like the main change is between the words *their*, *they're*, and *its* with a minor change between the words *citizen* and *citizens*. As such, this question seems to be asking *What is the appropriate pronoun to use in this context, and just how many citizens are we talking about?*

Start wherever is easiest. In this case, we're talking about many *citizens*, not just one, so (C) can be eliminated. Now, let's work with the pronoun. What does it refer back to? In this sentence, it seems that the pronoun refers back to *civilization*, which is a singular noun (even though it describes a lot of people). Therefore, the only possible answer that could work is (D), which contains the singular pronoun "its."

LEARN FROM THE ANSWER CHOICES

Let's think about the previous question a bit more. If someone said to you *a civilization's self-image can be assessed through what that civilization expects their citizens to know*, you might not necessarily hear that as wrong. That's because the way we speak is often very different from the way we write. The PSAT is more concerned on this test with how we write and with the stricter set of rules that go along with writing.

As such, not only can the answer choices tell us what a particular question is testing, they can also reveal mistakes that we might not have otherwise seen (in the original sentence) or heard (in our heads). In the previous question, we might not have noted the mistake at all if we hadn't looked at what was changing in the answer choices.

Let's see another.

A good standardized test can be an effective way **4** to try a different tact at assessing student learning.

4

A) NO CHANGE
B) to try a different tack
C) for those trying a different tact
D) for those trying a different tack

Here's How to Crack It

First, as always, check what's changing in the answer choices. In this case, that step is especially important because you can't really hear the error. People misuse this idiom all the time because they so rarely see it written; each pair of answer choices sounds basically the same. The fact that they are not the same, that they *change*, tells us precisely what to pay attention to when we use POE.

Start the Process of Elimination. There's no good reason to add a bunch of extra words that don't make things any more precise, so eliminate (C) and (D). Then, if you're not sure, take a guess. The correct form of the saying here is (B).

Notice, though, that looking at the answer choices revealed the problem that you might not have otherwise been able to see or hear. Then, POE got you the rest of the way.

POE DOES THE BIG WORK

Once you have a sense of what the question is testing, POE can get you closer and closer to the answer. POE is especially helpful when you're dealing with sentences that have lots of issues, like this one:

It may seem that what you learn in school is too different from what you **5** are doing on the test. However, they would say that the underlying skills are the same.

5

A) NO CHANGE
B) do on the test, however, they'd
C) are doing on the test; however, the creators of the test would
D) do on the test; however, the creators of the test would

Here's How to Crack It

First, as always, check what's changing in the answer choices. In this case, there are three things changing: the difference between *do* and *are doing*, the difference between *they* and *the creators of the test*, and some differences in punctuation. While this may seem like a lot, this is actually a huge POE opportunity! Start with the one you find easiest, and work backwards from there.

Because the semicolon is not commonly used, let's save the punctuation part for last. Hopefully we can get the right answer without having to deal with the punctuation at all. Let's start with the difference between *they* and *the creators of the test*. If we use the pronoun *they*, it's not entirely clear whom the sentence is talking about, so eliminate (A) and (B). Then, to choose between the last two, *do* is more concise and more consistent with the rest of the sentence than is *are doing*, which makes (D) better than (C). In this instance, we got to the correct answer without having to deal with all of the messiness in the question!

ALL OF THE QUESTIONS CAN'T BE WRONG ALL OF THE TIME

Now that our strategy is basically set, let's look at one more tough one.

---

 6 Your attitude toward these test creators may not be entirely sympathetic, but it might make you feel better to know that the tests were designed with you in mind.

6

A) NO CHANGE

B) You're attitude toward these test creators may not be entirely sympathetic,

C) Your attitude toward these test creators may not be sympathetically entire,

D) You're attitude toward these test creators may not be sympathetic or entire,

Here's How to Crack It

As always, check the answers first. In this case, here's what's changing: the answers are switching between *your* and *you're* and some weirdness with *entire* and *sympathetic*. Let's do the easy parts first!

First of all, we'll need the word *your*, because this is the attitude that belongs to *you*, thus eliminating (B) and (D). Then the choice is between *entirely sympathetic*, which is fine, and between *sympathetically entire*, which is really weird, so (C) is no good either. Choice (A) must be the one.

Remember, NO CHANGE is right sometimes! Some people pick it too much. Some people don't pick it enough, but if you've done the other steps in the process and have eliminated all the other choices, go ahead and pick (A)!

HOW TO ACE THE WRITING AND LANGUAGE SECTION: A STRATEGY

- Check what's changing in the answer choices.
- Figure out what the question is testing and let the differences reveal potential errors.
- Use Process of Elimination.
- If you haven't eliminated three answers, pick the shortest one that is most consistent with the rest of the sentence.

In the next few chapters, we'll get into some of the more technical issues in Writing and Language, but we'll be using this strategy throughout. Try the drill on the next page to get some of the basics down.

Writing and Language Drill 1

The purpose of this drill is to get a basic idea of what each question is testing from only the answer choices. Check your answers in Part III.

1

A) NO CHANGE
B) singers' preferred songwriters
C) singer's preferred songwriter's
D) singers' preferred songwriters'

What's changing in the answer choices?

_____

What is this question testing?

_____

2

A) NO CHANGE
B) had
C) has
D) has had

What's changing in the answer choices?

_____

What is this question testing?

_____

3

A) NO CHANGE
B) Even though
C) If
D) Since

What's changing in the answer choices?

_____

What is this question testing?

_____

4

A) NO CHANGE
B) seem attractive for their
C) seems attractive for its
D) seems attractive for their

What's changing in the answer choices?

_____

What is this question testing?

_____

5

A) NO CHANGE
B) smooth, as in completely lumpless.
C) smooth, like talking not a single lump.
D) smooth.

What's changing in the answer choices?

_____

What is this question testing?

_____

Chapter 6
Punctuation

WAIT; THE PSAT WANTS ME TO KNOW HOW TO USE A SEMICOLON?

Kurt Vonnegut once wrote, "Here is a lesson in creative writing. First rule: Do not use semi-colons…All they do is show you've been to college." Unfortunately, the writers of the PSAT don't quite agree. They want you to know how to use the semicolon and a few other types of weird punctuation as well. In this chapter, we're going to talk about the varieties of punctuation that the PSAT wants you to know how to use. Learn these few simple rules, and you'll be all set on the punctuation questions.

First and foremost, remember how you can spot a question that's asking about punctuation. Start by asking,

> What's changing in the answer choices?

If you see punctuation marks—commas, periods, apostrophes, semicolons, colons—changing, then the question is testing punctuation. Then, as you work the problem, make sure to ask the big question:

> Does this punctuation need to be here?

The particular punctuation mark you are using—no matter what it is—must have a specific role within the sentence. You wouldn't use a question mark without a question, would you? Nope! Well, all punctuation works that way, and in what follows, we'll give you about seven basic instances in which you would use some type of punctuation. Otherwise, let the words do their thing unobstructed!

STOP, GO, AND THE VERTICAL LINE TEST

Let's get the weird ones out of the way first. Everyone knows that a period ends a sentence, but even particularly nerdy grammarians can get lost when things get more complicated. Because of this confusion, we've come up with a basic chart that summarizes the different times you might use what the PSAT calls "end-of-sentence" and "middle-of-sentence" punctuation.

When you are linking ideas,

STOP	HALF-STOP	GO
• Period	• Colon	• Comma
• Semicolon	• Long dash	• No punctuation
• Comma + FANBOYS		
• Question mark		
• Exclamation Mark		

FANBOYS stands for **F**or, **A**nd, **N**or, **B**ut, **O**r, **Y**et, and **S**o.

> STOP punctuation can link *only* complete ideas.
>
> HALF-STOP punctuation must be *preceded* by a complete idea.
>
> GO punctuation can link anything *except* two complete ideas.

Let's see how these work. Here is a complete idea:

> *Samantha studied for the PSAT.*

Notice that we've already used one form of STOP punctuation at the end of this sentence: a period.

Now, if we want to add a second complete idea, we'll keep the period.

> *Samantha studied for the PSAT. She ended up doing really well on the test.*

In this case, the period is linking these two complete ideas. But the nice thing about STOP punctuation is that you can really use any of the punctuation in the list to do the same thing, so we could also say this:

> *Samantha studied for the PSAT; she ended up doing really well on the test.*

What the list of STOP punctuation shows us is that essentially, a period and a semicolon are the same thing. We could say the same for the use of a comma plus one of the FANBOYS.

> *Samantha studied for the PSAT, and she ended up doing really well on the test.*

You can also use HALF-STOP punctuation to separate two complete ideas, so you could say

Samantha studied for the PSAT: she ended up doing really well on the test.

Or

Samantha studied for the PSAT—she ended up doing really well on the test.

There's a subtle difference, however, between STOP and HALF-STOP punctuation: for STOP, both ideas have to be complete, but for HALF-STOP, only the first one does.

Let's see what this looks like. If we want to link a complete idea and an incomplete idea, we can use HALF-STOP punctuation as long as the complete idea is first. For example,

Samantha studied for the PSAT: all three sections of it.

Or

Samantha studied for the PSAT: the silliest test in all the land.

When you use HALF-STOP, there has to be a complete idea before the punctuation, so these examples wouldn't be correct:

Samantha studied for: the PSAT, the SAT, and every AP test in between.

The PSAT—Samantha studied for it and was glad she did.

When you are not linking two complete ideas, you can use GO punctuation. So you could say, for instance,

Samantha studied for the PSAT, the SAT, and every AP test in between.

Or

Samantha studied for the PSAT, all three sections of it.

These are the three types of mid-sentence or end-of-sentence punctuation: STOP, HALF-STOP, and GO. You'll notice that there is a bit of overlap between the concepts, but the writers of the PSAT couldn't possibly make you get into the minutiae of choosing between, say, a period and a semicolon. If you can figure out which of the big three (STOP, HALF-STOP, and GO) categories you'll need, that's all you need to be able to do.

In the following exercise, choose the type of punctuation that will correctly work in the blank. Some questions have more than one answer! Check your answers on page 84.

	STOP	HALF-STOP	GO
The other day I went to the stadium _____ and bought a ticket.			
I had saved up all week _____ I couldn't think of anything better to spend the money on!			
Some of my favorite sports include _____ hockey, baseball, and tennis.			
There's always something _____ for me to see at the stadium.			
When I arrived _____ I was thrilled to see that I had bought great seats.			
Some people from my school were sitting next to me _____ we're all in the same math class.			
The game was exciting _____ a goal in the first five minutes!			
The crowd was extremely diverse _____ men, women, and children in the stands.			
I didn't want to go home _____ even though I had school the next day.			
You can be sure of one thing _____ I'll be back as soon as I can.			

	STOP	HALF-STOP	GO
The other day I went to the stadium _____ and bought a ticket.			X
I had saved up all week _____ I couldn't think of anything better to spend the money on!	X	X	
Some of my favorite sports include _____ hockey, baseball, and tennis.			X
There's always something _____ for me to see at the stadium.			X
When I arrived _____ I was thrilled to see that I had bought great seats.			X
Some people from my school were sitting next to me _____ we're all in the same math class.	X	X	
The game was exciting _____ a goal in the first five minutes!		X	X
The crowd was extremely diverse _____ men, women, and children in the stands.		X	
I didn't want to go home _____ even though I had school the next day.			X
You can be sure of one thing _____ I'll be back as soon as I can.	X	X	

Let's see what this will look like on the PSAT.

Noah took the PSAT way more seriously than many of his **1** friends he was almost certain he would get a National Merit honor of some kind.

1.
A) NO CHANGE
B) friends, he was almost
C) friends he was almost,
D) friends; he was almost

Here's How to Crack It

As always, check what's changing in the answer choices. In this case, the words all stay the same. All that changes is the punctuation, and notice the types of punctuation that are changing: STOP and GO.

Now, when you see STOP punctuation changing in the answer choices, you can do a little something we like to call the Vertical Line Test.

Draw a line where you see the punctuation changing—in this case, between the words *friends* and *he*. Then, read up to the vertical line: *Noah took the PSAT way more seriously than many of his friends.* That's Complete. Now, read after the vertical line: *he was almost certain he'd get a National Merit honor of some kind.* That's also Complete.

By the time you're done, your page should look like this.

Complete | Complete

Noah took the PSAT way more seriously than many of his **1** friends | he was almost certain he would get a National Merit honor of some kind.

So let's think; we've got two complete ideas here. What kind of punctuation do we need? STOP or HALF-STOP. It looks like STOP is the only one available, so choose (D).

Let's try another.

He really wanted to make sure he had balanced **2** scores. Over 700 for both.

2.
A) NO CHANGE
B) scores; over
C) scores: over
D) scores, he wanted over

Here's How to Crack It

Check the answer choices. What's changing? It looks like the punctuation is changing, and some of that punctuation is STOP. Let's use the Vertical Line Test. Draw a vertical line where you see the punctuation: between *scores* and *over* in the underlined portion.

What's before the vertical line? *He really wanted to make sure he had balanced scores* is complete. Then, *over 700 for both* is not. Therefore, because we have one complete idea (the first) and one incomplete idea (the second), we can't use STOP punctuation, thus eliminating (A) and (B).

Now, what's different between the last two? Choice (C) contains HALF-STOP punctuation, which can work, so we'll keep that. Choice (D) adds some words, with which the second idea becomes *he wanted over 700 for both*, which is complete. That makes two complete ideas separated by a comma, but what do we need when we're separating two complete ideas? STOP punctuation! Eliminate (D)! Only (C) is left.

―――――――――◯―――――――――

Let's see one more.

―――――――――◯―――――――――

Every day after Noah got home from baseball **3** practice—he hit the books.

3

A) NO CHANGE

B) practice; he

C) practice, he,

D) practice, he

Here's How to Crack It

The punctuation is changing in the answer choices, and there's some STOP punctuation, so let's use the Vertical Line Test. Put the line between *practice* and *he*. The first idea, *Every day after Noah got home from baseball practice*, is incomplete, and the second idea, *he hit the books*, is complete. Therefore, we can't use STOP (which needs two complete ideas) or HALF-STOP (which needs a complete idea before the punctuation), thus eliminating (A) and (B). Then, because there is no good reason to put a comma after the word *he*, the best answer must be (D).

―――――――――◯―――――――――

A SLIGHT PAUSE FOR COMMAS

Commas can be a little tricky. In the last question (#3), we got down to two answers, (C) and (D), after having completed the Vertical Line Test. But then, how do you decide whether to keep a comma in or not? It seems a little arbitrary to say that you use a comma "every time you want to pause," so let's make that thought a little more concrete.

If you can't cite a reason to use a comma, *don't use one.*

On the PSAT, there are only four reasons to use a comma:
- in STOP punctuation, with one of the FANBOYS
- in GO punctuation, to separate incomplete ideas from other ideas
- in a list of three or more things
- in a sentence containing unnecessary information

We've already seen the first two concepts, so let's look at the third and fourth.

Try this one.

His favorite classes were

4 English, physics and history.

4

A) NO CHANGE

B) English, physics, and history.

C) English, physics, and, history.

D) English physics and history.

Here's How to Crack It

First, check what's changing in the answer choices. It looks like the commas in this list are changing. Because there's not any obvious STOP or HALF-STOP punctuation, the Vertical Line Test won't do us much good.

Then, it will help to know that that the PSAT wants a comma after every item in a series. Think of it this way. There's a potential misunderstanding in this sentence:

> *I went to the park with my parents, my cat Violet and my dog Stuart.*

Without a comma, it sure sounds like this guy has some interesting parents. If there's no comma, how do we know that this sentence isn't supposed to say his parents are *my cat Violet and my dog Stuart*? The only way to remove the ambiguity would be to add a comma like this:

> *I went to the park with my parents, my cat Violet, and my dog Stuart.*

Keep that in mind as we try to crack question 4. In this problem, *English, physics, and history* form a list or series, so they should be set off from one another by commas, as they are in (B).

———————◯———————

Let's try another.

———————◯———————

5 Noah, it was clear to everyone, had a really good shot at being a National Merit finalist.

5

A) NO CHANGE

B) Noah it was clear to everyone

C) Noah, it was clear to everyone

D) Noah it was clear to everyone,

Here's How to Crack It

First, check what's changing in the answer choices. Just commas. And those commas seem to be circling around the words *it was clear to everyone.* When you have a few commas circling around a word, phrase, or clause like this, the question is usually testing necessary versus unnecessary information.

A good way to test whether the idea is necessary to the meaning of the sentence is to take it out. Read the original sentence again. Now read this one: *Noah had a really good shot at being a National Merit finalist.*

Is the sentence still complete? Yes. Has the meaning of the sentence changed? No, we just lost a little extra thing. Therefore, the idea is *unnecessary* to the meaning of the sentence and should be set off with commas, as it is in (A).

———————◯———————

Let's try a few more. Try to figure out whether the word or idea in italics is necessary to the meaning of the sentence.

1. The student *with the highest score* has a good chance at a National Merit scholarship.
2. Katie wants to go to Yale *which has a really good theater program.*
3. The team *that scored five touchdowns* won the game in a landslide.
4. The National Merit competition *which began in 1955* had over 1.25 million applicants in 2005.
5. Rising senior *Liam* is hoping to be one of the chosen few this year.

Answers are on page 92.

Let's put it all together in this question.

All his teachers [6] believed, he had a
real shot, when he sat down to take the test.

6
A) NO CHANGE
B) believed, he had a real shot, when he
sat down,
C) believed, he had a real shot when he
sat, down,
D) believed he had a real shot when he
sat down

Here's How to Crack It

Check what's changing in the answer choices. There are varying numbers of commas in varying places. Remember, the rule of thumb with commas is that if you can't cite a reason to use
a comma, *don't use one*.

It looks like *he had a real shot* is being set off by commas. Let's see whether it's necessary or unnecessary information. Read the original sentence; then read the sentence again without that
piece of information: *All his teachers believed when he sat down to take the test.* It looks like the
sentence has changed meaning and is not really complete anymore. Therefore, that bit of information is necessary to the meaning of the sentence, so it doesn't need commas. Then, there are
no good reasons to put commas around or in the word *down*.

In the end, there aren't reasons to put commas anywhere in this sentence. The best answer is
(D). Sometimes the PSAT will test unnecessary punctuation explicitly, so make sure you have a
good reason to use commas when you use them!

YOUR GOING TO BE TESTED ON APOSTROPHE'S (AND INTERNET SPELLING IS A TERRIBLE GUIDE!)

As with commas, apostrophes have only a very limited set of applications. Apostrophes are a
little trickier, though, because you can't really hear them in speech, so people misuse them all
the time. Think about the header of this section. The apostrophes are wrong there. Here's the
correct way of punctuating it: *You're going to be tested on apostrophes.* Can you hear the difference? Neither can we.

Therefore, as with commas:

> If you can't cite a reason to use an apostrophe, *don't use one.*
>
> On the PSAT, there are only two reasons to use an apostrophe:
>
> * possessive nouns (NOT pronouns)
> * contractions

Here are some examples.

Some recognition from National Merit would help strengthen **7** his application's, especially for the high-end school's.

7

A) NO CHANGE

B) his applications, especially for the high-end schools'.

C) his application's, especially for the high-end schools.

D) his applications, especially for the high-end schools.

Here's How to Crack It

Check what's changing in the answer choices. In this case, the words are all staying the same, but the apostrophes are changing. Remember: we don't want to use apostrophes at all if we can't cite a good reason to do so.

Does anything belong to *schools* or *applications*? No! Are they forming contractions like *school is* or *application is*? No! Therefore, there's no reason to use apostrophes, and the only possible answer is (D), which dispenses with the apostrophes altogether.

As in the previous question, there's no need for any punctuation, and in a question like this, the PSAT is testing whether you can spot unnecessary punctuation.

But sometimes the apostrophes will be necessary. Let's have a look at another.

8 It's not easy to get you're score high enough for National Merit.

A) NO CHANGE
B) Its not easy to get your
C) Its not easy to get you're
D) It's not easy to get your

Here's How to Crack It

Check what's changing in the answer choices. The main changes have to do with apostrophes, particularly on the words *its/it's* and *your/you're*.

The first word, *its/it's*, needs an apostrophe: it creates the contraction *it is*. Therefore, because this one needs an apostrophe, get rid of (B) and (C). As for the other, this word is possessive (as in, the *score* belonging to *you*). Remember that possessive *nouns* need an apostrophe, but possessive *pronouns* don't. Therefore, because *you* is a pronoun, this word should be spelled *your*, as it is in (D).

Phew! These apostrophes can get a little tricky, so let's try a few more. On these (as on many parts of the PSAT), you'll find that using your ear, sounding things out, doesn't really help all that much.

Circle the option that works. The big question is this: apostrophes or no apostrophes?

1. *Salims/Salim's* teacher said *hes/he's* allowed to miss next *Tuesdays/Tuesday's* exam.
2. *Its/It's* really not going to hurt my feelings if you don't want to go to *they're/their* party with me.
3. Whatever the *justification's/justifications* for *your/you're* attitude, *there/they're* is no reason to be so obnoxious about it.
4. *Were/We're* going to get back to you as soon as your *application's/applications* processed.
5. *They're/Their they're/their* nachos, but they *wont/won't* share any unless *its/it's* absolutely necessary or we share *ours/our's*.

Answers are on page 92.

CONCLUSION

In sum, we've looked at all the punctuation you'd ever need on the PSAT. It's really not so much, and you probably knew a lot of it already. In general, checking what's changing in the answer choices can help reveal mistakes that you may not have heard, and POE can help you narrow those answers down.

Punctuation rules are easy to learn, as is the biggest rule of all about punctuation.

> Know why you are using punctuation, whether that punctuation is STOP, HALF-STOP, GO, commas, or apostrophes. If you can't cite reasons to use these punctuation marks, don't use them!

In the last few pages of this chapter, try out these skills on a drill.

Answers to Questions on Page 88:

1. NECESSARY to the meaning of the sentence (no commas). If you remove the italicized part, the sentence is not adequately specific.
2. UNNECESSARY to the meaning of the sentence (commas). If you remove the italicized part, the sentence is still complete and does not change meaning.
3. NECESSARY to the meaning of the sentence (no commas). If you remove the italicized part, the sentence is not adequately specific.
4. UNNECESSARY to the meaning of the sentence (commas). If you remove the italicized part, the sentence is still complete and does not change meaning.
5. NECESSARY to the meaning of the sentence (no commas). If you remove the italicized part, the sentence is no longer complete.

Answers to Questions on Page 91:

1. Salim's, he's, Tuesday's
2. It's, their
3. justifications, your, there
4. We're, application's
5. They're, their, won't, it's, ours

Writing and Language Drill 2

Time: 5-6 minutes. Check your answers in Part III.

There is no question that the United States is a country of **1** immigrants, the original countries of those immigrants varies so much that it can be tough to know who has contributed what. Moreover, different groups have come at **2** different time's for they're different reason's. In the late 1980s and **3** early 1990s, for instance, those, from the former Soviet Union arrived in large numbers on American shores.

1

A) NO CHANGE
B) immigrants, and the
C) immigrants and the
D) immigrants. And the

2

A) NO CHANGE
B) different time's for their different reason's.
C) different times for they're different reasons.
D) different times for their different reasons.

3

A) NO CHANGE
B) early 1990s, for instance those
C) early 1990s, for instance, those
D) early 1990s for instance those

This may seem a bit late, given that most of the USSR and USSR-affiliated empires fell around 1990 (starting with East Germany and **4** it's Berlin Wall in 1989) in fact the largest migrations of Soviets and ex-Soviets happened just *after* the Union had fallen. Indeed, whatever the shortcomings of the socialist republic, the real **5** poverty, depression and deprivation, began in earnest when the government was no longer tasked with providing basic necessities. As a result, while there had been a somewhat steady flow of immigration from the USSR since **6** the 1970s, the largest numbers came to the United States in the early 1990s.

4

A) NO CHANGE

B) its Berlin Wall in 1989), in fact,

C) it's Berlin Wall in 1989). In fact,

D) its Berlin Wall in 1989); in fact,

5

A) NO CHANGE

B) poverty, depression, and deprivation began

C) poverty, depression, and, deprivation began

D) poverty, depression, and deprivation, began

6

A) NO CHANGE

B) the 1970s the

C) the 1970s—the

D) the 1970s. The

Whether we realize it or not, the contributions of these Russian expatriates are with us everywhere. The [7] co-founder, of Google, Sergey Brin, came to the United States from Moscow at the age of 6 in 1979. Singer-songwriter Regina Spektor moved at the age of 9 in 1989, the same year that historian Artemy Kalinovsky arrived [8] with his parents. These and other children of the Soviet Union continue to shape the American experience in all kinds of positive and enlightening ways.

A) NO CHANGE

B) co-founder of Google. Sergey Brin,

C) co-founder of Google, Sergey Brin,

D) co-founder, of Google, Sergey Brin,

A) NO CHANGE

B) with his parents, today, these

C) with his parents. Today, these

D) with his parents today; these

In the same year and at the same age as Brin, **9** a writer, named David Bezmozgis, moved, with his family, from Riga, Latvia, then under Soviet control. While he has undoubtedly been one of the great success stories of Soviet immigration to North America (Canada in this case), he has found that success in detailing the difficult and often conflicting motivations that many people had for leaving the Soviet Union. While we have become comfortable believing that the Soviets came to North America looking for **10** freedom, whatever that term may mean. Bezmozgis shows that this was not always the case and that "freedom" could remain an elusive dream even for those who made the trip successfully. His first **11** novel *The Free World*, was published in 2011 to great critical acclaim.

As we think about the fact that ours is a nation of immigrants, we would be severely limited if we believed that people came from all over the world to assimilate to the American way of life. In fact, the peoples of the world may have become American, but they have done so while shaping and reshaping the meaning of that term in ever richer ways.

9

A) NO CHANGE

B) a writer, named David Bezmozgis moved with his family, from Riga,

C) a writer named, David Bezmozgis, moved, with his family, from Riga,

D) a writer named David Bezmozgis moved with his family from Riga,

10

A) NO CHANGE

B) freedom, whatever that term may mean: Bezmozgis

C) freedom, whatever that term may mean, Bezmozgis

D) freedom, whatever that term may mean; Bezmozgis

11

A) NO CHANGE

B) novel: *The Free World*,

C) novel—*The Free World*,

D) novel, *The Free World*,

Chapter 7
Words

THE WORDS CHANGE, BUT THE SONG REMAINS THE SAME

In the last chapter, we looked at what to do when the PSAT is testing punctuation. In this chapter, we're going to look at what to do when the PSAT is testing the parts of speech—mainly verbs, nouns, and pronouns.

Our basic strategy, however, has remained the same. As we saw in the previous two chapters, when faced with a PSAT Writing and Language question, you should always

> Check what's changing in the answer choices and use POE.

As you will notice, throughout this chapter, we talk a lot about certain parts of speech, but we don't really use a lot of grammar terms. That's because we find that on the PSAT, the best answers across a lot of different parts of speech can be summed up more succinctly with three basic terms: **consistency**, **precision**, and **concision**.

You don't need to know a ton of grammar if you can remember these three basic rules.

> **CONSISTENCY:** Correct answers are consistent with the rest of the sentence and the passage.
>
> **PRECISION:** Correct answers are as precise as possible.
>
> **CONCISION:** Barring other errors, correct answers are as concise as possible.

Let's look at some examples of each.

CONSISTENCY

The purveyors of the philosophy known as 1 Pragmatism is part of a long and complex movement.

1

A) NO CHANGE
B) Pragmatism has been
C) Pragmatism are
D) Pragmatism being

Here's How to Crack It

First, as always, check what's changing in the answer choices. In this case, *Pragmatism* stays the same, but the forms of the verb *to be* change. Therefore, because the verbs change, we know that the question is testing verbs.

When you see verbs changing in the answer choices, the first thing to check is the subject of the sentence. Is the verb consistent with the subject? In this case, it's not. The subject of this sentence is *purveyors*, which is plural. Therefore, (A) and (B) have to be eliminated, and (D) creates an incomplete idea. Only (C) can work in the context.

Thus, when you see verbs changing in the answer choices, check the subject first. Subjects and verbs need to be consistent with each other.

Let's have a look at another.

Pragmatism has entered the popular language as a kind of synonym for "realistic" or "cynical," but William James, perhaps the greatest of the American Pragmatists, **2** show that the movement can in fact be much more human and adaptable.

2

A) NO CHANGE

B) showed

C) will show

D) has shown

Here's How to Crack It

Check what's changing in the answer choices. The verbs are changing. Remember from the first question that whenever you see verbs changing, you want to make sure the verb is consistent with the subject. Because the subject of this part of the sentence is *William James*, a singular noun, you can eliminate (A), which isn't consistent.

Then, because all the others are consistent with the subject, make sure they are consistent with the other verbs. It looks like the other main verb in this sentence is *has been*, so the underlined verb should be in this form, as it is in (D). Choices (B) and (C) could work in some contexts, but not this one!

As you can see, verbs are all about consistency.

> When you see verbs changing in the answer choices, make sure those verbs are
>
> - CONSISTENT with their subjects
> - CONSISTENT with other verbs in the sentence and surrounding sentences

Let's try one that has a little bit of everything.

Reading James and the other theorists **3** reveal that as we make the big decisions in our lives, we think about those decisions in interestingly pragmatic ways.

3

A) NO CHANGE

B) reveal that we made the decisions in our lives, we have thought

C) reveals that as we make the big decisions in our lives, we could have been thinking

D) reveals that as we make the big decisions in our lives, we think

Here's How to Crack It

Check what's changing in the answer choices. It looks like lots of verbs!

Let's start with the first. See which one, *reveal* or *reveals*, is consistent with the subject. That subject is *Reading*, which is singular, thus eliminating (A) and (B).

Then, we have to choose between *think* and *could have been thinking*. Since both of these are consistent with the subject *we*, let's try to pick the one that is more consistent with other verbs. The only other verbs are *reveals* and *make*, both of which are in the present tense and don't use the odd *could have been* form. Therefore, if we have to choose between (C) and (D), (D) is definitely better.

Consistency applies across the test. Let's see another question in which the idea of Consistency might help us.

The early Pragmatists and their follower suggest that the big decisions in life should be measured by their possible outcomes alone.

4

A) NO CHANGE
B) they're followers suggest
C) their followers suggest
D) their follower suggests

Here's How to Crack It

Check the answer choices first. It looks like pretty much everything is changing here: *they're/their*, *followers/follower*, and *suggest/suggests*. Let's look at the ones we have done already.

We can't cite a good reason to use an apostrophe, so let's get rid of (B). Then, the verb changes, so let's check the subject. That subject is *The early Pragmatists and their follower/followers*, which is plural regardless of the word *follower* or *followers*. Keep the verb consistent with the plural subject and eliminate (D).

Then, we have to choose between *follower* and *followers*, two nouns. As with verbs, nouns are all about consistency. When you see nouns changing in the answer choices, make sure they are consistent with the other nouns in the sentence. In this case, we are talking about *The early Pragmatists*, all of them, who must have many *followers* as well, as (C) suggests.

Noun consistency can show up in other ways as well. Let's have a look the next question.

The logical processes of the Pragmatists are much different from other schools of thought.

5

A) NO CHANGE
B) other school's
C) those of other schools
D) schools that are otherwise

Here's How to Crack It

Look at what's changing in the answer choices. It looks like the main change is between the nouns—*schools* and *those*. We saw in the last problem that when nouns are changing in the answer choices, you want to make sure those nouns are consistent with other nouns in the sentence.

In this case, the nouns are being compared. *The logical processes of the Pragmatists* are being compared with the logical processes of people from other schools. Choices (A), (B), and (D) suggest that the *processes* are being compared with the *schools*, so both (B) and (D) are inconsistent. Only (C) is left.

SAT calls this concept "faulty comparison," but you don't have to know that name. Instead, just remember that *nouns have to be consistent with other nouns*. When the answer choices show a change in nouns, look for the sentence's other nouns. They'll provide the clue!

Pragmatism may be rooted in the German philosophers Immanuel Kant and Georg Friedrich Hegel, but it has found more popularity in Anglo-American communities than in **6** German or French ones.

6

A) NO CHANGE
B) German or French.
C) other ones.
D) European.

Here's How to Crack It

Check what's changing in the answer choices. There's a fairly significant change between *German or French* and *German or French ones*. As in the previous sentence, let's make sure this is consistent. The part of the sentence right before the underlined portion refers to *Anglo-American communities*, so we should make our part of the sentence consistent: *German or French communities*, not merely *German or French* or *European*, as in (B) and (D).

Then, we are down to (A) and (C). The difference here comes between the words *German or French* and *other*. While you do want to be concise when possible, you need to make sure first and foremost that we are being *precise*. Choice (A) is more precise than (C) in that it has a clearer relation to the *Anglo-American communities* with which it is being contrasted. Therefore, (A) is the best answer in that it is the most *consistent* with the rest of the sentence and the most *precise* of the remaining possible answers.

PRECISION

Consistency is probably the most important thing on the Writing and Language section of the PSAT, but precision is a close second. Once you've made sure that the underlined portion is consistent with the rest of the sentence, make sure that the underlined portion is as precise as possible. Perfect grammar is one thing, but it won't matter much if no one knows what the writer is talking about!

Let's hear that one more time.

> Once you are sure that a word or phrase is consistent with the non-underlined portion of the sentence, make that word or phrase as precise as you can.

Although purporting to be systems of universal truth, **7** most are bound to their countries of origin.

7

A) NO CHANGE

B) most of them

C) most from philosophy

D) most philosophical systems

Here's How to Crack It

Check what's changing in the answer choices. The changes could summed up with the question "*most* what?" We have four different options, so let's use our main guiding principles of consistency and precision.

Be as precise as possible. Choices (A) and (B) are very similar in that they say *most*, but they don't specify *what* that *most* refers to. Even though these are grammatically consistent with the rest of the sentence, they're not quite precise enough. Choice (C) is a little more precise, but it doesn't actually clarify what *most* refers to. With these answers out of the way, we can see that (D) is the best of the bunch because it is the only one that is sufficiently precise.

———————○———————

As this question shows, pronouns can be a bit of a challenge. They can appear in otherwise grammatically correct sentences. Still, precision is key when you're dealing with pronouns. Circle the potentially imprecise pronouns in each of the following sentences and rewrite each one.

1. Certain philosophers can be confusing, but it's still an important endeavor.
2. Each of us uses some of this philosophical logic in their everyday life.
3. Whether Anglo-American or Continental models, it can all tell us something important about how to live.
4. A philosopher's life cannot help but influence their work.
5. Self-help, psychology, economics are the cornerstones: it is each in a way part of the philosophical tradition.

Answers are on page 107.

Precision can show up in some other ways as well. Have a look at this question.

———————○———————

The Continental school's

8 approach has a tendency to problems to be far more abstract than the Anglo-American school's.

8

A) NO CHANGE

B) approach has a tendency to be far more abstract to problems

C) approach to problems has a tendency to be far more abstract

D) approach has a tendency to be to problems far more abstract

Here's How to Crack It
Check what's changing in the answer choices. This step is crucial here because there are no obvious grammatical errors, so the answer choices are essential to figuring out exactly what the question is asking you to do.

In the end, the only difference among the answer choices is that the phrase *to problems* is in different places. In the end, we will just need to put that phrase in the most precise place, hopefully right next to whatever it is modifying.

In this case, we can choose from among *approach, tendency, be,* and *abstract.* Which of these would have the most precise need for the phrase *to problems*? Because *problems* seem to have something to do with how those problems are solved, it would go best with *approach,* creating the phrase *approach to problems,* particularly because the other combinations don't make a lot of sense. What does it mean to be *abstract to problems*? Nothing! The best answer is (C).

Let's have a look at some more of these modifiers. Rewrite each sentence below so the modifier makes the *precise* sense that it should.

1. Given all its logical twists and turns, many people struggle with philosophy.
2. Readers in different times tend to gravitate toward different philosophers and places.
3. Once cracked, you can find incredible guidance and solace in philosophy.
4. I first learned about Pragmatism from a professor in college at 20.
5. Boring and uninteresting, Jack didn't care much for the work of William James.

Answers are on page 107.

CONCISION

This is not to say, however, that more words always mean more precision. In fact, fewer words are often better. For example, if you were to ask for directions, which answer would you rather receive?

> *Turn right at Main Street and walk four blocks.*

Or

> *Since this street, Elm Street, is facing in a northerly direction, and your destination is due northeast, go east when you arrive at the intersection of Elm and Main. Going east will entail making a right turn in quite that easterly direction. After having made this turn and arrived on the perpendicular street…*

The first one. Obviously.

And that's because concision is key when you want to communicate meaning. Really, as long as everything else is in order—as long as the grammar and punctuation are good to go—the best answer will almost always be the shortest.

Let's see an example.

I find Pragmatism to be one of the most **9** interesting and fascinating of the philosophical schools.

9

A) NO CHANGE

B) interesting

C) fascinatingly interesting

D) interestingly fascinating

Here's How to Crack It

Check what's changing in the answer choices. In this case, the word *interesting* appears in all the answer choices, and in some it is paired with the word *fascinating*. Typically, if you see a list of answer choices wherein one answer is short and the rest mean the same thing but are longer, the question is testing concision.

What, after all, is the difference between the words *interesting* and *fascinating*? There really isn't a very significant one, so there's no use in saying both of them, as in (A), or pairing them awkwardly, as in (C) and (D). In fact, the shortest answer, (B), does everything the other answers do, but it does so in the fewest words. Choice (B) is therefore the best answer.

Let's see one more.

10 Maybe it's just me but for me, Pragmatism in my view has the most applications to the most different kinds of problems.

10

A) NO CHANGE

B) Really and truly, Pragmatism

C) In my humble opinion, Pragmatism

D) Pragmatism

Here's How to Crack It

As always, check what's changing in the answer choices. The changes could be summed up like this. There's a bunch of stuff before the word *Pragmatism*. Does any of that stuff contribute in a significant way to the sentence? No. Does the word *Pragmatism* alone help the sentence to fulfill its basic purpose? Yes. Therefore, the best answer is (D).

As we have seen in this chapter, when the PSAT is testing *words* (i.e., any time the words are changing in the answer choices), make sure that those words are

- **Consistent.** Verbs, nouns, and pronouns should agree within sentences and passages.
- **Precise.** The writing should communicate specific ideas and events.
- **Concise.** When everything else is correct, the shortest answer is the best.

Answers to Questions on Page 104:

1. *it* is the problem. *Certain philosophers can be confusing, but the pursuit of philosophical knowledge can still be an important endeavor.*
2. *their* is the problem. *Each of us uses some of this philosophical logical in his or her everyday life.*
3. *it* is the problem. Take it out! *Anglo-American and Continental models can all tell us something important about how to live.*
4. *their* is the problem. *A philosopher's life cannot help but influence that philosopher's work.*
5. *it* is the problem. *Self-help, psychology, economics are the cornerstones: each of these is part of the philosophical tradition.*

Answers to Questions on Page 105:

1. Many people struggle with philosophy given all its logical twists and turns.
2. Readers in different times and places tend to gravitate toward different philosophers.
3. Once cracked, philosophy can provide incredible guidance and solace.
4. I first learned about Pragmatism from a college professor when I was 20 years old.
5. Jack didn't care much for the work of William James, which he found boring and uninteresting.

Writing and Language Drill 3

Time: 7-8 minutes. Check your answers in Part III.

William James's *Pragmatism* (1907) has been called the **1** greatest and best book of American philosophy. The series of lectures that were to become *Pragmatism* **2** encompasses James's adaptation of the great Pragmatists, such as Charles Peirce, who came before and adds a uniquely human element. **3** His work in psychology and religion laid the foundation for how theoretical work intersects with the concrete work of living.

In a way, pragmatism turns the philosophical endeavor on its head and **4** attacked the importance of its big questions. Philosophy is traditionally concerned with the big questions: What is the meaning of life? Are there many worlds like this one or only this one? What if none of us exist? Pragmatism is concerned with these questions as well, but it is equally concerned with another question: So what? Pragmatism is concerned, with what difference a particular truth means in the world **5** with *practice*.

1

A) NO CHANGE
B) best and truly greatest
C) greatly best
D) greatest

2

A) NO CHANGE
B) encompass
C) does encompass
D) are encompassing

3

A) NO CHANGE
B) James's
C) Their
D) Some

4

A) NO CHANGE
B) has been attacking
C) attacks
D) could be said to attack

5

If the punctuation were adjusted accordingly, the best placement for the underlined portion would be

A) where it is now.
B) after the word *Pragmatism*.
C) after the word *concerned*.
D) after the word *truth*.

Let's consider a basic example. Say you are stressed about an upcoming math test. You're afraid you might not get the grade you want, and the fear of it [6] keeps you up at night. Rather than asking, "Will you do well on this test?", the Pragmatists will want to know instead "What difference does it make whether you do well or poorly on the test?" If your answer is, "Well, no difference, I guess," then you've got [7] one. If your answer is, "I won't be able to get an A in the class!" then you've got another and a whole other series of questions. By constantly asking "So what?", the pragmatic approach helps to situate problems in their practice and their consequences rather than [8] abstracting.

6

A) NO CHANGE
B) keeping you up
C) awakens
D) kept you up

7

A) NO CHANGE
B) something.
C) one approach.
D) approaching.

8

A) NO CHANGE
B) abstractly.
C) in their abstraction.
D) by a process of abstraction.

The approach is especially interesting for life's big questions. One of James's particular favorites was, "Is life fated or free?" In other words, do we make our own choices, or are our lives completely predetermined? Well, for James, the question is an interesting but fundamentally irrelevant one. **9** Whether there is a cosmic order to our lives or not, we still have to live them responsibly, so it doesn't **10** differ whether our lives are "fated or free," because the distinction won't create practical differences.

These are two relatively simple examples of the pragmatic method in action, but give it a try yourself. Next time something is really stressing you out, ask the simple question: What difference does it make if that does happen? You may find that the real consequences are what help you to see through the problem, establish a plan, or **11** forgot about the issue entirely.

9

The writer is considering deleting the phrase *but fundamentally irrelevant*. Should the phrase be kept or deleted?

A) Kept, because it shows James's sense of humor as displayed in his writings.

B) Kept, because it sets up the subject of the remainder of the paragraph.

C) Deleted, because it dismisses the importance of Pragmatism as a movement.

D) Deleted, because the paragraph as a whole is focused on relevant subjects.

10

A) NO CHANGE

B) concern us or anyone else

C) count

D) make a significant difference

11

A) NO CHANGE

B) forget about them

C) forget about the issue

D) forget about the issues

Chapter 8
Questions

AND THEN THE PSAT WAS LIKE, "HEY, CAN I ASK YOU A QUESTION?"

In the previous two chapters, we saw most of the concepts that the PSAT will test on the Writing and Language portion of the exam. In this chapter, we're not going to learn a lot of new stuff in the way of grammar. Instead, we'll look at some of the questions that the PSAT asks.

As we've seen, a lot of the questions on the Writing and Language Test aren't technically questions at all. They're just lists of answer choices, and you start the process of answering them by asking a question of your own: "What's changing in the answer choices?" Because you need to move quickly through this test, you may fall into the habit of not checking for questions. Even when you do read the questions, you may read them hastily or vaguely. Well, we are here to tell you that neither of these approaches will work.

> The most important thing about Writing and Language questions is that you *notice* those questions and then *answer* those questions.

This may seem like just about the most obvious advice you've ever been given, but you'd be surprised how much less precise your brain is when you're working quickly.

Here's an example. Do these next 10 questions as quickly as you can.

1. $2 + 1 =$

2. $1 + 2 =$

3. $3 + 1 =$

4. $3 + 2 \neq$

5. $1 + 2 =$

6. $2 - 1 <$

7. $2 \pm 2 =$

8. $3 + 1 =$

9. $3 + 2 =$

10. $3 + 3 \neq$

Now check your answers.

1. 3

2. 3

3. 4

4. Anything but 5

5. 3

6. Any number greater than 1 (but not 1!)

7. 0 or 4

8. 4

9. 5

10. Anything but 6

Now, it's very possible that you got at least one of those questions wrong. What happened? It's not that the questions are hard. In fact, the questions are about as easy as can be. So why did you get some of them wrong? You were probably moving too quickly to notice that the signs changed a few times.

This is a lot like the Writing and Language section. You might miss some of the easiest points on the whole test by not reading carefully enough.

As you will see throughout this chapter, most of the questions will test concepts with which you are already familiar.

WORDS AND PUNCTUATION IN REVERSE

Many of the concepts we saw in the Punctuation and Words chapters show up explicitly with questions, but usually there's some kind of twist.

Here's an example.

It is well known that the film industry has largely eclipsed the once-booming theater business in the United **1** States: once the silver screen came along, audiences were more interested in the new medium.

1

Which of the following alternatives to the underlined portion would NOT be acceptable?

A) States; once

B) States. Once

C) States, for once

D) States, once

Here's How to Crack It

First and foremost, it's important to notice the question. This one is asking for the alternative that would NOT be acceptable, so we'll need to find an answer that doesn't work.

Go through the steps. What's changing in the answer choices? STOP, HALF-STOP, and GO punctuation. Use the Vertical Line Test between the words *States* and *once*. The idea before the line, *It is well known that the film industry has largely eclipsed the once-booming theater business in the United States*, is complete. The idea after the line, *once the silver screen came along, audiences were more interested in the new medium*, is also complete. Therefore, we need either STOP or HALF-STOP punctuation.

Choices (A) and (B) definitely provide the punctuation we want. Choice (C) doesn't look like it does, but remember! *For* is one of the FANBOYS, and comma + FANBOYS is one of the forms of STOP punctuation! The only one, therefore, that doesn't work in the context is (D), so it is the alternative that would NOT be acceptable because it uses GO punctuation.

Notice how important that word NOT was in this question. If you missed it, you might have thought the question had three correct answers!

Let's try another.

The [2] wonder that a beautiful film can inspire would seem to be unsurpassable.

2

Which of the following substitutions would be LEAST acceptable?

A) amazement

B) curiosity

C) awe

D) stupefaction

Here's How to Crack It

Again, the question asks for the LEAST acceptable, so find and eliminate answers that work. In this case, we need something similar in meaning to the word *wonder* as it is used in this sentence. All four words mean something similar to *wonder* in different contexts, but we want something that refers to just how *breathtaking* a beautiful film is, so (A), (C), and (D) would work.

Choice (B) does give a synonym for the word *wonder*, but it means something more like *pondering* than *breathtaking*, so it is the LEAST acceptable of the substitutions.

Even if you're not sure what *stupefaction* is (*astonishment* or *shock*), you can see that *curiosity* is clearly in a different category altogether. POE is your friend!

Let's look at another that deals with some of the topics we've seen earlier.

What many have forgotten, however, is that the theater remains a vibrant medium. The vibrancy of the medium comes partly from the particular intimacy of the connection between actors and audience. 3

 3

Which of the following gives the best way to combine these two sentences?

A) What many have forgotten, however, is that the theater remains a vibrant medium; the vibrancy of the medium comes partly from the particular intimacy of the connection between actors and audience.

B) What many have forgotten, however, is that the theater remains a vibrant medium, particularly given the intimacy of the connection between actors and audience.

C) A lot of people forget, however, about the vibrancy of theater as a medium when they don't think about how intimate the connection is between the actors in the theater and the audience in the seats.

D) What many have forgotten, however, is that the theater remains a vibrant medium. The connection between actors and audience is so intimate.

Here's How to Crack It

The question asks us to combine the two sentences. Your eyes were probably drawn immediately to (D), which is the most concise of the choices. There's just one problem: (D) doesn't answer the question! The question asks to *combine* the sentences, and while (D) shortens them, it doesn't combine them.

Choice (B) is therefore the best option. It combines the sentences and shortens them a bit, unlike (A) and (C), which combine the sentences but don't really do much beyond changing the punctuation or adding a bunch of words.

Questions like #3 are why...

> The most important thing about Writing and Language questions is that you *notice* those questions and then *answer* those questions.

PRECISION QUESTIONS

Not all questions will just be applications of punctuation and parts of speech. Some questions will ask you to do more specific things. Remember the three terms we kept repeating in the Words chapter: Consistency, Precision, and Concision. We'll start with the Precision-related questions. Even in those where Precision is not asked about directly, or when it is mixed with Consistency or Concision, remember this:

> Answer the question in the most precise way possible. Read literally!

Let's try one.

In fact, the history of the theater in the United States provides as riveting a story as the greatest stage drama. 4

4

The writer is considering deleting the phrase *of the theater in the United States* from the preceding sentence. Should this phrase be kept or deleted?

A) Kept, because removing it would remove a crucial piece of information from this part of the sentence.

B) Kept, because it stirs the reader's national sentiments and might generate extra interest in the story.

C) Deleted, because it wrongly implies that stage plays are not interesting on their own terms.

D) Deleted, because it gives information that has no bearing on this particular essay.

Here's How to Crack It

This question asks whether we should keep or delete the phrase *of the theater in the United States*. Without that phrase, the sentence reads: *In fact, the history provides as riveting a story as the greatest stage drama.* Because nothing in this sentence or any of the previous ones specifies what this *history* might be, keep the phrase. You want to be as precise as possible!

And, as (A) says, you want to keep the phrase because it is crucial to clarifying precisely what *the question* is. Choice (B) is a little too grandiose and vague a reason to keep the phrase. Choice (A) is therefore the best answer.

Let's try another.

The history of the theater in the United States is part of Revolutionary history. **5** The early provisional government banned all theaters during the War for Independence.

5

At this point, the writer is considering adding the following true statement:

> William Shakespeare was a British playwright, but his stature extends to all parts of the English-speaking world.

Should the writer make this addition here?

A) Yes, because it names an important figure in theatrical history.

B) Yes, because it shows that theater can bring nations together rather than drive them apart.

C) No, because it does not contribute in a significant way to the discussion of the history of the theater in the United States.

D) No, because other playwrights have had a large impact in the United States as well.

Here's How to Crack It

The proposed sentence does contain an interesting bit of information, but that piece of information has no clear place either in these few sentences or in the passage as a whole. Therefore, it should not be added, thus eliminating (A) and (B).

Then, because it does not play a significant role in the passage, the sentence should not be added for the reason stated in (C). While (D) may be true in a way, it does not reflect anything clearly relating to the role the sentence might play in the passage as a whole. Read literally, and answer as literally and precisely as you can.

CONSISTENCY QUESTIONS

Just as questions should be answered as *precisely* as possible, they should also be answered with information that is *consistent* with what's in the passage.

When answering consistency questions, keep this general rule in mind:

> Writing and Language passages should be judged on what they *do* say, not on what they *could* say. When dealing with Style, Tone, and Focus, make sure to work with the words and phrases the passage has already used.

Let's look at two questions that deal with the idea of consistency.

---

[1] The status of the theater was especially controversial in the pre-Revolutionary era. [2] These writings may have even influenced Shakespeare himself. [3] In particularly religious places, like Boston, the theater **6** has become a popular and respected profession in the twentieth century. [4] In Philadelphia, too, theater could have only a marginal influence over and above religious protests. [5] It was really in the southern colonies, especially around Virginia, that the real English love of the theater came through. [6] In fact, John Smith's writings of his trip to this early colony are full of imagery from the theater. **7**

6

Which of the following choices would best complete the idea presented in this sentence?

A) NO CHANGE

B) was thought to encourage unrighteous behavior in the audience and the actors.

C) may have hosted one of the first performances of the temperance play *The Drunkard.*

D) could be a pleasant way to spend a Sunday afternoon after church.

7

The best placement for sentence 2 would be

A) where it is now.

B) before sentence 1.

C) after sentence 5.

D) after sentence 6.

Here's How to Crack Them

Let's look at question 6 first. In this case, the question tells us exactly what to look for: something that would *complete the idea* in the sentence, an idea about how religious places were less likely to allow the theater. Choices (A) and (C) may be true, but they don't have anything to do with religion. Choice (D) addresses religion, but not in the way that the rest of the sentence or surrounding ideas do. Only (B) discusses religion in an appropriate way by noting how religious authorities saw the theater as promoting *unrighteous* behavior.

As for question 7, we need to find some very literal way to make sentence 2 consistent with the rest of the paragraph. Look for words and phrases that will link sentence 2 to other sentences. Remember, it's not what the passage *could* say; it's what the passage *does* say. Sentence 2, we should note, starts with *These writings*, thus clearly referring to writings that have been mentioned before it. As such, sentence 2 belongs definitively after sentence 6, which discusses the *writings* of John Smith. This is (D).

As we have seen, these questions are not difficult, but they do require very specific actions on your part. Make sure you read the questions carefully and that you answer those questions as precisely and consistently as you can.

The same goes for charts and graphs on the Writing and Language Test. Don't let the strangeness of the charts throw you off! Just read the graphs with as much precision as you can and choose the most precise answers possible.

Let's have a look at one.

For all the interest of its history, however, the theater has seen a remarkable decline in popularity. A recent study showed that in 2002 just 17.1%, 12.3%, and 3.2% of adults had seen a performance of an opera, a musical, or a non-musical play within the previous year. **8**

8

The writer wants the information in the passage to correspond as closely as possible with the information in the chart. Given that goal and assuming that the rest of the previous sentence would remain unchanged, in which sequence should the three cultural activities be listed?

A) NO CHANGE

B) Opera, non-musical, musical

C) Non-musical, musical, opera

D) Musical, non-musical, opera

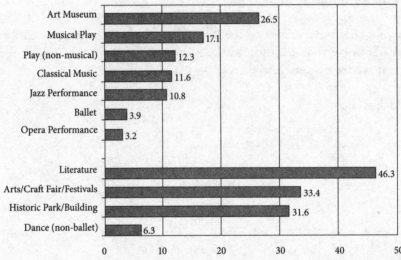

Participation in Arts and Cultural Activities – 2002

Art Museum	26.5
Musical Play	17.1
Play (non-musical)	12.3
Classical Music	11.6
Jazz Performance	10.8
Ballet	3.9
Opera Performance	3.2
Literature	46.3
Arts/Craft Fair/Festivals	33.4
Historic Park/Building	31.6
Dance (non-ballet)	6.3

Percent of Adults Who Participated at Least Once in the Past 12 Months

Here's How to Crack It

This question is asking for what agrees with the graph. From what we have seen, these questions are usually pretty straightforward. You don't have to do anything overly complex with the graphs, and that is certainly the case here.

There are three activities: opera, non-musical plays, and musical plays. Notice how the numbers are listed in the passage and match each of these numbers with the graph. The graph shows "Musical Play" at 17.1%, "Play (non-musical)" at 12.3%, and "Opera Performance" at 3.2%. This should therefore be the order in which the activities are listed, as in (D).

In general, graphs on the PSAT Reading and Writing and Language Tests are very straightforward, and the fundamental question they ask is this: "Can you read a graph?" These are easy points as long as you read the graphs carefully and use POE.

CONCLUSION

As we have seen in this chapter, the PSAT can ask a lot of different kinds of questions, but the test won't throw anything really crazy at you. The biggest things to remember, aside from the punctuation rules, are *PRECISION* and *CONSISTENCY*. If you pick answers that are precise and consistent with other information in the passage, you should be good to go. Just make sure to answer the question!

Take a Breather
You've made it through the entire Writing and Language section! Next up is Math, so feel free to take a break before diving in. Grab a snack, relax with a book, go for a walk—anything that will help you refresh before reviewing more content. Remember that study breaks can make you more productive, so don't deprive yourself of some needed relaxation time.

Writing and Language Drill 4

Time: 10 minutes. Check your answers in Part III.

— 1 —

1 In the 1980s and 1990s, cultural critics had begun to express concern that Americans watched too much television. The numbers varied, but it was widely touted that Americans spent anywhere from three to five hours a day in front of the tube. **2** Whether this was true, it certainly did present a startling finding, especially to those who were interested in promoting other media and activities.

1

Which of the following choices would best introduce the essay by identifying a way that a historical period understood a particular medium?

A) NO CHANGE

B) If you don't own a TV today, it's not considered that weird anymore.

C) It's very possible that the only thing you listen to on the radio is music.

D) The old cathode-ray-tube TVs are relics of the past by this point.

2

The writer is considering deleting the phrase *in front of the tube* and ending the sentence with a period after the word *day.* Should the phrase be kept or deleted?

A) Kept, because the meaning of the sentence is unclear without the phrase.

B) Kept, because it shows what the viewers of television find so compelling.

C) Deleted, because it does not clarify whether the number was closer to three or five.

D) Deleted, because this kind of slangy language should be avoided at all costs.

— 2 —

Therefore, in today's world, where the Internet seems to be the new medium of choice, we should not be so quick to criticize it in these terms. Still, as a recent survey has shown, American consumers spend more time online than they have on any other media platform in the last five years. **3** Spending more time on the Internet as of 2012, **4** American consumers in 2013 spent an average of over 5 hours a day on the Internet.

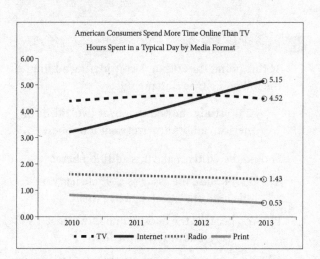

American Consumers Spend More Time Online Than TV
Hours Spent in a Typical Day by Media Format

- - - TV ——— Internet ┄┄┄┄ Radio ——— Print

3

The writer is considering replacing the word *spend* in the preceding sentence with the word *pay out*. Should the writer make the change or keep the sentence as it is?

A) Make the change, because the words *pay out* are more relatable to readers.

B) Make the change, because the words *pay out* provide a more direct indication of the action of the sentence.

C) Keep the sentence as it is, because the words *pay out* change the meaning in a way inconsistent with the passage as a whole.

D) Keep the sentence as it is, because the word *spend* hides the fact that the use of media platforms varies widely by socioeconomic status.

4

Which of the following gives information consistent with the graph?

A) NO CHANGE

B) the world's consumers in 2013 spent an average of over 3 hours a day on the Internet.

C) American consumers only a year earlier spent an average of as few as 2 hours a day on the Internet.

D) American consumers decided that the Internet was a better place to watch shows than was the television.

5 All the while, TV is as good now as it has ever been in its 60-year history. Political theorists warned that too much time in front of the television would dampen people's political awareness. Nutrition activists feared that such a sedentary activity would spur an obesity epidemic. **6** Movie-theater owners cautioned that the lower-quality television could destroy the high-end film industry. Lovers of literature fretted that people no longer had the time or attention span to read the great works.

5

Which of the following choices would offer the most effective transition between the previous paragraph and the current one?

A) NO CHANGE

B) In addition, this general movement toward the television seemed to bode ill for society at large.

C) The first televised presidential debate came during the 1960 election.

D) The technology of new TVs has improved by leaps and bounds even in the last ten years.

6

At this point, the author is considering adding the following true statement:

> A 2015 study showed that over two-thirds of American adults are overweight or obese.

Should the writer make this addition here?

A) Yes, because the essay as a whole has very little hard statistical data like this.

B) Yes, because the obesity rate shows that TV was truly a destructive medium.

C) No, because the mention of these statistics is cruel to those who are overweight.

D) No, because the essay as a whole is focused on a different subject.

7 While each of these criticisms certainly has its merits, each was in a way following in a long path of conservative skepticism at new media developments. Movies were controversial in the 1920s. The National Association of Librarians wrote a report in the 1940s. In this report, radio was excoriated for distracting children from life's real pursuits. **8** The criticisms went even further back. The printing press, even early in its history as mainly a printer of Bibles, was thought to give religious messages to too many who couldn't properly **9** understand the messages. Even newspapers, now a mainstay of the serious American consumer, were once considered politically subversive.

7

Which of the following alternatives to the underlined portion would NOT be acceptable?

A) Although each

B) However, each

C) Even if each

D) However, while each

8

Which of the following gives the most effective way to combine the previous two sentences, reproduced below?

> The National Association of Librarians wrote a report in the 1940s. In this report, radio was excoriated for distracting children from life's real pursuits.

A) (keep the sentences as they are)

B) The National Association of Librarians wrote a report in the 1940s. It was about the following: radio, they said, should be excoriated for distracting children from life's real pursuits.

C) In a 1940 report from the National Association of Librarians, radio was excoriated for distracting children from life's real pursuits.

D) The National Association of Librarians was so upset about radio's excoriating influence that they wrote a report on children in 1940.

9

Which of the following alternatives to the underlined portions would be LEAST acceptable?

A) comprehend

B) grasp

C) appreciate

D) intuit

Is this a troubling change? Well, history would seem to say that it's not. **10** After all, the Internet has the advantage of being significantly more active than all those other media. In short, effective use of the Internet requires your participation in a way that TV does not. Even so, upwards of six hours a day is a tremendous amount. There must at least be some kind of change, even if it's not necessarily for the worse.

Question 11 asks about the previous passage as a whole.

At this point, the writer wants to insert an idea that will support the idea given in the previous sentence ("Well, history . . . not"). Which of the following true statements would offer that support?

A) The rate of literacy remains at an all-time high, despite the introduction of the radio in the 1930s.

B) The number of creative-writing majors may soon eclipse the number of English majors, which will lead to an odd imbalance.

C) Then-candidate Richard Nixon looked really bad on TV in 1960, and how else would people have known his big scandal was coming?

D) The printing press, the newspapers, the radio, and even the television have all been integrated effectively into American culture.

Think about the previous passage as a whole as you answer question 11.

The best placement for paragraph 2 would be

A) where it is now.

B) after paragraph 3.

C) after paragraph 4.

D) after paragraph 5.

Chapter 9
Math Basics

Although we'll show you which mathematical concepts are most important to know for the PSAT, this book relies on your knowledge of basic math concepts. If you're a little rusty, this chapter is for you. Read on for a review of the math basics you'll need to know before you continue.

HOW TO CONQUER PSAT MATH

So what do you need to do? There are three important steps:

1. **Know the basic content.** Obviously you do need to know the basics of arithmetic, algebra, and geometry. We'll cover what you need to know in this chapter.
2. **Learn some PSAT-specific problem-solving skills.** Since these basic concepts appear in ways you're probably not used to from math class, you need to prepare yourself with a set of test-specific problem-solving skills designed to help you solve PSAT Math problems. We'll cover the most important ones in the next chapter.
3. **Have a sound overall testing strategy.** This means knowing what to do with difficult questions or when calculator use is not allowed, and having a plan to pace yourself to get the maximum number of points in the time allotted. Be sure to read carefully the material in Chapter 3, to make sure you're using the strategy that will get you the greatest number of points in the time you have.

(PERSONAL) ORDER OF DIFFICULTY

The Math sections on the PSAT are Sections 3 and 4. Section 3 contains 13 multiple-choice questions and 4 grid-in questions. Section 4 contains 27 multiple-choice questions and 4 grid-in questions. Within each question type, there is a loose order of difficulty, with most of the questions being of medium difficulty. (This means that the first few multiple choice and first few grid-in questions are likely to be rated as easy, and the last few multiple choice and last few grid-ins are typically considered the most difficult.) More important than any order of difficulty is your own Personal Order of Difficulty. Though the last questions of each type in a section are likely to be the hardest, use your own personal strengths and weaknesses to decide which questions to do and which to skip.

No Calculator

Yes Calculator

1
2
3
4
5
6
7
8
9
10
11
12
13
Grid-In
14
15
16
17

17 Questions /
25 minutes

1
2
3
4
5
6
7
8
9
10
11
12
13
14
15
16
17
18
19
20
21
22
23
24
25
26
27
Grid-In
28
29
30
31

31 Questions /
45 minutes

USING YOUR CALCULATOR

You are allowed to use a calculator on Section 4 of the PSAT, and you should definitely do so. You can use any graphing, scientific, or plain old four-function calculator, **provided that it doesn't have a keyboard.**

There are a few simple rules to remember when dealing with your calculator:

1. Use the calculator you're most comfortable with. You definitely don't want to be trying to find the right button on test day. Ideally, you should be practicing with the same calculator you'll use on test day.
2. Change your batteries the week before the test. If they run out during the test, there's nothing you can do about it.

3. Be sure to hit the "clear" or "on/off" button after each calculation to reset the calculator after an operation. A common mistake to make when using your calculator is to forget to clear your last result.

4. Your calculator is very good at calculating, but watch out for mis-keying information. (If you type the wrong numbers in, you'll get the wrong result.) Check each number on the display as you key it in.

5. For the most part, you'll use your calculator for the basic operations of addition, subtraction, multiplication, and division; the ability to convert fractions to decimals and vice versa; and the ability to do square roots and exponents. Don't forget, though, that it has handy buttons for things like sine, cosine, and i, should you encounter those on the test.

6. Then, there's one really big, important rule whenever you think about using your calculator:

> A calculator can't think; it can only calculate.

What does this mean? It means that a calculator can't think through a problem for you. You have to do the work of understanding and setting up the problem correctly to make sure you know what the right calculation will be to get the answer. Only then can you use the calculator, when it is allowed, to calculate the answer.

So use your paper and pencil to practice your problem-solving skills on all Math questions. You should always be sure to set up the problem in your test booklet—writing it down is still the best method—which will help you catch any errors you might make and allow you to pick up where you left off if you lose focus. Then, for questions in Section 4, move quickly to your calculator to chug your way through the arithmetic, and be careful to enter each number and operator correctly. Remember, using your calculator is already saving you time on these questions—don't rush and lose the advantage that it gives you.

As you work through this book, look for calculator symbols next to questions on which calculator use would be allowed. If you don't see the symbol, don't use your calculator!

Drill 1

DEFINITIONS

One of the reasons that good math students often don't get the credit they deserve on the PSAT is that they've forgotten one or more of these definitions—or they read too fast and skip over these "little" words. Be sure you know them cold and watch out for them!

Match the words with their definitions, and then come up with some examples. Answers can be found in Part III.

1. integers

2. positive numbers

3. negative numbers

4. even numbers

5. odd numbers

6. factors

7. multiples

8. prime numbers

9. distinct

10. digit

a. numbers that a certain number can be divided by, leaving no remainder
Examples: _____

b. integers that cannot be divided evenly by 2
Examples: _____

c. numbers that have no fractional or decimal parts
Examples: _____

d. numbers that are greater than zero
Examples: _____

e. having a different value
Examples: _____

f. integers that can be divided by 2 evenly (with no remainder)
Examples: _____

g. numbers that are less than zero
Examples: _____

h. numbers that have exactly two distinct factors: themselves and 1
Examples: _____

i. numbers that can be divided by a certain number with no remainder
Examples: _____

j. a figure from 0 through 9 that is used as a placeholder
Examples: _____

11. consecutive numbers

12. divisible

13. remainder

14. sum

15. product

16. difference

17. quotient

18. absolute value

k. the result of addition
Examples: _____

l. a whole number left over after division
Examples: _____

m. the result of subtraction
Examples:_____

n. can be divided with no remainder
Examples: _____

o. a number's distance from zero; always a
positive value
Examples: _____

p. numbers in a row
Examples: _____

q. the result of division
Examples: _____

r. the result of multiplication
Examples: _____

EXPONENTS AND SQUARE ROOTS

Exponents are just a shorthand for multiplication. Instead of writing $3 \times 3 \times 3 \times 3$, you can write 3^4. Thus, you can handle exponents by expanding them out if necessary.

$$y^2 \times y^3 = y \times y \times y \times y \times y = y^5$$

$$\frac{y^4}{y^2} = \frac{y \times y \times y \times y}{y \times y} = y \times y = y^2$$

However, you can also multiply and divide exponents that have the same base using a shortcut called MADSPM. MADSPM also helps you remember how to deal with raising exponents to another power. Let's see the breakdown:

- **MA** means when you see a MULTIPLICATION sign, ADD the exponents. So $y^2 \times y^3 = y^{2+3} = y^5$.
- **DS** means when you see a DIVISION sign (or fraction), SUBTRACT the exponents. So $\frac{y^5}{y^2} = y^{5-2} = y^3$.

- **PM** means when you see an exponent raised to a POWER, MULTIPLY the exponents. So $(y^2)^3 = y^{2 \times 3} = y^6$. (This is really easy to confuse with multiplication, so watch out!)

Be careful, because the rules of MADSPM don't work for addition and subtraction. For example, $3^2 + 3^5$ does NOT equal 3^7. (Crunch it on your calculator if you want to prove it.)

Here are some additional rules to remember about exponents:

- Anything to the zero power equals 1: $3^0 = 1$. Mathematicians argue about whether 0^0 is 1 or is undefined, but that won't come up on the PSAT.
- Anything to the first power equals itself: $3^1 = 3$.
- 1 to any power equals 1: $1^{3876} = 1$.
- A **negative exponent** means to take the reciprocal of what would be the result as if the negative weren't there: $2^{-2} = \frac{1}{2^2} = \frac{1}{4}$.
- A **fractional exponent** has two parts (like any other fraction), the numerator, which is the power the base is raised to, and the denominator, which is the root of the base. For example, $8^{2/3} = \sqrt[3]{8^2} = \sqrt[3]{64} = 4$.

> **Warning**
> The rules for multiplying and dividing exponents do not apply to addition or subtraction:
> $2^2 + 2^3 = 12$
> $(2 \times 2) + (2 \times 2 \times 2) = 12$
> It does not equal 2^5 or 32.

Remember that in calculating the value of a root, you're looking for what number multiplied by itself results in the number under the radical. In the above example, $\sqrt[3]{64} = 4$ because $4 \times 4 \times 4 = 64$.

When you see the square root sign, that means to take the positive root only. So, $\sqrt{9} = 3$, but not -3.

Square roots work just like exponents: You can *always* multiply and divide roots, but you can add and subtract only with the *same* root.

Multiplication and Division:

$$\sqrt{8} \times \sqrt{2} = \sqrt{8 \times 2} = \sqrt{16} = 4$$

$$\sqrt{\frac{1}{4}} = \frac{\sqrt{1}}{\sqrt{4}} = \frac{1}{2}$$

$$\sqrt{300} = \sqrt{100 \times 3} = \sqrt{100} \times \sqrt{3} = 10\sqrt{3}$$

Addition and Subtraction:

$$2\sqrt{2} + 3\sqrt{2} = 5\sqrt{2}$$

$$4\sqrt{3} - \sqrt{3} = 3\sqrt{3}$$

$2\sqrt{3} + 3\sqrt{2}$ *Cannot be added without a calculator since the terms do not have the same root.*

Drill 2

Answers can be found in Part III.

a. $3^3 \times 3^2 = $ _____

b. $\dfrac{3^3}{3^2} = $ _____

c. $\left(3^3\right)^2 = $ _____

d. $x^6 \times x^2 = $ _____

e. $\dfrac{x^6}{x^2} = $ _____

f. $\left(x^6\right)^2 = $ _____

g. $\sqrt{8} = $ _____

h. $\sqrt[3]{-64} = $ _____

i. $\sqrt{12} + 5\sqrt{3} = $ _____

j. $\sqrt{y^3} = $ _____

k. $\sqrt[3]{-y^3} = $ _____

l. $\sqrt{x^2 y} + 5x\sqrt{y} = $ _____

3

If $3^4 = 9^x$, what is the value of x ?

A) 2

B) 3

C) 4

D) 5

6

$$\sqrt{m^2 + 39} = 8$$

In the equation above, what is a possible value of m ?

A) 3

B) 4

C) 5

D) 6

5

If $\left(3^x\right)^3 = 3^{15}$, what is the value of x ?

A) 3

B) 5

C) 7

D) 9

8

If $x^y x^6 = x^{54}$ and $\left(x^3\right)^z = x^9$, what is the value of $y + z$?

A) 11

B) 12

C) 48

D) 51

7

If $\sqrt{s} - 3 = 9$, which of the following is a possible value of s ?

A) 12

B) 36

C) 81

D) 144

8

Which of the following is equivalent to the expression $x^6 y^{-3} z^{\frac{1}{2}}$?

A) $\dfrac{x^6 \sqrt{z}}{3y}$

B) $\dfrac{x^6 \sqrt{2z}}{y^3}$

C) $\dfrac{6x\sqrt{z}}{y^3}$

D) $\dfrac{x^6 \sqrt{z}}{y^3}$

9

Which of the following expressions is equivalent to $\sqrt[4]{81b^3c}$?

A) $3b^{\frac{3}{4}}c^{\frac{1}{4}}$

B) $3b^3c$

C) $20.25b^{\frac{3}{4}}c^{\frac{1}{4}}$

D) $20.25b^3c$

9

The function $f(x) = k^{0.3x}$, where k is a constant, can also be expressed as $f(x) = k^{\frac{Bx}{9}}$ for what value of B ?

A) 2.7

B) 9.3

C) 27

D) 30

10

If $x^{\frac{5}{2}} = 8x$, which of the following could be the value of x ?

A) 2

B) 4

C) 6

D) 8

11

Which of the following expressions is equivalent to $\left(3m^2n^{-3}\right)^{\frac{2}{3}}$?

A) $2m^{\frac{4}{3}}n^{-2}$

B) $\sqrt[3]{9}m^{\frac{4}{3}}n^{-2}$

C) $3m^{\frac{4}{3}}n^{-2}$

D) $3m^4n^{-6}$

16

$$b\sqrt[3]{64a^2} = \left(4\sqrt{3a}\right)^2$$

Which of the following values of b makes the equation above true?

A) 4

B) 6

C) 8

D) 12

23

Which of the following shows the expression $\dfrac{9 \cdot 8^y}{5 \cdot 16^{y+\frac{1}{2}}}$ in the form of $A \cdot (B)^y$?

A) $\dfrac{9}{20} \cdot \left(\dfrac{1}{2}\right)^y$

B) $\dfrac{9}{10} \cdot (1)^{\frac{y}{2}}$

C) $\dfrac{9}{5} \cdot \left(\dfrac{1}{2}\right)^{\frac{y}{2}}$

D) $\dfrac{9}{5} \cdot \left(\dfrac{1}{2}\right)^y$

EQUATIONS AND INEQUALITIES

An **equation** is a statement that contains an equals sign, such as $3x + 5 = 17$.

To solve an equation, you must get the variable x alone on one side of the equals sign and everything else on the other side.

The first step is to put all of the variables on one side of the equation and all of the numbers on the other side, using addition and subtraction. As long as you perform the same operation on both sides of the equals sign, you aren't changing the value of the variable.

Then you can divide both sides of the equation by the *coefficient*, which is the number in front of the variable. If that number is a fraction, you can multiply everything by its reciprocal.

For example:

$$\begin{array}{rcl} 3x + 5 & = & 17 \\ -5 & & -5 \\ \hline 3x & = & 12 \\ \div 3 & & \div 3 \\ \hline x & = & 4 \end{array}$$

Subtract 5 from each side.

Divide each side by 3.

Always remember the rule of equations:

Whatever you do to one side of the equation, you must also do to the other side.

The example above was fairly simple. The PSAT may test this idea with more complex equations and formulas, though. Just keep trying to isolate the variable in question by undoing the operations that have been done to it. Here's an example.

14

Logging companies can use Doyle's Log Rule to estimate the amount of usable lumber, in board feet B, that can be milled from logs. The rule is defined as $B = L\left(\dfrac{d-4}{4}\right)^2$, where d is the diameter inside the bark measured in inches at the small end of the log and L is the log length measured in feet. Which of the following gives the value of d, in terms of B and L ?

A) $d = \dfrac{1}{4}\left(\sqrt{\dfrac{B}{L}} + 16\right)$

B) $d = 4\left(\sqrt{BL} + 1\right)$

C) $d = 4\left(\sqrt{\dfrac{B}{L}} - 1\right)$

D) $d = 4\left(\sqrt{\dfrac{B}{L}} + 1\right)$

Here's How to Crack It

Start with the L on the outside of the parentheses on the right. Divide both sides by L to get $\dfrac{B}{L} = \left(\dfrac{d-4}{4}\right)^2$. Now undo the power of 2 outside the parentheses. Take the square root of both sides of the equation to get $\sqrt{\dfrac{B}{L}} = \dfrac{d-4}{4}$. Multiply both sides by 4 to get $4\sqrt{\dfrac{B}{L}} = d - 4$. Add 4 to both sides to get $4\sqrt{\dfrac{B}{L}} + 4 = d$. Factor out the 4 to get $4\left(\sqrt{\dfrac{B}{L}} + 1\right) = d$. The correct answer is (D).

An **inequality** is any statement with one of these signs:

> <   (less than)
> \>   (greater than)
> ≤   (less than or equal to)
> ≥   (greater than or equal to)

You can solve inequalities in the same way you solve equations, with one exception: whenever you multiply or divide an inequality by a negative value, you must change the direction of the sign: < becomes >, and ≤ becomes ≥.

For example:

$$
\begin{array}{rl}
3x + 5 > 17 & \\
\underline{-5 \quad -5} & \text{Subtract 5 from each side.} \\
3x \quad\;\; > 12 & \\
\underline{\div 3 \qquad \div 3} & \text{Divide each side by 3.} \\
x \quad\;\; > \;\; 4 &
\end{array}
$$

In this case, we didn't multiply or divide by a negative value, so the direction of the sign didn't change. However, if we were to divide by a negative value, we would need to change the direction of the sign.

$$
\begin{array}{rl}
-4x + 3 > 15 & \\
\underline{-3 \quad -3} & \text{Subtract 3 from each side.} \\
-4x \quad\;\; > 12 & \\
\underline{\div -4 \qquad \div -4} & \text{Divide each side by } -4. \\
x \quad\;\; < -3 &
\end{array}
$$

Now let's look at how the PSAT may make things more complicated with a question about a range of values.

6

Which of the following is equivalent to $-12 \le 3b + 3 \le 18$?

A) $-5 \le b \le 5$

B) $-5 \le b \le 6$

C) $-4 \le b \le 6$

D) $\;\;3 \le b \le 5$

Here's How to Crack It

Like many problems on the PSAT, this question will be difficult if you try to do it all at once. Instead, break it down into Bite-Sized Pieces. Start with just part of the inequality, $-12 \le 3b + 3$. Remember that you can solve inequalities just like equations—provided that if you multiply or divide by a negative value, you swap the direction of the inequality sign. To solve this part of the inequality, though, you just need to subtract 3 from each side (giving you $-15 \le 3b$) and then divide each side by 3, which leaves you with $-5 \le b$. Now you can eliminate any choices that you know won't work: (C) and (D) don't have -5 in them. Now take the other part of the inequality: $3b + 3 \le 18$. If you subtract 3 from each side and then divide by 3, you get $b \le 5$. Now you can cross off (B), and you're left with (A).

SOLVING RATIONAL EQUATIONS

Since you are not always allowed to use your calculator on the PSAT, there will be some instances in which you will need to solve an equation algebraically. Even on the sections in which calculator use is permitted, you may find it faster and more effective to use your mathematical skills to efficiently answer a question. Another way ETS and the College Board may make your calculator less effective is by asking you to solve for an expression. A lot of the time, algebraic manipulation will be the means by which you can solve that problem.

Here is an example:

5

Which of the following is equivalent to $\dfrac{f}{f-2} - \dfrac{5}{f+3}$?

A) $\dfrac{f-5}{2f+1}$

B) $\dfrac{-5f}{f^2-6}$

C) $\dfrac{f^2-2f+10}{f^2+f-6}$

D) $\dfrac{f^2+8f-10}{f^2+f-6}$

Here's How to Crack It

In order to be able to add these fractions, you need a common denominator. Multiply both the top and the bottom of the left fraction by $(f + 3)$ and multiply both the top and bottom of the right fraction by $(f - 2)$. The expression becomes $\dfrac{f(f + 3)}{(f - 2)(f + 3)} - \dfrac{5(f - 2)}{(f + 3)(f - 2)}$ or $\dfrac{f^2 + 3f}{f^2 + f - 6} - \dfrac{5f - 10}{f^2 + f - 6}$. Now the numerators can be combined over the common denominator and you get $\dfrac{f^2 + 3f - 5f + 10}{f^2 + f - 6} = \dfrac{f^2 - 2f + 10}{f^2 + f - 6}$, which is (C).

EXTRANEOUS SOLUTIONS

Sometimes solving a rational or radical expression makes funny things happen. Let's look at an example.

$$\frac{1}{z + 2} + \frac{1}{z - 2} = \frac{4}{(z + 2)(z - 2)}$$

Given the equation above, what is the value of z?

To add the fractions on the left side, you need a common denominator. Multiply the numerator and the denominator of the first fraction by $(z - 2)$ and the numerator and denominator of the second fraction by $(z + 2)$. Now the fractions can be added together.

The equation becomes

$$\frac{(z - 2) + (z + 2)}{(z + 2)(z - 2)} = \frac{4}{(z + 2)(z - 2)}$$

Since the denominators are equal, the numerators are equal. This gives you

$$(z - 2) + (z + 2) = 4$$

When you simplify the left side, you get $2z = 4$, so $z = 2$. Sounds great, right? However, you need to plug this solution back into the original equation to make sure that it works. You get

$$\frac{1}{2 + 2} + \frac{1}{2 - 2} = \frac{4}{(2 + 2)(2 - 2)}$$

Extra Answers
Any time you are solving for a variable, make sure your solutions actually work. If they do not, they are "extraneous," or extra.

Once simplified, two of the three denominators become zero. That is not allowed, so the solution you found isn't really a solution at all. It is referred to as an "extraneous solution." That term refers to any answer you get to an algebraic equation that results in a false statement when plugged back in to the original equation.

Here's how it might look on the PSAT.

3

$$\frac{3p}{p-2} = \frac{6}{p-2}$$

Which of the following is a true statement about the equation above?

A) There are no solutions to the equation.

B) The solution is $p = 2$.

C) The solution is $p = 3$.

D) There are infinitely many solutions to the equation.

Here's How to Crack It

When given two fraction sets equal to one another, you often have to cross-multiply to solve. In this case, though, the fractions have the same denominator. This tells you that their numerators are equal. Therefore, $3p = 6$, so $p = 2$, right? But what if you put that value back into the denominators? They become 0, which can't happen. Therefore, 2 is an extraneous solution and the answer is (A).

An answer like (D) would occur if literally any value for a variable would make the equation true, such as would be the case in $x + 3 = x + 3$.

ABSOLUTE VALUES

Absolute value is just a measure of the distance between a number and 0. Since distances are always positive, the absolute value of a number is also always positive. The absolute value of a number is written as $|x|$.

When solving for the value of a variable inside the absolute value bars, it is important to remember that variable could be either positive or negative. For example, if $|x| = 2$, then $x = 2$ or $x = -2$ since both 2 and –2 are a distance of 2 from 0.

Here's an example:

9

$$|x + 3| = 6$$
$$|y - 2| = 7$$

For the equations shown above, which of the following is a possible value of $x - y$?

A) –14

B) –4

C) –2

D) 14

Here's How to Crack It

To solve the first equation, set $x + 3 = 6$ and set $x + 3 = -6$. If $x + 3 = -6$, then the absolute value would still be 6. So, x can be either 3 or –9. Now, do the same thing to solve for y. Either $y = 9$ or $y = -5$.

To get the credited answer, you need to try the different combinations. One combination is $x = -9$ and $y = -5$. So, $x - y = -9 - (-5) = -4$, which is (B).

SIMULTANEOUS EQUATIONS

Simultaneous equations occur when you have two equations at the same time. Occasionally, all you have to do is stack the equations, and then add or subtract them, so try that first. Sometimes, it won't get you exactly what you want, but it will get you close to it.

6

$$x + 2y = 12$$
$$2x + y = 9$$

Given the system of equations above, what is the value of $x + y$?

A)   3

B)   7

C) $\dfrac{21}{2}$

D)   21

Here's How to Crack It

This question involves simultaneous equations, so first try to stack and combine them. You're being asked for $x + y$, so even getting the same number of x variables as y variables would be useful.

Let's see what happens when you add the equations:

$$x + 2y = 12$$
$$\underline{+\ 2x + \ y = \ 9}$$
$$3x + 3y = 21$$

Now all you need to do is divide both sides of the equation by 3 to get the expression you're being asked for, $x + y$, and you end up with the answer, 7. The correct answer is (B).

That was pretty simple, but simultaneous equations on the PSAT are rarely that straightforward. Let's look at a really challenging one.

27

Two competing fast food restaurants sell both hamburgers and orders of French fries at the same prices. Burger Planet's lunchtime sales can be modeled as $40h + 70f = \$260.00$, where h is the cost of a hamburger and f is the cost of an order of French fries. If Slider Heaven sells 80 hamburgers and 60 orders of French fries over the same period and outsells Burger Planet by $100, what is the total cost of three hamburgers and three orders of French fries at either establishment?

A) $5.00

B) $9.00

C) $11.00

D) $15.00

Here's How to Crack It

The sales equation at Burger Planet is given in the question. Create an equation for Slider Heaven's lunchtime sales so you can solve them. Slider Heaven's sales can be modeled as $80h + 60f = 260 + 100 = 360$. Adding these equations together or subtracting one from the other won't give you the 3 burgers and 3 fries that you want. Instead, you need to create a common coefficient for one of the variables and then add or subtract the two equations from each other to get rid of that variable. In this case, multiply the Burger Planet equation by -2 to get $-80h - 140f = -520$. Place the two equations on top of each other and add:

$$\begin{aligned} -80h - 140f &= -520 \\ +80h + 60f &= 360 \\ \hline -80f &= -160 \end{aligned}$$

Divide both sides by -80 to get $f = 2$. Plug 2 into the Burger Planet equation to get $40h + 70(2) = 260$. Solve for h to get $40h + 140 = 260$, or $40h = 120$, so $h = 3$. Therefore, the total cost of 3 hamburgers and 3 orders of French fries is $3(3) + 3(2) = 9 + 6 = 15$. The correct answer is (D).

WRITING YOUR OWN EQUATIONS

For the most part, we've been looking at solving equations given to you in questions. That last question, though, required you to create one of your own. The PSAT Math sections are testing not only your math skills, but also, and possibly even more important to your score improvement, your reading skills. It is imperative that you read the questions carefully and translate the words in the problem into mathematical symbols.

ENGLISH	MATH EQUIVALENTS
is, are, were, did, does, costs	=
what (or any unknown value)	*any variable (x, y, k, b)*
more, sum	+
less, difference	−
of, times, product	× *(multiply)*
ratio, quotient, out of, per	÷ *(divide)*

Sometimes you'll be asked to take a word problem and create equations or inequalities from that information. Usually they will not ask you to solve these equations/inequalities, so if you are able to locate and translate the information in the problem, you have a good shot at getting the correct answer. Always start with the most straightforward piece of information. What is the most straightforward piece of information? Well, that's up to you to decide. Consider the following problem.

> 3
>
> Elom joined a gym that charges a monthly fee of $35. A one-time enrollment fee of $40 is charged when he joins. Which of the following represents the total amount of fees that Elom has paid to his gym after *m* months, in dollars?
>
> A) $35m + 40$
>
> B) $35 + 40m$
>
> C) $35m - 40$
>
> D) $(35 + 40)m$

Here's How to Crack It

The question states that there is a monthly fee of $35 and that the variable *m* represents the number of months. Therefore, the correct answer should include $35m$, so you can eliminate (B). The one-time enrollment fee of $40 has nothing to do with the number of months, so the 40 should be by itself. Eliminate (D), which multiplies the 40 by *m*. The fee should be added on, so the correct answer is (A).

Now let's look at harder one. The following question has a lot more words and more than one inequality in each answer choice. This makes it even more important to translate one piece at a time and eliminate after each step.

5

Kai has two different after-school jobs, one at a bookstore and one at a grocery store. He can only work a total of 10 hours each week due to his heavy homework load. When he works at the bookstore, he earns $10 per hour, and when he works at the grocery store, he earns $13 per hour. He never earns less than $100 in a week, and he always works more hours at the bookstore because he can get free coffee from the café. Solving which of the following systems of inequalities yields the number of hours at the bookstore, b, and the number of hours at the grocery store, g, that Kai can work in one week?

A) $\begin{cases} b - g \le 10 \\ b < g \\ 10b + 13g \ge 100 \end{cases}$

B) $\begin{cases} b + g \le 10 \\ b > g \\ 10b + 13g \ge 100 \end{cases}$

C) $\begin{cases} b + g \le 10 \\ b > g \\ 13b + 10g \ge 100 \end{cases}$

D) $\begin{cases} bg \le 100 \\ b > g \\ 10b + 13g \le 100 \end{cases}$

Here's How to Crack It

Start with a straightforward piece of information to translate. If you start with the fact that Kai works more hours at the bookstore than at the grocery store, you can translate that into $b > g$. This would eliminate (A). If you start with the fact that Kai works no more than 10 hours each week, you can translate that into $b + g \le 10$. This would eliminate (D). Now, to decide between (B) and (C), compare the answers and see what the differences are. Choice (B) has a coefficient of 10 in front of the variable b. Check the question to see if 10 should be associated with b. Since b is the number of hours Kai works at the bookstore, and he earns $10 per hour there, the correct answer should have $10b$, not $13b$. Eliminate (C) and choose (B).

Drill 3

Answers can be found in Part III.

3

If a certain number is 3 more than 7 times itself, what is the number?

A) −3

B) $-\dfrac{3}{2}$

C) $-\dfrac{1}{2}$

D) $-\dfrac{3}{8}$

2

If $\dfrac{7}{x+4} = \dfrac{x+3}{y}$, then which of the following represents an equivalent equation for y, in terms of x ?

A) $y = \dfrac{7(x+3)}{x+4}$

B) $y = \dfrac{x^2 + 7x + 12}{7}$

C) $y = \dfrac{x+3}{7(x+4)}$

D) $y = \dfrac{7}{x^2 + 7x + 12}$

5

Ann is writing a book that will include up to 98 recipes. She currently has 32 main dish recipes and 18 dessert recipes. If r represents the number of additional recipes that Ann could include in her book, which of the following inequalities represents all possible values of r?

A) $r - 50 \geq 98$

B) $r - 50 \leq 98$

C) $98 - (32 + 18) - r \leq 0$

D) $98 - (32 + 18) - r \geq 0$

4

If $\dfrac{3a}{4b} = \dfrac{5c}{6d}$, then which of the following is equal to bc?

A) $\dfrac{a}{2d}$

B) $\dfrac{5a}{8d}$

C) $\dfrac{9ad}{10}$

D) $18ad$

28

A fitness tracking watch collects data on how many miles a user walks per day. The data is collected from 12:00 A.M. each morning until 12:00 A.M. the following day, and resets each day at midnight. After one month of use, Debbie reviews her data in the fitness tracker. She discovers that her average daily miles walked are equal to one-hundredth of the square of the number of hours in one day. How many miles does Debbie walk in one day, on average, rounded to the nearest mile?

7

$$\frac{2(p-2)+2(3-p)}{p-2} = \frac{2(3p-6)+3(6-2p)}{p-2}$$

Which of the following is a true statement about the equation above?

A) There are no solutions to the equation.

B) The solution is $p = 2$.

C) The solution is $p = 3$.

D) There are infinitely many solutions to the equation.

8

A ski resort is renting skis for $30 and snowboards for $20 over a weekend. On Friday, 40 skis and snowboards were rented, and the resort collected $1,100 in rental fees. On Saturday, 55 skis and snowboards were rented and the resort collected $1,400 in rental fees. On Sunday, the resort rented 85 skis and snowboards and collected $2,100 rental fees. Solving which of the following system of equations yields the number of skis, s, and the number of snowboards, b, that were rented over the three-day weekend?

A) $s + b = 50$
$30s + 20b = 180$

B) $s + b = 180$
$30s + 20b = 460$

C) $s + b = 180$
$30s + 20b = 4,600$

D) $s + b = 4,600$
$30s + 20b = 180$

12

$$\frac{m+9}{3} + 2 = \frac{m-2}{7} + 3$$

In the equation above, what is the value of m ?

A) −17

B) −12

C) 5

D) 10

9

$$-4(h + 5) = -3(2 - h) + 14$$

In the equation above, what is the value of h ?

A) −18

B) −4

C) $\dfrac{18}{7}$

D) 18

23

A group of students sells different types of cookies at a bake sale to raise funds for a school trip. When the students sell two snickerdoodle cookies, s, and seven cinnamon cookies, c, they raise $14.00. When the students sell eight snickerdoodle cookies and three cinnamon cookies, they raise $17.50. Assuming the price per cookie does not change, which of the following equations represents a sale the students could make during the fundraiser?

A) $2s + 3c = \$8.00$

B) $4s + 6c = \$16.25$

C) $6s + 5c = \$17.36$

D) $8s + 7c = \$24.50$

13

$$10(3x + a) - a(4x + 2) = 2a(x + 4)$$

If the equation above has infinitely many solutions for x, what is the value of a ?

A) 5

B) 4

C) 3

D) 1

25

Laura has a recipe for cake that calls for both eggs and cups of flour. Laura can purchase five eggs and four cups of flour for $5.50 and nine eggs and eight cups of flour for $10.50. Based on these costs, what is the cost of the ten eggs that Laura will need for her recipe?

A) $5.00

B) $5.50

C) $7.50

D) $10.50

THE COORDINATE PLANE

You will definitely see some questions in the coordinate plane, or *xy*-plane, on the PSAT. Let's start by covering the basics here. You'll see more advanced concepts in the Advanced Math Principles chapter. So let's just review:

The *x*-axis is the horizontal axis, and the *y*-axis is the vertical axis. Points are given on the coordinate plane with the *x*-coordinate first. Positive *x*-values go to the right, and negative ones go to the left; positive *y*-values go up, and negative ones go down. So point *A* (3, 1) is 3 points to the right on the *x*-axis and 1 point up from the *y*-axis. Point *B* (2, −1) is 2 points to the right on the *x*-axis and 1 point down from the *y*-axis.

Slope is a measure of the steepness of a line on the coordinate plane. On most slope problems, you need to recognize only whether the slope is positive, negative, or zero. A line that goes up and to the right has positive slope; a line that goes down and to the right has negative slope, and a flat line has zero slope. In the figure below, ℓ_1 has positive slope, ℓ_2 has zero slope, and ℓ_3 has negative slope.

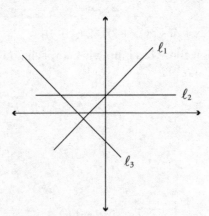

If you do need to calculate the slope, and the graph is drawn for you, here's how: slope = $\frac{y_2 - y_1}{x_2 - x_1}$. The *slope* of a line is equal to $\frac{rise}{run}$. To find the slope, take any two points on the line and count off the distance you need to get from one of these points to the other.

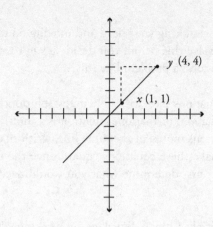

In the graph above, to get from point x to point y, we count up (rise) 3 units, and count over (run) 3 units. Therefore, the slope is $\dfrac{rise}{run} = \dfrac{3}{3} = 1$. Always remember to check whether the slope is positive or negative when you use $= \dfrac{rise}{run}$.

If you're not given a figure and you can't draw one easily using the points given, you can find the slope by plugging the coordinates you know into the slope formula. Just remember to plug the numbers into the formula carefully!

Knowing how to find the slope is useful for solving questions about perpendicular and parallel lines. **Perpendicular lines** have slopes that are negative reciprocals of one another. **Parallel lines** have the same slope and no solutions. You may also be given two equations that have infinitely many solutions.

Take a look at an example.

———————————○———————————

20

$$gx - hy = 78$$
$$4x + 3y = 13$$

In the system of equations above, g and h are constants. If the system has infinitely many solutions, what is the value of gh ?

A) −432

B) −6

C) 6

D) 432

To Infinity…and Beyond!
When given two equations with infinitely many solutions, find a way to make them equal. The equations represent the same line.

Here's How to Crack It

This question may have you scratching your head and moving on to the next question, but let's explore what you can do to solve this before you decide it's not worth your time. You may be surprised by how easy it is to solve a problem like this.

When they say that these equations have infinitely many solutions, what they are really saying is that these are the same equation, or that one equation is a multiple of the other equation. In other words, these two equations represent the same line. With that in mind, try to determine what needs to be done to make these equations equal. Since the right side of the equation is dealing with only a constant, first determine what you would need to do to make 13 equal to 78.

In this case, you need to multiply 13 by 6. Since we are working with equations, we need to do the same thing to both sides of the equation in order for the equation to remain equal.

$$6(4x + 3y) = 6 \times 13$$
$$24x + 18y = 78$$

Since both equations are now equal to 78, you can set them equal to one another, giving you this equation:

$$24x + 18y = gx - hy$$

You may know that when you have equations with the same variables on each side the coefficients on those variables must be equal, so you can deduce that $g = 24$ and $h = -18$. (Be cautious when you evaluate this equation. The test writers are being sneaky by using addition in one equation and subtraction in another.) Therefore, gh equals $24 \times -18 = -432$. Choice (A) is correct.

The equation of a line can take multiple forms. The most common of these is known as the **slope-intercept form**. If you know the slope and the y-intercept, you can create the equation of a given line. A slope-intercept equation takes the form $y = mx + b$, where m is the slope and b is the y-intercept.

Here's an example.

○

5

If c is a constant less than 0, which of the following could be the graph of $y = c(x + y)$ in the xy-plane?

A)

B)

C)

D)

Here's How to Crack It

No points are labeled on the graphs in the answers, and the equation of the line has a mysterious c in it. If you knew the slope or y-intercept of the equation, you could use Process of Elimination. To see what is going on with this problem, make up a value for c that is less than 0. Let's say that $c = -2$, in which case $y = -2(x + y)$. Distribute the -2 to get $y = -2x - 2y$. Rewrite the equation so that it is in the slope-intercept form $y = mx + b$, to get $3y = -2x$ or $y = -\dfrac{2}{3}x$. Therefore, the slope is $-\dfrac{2}{3}$ and the

y-intercept is 0. In fact, no matter what value you picked for c, if c is a constant less than 0, the slope will be negative, and the y-intercept will be 0. Eliminate (A) and (C) since both of these lines have positive slopes. Eliminate answer (B) because the y-intercept is not 0. The correct answer is (D).

The **distance formula** looks quite complicated. The easiest way to solve the distance between two points is to connect them and form a triangle. Then use the Pythagorean Theorem. Many times, the triangle formed is one of the common Pythagorean triplets (3-4-5 or 5-12-13). We'll talk more about the Pythagorean Theorem in the Additional Math Topics chapter.

The **midpoint formula** gives the midpoint of a line segment on the coordinate plane. For example, the line ST has points $S(x_1, y_1)$ and $T(x_2, y_2)$. To find the midpoint of this line segment, simply find the average of the x-coordinates and the y-coordinates. In our example, the midpoint would be $\left(\dfrac{x_1 + x_2}{2}, \dfrac{y_1 + y_2}{2} \right)$.

To find the **point of intersection** of two lines, find a way to set them equal and solve for the variable. If the equations are already in $y = mx + b$ form, set the $mx + b$ part of the two equations equal and solve for x. If the question asks for the value of y, plug the value of x back into either equation to solve for y. It may also be possible to Plug In the Answers (see Chapter 10 for more on this) or graph the equations on your calculator. These skills will also help find the points of intersection between a line and a non-linear graph such as a parabola.

Sometimes, it's a little trickier. Let's look at a difficult question that combines several of the previous concepts.

24

Line 1 contains the points (2, 1) and (1, –2), and line 2 contains the points (–2, 9) and (10, –3). What is the y-coordinate of the point of intersection of lines 1 and 2 ?

A) –1

B) 3

C) 4

D) 7

Here's How to Crack It

To solve this problem, first you need to find the equations of the two lines in order to set the equations equal to each other and find the value of x. Given two points on a line, you can find the slope using $\dfrac{y_2 - y_1}{x_2 - x_1}$. Therefore, the slope of line 1 can be calculated as $\dfrac{-2 - 1}{1 - 2} = \dfrac{-3}{-1} = 3$. Plug this and the coordinates of the easier point, (2, 1), into $y = mx + b$ to find the value of b. The equation for line 1 becomes $1 = 3(2) + b$. Solve for b to find that the value is -5, so line 1 is $y = 3x - 5$. The slope of line 2 can be calculated as $\dfrac{-3 - 9}{10 - (-2)} = \dfrac{-12}{12} = -1$. Find the value of b: $9 = -1(-2) + b$, so $b = 7$. The equation for line 2 is $y = -x + 7$. Set the two equations equal to each other to get $3x - 5 = -x + 7$. Solve for x to get $4x - 5 = 7$ or $4x = 12$, so $x = 3$. Finally, plug x into one of the equations to solve for y. Plug x into the equation $y = -x + 7$, to get $y = -3 + 7 = 4$. Therefore, the correct answer is 4, which is (C).

Drill 4

Answers can be found in Part III.

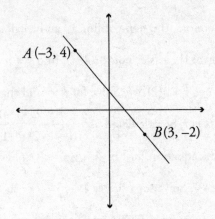

a. How many units do you count up (rise) to get from point B to point A?
_____

b. How many units must you count over (run) to get from point A to point B?
_____

c. What is the slope of the line above? _____

(Remember, the line is going down to the right, so it must have a negative slope.)

d. What would be the slope of a line parallel to AB? _____

e. What would be the slope of a line perpendicular to AB? _____

f. What is the distance from point A to point B? _____

g. What is the midpoint of line segment AB? _____

If $y = 6x + 3$ and $y = cx + 3$ are the equations of perpendicular lines, then what is the value of c ?

A) -6

B) $-\dfrac{1}{6}$

C) $\dfrac{1}{6}$

D) 6

Line l is shown in the graph above. If line m is parallel to line l, which of the following could be the equation of line m ?

A) $y = -3x - 1$

B) $y = -\dfrac{1}{3}x + 2$

C) $y = \dfrac{1}{3}x - 3$

D) $y = 3x + 2$

3

What is the *y*-intercept of the line with equation
$2x + 3y = 12$?

A) 4

B) 3

C) 2

D) $\dfrac{1}{4}$

12

What is the *x*-intercept of the line in the graph above?

A) −1

B) 0

C) 1

D) 2

Which of the following could be the equation of the line in the graph above?

A) $2y - x = -8$

B) $4y + x = -8$

C) $8y - 3x = 8$

D) $8y + x = 8$

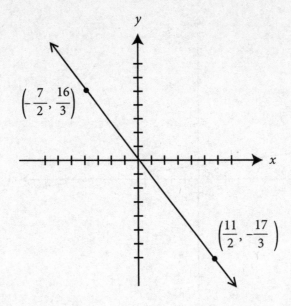

Which of the following is the slope of the line in the graph above?

A) $-\dfrac{11}{6}$

B) $-\dfrac{11}{9}$

C) $-\dfrac{9}{8}$

D) $-\dfrac{9}{11}$

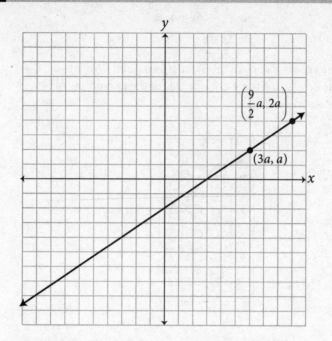

The graph of a line is shown in the *xy*-plane above. It

contains the points $(3a, a)$ and $\left(\dfrac{9}{2}a, 2a\right)$, where a is a

positive constant. Which of the following could be the

equation of this line?

A) $y = \dfrac{2}{3}x - 2$

B) $y = \dfrac{2}{3}x + 2$

C) $y = \dfrac{4}{3}x - 2$

D) $y = \dfrac{3}{2}x - 2$

$$y = 4x^2 - 6x + 4$$
$$y = 2x + 4$$

The equations above intersect at two points. What is the product of the *y*-coordinates of the two points of intersection?

CHARTS AND GRAPHS

Another basic math skill you will need for the PSAT is the ability to read charts and graphs. The PSAT now includes charts, graphs, and tables throughout the test (not just in the Math sections) to present data for students to analyze. The test writers believe this will better reflect what students learn in school and need to understand in the real world. The situations will typically include real-life applications, such as finance and business situations, social science issues, and science.

Since you'll be seeing graphics throughout the test, let's look at the types you may encounter and the skills you'll need to be familiar with when you work with charts and graphs.

The Scatterplot

A scatterplot is a graph with distinct data points, each representing one piece of information. On the scatterplot below, each dot represents the number of televisions sold at a certain price point.

Here's How to Read It

To find the cost of a television when 225 televisions are sold, start at 225 on the vertical axis and draw a horizontal line to the right until you hit a data point. Use the edge of your answer sheet as a straightedge if you have trouble drawing your own straight lines. Once you hit a point, draw a straight line down from it to the horizontal axis and read the number the line hits, which should be $1,500. To determine the number of televisions sold when they cost a certain amount, reverse the steps—start at the bottom, draw up until you hit a point, and then move left until you intersect the vertical axis.

A question may ask you to draw a "line of best fit" on a scatterplot diagram. This is the line that best represents the data. You can use the edge of your answer sheet as a ruler to help you draw a line that goes through most of the data.

The Line Graph

A line graph is similar to a scatterplot in that it shows different data points that relate the two variables. The difference with a line graph, though, is that the points have been connected to create a continuous line.

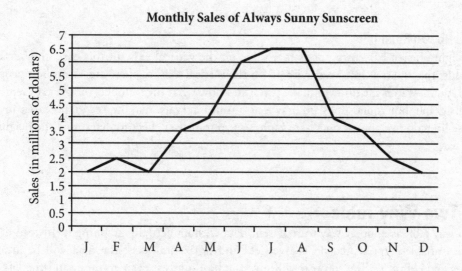

Monthly Sales of Always Sunny Sunscreen

Here's How to Read It

Reading a line graph is very similar to reading a scatterplot. Start at the axis that represents the data given, and draw a straight line up or to the right until you intersect the graph line. Then move left or down until you hit the other axis. For example, in February, indicated by an F on the horizontal axis, Always Sunny Sunscreen had 2.5 million in sales. Make sure to notice the units on each axis. If February sales were only $2.50, rather than $2.5 million, then this company wouldn't be doing very well!

The Bar Graph (or Histogram)

Instead of showing a variety of different data points, a bar graph will show how many items belong to a particular category. If the variable at the bottom is given in ranges, instead of distinct items, the graph is called a histogram, but you read it the same way.

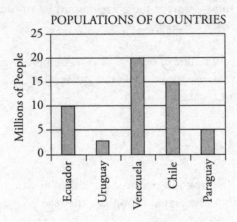

POPULATIONS OF COUNTRIES

Here's How to Read It

The height of each bar corresponds to a value on the vertical axis. In this case, the bar above Chile hits the line that intersects with 15 on the vertical axis, so there are 15 million people in Chile. Again, watch the units to make sure you know what the numbers on the axes represent. On this graph, horizontal lines are drawn at 5-unit intervals, making the graph easier to read. If these lines do not appear on a bar graph, use your answer sheet to determine the height of a given bar.

The Two-Way Table

A two-way table is another way to represent data without actually graphing it. Instead of having the variables represented on the vertical and horizontal axes, the data will be arranged in rows and columns. The top row will give the headings for each column, and the left-most column will give the headings for each row. The numbers in each box indicate the data for the category represented by the row and the column the box is in.

	Computer Production	
	Morning Shift	**Afternoon Shift**
Monday	200	375
Tuesday	245	330
Wednesday	255	340
Thursday	250	315
Friday	225	360

Here's How to Read It

If you wanted to see the number of computers produced on Tuesday morning, you could start in the Morning Shift column and look down until you found the number in the row that says "Tuesday," or you could start in the row for Tuesday and look to the right until you found the Morning Shift column. Either way, the result is 245. Some tables will give you totals in the bottom row and/or the right-most column, but sometimes you will need to find the totals yourself by adding up all the numbers in each row or in each column. More complicated tables will have more categories listed in rows and/or columns, or the tables may even contain extraneous information.

Figure Facts

Every time you encounter a figure or graphic on the PSAT, you should make sure you understand how to read it by checking the following things:

- What are the variables for each axis or the headings for the table?
- What units are used for each variable?
- Are there any key pieces of information (numbers, for example) in the legend of the chart that you should note?
- What type of relationship is shown by the data in the chart? For instance, if the chart includes curves that show an upward slope, then the graph shows a *positive association*, while curves that show a downward slope show a *negative association*.
- You can use the edge of your answer sheet as a ruler to help you make sure you are locating the correct data in the graph or to draw a line of best fit if necessary.

PROBABILITY

One topic that is often tested with two-way tables is probability. Probability refers to the chance that an event will happen, and it is given as a percent or a fractional value between 0 and 1, inclusive. A probability of 0 means that the event will never happen; a probability of 1 means that it is certain to happen.

$$\text{Probability} = \frac{\text{number of outcomes you want}}{\text{number of possible outcomes}}$$

For instance, if you have a die with faces numbered 1 to 6, what is the chance of rolling a 2?

There is one face with the number 2 on it, out of 6 total faces. Therefore, the probability of rolling a 2 is $\frac{1}{6}$.

What is the chance of rolling an even number on one roll of this die? There are 3 faces of the die with an even number (the sides numbered 2, 4, and 6) out of a total of 6 faces. Therefore, the probability of rolling an even number is $\frac{3}{6}$, or $\frac{1}{2}$.

Let's look at how this concept will be tested on the PSAT.

18

A survey was conducted among a randomly chosen sample of full-time salaried workers about satisfaction in their current jobs. The table below shows a summary of the survey results.

Reported Job Satisfaction by Education Level (in thousands)

Highest Level of Education	Satisfied	Not Satisfied	No Response	Total
High School Diploma	17,880	12,053	2,575	32,508
Bachelor's Degree	24,236	8,496	3,442	36,174
Master's Degree	17,605	5,324	1,861	24,790
Doctoral Degree	12,210	2,081	972	15,263
Total	71,931	27,954	8,850	108,735

All persons who have earned a Master's or Doctoral degree must have previously earned a Bachelor's degree. What is the probability that a full-time salaried worker does NOT have a Bachelor's degree?

A) 29.9%

B) 33.3%

C) 36.8%

D) 66.7%

Here's How to Crack It

If everyone with a Master's or Doctoral degree has a Bachelor's degree, then the only people who do NOT have a Bachelor's degree are those whose highest level of education is a High School Diploma. Find the probability of choosing someone with a High School Diploma out of the total: $\frac{32,508}{108,735} = 0.299 = 29.9\%$, which is (A).

GRIDS-INS: THE BASICS

You will see 8 questions on the PSAT that ask you to bubble in a numerical answer on a grid, rather than answer a multiple-choice question. These Grid-In questions are arranged in a loose order of difficulty, meaning they start easier and get progressively harder, and can be solved according to the methods outlined for the multiple-choice problems on the test. The last two grid-ins in Section 4 will be a paired set, but each question can be answered separately. Don't worry that there are no answer choices—your approach is the same.

Keep Left
No matter how many digits in your answer, always start gridding in the leftmost column. That way, you'll avoid omitting digits and losing points.

The only difficulty with grid-ins is getting used to the way in which you are asked to answer the question. For each question, you'll have a grid like the following:

We recommend that you write the answer on top of the grid to help you bubble, but it's important to know that the scoring machine reads only the bubbles. *If you bubble incorrectly, the computer will consider the answer to be incorrect.*

Here are the basic rules of gridding:

1. If your answer uses fewer than four boxes, you can grid it anywhere you like. To avoid confusion, we suggest that you start at the leftmost box. For example:

2. You can grid your answer as either a fraction or a decimal, *if* the fraction will fit.

You can grid an answer of .5 as either .5 or $\frac{1}{2}$.

Relax
If your answer is a fraction and it fits in the grid (fraction bar included), don't reduce it. Why bother? You won't get an extra point for doing so. However, if your fraction doesn't fit, reduce it or turn it into a decimal on your calculator.

or

3. You do not need to reduce your fractions, *if* the fraction will fit.

If your answer is $\frac{2}{4}$, you can grid it as $\frac{2}{4}$, $\frac{1}{2}$, or .5.

or   or

4. If you have a decimal that will not fit in the spaces provided, you *must grid as many places as will fit.*

    If your answer is $\frac{2}{3}$, you can grid it as $\frac{2}{3}$, .666, or .667, but .66 is *not* acceptable.

    You do *not* need to round your numbers, so we suggest that you don't. There's no reason to give yourself a chance to make a mistake if you don't have to.

 or or

5. You cannot grid mixed numbers. Convert all mixed numbers to ordinary fractions.

    If your answer is $2\frac{1}{2}$, you must convert it to $\frac{5}{2}$ or 2.5; otherwise the computer will read your 2 1/2 as 21/2.

 or

Don't Mix
Never grid in a mixed number. Change it into an improper fraction or decimal. To convert mixed fractions into improper fractions, all you have to do is multiply the denominator with the whole number in front of the fraction, then add that product to the numerator, and finally put that number over the denominator you started with.

6. You can't grid π, square roots, variables, or negative numbers, so if you get an answer with one of those terms, you've made a mistake. Check your work.

Drill 5

Answers can be found in Part III.

28

**Estimated Numbers of Cell Phone Users by Type
(in millions)**

	Prepaid users	Contracted users	Totals
2008	45	225	270
2012	75	250	325
Totals	120	475	595

If a cell phone user is selected at random in 2008, what is the probability that user is a contracted user?

14

If $5x^2 = 125$, what could be the value of $5x^3$?

15

$$z = 5 - 5[5z - 2(1 - z)]$$

In the equation above, what is the value of z ?

29

If $5 - \sqrt{z} = \sqrt{z - 5}$, what is the value of z ?

16

If $3a + 2b = 37$ and $7a + 4b = 85$, what is the value of $b^2 + 6b - 10$?

30

Linh travels from his home in Canada, where temperature is measured in degrees Celsius, to Houston, where temperature is measured in degrees Fahrenheit. The weather channel forecasts the high temperature in Houston for the next 2 days as 95 degrees and 86 degrees Fahrenheit, respectively. He wants to convert these temperatures from Fahrenheit to Celsius. To do so, he subtracts 32 from the degrees in Fahrenheit for each day and multiplies the difference by $\frac{5}{9}$. How many degrees higher is the predicted temperature for the first day than the predicted temperature for the second day, in degrees Celsius?

Mathew and Moriah purchased a tandem bicycle for $540. If the amount Moriah paid was $30 less than twice the amount Mathew paid, how much, in dollars, did Moriah pay? (Disregard the dollar sign when gridding in your answer.)

Kimberly is an apiologist studying the sugar content of different sugar-water solutions to determine which is preferred by her hive of honeybees. After trying Solution 1, which has a sugar content of 25%, and Solution 2, which has a sugar content of 10%, she decides to make a new solution. She mixes 50 ounces of Solution 1 with some quantity of Solution 2 to make Solution 3, which has a sugar content of 15%. How many ounces of Solution 2 did Kimberly use to make Solution 3 ?

Summary

- The Math sections are arranged in a loose Order of Difficulty, which can make it easier to spot the less difficult problems. However, remember that the test writers' idea of "easier" problems is not necessarily the same as your idea. Let your Personal Order of Difficulty be your guide.

- Write in your test booklet to set up problems, and then use your calculator (when allowed) to figure out solutions. And remember to type carefully—your calculator won't check for mistakes.

- Review basic definitions again before the test to make sure you don't get stuck on the "little words."

- When you have to manipulate exponents, remember your MADSPM rules.

- To solve equations for a variable, isolate the variable. Make sure you perform the same operations on both sides of the equation.

- Inequalities can be worked just like equations, until you have to multiply or divide by a negative number. Then you need to flip the inequality sign.

- When solving radical and rational equations, be on the lookout for extraneous solutions. They are answers you get that don't work when plugged back into the original equation.

- The absolute value of a number is the positive distance from zero, or practically, making the thing inside the | | sign positive. Everything inside the | | is equal to the positive and the negative value of the expression to which it is equal. Also remember that | | work like ( ); you need to complete all the operations inside the | | before you can make the value positive.

- To solve simultaneous equations, simply add or subtract the equations. If you don't have the answer, look for multiples of your solutions. When the simultaneous equation question asks for a single variable and addition and subtraction don't work, try to make something disappear. Multiply the equations by a constant to make the coefficient(s) of the variable(s) you want go to zero when the equations are added or subtracted.

- When writing a system of equations, start with the most straightforward piece of information.

o   You can also use the equations in the answer choices to help you narrow down the possibilities for your equations. Eliminate any answers in which an equation doesn't match your equation.

o   Parallel lines have the same slope and no solutions. If two lines have the same slope and infinitely many solutions, they are actually the same line. Perpendicular lines have slopes that are negative reciprocals of one another.

o   Rather than worrying about the distance formula, connect the two points and make the resulting line the hypotenuse of a right triangle. Then you can use the Pythagorean Theorem to find the distance.

o   The coordinates of the midpoint of a line segment with endpoints (x_1, y_1) and (x_2, y_2) will be $\left(\dfrac{x_1 + x_2}{2}, \dfrac{y_1 + y_2}{2} \right)$.

o   When you encounter charts, carefully check the chart for information you should note, and remember that you can use your answer sheet as a ruler to help you locate information or to draw a line of best fit.

o   Probability is a fractional value between 0 and 1 (inclusive), and it is equal to the number of outcomes the question is asking for divided by the total number of possible outcomes. It can also be expressed as a percent.

o   When doing Grid-In questions, be sure to keep to the left, and don't bother reducing fractions if they fit in the allotted spaces.

Chapter 10
Math Techniques

In the previous chapter, we mentioned that one of the keys to doing well on the PSAT is to have a set of test-specific problem-solving skills. This chapter discusses some powerful strategies, which—though you may not use them in school—are specifically designed to get you points on the PSAT. Learn them well!

PLUGGING IN

One of the most powerful problem-solving skills on the PSAT is a technique we call Plugging In. Plugging In will turn nasty algebra problems into simple arithmetic and help you through the particularly twisted problems that you'll often see on the PSAT. There are several varieties of Plugging In, each suited to a different kind of question.

Plugging In Your Own Numbers

The problem with doing algebra is that it's just too easy to make a mistake.

> Whenever you see a problem with variables in the answer choices, Plug In.

Start by picking a number for the variable in the problem (or for more than one variable, if necessary), solve the problem using your number, and then see which answer choice gives you the correct answer.

Take a look at the following problem:

13

If $2x + x + \dfrac{1}{x} = y$, what is the value of $xy - 1$, in terms of x?

A) $\dfrac{3x^2 + 1}{x}$

B) $3x^2 - 1$

C) $3x^2 + 1$

D) $3x^2$

When to Plug In
- Phrases like "in terms of" or "equivalent form" in the question
- Variables in the question and/or answers choices

Here's How to Crack It

First, start by choosing a value for one of the variables. Here, all the action is happening to the x, so choose a value for x. Make $x = 2$. Next, work the problem in Bite-Sized Pieces until you've come up with a numerical answer for the question. If $x = 2$, then the equation becomes

$2(2) + 2 + \dfrac{1}{2} = y$. Multiply; then add on the left side: $4 + 2 + \dfrac{1}{2} = y$; $\dfrac{13}{2} = y$. Note the question doesn't want the value of y, but rather $xy - 1$. Because $x = 2$ and $y = \dfrac{13}{2}$, $xy - 1 = (2)\left(\dfrac{13}{2}\right) - 1 = 13 - 1 = 12$. This is the target number; circle it.

Now that you have a target number, work your answer choices using Process of Elimination. Make $x = 2$ in each answer choice and eliminate any choice that doesn't equal your target number of 12:

A) $\dfrac{3(2)^2 + 1}{2} = \dfrac{13}{2}$ Not 12; eliminate!

B) $3(2)^2 - 1 = 11$ Not 12; eliminate!

C) $3(2)^2 + 1 = 13$ Not 12; eliminate!

D) $3(2)^2 = 12$ Is 12; keep!

Only (D) matches your target number, so it must be the answer!

———————◯———————

As you can see, Plugging In can turn messy algebra questions into more straightforward arithmetic questions. This technique is especially powerful when the PSAT asks you to find the equivalent form of an expression:

———————◯———————

16

The expression $x^2 + 4x - 4$ is written in the equivalent form $N^2 - 8$. What is the value of N?

A) $x^2 + 4x - 4$

B) $x^2 + 4x + 4$

C) $x - 2$

D) $x + 2$

> **Plugging In: Quick Reference**
> - When you see *in terms of* or *equivalent form* and there are variables in the answer choices, you can Plug In.
> - Pick your own number for an unknown in the problem.
> - Do the necessary math to find the answer you're shooting for, which is the target number. Circle the target number.
> - Use POE to eliminate every answer which doesn't match the target number.

Here's How to Crack It

The variable x is all over the place, so assign a value for x. Try $x = 2$. Next, work the problem in Bite-Sized Pieces. The first expression becomes $2^2 + 4(2) - 4 = 4 + 8 - 4 = 8$. The question then states that this is "written in the equivalent form" of $N^2 - 8$. If these expressions are equivalent, then $N^2 - 8$ must also equal 8. So set it equal to 8 and solve for N : $N^2 - 8 = 8$; $N^2 = 16$; $N = \pm 4$. The question is asking for N, so you're looking for any answer that equals either -4 or 4 (because there are two possible values). These are your target numbers; circle them. Make $x = 2$ in each answer choice and eliminate any option that doesn't match one of the target numbers:

A) $2^2 + 4(2) - 4 = 4 + 8 - 4 = 8$ Not -4 or 4; eliminate!

B) $2^2 + 4(2) + 4 = 4 + 8 + 4 = 16$ Not -4 or 4; eliminate!

C) $2 - 2 = 0$ Not -4 or 4; eliminate!

D) $2 + 2 = 4$ Yes!

The answer is (D).

Plugging In is such a great technique because it turns hard algebra problems into medium and sometimes even easy arithmetic questions. Remember this when you're thinking of your POOD and looking for questions to do among the hard ones; if you see variables in the answers, there's a good chance it's one to try.

Don't worry too much about what numbers you choose to plug in; just plug in easy numbers (small numbers like 2, 5, or 10 or numbers that make the arithmetic easy, like 100 if you're looking for a percent). Also, be sure your numbers fit the conditions of the questions (for example, if they say $x \leq 11$, don't plug in 12).

What If There's No Variable?

Sometimes you'll see a problem that doesn't contain an x, y, or z, but which contains a hidden variable. If your answers are percents or fractional parts of some unknown quantity (total number of marbles in a jar, total miles to travel in a trip), try Plugging In.

Take a look at this problem:

27 _____

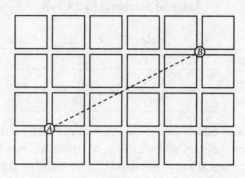

A neighborhood is comprised of square blocks, as shown above. Genna launches a drone from point A. The drone flies directly to point B, as shown by the dotted line. Genna then walks from point A to point B by following the streets by the shortest route possible. By approximately what percent was the distance Genna walked greater than the distance the drone flew?

A)   25%

B)   34%

C)   75%

D)   134%

Here's How to Crack It

Plug In for the size of the blocks. Assume each block is 1 unit by 1 unit. Genna must travel 4 blocks east and 2 blocks north, so she must travel 6 units total. (Note that it doesn't matter whether she goes north then east, east then north, or a zigzag pattern from A to B; the shortest path will always be 6 units).

To find the distance the drone travels, make a right triangle with legs 4 units (the distance east) and 2 units (the distance north). Find the hypotenuse (which is the direct distance from A to B) using the Pythagorean Theorem. The Pythagorean Theorem is $a^2 + b^2 = c^2$, where c is the hypotenuse. Therefore, $4^2 + 2^2 = c^2$; $16 + 4 = c^2$; $20 = c^2$; $\sqrt{20} = c$.

> We'll cover the Pythagorean Theorem in more detail in Chapter 12.

To find the percent difference, use the formula $\dfrac{\text{difference}}{\text{original}} \times 100$. Because you want percent greater, the original is the smaller value (in this case $\sqrt{20}$): $\dfrac{6 - \sqrt{20}}{\sqrt{20}} \times 100 \approx 34.16$, which is closest to (B).

Try another one.

16

Ratio of Students in a Club

	Male	Female	Total
Junior	0.18	0.27	0.45
Senior	0.24	0.31	0.55
Total	0.42	0.58	1.00

The two-way table above shows the ratio of males and females and juniors and seniors in a particular club. If a male is chosen at random, what is the probability that he will be a junior?

A) $\dfrac{9}{50}$

B) $\dfrac{3}{7}$

C) $\dfrac{27}{58}$

D) $\dfrac{3}{4}$

Here's How to Crack It

The total ratio of students is 1.00, so Plug In for the total number of students. Make the number of students 100. To find the number of students in each category, you only need to multiply each number in the table by 100. This gives you the following:

	Male	Female	Total
Junior	18	27	45
Senior	24	31	55
Total	42	58	100

You're asked to find the probability of choosing a junior if you choose from the males. Probability is $\dfrac{what\ you\ want}{total\ possible\ outcomes}$. There are 18 male juniors and 42 total males, making the probability of choosing a junior from the males $\dfrac{18}{42}$, which reduces to $\dfrac{3}{7}$. This matches (B).

Drill 1

Answers can be found in Part III.

5

David acquired a data plan for his smart phone. Every month he pays a flat rate of $25 and an additional $0.05 for every megabyte he goes over his monthly limit. Which of the following represents David's monthly data bill when he goes over his limit by m megabytes?

A) $25 + 1.05m$

B) $25 + 0.05m$

C) $0.05(25 + m)$

D) $1.05(25 + m)$

4

If $a = \dfrac{b}{c^2}$ and $c \neq 0$, what is the value of $\dfrac{1}{b^2}$?

A) ac^2

B) a^2c^4

C) $\dfrac{1}{ac^2}$

D) $\dfrac{1}{a^2c^4}$

11

Luciano measured the amount of water that evaporated over a period of time from a container holding w ounces of water, where w is greater than 12. By the end of the first day, the cup had lost 2 ounces of water. By the end of the 7th day, the cup had lost an additional 8 ounces of water. By the end of the 11th day, the cup had lost half of the water that remained after the 7th day. Which of the following represents the remaining amount of water, in ounces, in Luciano's container at the end of the 11th day?

A) $\dfrac{w-2}{8}$

B) $\dfrac{w-2}{2} - 10$

C) $\dfrac{1}{2}w - 10$

D) $\dfrac{w-10}{2}$

7

If $p \neq 0$, what is the value of $\dfrac{\frac{1}{8}}{2p}$?

A) $\dfrac{1}{16p}$

B) $\dfrac{p}{4}$

C) $\dfrac{4}{p}$

D) $4p$

9

A certain standardized test has 50 questions. A student receives 1 point for each correct answer and loses $\dfrac{1}{4}$ of a point for each incorrect answer. Which of the following equations best models the net score, S, in points, for a student who completes all 50 questions and answers c of the questions correctly?

A) $S = 50 - 0.25c$

B) $S = 50 - 0.75c$

C) $S = c - 0.25(50 - c)$

D) $S = c - 0.75(50 - c)$

18

Jodi has x dollars in her bank account. She withdraws $\dfrac{1}{6}$ of the money in her account to pay her rent and another $\dfrac{1}{6}$ of the money in her account to make her car payment. Jodi then deposits her paycheck of y dollars into her account. A week later, she withdraws $\dfrac{1}{2}$ of the money in her account to spend on a new set of knives. In terms of x, how many dollars are left in Jodi's account?

A) $\dfrac{(4x - 3y)}{6}$

B) $\dfrac{(3x - 5y)}{6}$

C) $\dfrac{(3x - y)}{6}$

D) $\dfrac{(2x + 3y)}{6}$

12

$$2\left|4y-5\right|<24$$

What is the sum of all the integer solutions to the inequality above?

A)   7

B)   9

C) 10

D) 14

29

15% of the members of the incoming freshmen class at a certain university are left-handed, and the remaining members are right-handed. 65% of the same incoming freshmen class are female, and the rest are male. If $\dfrac{2}{3}$ of the left-handed students are male, then what percent of the female class is right-handed, to the nearest tenth of a percent? (Disregard the percent sign when gridding your answers. For example, if the answer is 43.2%, grid in 43.2.)

PLUGGING IN THE ANSWERS (PITA)

You can also Plug In when the answer provided to a problem is an actual value, such as 2, 4, 10, or 20. Why would you want to do a lot of complicated algebra to solve a problem, when the answer is right there on the page? All you have to do is figure out *which* choice it is.

How can you tell which is the correct answer? Try every choice *until you find the one that works*. Even if this means you have to try all four choices, PITA is still a fast and reliable means of getting the right answer.

If you work strategically, however, you almost never need to try all four answers. If the question asks for either the greatest or the least answer, start there. Otherwise, start with one of the middle answer choices. If that answer works, you're done. If the answer you started with was too big, try a smaller answer. If the answer you started with was too small, try a bigger answer. You can almost always find the answer in two or three tries this way. Let's try PITA on the following problem.

4

If the average (arithmetic mean) of 8 and x is equal to the average of 5, 9, and x, what is the value of x ?

A) 1

B) 2

C) 4

D) 8

PITA = Plugging In the Answers
Don't try to solve problems like this by writing equations and solving for *x* or *y*. Plugging In the Answers lets you use arithmetic instead of algebra, so you're less likely to make errors.

Here's How to Crack It
Let's start with (C) and plug in 4 for x. The problem now reads:

If the average (arithmetic mean) of 8 and 4 is equal to the average of 5, 9, and 4 . . .

Does this work? The average of 8 and 4 is 6, and the average of 5, 9, and 4 is also 6. Therefore, (C) is the answer.

Neat, huh? Of course, the first answer you choose won't always be the correct one. Let's try one more.

10

If $(x - 2)^2 = 2x - 1$, which of the following is a possible value of x ?

A) 1

B) 2

C) 3

D) 6

Here's How to Crack It

If we try plugging in (C), 3, for x, the equation becomes $1 = 5$, which is false. So (C) can't be right. If you're not sure which way to go next, just pick a direction. It won't take very long to figure out the correct answer. If we try plugging in (B), 2, for x, the equation becomes $0 = 3$, which is false. If we try plugging in (A), 1, for x, the equation becomes $1 = 1$, which is true. There's no need to try other answers, because there are no variables; only one answer choice can work. So the answer is (A).

Drill 2

Answers can be found in Part III.

3

$$2(n + 5) = 3(n - 2) + 8$$

In the equation above, what is the value of n ?

A) 1

B) 3

C) 4

D) 8

8

If $3^{x+2} = 243$, what is the value of x ?

A) 1

B) 2

C) 3

D) 4

7

$$2x - y > -3$$

$$4x + y < 5$$

$$y > -6$$

Which of the following points is in the solution set of the systems of inequalities above?

A) $(-4, -1)$

B) $(-3, -2)$

C) $(-1, -1)$

D) $(3, -5)$

If $\dfrac{24x}{4} + \dfrac{1}{x} = 5$, what is the value of x ?

A) $-\dfrac{1}{6}$

B) $\dfrac{1}{6}$

C) $\dfrac{1}{4}$

D) $\dfrac{1}{2}$

$$-\dfrac{5}{7} - \dfrac{11}{7}u = -v$$
$$2v = 7 + 5u$$

Based on the system of equations above, what is the value of v ?

A) −4

B) −3

C) −1

D) 0

An alloy needs to contain between 10 and 15% of titanium. Which of the following expressions represents the amount in kilograms, x, of a 20% titanium alloy that should be mixed with a 5% titanium alloy to produce 10 kilograms of an alloy with the acceptable percentage of titanium?

A) $1.33 \le x \le 1.67$

B) $2.25 \le x \le 3.25$

C) $3.33 \le x \le 6.67$

D) $7.25 \le x \le 9.75$

DATA ANALYSIS

In the calculator-allowed math section (Section 4), there will be questions that will ask you to work with concepts such as averages, percentages, and unit conversions. Luckily, The Princeton Review has you covered! The rest of this chapter will give you techniques and strategies to help you tackle these questions.

The Average Pie

You probably remember the average formula from math class, which says

Average (arithmetic mean) = $\dfrac{\text{total}}{\text{\# of things}}$. However, the PSAT rarely will ask you to take a simple average. Of the three parts of an average problem—the average, the total, and the number of things—you're usually given two of these parts, but often in tricky combinations.

Therefore, the most reliable way to solve average problems is always to use the Average Pie:

What the pie shows you is that if you know any two of these parts, you can always solve for the third. Once you fill in two of the elements, the pie shows you how to solve for the third part. If you know the total and the number of things, you can solve for the average (total divided by number); if you know the total and the average, you can solve for the number of things (total divided by average); if you know the number of things and average, you can solve for the total (number times average).

Let's try this example.

> **9**
>
> The average (arithmetic mean) of 3 numbers is 22 and the smallest of these numbers is 2. If the remaining two numbers are equal, what are their values?
>
> A) 22
>
> B) 32
>
> C) 40
>
> D) 64

Total

When calculating averages, always find the total. It's the one piece of information that ETS loves to withhold.

Here's How to Crack It

Let's start by filling in our Average Pie. We know that 3 numbers have an average of 22. So we can fill in our pie, and the pie shows us that the sum total of these numbers must be 22 × 3, or 66.

We know that one of the numbers is 2, so we can subtract it from the total we've just found, which leaves 64. What else do we know from the question? The remaining two numbers are equal, so 64/2 = 32. So the answer is (B).

Try one more.

8

Caroline scored 85, 88, and 89 on three of her four history tests. If her average (arithmetic mean) score for all four tests was 90, what did she score on her fourth test?

A) 90

B) 93

C) 96

D) 98

Here's How to Crack It

Let's start with what we know: We know that the average of all four of her tests was 90. So we can fill in an Average Pie with this information:

Now the pie tells us that the sum total of the scores on these four tests will be 4×90, or 360. Since three of these tests have a sum of $85 + 88 + 89$, or 262, we know that the score on the fourth test must be equal to $360 - 262$, or 98. This makes the answer (D).

Median and Mode

Another two terms that are often tested along with average are median and mode.

The **median** of a group of numbers is the number in the middle, just as the "median" is the large divider in the middle of a road. To find the median, here's what you do:

Finding a Median
To find the median of a set containing an even number of items, take the average of the two middle numbers after putting the numbers in order.

- First, put the elements in the group in numerical order from lowest to highest.
- If the number of elements in your group is *odd*, find the number in the middle. That's the median.
- If you have an *even* number of elements in the group, find the two numbers in the middle and calculate their average (arithmetic mean).

Try this on the following problem:

3

If the 5 students in Ms. Jaffray's math class scored 91, 83, 84, 90, and 85 on their final exams, what is the median score for her class on the final exam?

A) 84

B) 85

C) 86

D) 88

Here's How to Crack It

First, let's place these numbers in order from lowest to highest: 83, 84, 85, 90, 91. The number in the middle is 85, so the median of this group is 85 and the answer is (B).

The **mode** of a group of numbers is the number that appears the most. (Remember: *Mode* sounds like *most*.) To find the mode of a group of numbers, simply see which element appears the greatest number of times.

28

If the 7 students in Ms. Holoway's math class scored 91, 83, 92, 83, 91, 85, and 91 on their final exams, what is the mode of her students' scores?

Here's How to Crack It

Since the number 91 is the one that appears most often in the list, the mode of these numbers is 91. Pretty simple!

Range

Another measure of the spread of data is range. The range of a list of numbers is the difference between the greatest number on the list and the least number on the list. For the list 4, 5, 5, 6, 7, 8, 9, 10, 20, the greatest number is 20 and the least is 4, so the range is 20 − 4 = 16.

Let's look at a problem:

184	176	181	157	168
154	148	165	190	162

A group of patients is recruited for a clinical trial. Their heights, recorded in centimeters, are listed in the table above. Two more patients are recruited to the study. After these patients join, the range of the heights is 42 cm. Which of the following could NOT be the heights of the two new patients?

A) 154 cm and 186 cm

B) 146 cm and 179 cm

C) 150 cm and 188 cm

D) 148 cm and 185 cm

Here's How to Crack It

To determine the current range, take the difference of the greatest and least values: 190 − 148 = 42 cm. If the range is to remain 42 cm, then the new patients cannot be greater than 190 cm or less than 148 cm tall. Choice (B) violates this restriction. Because the question wants what could NOT be the heights of the new patients, the answer is (B).

Rates

Rate is a concept related to averages. Cars travel at an average speed. Work gets done at an average rate. Because the ideas are similar, you can also use a pie to organize your information on rate questions.

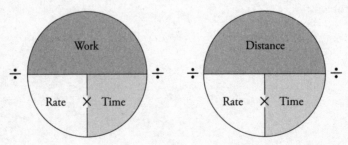

Here's a simple example:

Problem: If a fisherman can tie 9 flies for fly fishing in an hour and a half, how long does it take him to tie one fly, in minutes?

Solution: First, convert the hour and a half to 90 minutes, so your units are consistent. Then fill in the top of the pie with the amount (9 flies) and the lower right part with the time (90 minutes). Divide 9 by 90 to get the rate, $\frac{1}{10}$, or one fly every 10 minutes.

Let's look at another example:

28

Sally, Abdul, and Juanita have volunteered to stuff a certain number of envelopes for a local charity. Working by herself, Sally could stuff all the envelopes in exactly 3 hours. Working by himself, Abdul could stuff all the envelopes in exactly 4 hours. Working by herself, Juanita could stuff all the envelopes in exactly 6 hours. If Sally, Abdul, and Juanita work together at these rates to stuff all the envelopes, what fraction of the envelopes will be stuffed by Juanita?

Here's How to Crack It

Since the question doesn't tell you how many envelopes to stuff, this is a great problem to Plug In on in addition to using the Rate Pie. Because Sally takes 3 hours, Abdul takes 4 hours, and Juanita takes 6 hours, you want to choose a multiple of all those numbers. Make the total number of envelopes to stuff 120. Next, use the Rate Pie to determine each person's rate:

Sally

Abdul

Juanita

If all three people work together, their total rate will be 40 + 30 + 20 = 90 envelopes/hour.

During that hour Juanita will stuff 20 envelopes, meaning she does $\frac{20}{90}$, or $\frac{2}{9}$, of the job.

PERCENTS

Percent just means "divided by 100." So 20 percent $= \dfrac{20}{100} = \dfrac{1}{5}$, or .2.

Likewise, 400 percent $= \dfrac{400}{100} = \dfrac{4}{1} = 4$.

Any percent question can be translated into algebra—just use the following rules:

Percent	÷ 100
Of	×
What	x (or any variable)
Is, Are, Equals	=

Take a look at some examples of phrases you might have to translate on the PSAT:

	becomes	
8 percent of 10		$.08 \times 10 = .8$
10 percent of 80		$.1 \times 80 = 8$
5 is what percent of 80?		$5 = \dfrac{x}{100} \times 80$
5 is 80 percent of what number?		$5 = \dfrac{80}{100} x$
What percent of 5 is 80?		$\dfrac{x}{100} \times 5 = 80$

Percent Increase/Decrease

Percent Increase or *Percent Decrease* $= \dfrac{difference}{original\ amount} \times 100$

For example, if an $80 item is reduced to $60 during a sale, the percent decrease is the change in price ($80 − $60 = $20) divided by the original amount ($80), which gives us .25. Multiply by 100 to get 25 percent.

Try a question:

| 26 |

Estimated Numbers of Cell Phone Users by Type
(in millions)

	Prepaid users	Contracted users	Totals
2008	45	225	270
2012	75	250	325
Totals	120	475	595

By how much greater was the percent increase in prepaid users from 2008 to 2012 than the percent increase in contracted users over the same period, to the nearest percent?

A) 6%

B) 10%

C) 30%

D) 56%

Here's How to Crack It

First, find the percent increase in each group. Remember that percent increase is $\frac{\text{difference}}{\text{original}} \times 100$. For prepaid users, the equation would be $\frac{75-45}{45} \times 100 = 66\frac{2}{3}\%$. Contracted users: $\frac{250-225}{225} \times 100 = 11\frac{1}{9}\%$. Finally, subtract: $66\frac{2}{3} - 11\frac{1}{9} = 55\frac{5}{9}\%$, which is closest to (D).

GROWTH AND DECAY

Another aspect of percent questions may relate to things that increase or decrease by a certain percent over time. This is known as "growth and decay." Real-world examples include population growth, radioactive decay, and credit payments, to name a few. While Plugging In can help on these, it is also useful to know the growth and decay formula.

When the growth or decay rate is a percent of the total population:

$$final\ amount = original\ amount\ (1 \pm rate)^{number\ of\ changes}$$

Let's see how this formula can make quick work of an otherwise tedious question.

14

The population of Bethesda, Maryland is currently 61,000 and is growing at a rate of 2.5% every three months. If Bethesda's population, P, is a function of time in years, t, then which of the following functions represents the town's population growth?

A) $P(t) = 61,000(1.025)^t$

B) $P(t) = 61,000(1.1)^t$

C) $P(t) = 61,000(1.025)^{4t}$

D) $P(t) = 61,000(1.1)^{3t}$

Here's How to Crack It

Because the rate of growth is 2.5%, you need to add 0.025 (2.5% in decimal form) to 1 within the parenthesis. This would be $1 + 0.025 = 1.025$. Eliminate (B) and (D) because they do not have this piece. The only difference between (A) and (C) is the exponent, which represents the number of changes. Here, t is in years, but the population increases every 3 months, which is 4 times a year. This means you want 4 changes when $t = 1$; this gives you (C) as your answer.

RATIOS AND PROPORTIONS

Some questions in the calculator-allowed math section (Section 4) will ask about ratios and proportions. With the strategies that you'll learn on the next few pages, you'll be well prepared to tackle these concepts on the PSAT.

Ratios

$$\text{Fraction} = \frac{\text{part}}{\text{whole}}$$

$$\text{Ratio} = \frac{\text{part}}{\text{part}}$$

Ratios are about relationships between numbers. Whereas a fraction is a relationship between a part and a whole, a ratio is about the relationship between parts. So, for example, if there were 3 boys and 7 girls in a room, the fraction of boys in the room would be $\frac{3}{10}$. But the ratio of boys to girls would be 3:7. Notice that if you add up the parts, you get the whole: 7 + 3 = 10. That's important for PSAT ratio problems, and you'll see why in a moment.

Ratio problems usually aren't difficult to identify. The problem will tell you that there is a "ratio" of one thing to another, such as a 2:3 ratio of boys to girls in a club. When you see a ratio problem, drawing a Ratio Box will help you organize the information in the problem and figure out the correct answer.

For instance, suppose a problem tells you that there is a ratio of 2 boys to 3 girls in the physics club, which has 40 members total. Here's how you would put that information into a Ratio Box so that you can answer the question being asked:

The first line of a Ratio Box is where you put the *ratio* from the problem. These are parts of the whole; they're not actual numbers of people, animals, books, or anything else. By themselves, they don't tell you *how many* of anything you have.

The second line of a Ratio Box is for the **multiplier**. The multiplier tells you how much you have to multiply the ratio by to get an actual number of something. The multiplier is the same all the way across; it doesn't change from column to column. And usually, the multiplier isn't in the problem; you have to figure it out yourself.

The third line is for *actual numbers*, so when the problem gives you a number of people (or animals, books, or whatever), that information goes in the third line.

One more thing to notice: See how there's a column for "whole"? This is where you add up the numbers in the ratio row and actual numbers row. Don't forget to add a column for the whole—it's usually key in figuring out the problem.

Now that you know some information from the problem and you know how the Ratio Box works, you can fill in the rest of the box.

Boys		Girls		Whole	
2	+	3	=	5	← Ratio
×		×		×	
8	=	8	=	8	← Multiplier
=		=		=	
16	+	24	=	40	← Actual #s

The first step is adding the ratio columns to find the whole, which is 5. Then you can find the multiplier by figuring out what you need to multiply 5 by to get 40. Once you fill in 8 for the multiplier all the way across the middle row, finding the actual number of boys and girls in the club is a snap.

Now you can answer all kinds of questions about the membership of the physics club.

There are 16 boys and 24 girls. Take the $\frac{part}{whole}$ from the ratio row to figure out that $\frac{3}{5}$, or 60 percent, of the members are girls. That means $\frac{2}{5}$, or 40 percent, of the members are boys.

Sometimes you won't need to use the Ratio Box to solve a ratio problem. Instead, remember that you can treat ratios as fractions and, like fractions, you can use your calculator to turn the ratio into a decimal to simplify your calculations.

Gridding In
A ratio is usually expressed as 2:3 or 2 to 3, but if you need to grid a ratio, grid it as $\frac{2}{3}$.

Try this one.

The ice cream flavor preferences of a randomly selected group of young Americans aged 3–18 are represented in the table below. Survey participants were asked to choose their favorite flavor among the following five: Vanilla, Chocolate, Mint Chocolate Chip, Cookies and Cream, and Coffee.

Reported favorite ice cream flavor by age group

Age	Vanilla	Chocolate	Mint Chocolate Chip	Cookies and Cream	Coffee
3–6	8,534	7,835	6,135	4,526	254
7–10	9,250	10,936	4,019	7,530	497
11–15	5,093	7,591	9,495	1,076	760
16–18	11,024	7,345	2,026	4,620	1,062

According to the data in the table above, the ratio of the most- to least-favorite flavors among the 7–10 age group is approximately how many times greater than the ratio of the most- to least-favorite flavors among the 11–15 age group?

A) 1.8

B) 3.4

C) 4.2

D) 6.7

Here's How to Crack It

First, you need to find the ratio of the most- to least-favorite flavor for each of the two age groups in question. For the 7–10 age group, the most favorite flavor is chocolate, with 10,936 votes, and the least favorite is coffee, with 497 votes. The ratio is thus $\frac{10,936}{497}$ = 22.0. For the 11–15 age group, the most favorite flavor is mint chocolate chip, with 9,495 votes, and the least favorite flavor is coffee, with 760 votes. The ratio is thus $\frac{9,495}{760}$ = 12.5. To find out how many times greater the first ratio is, divide these numbers: $\frac{22.0}{12.5}$ = 1.8, which is (A).

Direct Proportion/Variation

Direct proportion problems generally ask you to make a conversion (such as from ounces to pounds) or to compare two sets of information and find a missing piece. For example, a proportion problem may ask you to figure out the amount of time it will take to travel 300 miles at a rate of 50 miles per hour.

> To solve proportion problems, just set up two equal fractions. One will have all the information you know, and the other will have a missing piece that you're trying to figure out.

$$\frac{50 \text{ miles}}{1 \text{ hour}} = \frac{300 \text{ miles}}{x \text{ hours}}$$

Be sure to label the parts of your proportion so you'll know you have the right information in the right place; the same units should be in the numerator on both sides of the equals sign and the same units should be in the denominator on both sides of the equals sign. Notice how using a setup like this helps us keep track of the information we have and to find the information we're looking for, so we can use Bite-Sized Pieces to work through the question.

Now we can cross-multiply and then solve for x: $50x = 300$, so $x = 6$ hours.

Let's try the following problem.

2

John receives $2.50 for every 4 pounds of berries he picks. How much money will he receive if he picks 90 pounds of berries?

A) $36.00

B) $42.25

C) $48.50

D) $56.25

Here's How to Crack It

To solve this, set up a proportion.

$$\frac{\$2.50}{4\,pounds} = \frac{x}{90\,pounds}$$

Now we can cross-multiply: $4x = 2.50 \times 90$, so $4x = 225$, and $x = 56.25$. The answer is (D).

Occasionally, you may see a problem that tells you there are two equal ratios. For example, if a problem says that the ratio of 24 to 0.6 is equal to the ratio of 12 to y, you can solve for y by setting up a proportion. A proportion, after all, is really just two ratios set equal to each other.

$$\frac{24}{0.6} = \frac{12}{y}$$

Then you can cross-multiply and solve to get 0.3 for your answer.

Inverse Proportion/Variation

Inverse proportion is simply the opposite of a direct, or ordinary, proportion. In a direct proportion when one variable increases, the other variable also increases; however, in an inverse variation or proportion, when one variable *increases*, the other variable *decreases*, or vice versa. These types of problems are generally clearly labeled and all you have to do is apply the inverse variation formula:

$$x_1 y_1 = x_2 y_2$$

Once you memorize the formula, applying it will become second nature to you.

Now try this one.

18

On a particular test, the percentage of people answering a question with the same response is inversely proportional to the number of the question. If 80% of test takers answered the 8th question correctly, then, approximately, what percentage of test takers gave the correct response to the 30th question?

A) 3%

B) 13%

C) 18%

D) 21%

Here's How to Crack It

The problem tells us that the numbers are inversely proportional, so we need to figure out what to put into the formula. The first piece of information is that 80 percent of the people answered the 8th question correctly; we need to know the percent of people who answered the 30th question correctly. Let's make x the percent and y the question number. Your equation should look like this:

$$(80)(8) = (x_2)(30)$$

When you solve the equation, you should end up with $\frac{640}{30}$ or $21\frac{1}{3}$, which is (D) (remember, when the problem says "approximately," you'll probably have to round up or down).

Remember, answers to these drill questions can be found in Part III!

Drill 3

a. If a student scores 70, 90, 95, and 105, what is the average (arithmetic mean) for these tests? _____

b. If a student has an average (arithmetic mean) score of 80 on 4 tests, what is the total of the scores received on those tests? _____

c. If a student has an average of 60 on tests, with a total of 360, how many tests has the student taken? _____

d. If the average of 2, 8, and x is 6, what is the value of x? _____

2, 3, 3, 4, 6, 8, 10, 12

e. What is the median of the group of numbers above? _____

f. What is the mode of the group of numbers above? _____

g. What is the range of the group of numbers above? _____

h. What percent of 5 is 6? _____

i. 60 percent of 90 is the same as 50 percent of what number? _____

j. Jenny's salary increased from $30,000 to $33,000. By what percent did her salary increase? _____

k. In 1980, factory X produced 18,600 pieces. In 1981, factory X produced only 16,000 pieces. By approximately what percent did production decrease from 1980 to 1981? _____

The amount of money in a savings account after m months is modeled by the function $f(m) = 1{,}000(1.01)^m$.

l. What was the original amount in the bank account? _____

m. By what percent does the amount in the account increase each month? _____

n. In a certain bag of marbles, the ratio of red marbles to green marbles is 7:5. If the bag contains 96 marbles, how many green marbles are in the bag? _____

o. One hogshead is equal to 64 gallons. How many hogsheads are equal to 96 gallons? _____

p. The pressure and volume of a gas are inversely related. If the gas is at 10 kPa at 2 liters, then what is the pressure when the gas is at 4 liters? _____

2

If 10 pecks are equivalent to 2.5 bushels, then 4 bushels are equivalent to how many pecks?

A) 4

B) 10

C) 12.5

D) 16

28

Estimated Numbers of Cell Phone Users by Type
(in millions)

	Prepaid users	Contracted users	Totals
2008	45	225	270
2012	75	250	325
Totals	120	475	595

If a cell phone user is selected at random in 2008, what is the probability that user is a contracted user?

12

A forest fire is burning an area of forest that is 10 square miles. An air squad is able to reduce the size of the fire by 7% every 12 hours. If $F(t)$ is the area being burned by the fire, which expression for $F(t)$ represents the area of forest still on fire after t hours?

A) $10 - (0.93)^{12t}$

B) $10 \times (1 - 0.07)^{\frac{t}{12}}$

C) $10 - 93^{12t}$

D) $0.93^{10 - 12t}$

15

A student took five tests. He scored an average (arithmetic mean) of 80 on the first three tests and an average of 90 on the other two. Which of the following must be true?

    I.   The student scored more than 85 on at least one test.

    II. The average (arithmetic mean) score for all five tests is less than 85.

    III. The student scored less than 80 on at least two tests.

A) I only

B) II only

C) I and II

D) II and III

19

Maggie and Glenn's Distance from Home During Jog

Maggie and Glenn both leave from the same house to go for a jog along a trail. Shortly after leaving, Maggie realizes she forgot her iPod and returns home to find it before heading back out onto the same trail. The graph above shows how far each of them is from home for the first fifteen minutes of their jogs.

Excluding the time she spends at home, which of the following is closest to Maggie's average speed, in meters per second, during the portion of her jog shown?

A)   2.3

B)   5

C)   6.3

D) 140

28

Marcia can type 18 pages per hour, and David can type 14 pages per hour. If they work together, how many minutes will it take them to type 24 pages?

22

In a political poll, 500 voters were first asked whether they were registered as Democrat, Republican, or Independent. The voters were then asked whether they planned to vote for Candidate A, for Candidate B, or were Undecided. The table below shows the results of the poll.

	Candidate A	Candidate B	Undecided	Total
Democrat	24	56	70	150
Republican	117	70	50	237
Independent	15	18	80	113
Total	156	144	200	500

The number of registered Republicans who plan to vote for Candidate B is what percent greater than the number of registered Democrats who plan to vote for Candidate B ?

A) 14%

B) 20%

C) 25%

D) 28%

The college that Everett attends in Chicago is exactly 200 miles from his parents' home. When his parents come to visit him at school, they drive at an average speed of 45 miles per hour for maximum safety. When Everett drives home for winter break, his average speed is $x\%$ greater than the average speed at which his parents drive when they make the trip. Which of the following represents the time Everett saves on the 200-mile trip compared with his parents' average time, in hours?

A) $\dfrac{-2x}{45\left(1+\dfrac{x}{100}\right)}$

B) $\dfrac{2x}{45\left(1-\dfrac{x}{100}\right)}$

C) $\dfrac{2x}{45\left(1+\dfrac{x}{100}\right)}$

D) $\dfrac{45\left(\dfrac{x}{100}\right)}{200\left(1+\dfrac{x}{100}\right)}$

27

A survey company gathered data regarding people's transportation habits in four major U.S. cities. The survey asked participants in each of these cities to indicate whether they regularly used a personal vehicle, public transportation, or neither to commute. Participants were not limited to one response and could check both personal vehicle and public transportation. The results are shown below.

	Personal Vehicle	Public Transportation	Neither	Total Responses
Washington, D.C.	5,687	3,134	1,232	8,505
New York	2,476	5,738	1,459	7,789
Boston	5,281	3,504	1,025	7,556
San Francisco	4,122	4,629	1,192	7,934

Which one of the following statements is supported by the data shown above?

A) Approximately 20% more people checked both personal vehicle and public transportation in Boston than in New York.

B) Washington, D.C. has the highest proportion of people that regularly use both public transportation and a personal vehicle.

C) The number of people that reported regularly using public transportation in New York is approximately 230% more than the number that reported regularly using a personal vehicle.

D) The ratio of personal vehicle use to public transportation use was lowest in San Francisco.

Summary

o The test is full of opportunities to use arithmetic instead of algebra—just look for your chances to use Plugging In and Plugging In the Answers (PITA).

o If a question has *in terms of* or variables in the answer choices, it's a Plugging In problem. Plug in your own number, do the math, find the target number, and use POE to get down to one correct answer.

o If a question doesn't have variables but asks for a fraction or a percent of an unknown number, you can also Plug In there. Just substitute your own number for the unknown and take the rest of the problem step by step.

o If a question has an unknown and asks for a specific amount, making you feel like you have to write an equation, try PITA instead.

o The Average Pie can help you tackle any question about the average (arithmetic mean)—just fill what you know from the problem into the correct spots for *Total*, *Number of Things*, and *Average*.

o The median is the middle value in a list of consecutive numbers. If there are an odd number of elements, the median is the average of the two middle values.

o The mode is the most commonly occurring value in a list of numbers.

o The range is the difference between the greatest and least values in a list of numbers.

o Rates are closely related to averages. Use the Rate Pie just like you use the Average Pie. Remember that the PSAT likes to make you find the totals (distance or work in the Rate Pie).

o Percent simply means "per 100." Many percent questions can be tackled by translating English to math.

o Percent increase or decrease is $\dfrac{difference}{original} \times 100$.

o Growth and decay are given by the formula *final amount = original amount*$(1 \pm rate)^{number\ of\ changes}$.

o Use the Ratio Box on questions that ask about a ratio. Fill in the Ratio Box with information from the problem, calculate the missing piece, and then solve for whatever the problem is asking for.

o Sometimes you'll need to treat ratios like fractions or decimals. Use your calculator to turn the numbers into the easiest form to work the problem.

o Direct proportion means as one value goes up, the other goes up. The formula is $\dfrac{x_1}{y_1} = \dfrac{x_2}{y_2}$.

o Inverse proportion means as one value goes up, the other goes down. The formula is $x_1 y_1 = x_2 y_2$.

Chapter 11
Advanced Math Principles

So far we've covered basic knowledge and some PSAT-specific problem-solving skills. Now we'll look at some of the more advanced skills tested on the PSAT.

FUNCTIONS

In the Math Basics chapter, we looked at some concepts related to the *xy*-plane. Here, we will look at some more complicated topics involving functions and graphs. The functions on the PSAT mostly look like this:

$$f(x) = x^2 + 6x + 24$$

Just Follow the Instructions

Functions are like recipes. Each one is just a set of directions for you to follow. ETS and the College Board provide the ingredients and you work your magic.

Most questions of this type will give you a specific value to plug in for *x* and then ask you to find the value of the function for that *x*. Each function is just a set of instructions that tells you what to do to *x*—or the number you plug in for *x*—in order to find the corresponding value for $f(x)$ (a fancy name for *y*). Just plug your information into that equation and follow the instructions.

Let's try an easy one.

○

2

If $f(x) = x^2 + 3x - 3$, what is the value of $f(7)$?

A) 14

B) 20

C) 32

D) 67

Here's How to Crack It

Function questions are just trying to see if you can follow the directions, so follow them! The instructions, in this case, are in the equation. So plug 7 into the equation and it should look like this: $f(7) = (7)^2 + 3(7) - 3$. Do the math and $f(7) = 67$. Therefore, the answer is (D).

○

Sometimes you'll get more complicated questions. As long as you know that when you put in *x*, your function will spit out another number, you'll be fine. Try this next one:

20

Let the function g be defined by $g(x) = 5x + 2$. If $\sqrt{g\left(\dfrac{a}{2}\right)} = 6$,

what is the value of a ?

A) $\dfrac{1}{\sqrt{6}}$

B) $\dfrac{1}{\sqrt{2}}$

C) $\dfrac{34}{5}$

D) $\dfrac{68}{5}$

Here's How to Crack It

This may look complicated, but just follow the directions. You know that

$g(x) = 5x + 2$. You also know that $\sqrt{g\left(\dfrac{a}{2}\right)} = 6$. First, get rid of the square root

by squaring both sides. Now you have $g\left(\dfrac{a}{2}\right) = 36$. Usually there's an x inside

the parentheses. Treat this the same. This statement says that g of some num-

ber equals 36. We also know that g of some number is the same as $5x + 2$. So

$5x + 2 = 36$. Simplify and you get $\dfrac{34}{5}$. Careful, you're not done. You now know that $\dfrac{a}{2} = \dfrac{34}{5}$, so

$a = \dfrac{68}{5}$, or (D).

> **PITA!**
> Don't forget that you can often Plug In the Answers on function questions.

Another way the PSAT can make functions more complicated is to give you two functions to deal with together. If you approach these problems one piece at a time, they will be easier to handle.

Here's an example:

---○---

15

If $f(x) = -x + \dfrac{1}{x}$ and $g(x) = x^2 - 7$, what is the value of $f(g(-2))$?

Here's How to Crack It

With compound functions like this one, start from the inside and work your way out. Plug –2 into the g function to get $g(-2) = (-2)^2 - 7 = 4 - 7 = -3$. Plug this value into the f function to get $f(-3) = -(-3) + \dfrac{1}{-3} = 3 - \dfrac{1}{3} = 2\dfrac{2}{3}$. You can't grid in mixed fractions, so convert it to an improper fraction $\dfrac{8}{3}$ or the decimal 2.66 or 2.67. Any of these would be acceptable answers.

---○---

Sometimes the PSAT will use a word problem to describe a function, and then ask you to "build a function" that describes that real-world situation.

Try one of those:

6

A scientist noted that the rate of growth of a tree which he had been observing is directly proportional to time. The scientist first measured the height of the tree to be 20 feet; two years later, the tree was 21 feet tall. If the tree continues to grow at a constant rate, which of the following represents the height of the tree in feet, y, as a function of time, x, in years since the scientist's first measurement?

A) $y(x) = 0.5x + 20$

B) $y(x) = 21x + 20$

C) $y(x) = x + 20$

D) $y(x) = 20x + 21$

Here's How to Crack It

Instead of trying to write your own equation, use the ones in the answer choices. According to the question, 2 years after the first measurement, the tree was 21 feet tall. Therefore, when $x = 2$, $y(x) = 21$. Plug these points into the answers to see which answer works. Choice (A) becomes $21 = 0.5(2) + 20$. Solve the right side of the equation to get $21 = 1 + 20$, or $21 = 21$. The correct answer is (A).

Roots of a Function

You may also be asked about the roots of a function. These are the solutions for x that you get when you solve the function or the places where the graph of the function crosses the x-axis. Here's how this concept may be tested on the PSAT.

11

The graph of the function f in the xy-plane contains the points $(-3, 0)$, $(0, -2)$, and $(4, 0)$. Which of the following is a factor of function f?

A) $x - 2$

B) $x + 2$

C) $x + 3$

D) $x + 4$

Here's How to Crack It

The roots of an equation, found by setting the factors equal to 0, are the same as the x-intercepts of the equation. At the x-intercept, $y = 0$. Therefore, the point $(0, -2)$ is not a root, so you can eliminate (A) and (B) because they include 2. According to the question, one of the x-intercepts is at $(-3, 0)$. This means that one solution to the function can be found by $x + 3 = 0$, and one of the factors of the function is $x + 3$. The other factor would be $(x - 4)$, but that's not a choice. The correct answer is (C).

Drill 1

Answers can be found in Part III.

3

Which of the following equivalent forms of the equation $x^2 + 8x + 15 = 0$ would be the most useful for finding the x-intercepts of the equation?

A) $x(x) + 8(x) + 15 = 0$

B) $x^2 + 3x + 5x + 15 = 0$

C) $(x + 3)(x + 5) = 0$

D) $x^2 + 8x + 4 + 11 = 0$

4

Monster Truck Inc. leases a new truck for a down payment of $3,200 plus monthly payments of $380 per month for 36 months. Which of the following functions, f, represents the total amount paid, in dollars, after m months, where $0 \le m \le 36$?

A) $f(m) = 380 + 3,200m$

B) $f(m) = 3,200 + 36m$

C) $f(m) = 3,200 + 380m$

D) $f(m) = 10,480 - 380m$

15

If $f(x) = x^2 - x + 4$, a is non-negative, and $f(a) = 10$, what is the value of a ?

9

The number of bonus points, $B(p)$, that a credit card holder receives is given by the function $B(p) = ap + 7$, where p represents the number of purchases made and a is a constant. If the number of purchases is increased by 4, the number of bonus points increases by 25. What is the value of a ?

A)   4

B)   4.5

C)   6.25

D) 11

21

If $f(x) = x^{-\frac{2}{3}}$, what is the value of $\dfrac{f(8)}{f(3)}$?

A) $\dfrac{4}{\sqrt[3]{9}}$

B) $\dfrac{8}{3}$

C) $\sqrt{\dfrac{512}{27}}$

D) $\dfrac{\sqrt[3]{9}}{4}$

23

The temperature, T, in degrees Celsius on a winter day can be written as a function of x, the time in hours since midnight (12:00 A.M.), as shown below.

$$T(x) = -\frac{1}{10}x^2 + \frac{24}{10}x - \frac{44}{10}$$

If $100 = x^2 - 24x + 144$ is an equivalent form of the equation when $T(x) = 0$, which of the following gives a time on that day when the temperature was 0°C ?

A)   6 P.M.

B)   10 P.M.

C)   3 A.M.

D)   9 A.M.

x	-1	j	5
$f(x)$	2	j	-6

The table above shows selected values for the linear function $f(x)$. What is the value of j ?

A) $-\dfrac{1}{6}$

B) $\dfrac{2}{7}$

C) $\dfrac{5}{7}$

D) $\dfrac{7}{6}$

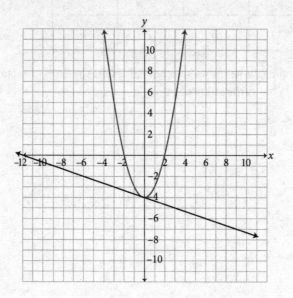

In the above graph, parabola $f(x)$ is represented by the equation $f(x) = x^2 - 4$ and line $g(x)$ is represented by the equation $g(x) = -\dfrac{1}{3}x - 4$. Line $g(x)$ intersects parabola $f(x)$ at point $(0, -4)$.

30

For $x = 12$, how much greater is the value of $f(x)$ than $g(x)$?

31

A new line, $h(x)$, is added to the graph. The line $h(x)$ is perpendicular to line $g(x)$, intersecting with line $g(x)$ at the point $(-12, 0)$. What is the x-coordinate of the point where line $h(x)$ will intersect parabola $f(x)$ in Quadrant I ?

QUADRATIC EQUATIONS

Ah, quadratics. You're likely to see several questions on the PSAT that require you to expand, factor, or solve quadratics. You may even need to find the vertex of a parabola or the points of intersection of a quadratic and a line. So let's review, starting with the basics.

Expanding

Most often you'll be asked to expand an expression simply by multiplying it out. When working with an expression of the form $(x + 3)(x + 4)$, multiply it out using the following rule:

> FOIL = First Outer Inner Last

Start with the *first* figure in each set of parentheses: $x \times x = x^2$.

Now do the two *outer* figures: $x \times 4 = 4x$.

Next, the two *inner* figures: $3 \times x = 3x$.

Finally, the *last* figure in each set of parentheses: $3 \times 4 = 12$.

Add them all together, and we get $x^2 + 4x + 3x + 12$, or $x^2 + 7x + 12$.

Factoring

If you ever see an expression of the form $x^2 + 7x + 12$ on the PSAT, there is a good chance that factoring it will be the key to cracking it.

The key to factoring is figuring out what pair of numbers will multiply to give you the constant term (12, in this case) and add up to the coefficient of the x term (7, in this question).

Let's try an example:

$$x^2 + 7x + 12$$

Step 1: Draw two sets of parentheses next to each other and fill an x into the left side of each. That's what gives us our x^2 term.

$$(x\ \ \ )(x\ \ \ )$$

Step 2: 12 can be factored a number of ways: 1×12, 2×6, or 3×4. Which of these adds up to 7? 3 and 4, so place a 3 on the right side of one parenthesis and a 4 in the other.

$$(x\ \ \ 3)(x\ \ \ 4)$$

Step 3: Now we need to figure out what the correct signs should be. They should both be positive in this case, because that will sum to 7 and multiply to 12, so fill plus signs into each parenthesis.

$$(x + 3)(x + 4)$$

If you want to double-check your work, try expanding out $(x + 3)(x + 4)$ using FOIL and you'll get the original expression.

Now try the following problem.

8

Travis determines that the average speed of his kayak traveling down the river when he is not paddling can be calculated using the formula $4r^2 - 40r + 100$, where r represents the strength of the river's current in feet per second. Which of the following expressions would be an equivalent formula that Travis could use to determine his kayak's speed?

A) $(2r + 10)^2$

B) $(2r + 10)(2r - 10)$

C) $4(r + 5)^2$

D) $4(r - 5)^2$

Here's How to Crack It

To compare the equation in the question with the answer choices, you need to either factor the equation in the question or expand out the answer choices. The first option is probably faster. Start by factoring a 4 out of the entire equation to get $4(r^2 - 10r + 25)$. Now, determine what two numbers can be added to get −10 and multiplied to get 25. In this case, it's −5 and −5. The equation becomes $4(r - 5)(r - 5)$ or $4(r - 5)^2$, which is (D).

Don't forget that you can also Plug In on a question like the last one. Let's look at one in which Plugging In makes a strange question much more manageable.

8

If the expression $x + 2(x - 4)$ is multiplied by R to form the expression $3x^2 - 5x - 8$, then which of the following is equivalent to R?

A) $x + 1$

B) $x + 2$

C) $x + 3$

D) $x + 4$

Here's How to Crack It

Whenever the question and the answers include variables, see if you can Plug In. If $x = 2$, the first expression becomes $2 + 2(2 - 4) = 2 + 2(-2) = 2 + (-4) = -2$, and the second expression becomes $3(2^2) - 5(2) - 8 = 3(4) - 10 - 8 = 12 - 10 - 8 = -6$. To find R, set up the following equation: $-2R = -6$. Solve for R to get $R = 3$. Plug 2 in for x in the equations to see which answer equals the target number of 3. Choice (A) becomes $2 + 1 = 3$. Keep (A), but check the remaining answers just in case. Choice (B) becomes $2 + 2 = 4$, (C) becomes $2 + 3 = 5$, and (D) becomes $2 + 4 = 6$. Eliminate (B), (C), and (D). The correct answer is (A).

Solving Quadratic Equations

Sometimes you'll want to factor to solve an equation. In this case, there will be two possible values for x, called the roots of the equation. To solve for x, use the following steps:

Step 1: Make sure that the equation is set equal to zero.

Step 2: Factor the equation.

Step 3: Set each parenthetical expression equal to zero. So if you have $(x + 2)(x - 7) = 0$, you get $(x + 2) = 0$ and $(x - 7) = 0$. When you solve for each, you get $x = -2$ and $x = 7$. Therefore, −2 and 7 are the solutions or roots of the equation.

Try the following problem.

4

If $b^2 + 2b - 8 = 0$, and $b < 0$, what is the value of b ?

A) –6

B) –4

C) –2

D) 0

Here's How to Crack It

Begin by using Process of Elimination. Since the question states that $b < 0$, eliminate (D). Now follow the steps:

1. The equation is already set equal to zero.
2. You can now factor the left side of the equation to get $(b + 4)(b - 2) = 0$.
3. When you set each parenthetical expression equal to zero, you get $b = -4$ and $b = 2$. Since $b < 0$, the answer is (B).

An alternative approach to this question is to Plug In the Answers. For (A), plug $b = -6$ into the equation to get $(-6)^2 + 2(-6) - 8 = 0$. Solve the left side of the equation to get $36 - 12 - 8 = 0$, or $16 = 0$. Since this statement is not true, eliminate (A). For (B), plug $b = -4$ into the equation to get $(-4)^2 + 2(-4) - 8 = 0$. Solve the left side of the equation to get $16 - 8 - 8 = 0$, or $0 = 0$. Since this statement is true, the correct answer is (B).

Sometimes, solving will get a little trickier. When quadratics do not factor easily and there are no answer choices to plug in, you can use the quadratic formula to solve.

The values of x for a quadratic equation in the form $y = ax^2 + bx + c$ are

$$x = \frac{-b \pm \sqrt{b^2 - 4ac}}{2a}$$

Let's try one.

29

If $y = x^2 - 4x + 3.75$, what is one possible value of x ?

Here's How to Crack It

This one is not easy to factor, so try the quadratic formula. In the given equation, $a = 1$, $b = -4$, and $c = 3.75$. Therefore,

$$x = \frac{-(-4) \pm \sqrt{(-4)^2 - 4(1)(3.75)}}{2(1)} = \frac{4 \pm \sqrt{16 - 15}}{2} = \frac{4 \pm 1}{2}.$$

So x equals $\frac{5}{2}$ (or 2.5) and $\frac{3}{2}$ (or 1.5). Any of these 4 options could be entered into the grid.

You may have noticed that this is a calculator question. Another option for this one would be to graph the equation on your calculator to determine the x-intercepts, which are the roots, or solutions, to the equation.

Other Quadratic Questions

Sometimes, quadratic equations will be tested with word problems or charts. Let's look at these types of questions.

29

An Olympic shot-putter throws a heavy spherical object that follows a parabolic trajectory. The equation describing the trajectory of the shot-putter's throw is $y = -0.04x^2 + 2.02x + 5.5$, where y represents the height of the object in feet and x represents the horizontal distance in feet traveled by the object. What is the original height of the object (in feet) immediately before it leaves the shot-putter's hand?

Here's How to Crack It

According to the question, x represents the horizontal distance in feet traveled by the object, and y represents the height. Before the shot-putter throws the object, $x = 0$. Plug 0 into the equation and solve for y. The equation becomes $y = -0.04(0^2) + 2.02(0) + 5.5 = 0 + 0 + 5.5 = 5.5$. The correct answer is 5.5.

Now look at an example of a chart-based quadratic question.

14

Trajectory of a Dolphin's Jump

Horizontal Distance (feet)	Vertical Height (feet)
0	0
1	2.7
2	4.8
3	6.3
4	7.2
5	7.5
6	7.2
7	6.3
8	4.8
9	2.7
10	0

The table above shows the horizontal distance and vertical height, both in feet, of a typical dolphin jumping out of the water (a height of 0 represents the surface of the water). If d represents the horizontal distance and h represents the vertical height, which of the following equations would best represent the trajectory of the dolphin's jump?

A) $h = -0.3d^2 + 3d$

B) $h = -0.4d^2 + 4d$

C) $h = -0.5d^2 + 5d$

D) $h = -0.6d^2 + 6d$

Here's How to Crack It

This is a similar task to "building a function" that we discussed earlier in this chapter. You should plug values from the table into the equations in the answer choices to see which equation works. According to the table, when $d = 1$, $h = 2.7$. Plug these values into (A) to get $2.7 = -0.3(1^2) + 3(1)$. Solve the right side of the equation to get $2.7 = -0.3 + 3$ or $2.7 = 2.7$. Keep (A), but check the remaining answers just in case. Choice (B) becomes $2.7 = -0.4(1^2) + 4(1)$. Solve the right side of the equation to get $2.7 = -0.4 + 4$ or $2.7 = 3.6$. This is not true, so eliminate (B). Choice (C) becomes $2.7 = -0.5(1^2) + 5(1)$. Solve the right side of the equation to get $2.7 = -0.5 + 5$ or $2.7 = 4.5$. Eliminate (C). Choice (D) becomes $2.7 = -0.6(1^2) + 6(1)$. Solve the right side of the equation to get $2.7 = -0.6 + 6$ or $2.7 = 5.4$. Eliminate (D). The correct answer is (A).

Forms of Quadratics

When graphed in the xy-plane, quadratics form a parabola. The PSAT will ask questions using two different forms of the equation for a parabola.

> The standard form of a parabola equation is as follows:
>
> $$y = ax^2 + bx + c$$

In the standard form of a parabola, the value of a tells whether a parabola opens upwards or downwards (if a is positive, the parabola opens upwards, and if a is negative, the parabola opens downwards).

> The vertex form of a parabola equation is as follows:
>
> $$y = a(x - h)^2 + k$$
>
> In the vertex form, the point (h, k) is the vertex of the parabola.

Simply knowing what the vertex form looks like may help you answer a question, like the following example.

Which of the following equations has its vertex at
(−4, 3) ?

A) $y = (x - 4)^2 + 3$

B) $y = (x + 4)^2 + 3$

C) $y = (x - 3)^2 + 4$

D) $y = (x + 3)^2 - 4$

Here's How to Crack It

If you know the vertex form, you can create the correct equation for the parabola. Be careful with the signs, though, as the signs are all changing in the answer choices. In the vertex (−4, 3), −4 is h and 3 is k. The correct answer should end in + 3, so eliminate (C) and (D). For the $(x - h)^2$ part of the equation, it becomes $(x - (-4))^2$, or $(x + 4)^2$, so the correct answer is (B).

Knowing the form makes Process of Elimination a quick way to answer these, but if you forget the form, you can always plug in the given point to see which equation is true.

The vertex form is great for answering questions about the minimum or maximum value a parabolic function will reach or the x-value that results in that minimum or maximum y-value. So another good thing to know is the method for turning a quadratic in the standard form into the vertex form. Here are the steps to do that.

To convert a parabola equation in the standard form to the vertex form, complete the square.

1. Make $y = 0$, and move any constants over to the left side of the equation.
2. Take half of the coefficient on the x-term, square it, and add it to both sides of the equation.
3. Convert the x terms and the number on the right to square form: $(x - h)^2$.
4. Move the constant on the left back over to the right and set it equal to y again.

Say you were given the equation $y = x^2 - 4x - 12$. You would make it $0 = x^2 - 4x - 12$, and then $12 = x^2 - 4x$. You'd add 4 to both sides to get $16 = x^2 - 4x + 4$, and then convert the right side to the square form to get $16 = (x - 2)^2$. Finally, you'd move the 16 back over and set it equal to y to get $y = (x - 2)^2 - 16$.

Drill 2

Answers can be found in Part III.

3

In his physics class, Yigit determined that the height in feet (h) of a projectile t seconds after being launched can be expressed using the function $h(t) = -5t^2 + 20t + 45$. Which of the following values of t would be most helpful in finding the initial height of the projectile?

A) $t = 0$

B) $t = 1$

C) $t = 2$

D) $t = 3$

4

If $12 - (t + 2)^2 = 3$, which of the following could be the value of t?

A) -9

B) -5

C) 5

D) 7

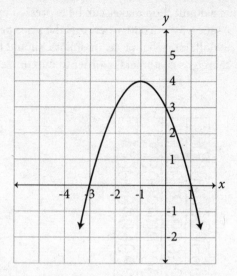

Which of the following equations is shown in the graph above?

A) $y = -(x - 3)(x + 1)$

B) $y = -(x + 3)(x - 1)$

C) $y = -(x + 3)(x + 4)$

D) $y = -(x - 1)(x + 4)$

Aubri determines that her score in a particular video game can be calculated using the formula $x^4 - y^4$, where x represents the number of treasures she discovers, and y represents the number of hidden traps she falls into. Which of the following expressions would be a suitable equivalent for Aubri's score calculation formula?

A) $(x + y)(x - y)(x^2 + y^2)$

B) $(x + y)^2(x^2 + y^2)$

C) $(x - y)^2(x^2 + y^2)$

D) $(x + y)(x - y)(x^2 - y^2)$

Which of the following equations has a vertex of $(-5, 2)$?

A) $y = (x + 5)^2 - 2$

B) $y = (x - 5)^2 - 2$

C) $y = 2(x + 5)^2 + 2$

D) $y = 2(x - 5)^2 + 2$

The profit that a donut shop makes can be expressed by the equation $P = -4(x - 3)^2 + 2,000$, where x is the price per donut sold (in dollars). What price, in dollars, should the donut shop charge its customers in order to maximize its profit?

23

In the equation $x^2 + 24x + c = (x + 9)(x + p)$, c and p are constants. If the equation is true for all values of x, what is the value of c?

A)   33

B)   135

C)   144

D)   216

26

The stream of water that shoots out of a public fountain in Central Park takes the form of a parabola. The water shoots from a spout that is 8 feet above the ground and reaches a maximum height of 39.25 feet. If y represents the height of the water and x represents the time (in seconds), which of the following equations could describe the trajectory of the stream of water?

A) $y = -x^2 + 15$

B) $y = -5x^2 + 25x + 8$

C) $y = 2x^2 + 32x + 8$

D) $y = 8x + 39.25$

ANALYSIS IN SCIENCE

If some of the questions you've seen so far are reminding you of science class, you're not crazy. One of the cross-test scores the PSAT aims to measure is called Analysis in Science. This means that questions on science-based ideas will show up in Reading and Writing passages and also in Math questions.

One way this concept will be tested is through word problems. Many of the strategies we've already discussed, such as translating or Plugging In, will help you to answer these questions, regardless of the scientific context.

Here's an example.

17

The electric potential of a point charge Q is given by the equation $V = \dfrac{kQ}{r}$, where V is the charge in volts or Joules per Coulomb, Q is the charge in Coulombs, r is the distance from the charge in meters, and k is a constant equal to 9.0×10^9 Nm^2/C^2. If a point charge has an electric potential of 225 volts at a distance of 1 meter from the charge, what is the charge in nanocoulombs? (Note: 1 Coulomb = 10^9 nanocoulombs.)

Here's How to Crack It

Start by identifying the values of all of the variables given. According to the question, $r = 1$, $k = 9.0 \times 10^9$, and $V = 225$ coulombs. The question asks for the charge in nanocoulombs, so multiply 225 by 10^9 and you find that $V = 225 \times 10^9$. Plug these values into the equation to get $225 \times 10^9 = \dfrac{(9.0 \times 10^9)Q}{1}$. Solve for Q by dividing both sides by 9.0×10^9 to get $\dfrac{225 \times 10^9}{9.0 \times 10^9} = Q$, or $\dfrac{225}{9.0} = Q$. So $25 = Q$, and that's your answer.

Sometimes, you will be asked science questions based on a chart or graph. In those cases, carefully look up the numbers in question, do the required calculations, and eliminate answers that aren't true.

Let's look at one.

4

Marble Ramp Rolling Times

A student is rolling a marble down ramps of varying lengths.
The scatterplot above shows the time, in seconds, it takes the
marble to roll down each ramp. Based on the curve of best fit
to the data represented, which of the following is the closest
to the expected length of a ramp if a marble takes 12 seconds
to roll down?

A) 61

B) 72

C) 79

D) 84

Here's How to Crack It

Roll time is shown on the horizontal axis of the graph, given in seconds. Look for the mark
indicating 12 seconds on this axis; then draw a vertical line from that mark to the curve of best
fit. Once you hit it, draw a horizontal line over to the vertical axis. It should hit between 60
and 80 centimeters, right around 70. This makes (B) the credited response, since it is slightly
closer to the mark for 70. Draw your lines carefully, using your answer sheet as a straightedge if
necessary, since three of these answer choices are between 60 and 80.

You may also be asked to graph the data presented in a table. Your knowledge of graphing in the *xy*-plane should help you with most of those. If anything gets too tricky, consider skipping it and spending your time on something else.

The last science-based question type you may see doesn't involve charts, graphs, or equations. In fact, these don't even look much like math problems at all. They will have a lot of words to describe a scientific situation and ask about the conclusion that can be drawn. Just use a lot of Process of Elimination and a little knowledge of what makes a good experiment, and you should be fine.

Try this one.

15

A psychologist wants to know whether there is a relationship between increased water consumption and exam scores. He obtains survey responses from a random sample of 3,500 20-year-old college students in the United States and finds a strong positive correlation between increased water consumption and test scores. Which of the following conclusions is well-supported by the data?

A) There is a positive association between increased water consumption and test scores for 20-year-olds in the United States.

B) There is a positive association between increased water consumption and test scores for adults in the United States.

C) High test scores are caused by increased water consumption for 20-year-olds in the United States.

D) High test scores are caused by increased water consumption for adults in the United States.

Here's How to Crack It

Consider each answer choice one at a time and use Process of Elimination. Choice (A) merely restates what the evidence says, which makes it a safe conclusion, so keep it. Choice (B) is similar but shifts from "20-year-old college students" to "adults." This is a less safe conclusion than (A), because it generalizes from a more particular group, so eliminate (B). Choices (C) and (D) both introduce the idea of causation. This is a problem—no information was given about cause. Maybe people who tend to score higher on tests are also smart enough to drink more water, or maybe there is another factor causing both high test scores and increased water consumption. Eliminate (C) and (D) and choose (A).

MEANING IN CONTEXT

Some questions, instead of asking you to come up with an equation, just want you to recognize what a part of the equation stands for. It sounds like a simple enough task, but when you look at the equation, they have made it really hard to see what is going on. For this reason, Meaning in Context questions are a great opportunity to plug in real numbers and start to see how the equation really works!

First things first, though, you want to think about your POOD. Does this question fit into your pacing goals? It might take a bit of legwork to get an answer, and you may need that time to go collect points on easier, quicker questions.

If this question does fit into your pacing plan, you should read carefully, label everything you can in the equation, and POE to get rid of any answer choices that are clearly on the wrong track. Then, it's time to plug some of your own numbers in to see what is going on in there.

Here's an example:

7

$$n = 1,273 - 4p$$

The equation above was used by the cafeteria in a large public high school to model the relationship between the number of slices of pizza, n, sold daily and the price of a slice of pizza, p, in dollars. What does the number 4 represent in this equation?

A) For every \$4 the price of pizza decreases, the cafeteria sells 1 more slice of pizza.

B) For every dollar the price of pizza decreases, the cafeteria sells 4 more slices of pizza.

C) For every \$4 the price of pizza increases, the cafeteria sells 1 more slice of pizza.

D) For every dollar the price of pizza increases, the cafeteria sells 4 more slices of pizza.

Here's How to Crack It

First, read the question very carefully, and use your pencil to label the variables. You know that p is the price of pizza, and n is the number of slices, so you can add that information to the equation. If you can, eliminate answer choices that don't make sense. But what if you can't eliminate anything, or you can eliminate only an answer choice or two?

Even with everything labeled, this equation is difficult to decode, so it's time to Plug In! Try a few of your own numbers in the equation, and you will get a much better understanding of what is happening.

Let's try it out with $p = 2$. When you put 2 in for p, $n = 1{,}273 - 4(2)$ or $1{,}265$.

So, when $p = 2$, $n = 1{,}265$. In other words, at \$2 a slice, the cafeteria sells 1,265 slices.

When $p = 3$, $n = 1{,}261$, so at \$3 a slice, the cafeteria sells 1,261 slices.

When $p = 4$, $n = 1{,}257$, so at \$4 a slice, the cafeteria sells 1,257 slices.

So now, let's use POE. First of all, is the cafeteria selling more pizza as the price goes up? No, as the price of pizza goes up, the cafeteria sells fewer slices of pizza. That means you can eliminate (C) and (D).

Choice (A) says that for every \$4 the price goes down, the cafeteria sells 1 more slice of pizza. Does your plugging in back that up? No. The cafeteria sells 8 more slices of pizza when the price drops from \$4 to \$2, so (A) is no good.

Now, let's take a look at (B). Does the cafeteria sell 4 more slices of pizza for every dollar the price drops? Yes! Choice (B) is the correct answer.

Here are the steps for using Plugging In to solve Meaning in Context questions:

Meaning In Context

1. Read the question carefully. Make sure you know which part of the equation you are being asked to identify.
2. Use your pencil to label the parts of the equation you can identify.
3. Eliminate any answer choices that clearly describe the wrong part of the equation, or go against what you have labeled.
4. Plug In! Use your own numbers to start seeing what is happening in the equation.
5. Use POE again, using the information you learned from plugging in real numbers, until you can get it down to one answer choice. Or, get it down to as few choices as you can, and guess.

Let's look at a slightly different one now.

$$7x + y = 133$$

Jeffrey has set a monthly budget for purchasing frozen blended mocha drinks from his local SpendBucks coffee shop. The equation above can be used to model the amount of his budget, y, in dollars that remains after buying coffee for x days in a month. What does it mean that $(19, 0)$ is a solution to this equation?

A) Jeffrey starts the month with a budget of $19.

B) Jeffrey spends $19 on coffee every day.

C) It takes 19 days for Jeffrey to drink 133 cups of coffee.

D) It takes 19 days for Jeffrey to run out of money in his budget for purchasing coffee.

Here's How to Crack It

Start by labeling the x and the y in the equation to keep track of what they stand for. Use your pencil to write "days" above the x and "budget" above the y. So 7 × days + budget = 133. Hmm, still not very clear, is it? One way to approach this is to plug in the point $(19, 0)$. If x = days = 19 when y = budget = 0, then Jeffrey will have no budget left after 19 days. This matches (D).

If you have trouble seeing this, you can use the answer choices to help you Plug In. If (A) is true, the budget at the start of the month, when days = 0, is $19. Plug these values into the equation to see if it is true. Is 7 × 0 + 19 = 133? Not at all, so eliminate (A). If (B) is true, Jeffrey drinks a lot of coffee! Let's try some numbers and see if it works. For $x = 1$, the equation becomes $7(1) + y = 133$ or $y = 126$, and for $x = 2$, it is $7(2) + y = 133$ or $y = 119$. The difference in y, the budget remaining, is $126 - 119 = 7$, so that's not $19 per day. Eliminate (B), so only (C) and (D) remain. These both have 19 for the number of days, and the point $(19, 0)$ would indicate that 19 is the x value, or days. If you saw that right away—great! That would allow you to skip right to testing (C) and (D).

For (C), you can plug in 19 for days in the equation to get 7 × 19 + budget = 133, or budget = 0. Does that tell you how many cups of coffee Jeffrey drank? You have no information about the cost of a single cup of coffee, so the answer can't be (C). It does tell you, however, that after 19 days, Jeffrey has no budget left, so (D) is not only the one remaining answer, but it is also the correct one!

Drill 3

Answers can be found in Part III.

3

An oceanographer is trying to determine the concentration profile of dissolved oxygen in the ocean at depths lower than 10 meters. He determines that the dissolved oxygen concentration is 0.0022 g/L at a depth of 15 meters, and it is 0.00125 g/L at a depth of 20 meters. If $C(d)$ is the concentration of dissolved oxygen at d meters, which of the follow equations best describes the profile below 10 meters?

A) $C(d) = \dfrac{1}{2} - \dfrac{1}{d^2}$

B) $C(d) = \dfrac{1}{100d}$

C) $C(d) = \dfrac{1}{d}$

D) $C(d) = \dfrac{1}{2d^2}$

6

A shipping company pays a driver a fixed fee for each delivery, and deducts a separate fee daily for the use of the company's delivery truck. The driver's net pay in dollars, P, for one day is given by the equation $P = 8d - 40$, where d is the number of deliveries made in one day. What does the number 40 most likely represent?

A) The amount, in dollars, that the company deducts for use of the delivery truck

B) The amount, in dollars, that the driver is paid for each delivery

C) The average number of deliveries per hour made by the driver

D) The total number of deliveries made per day by the driver

9

At a buffet restaurant, students pay $5 per meal and non-students pay $7. The total revenue, R, in dollars, earned per day by the restaurant is given by the equation $R = 5s + 7n$, where s is the number of student customers and n is the number of non-student customers. Which of the following represents the total number of customers on a given day?

A) $s - n$

B) $s + n$

C) sn

D) $\dfrac{s}{n}$

7

$$T(t) = \Delta T^{(-kt)}$$

The simple cooling of an object can be represented by the equation above, where T is temperature in degrees Celsius, k is a rate constant, and t is time. What might the quantity ΔT represent?

A) Temperature at a certain time

B) The difference between the initial temperature of the object and the temperature of its surroundings

C) A conversion from Celsius to Fahrenheit

D) A constant factor that is dependent on the object

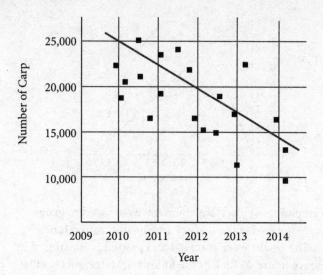

Between 2009 and 2014, researchers tracked populations of Crucian carp in the Ohio River. The graph above displays population sizes as counted by the researchers. According to the best-fit line, what is the approximate average yearly decrease in the number of Crucian carp?

A)   1

B)   2.5

C) 1,200

D) 2,500

A group of students decided to have a car wash to raise funds for the school. The students charged the same rate to wash each car, and they paid for cleaning supplies out of the proceeds. If the net amount, $N(c)$, in dollars, raised from washing c cars is given by the function $N(c) = 8c - 0.40c$, which of the following can be deduced from the function?

A) The students paid a total of $8 for cleaning supplies.

B) The students paid a total of $40 for cleaning supplies.

C) The students paid $0.40 per car for cleaning supplies.

D) The students paid $8 per car for cleaning supplies.

Two employees at a certain company were asked to gauge their energy levels on a scale of 1 to 10 after eating lunch at noon. The results were averaged and plotted as illustrated in the above figure. Which of the following statements is most consistent with the given data?

A) Both employees experienced the same fluctuation in energy during the afternoon hours.

B) Both employees were drowsy after eating big lunches.

C) One of the employees consumed energy-boosting foods and drinks and became less energetic throughout the afternoon.

D) One of the employees consumed foods that resulted in her feeling more energetic throughout the day.

Delphine is studying the growth of bacteria in a petri dish. She grows 100 colonies of bacteria in dishes at varying temperatures to find the optimal temperature for bacteria growth. The temperature of the 10 colonies with the most rapid growth is used to determine the optimal temperature range, which Delphine finds to be from 30° to 37°C, inclusive. Which of the following inequalities represents the optimal temperature range, t, for bacteria growth?

A) $|t + 7| \le 37$

B) $|t - 3.5| \le 33.5$

C) $|t - 30| \le 7$

D) $|t - 33.5| \le 3.5$

13

The sum, S, of a set of consecutive integers, n, is given by the

equation $S = \left(\dfrac{a+k}{2} \right) n$. What does $a + k$ represent?

A) The sum of the two least integers

B) The sum of the least and greatest integers

C) The sum of the two middle integers

D) The sum of the two greatest integers

23

If interest deposits are made monthly into an account with a beginning balance of $250, supposing no withdrawals are made from the account, the balance B of an account with an annual interest rate of 5% after t years can be computed using the equation below.

$$B = 250 \left(1 + \frac{0.05}{12} \right)^{12t}$$

Which of the following describes what the quantity $\dfrac{0.05}{12}$ represents in the equation?

A) The amount of money deposited into an account with balance B during a given month

B) The amount of money in an account with balance B after a monthly interest deposit is made

C) The percentage of the starting balance B added during a monthly interest deposit

D) The number of months over which interest payments will be made in a year

Summary

o   Given a function, you put an x value in and get an $f(x)$ or y value out.

o   Look for ways to use Plugging In and PITA on function questions.

o   For questions about the graphs of functions, remember that $f(x) = y$.

o   If the graph contains a labeled point or the question gives you a point, plug it into the equations in the answers and eliminate any that aren't true.

o   To find a point of intersection, set the equations equal, plug a given point into both equations to see if it works, or graph the equations on your calculator when it is allowed.

o   When solving quadratic equations, you may need to FOIL or factor to get the equation into the easiest form for the question task.

o   To solve for the roots of a quadratic equation, set it equal to zero by moving all the terms to the left side of the equation, or use the quadratic formula:

$$x = \frac{-b \pm \sqrt{b^2 - 4ac}}{2a}$$

o   The vertex form of a parabola equation is $y = a(x - h)^2 + k$, where (h, k) is the vertex. To get a parabola in the standard form into vertex form, complete the square.

o   Plugging In can also be used on Meaning In Context questions. If a question asks you to identify a part of an equation, plug your own amounts into the equation so you can start to see what is going on.

○ Analysis in Science questions may seem weird, but they can usually be handled with the same strategies as those used for other math questions. Plug In or translate, read the chart or text carefully, and always use Process of Elimination to get rid of answers that don't match the data or don't make sense.

○ If you come across a hard Meaning in Context question or Science question, see if you can eliminate anything and make a guess. If not, find another question to do!

Chapter 12
Additional Math Topics

The PSAT has a clever name for the rest of the math concepts tested—Additional Topics. Well, maybe it's not that clever. It consists of some geometry concepts and possibly a question about imaginary numbers. While there are many geometry ideas that could be tested, these Additional Topics will really make up only a small fraction of the PSAT. Spend time on this chapter only after you have mastered the topics and techniques in the previous three chapters.

The number of degrees of arc in a circle is 360.

The number of radians of arc in a circle is 2π.

The sum of the measures in degrees of the angles of a triangle is 180.

GEOMETRY

Lines and Angles

Common sense might tell you what a line is, but for this test you are going to have to learn the particulars of a line, a ray, and a line segment.

A **line** continues on in each direction forever. You need only two points to form a line, but that line does not end at those points. A straight line has 180 degrees on each side.

A **ray** is a line with one distinct endpoint. Again, you need only two points to designate a ray, but one of those points is where it stops—it continues on forever in the other direction. A ray has 180 degrees as well.

A **line segment** is a line with two distinct endpoints. It requires two points, and it is the length from one point to the other. A line segment has 180 degrees.

Whenever you have angles on a line, remember *the rule of 180*: The angles on any line must add up to 180. These angles are called *supplementary angles*. In the figure below, what is the value of x? We know that $2x + x$ must add up to 180, so we know that $3x = 180$. This makes $x = 60$.

If two lines cross each other, they make *vertical angles*—that is, angles opposite each other when two lines intersect. These angles will always have the same measure. In the figure below, z and x are vertical angles, and y and the 130° angle are vertical angles. Also, we know that z must equal 50, since $130 + z$ must equal 180. We know that y is 130, since it is across from the angle 130. We also know that x is 50, since it is across from z.

Any time you have two parallel lines and a line that crosses them, you have two kinds of angles: big angles and small angles. All of the big angles have the same measure, and all of the small angles have the same measure. In the following figure, angles a, d, e, and h all have the same measure; angles b, c, f, and g also all have the same measure. The sum of the measure of any big angle plus any small angle equals 180 degrees.

Four-Sided Figures

Thinking Inside the Box

Here's a progression of quadrilaterals from least specific to most specific:

quadrilateral = 4-sided figure
↓
parallelogram = a quadrilateral in which opposite sides are parallel
↓
rectangle = a parallelogram in which all angles equal 90°
↓
square = a rectangle in which all angles and all sides are equal

Parallelogram   Rectangle   Square

A figure with two sets of parallel sides is a **parallelogram**. In a parallelogram, the opposite angles are equal, and any adjacent angles add up to 180 degrees. (In the left-hand figure above, $x + y = 180$ degrees.) Opposite sides are also equal. The sum of all angles of a parallelogram is 360 degrees.

If all of the angles are also right angles, then the figure is a **rectangle**. And if all of the sides are the same length, then the figure is a **square**.

The *area* of a square, rectangle, or parallelogram is *length × width*. (In the parallelogram above, the length is shown by the dotted line.)

The *perimeter* of any figure is the sum of the lengths of its sides. A trapezoid with sides of 6, 8, 10, and 8 has a perimeter of 32.

Drill 1

Answers can be found in Part III.

a. What is the area of square *ABCD* above? _____

b. What is the perimeter of square *ABCD* above? _____

c. If *ABCD* is a rectangle, $x =$ _____ $y =$ _____

d. What is the perimeter of rectangle *ABCD* above? _____

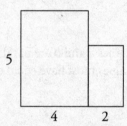

e. If the above figure is composed of two rectangles, what is the perimeter of the figure?
_____

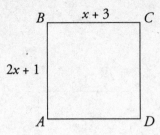

If *ABCD* is a square, what is the area of the square?

A)   2

B)   4

C) 20

D) 25

3

In the figure above, lines *a* and *b* are parallel. Which of the following pairs of angles must have equal degree measures?

   I.   1 and 5

   II. 2 and 7

   III. 3 and 9

A) I only

B) II only

C) III only

D) II and III only

The diagonal of rectangle *ABCD* is 13 inches long. What is the area of rectangle *ABCD* ?

In the figure above, $\overline{BC} \parallel \overline{AD}$. What is the measure of $\angle ACD$?

A) 35

B) 40

C) 50

D) 55

TRIANGLES

The sum of the angles inside a triangle must equal 180 degrees. This means that if you know two of the angles in a triangle, you can always solve for the third. Since you know that two of the angles in the following figure are 90 and 60 degrees, you can solve for the third angle, which must be 30 degrees. (Note: The little square in the bottom corner of the triangle indicates a right angle, which is 90°.)

An **isosceles triangle** has two sides that are equal. Angles that are opposite equal sides must be equal. The figure below is an isosceles triangle. Since $AB = BC$, you know that angles x and y are equal. And since their sum must be 150 degrees (to make a total of 180 degrees when you add the last angle), they each must be 75 degrees.

The **area** of a triangle is $\frac{1}{2}$ *base* × *height*. Note that the height is always perpendicular to the base.

$$\text{Area} = \frac{1}{2} \times 10 \times 4 = 20 \qquad \text{Area} = \frac{1}{2} \times 6 \times 4 = 12$$

An **equilateral triangle** has all three sides equal and all of its angles equal to 60 degrees.

Here's a typical example of a PSAT question on triangles.

5

In triangle *ABC* above, what is the value of *x* ?

A) 30

B) 40

C) 50

D) 60

Here's How to Crack It

We know that the angle adjacent to the 100-degree angle must equal 80 degrees since we know that a straight line is 180 degrees. Fill it in on your diagram. Now, since we know that the sum of the angles contained in a triangle must equal 180 degrees, we know that $80 + 60 + x = 180$, so $x = 40$. That's (B).

Being Aggressive on Geometry Problems

The most important problem-solving technique for tackling PSAT geometry is to learn to be aggressive. This means, whenever you have a diagram, ask yourself *What else do I know?* Write everything you can think of on your booklet. You may not see right away why it's important, but write it down anyway. Chances are good that you will be making progress toward the answer, without even knowing it.

ETS is also fond of disguising familiar figures within more complex shapes by extending lines, overlapping figures, or combining several basic shapes. So be on the lookout for the basic figures hidden in complicated shapes.

The Pythagorean Theorem

Whenever you have a right triangle, you can use the Pythagorean Theorem. The theorem says that the sum of the squares of the legs of the triangle (the sides that form the right angle) will equal the square of the hypotenuse (the side opposite the right angle).

$$a^2 + b^2 = c^2$$

Two of the most common ratios of sides that fit the Pythagorean Theorem are $3 : 4 : 5$ and $5 : 12 : 13$. Since these are ratios, any multiples of these numbers will also work, such as $6 : 8 : 10$ and $30 : 40 : 50$.

Try the following example.

14

If *ABCD* is a rectangle, what is the perimeter of triangle *ABC*?

Here's How to Crack It

We can use the Pythagorean Theorem to figure out the length of the diagonal of the rectangle —since it has sides 6 and 8, its diagonal must be 10. (If you remembered that this is one of those well-known Pythagorean ratios, you didn't actually have to do the calculations.) Therefore, the perimeter of the triangle is 6 + 8 + 10, or 24.

Special Right Triangles

There are two specific right triangles, the properties of which may play a role in some harder PSAT math problems. They are the right triangles with angles 45°-45°-90° and 30°-60°-90°. These triangles appear at the front of each Math section, so you don't have to memorize them.

An isosceles right triangle has angles that measure 45, 45, and 90 degrees. Whenever you have a 45°-45°-90° triangle with sides of x, the hypotenuse will always be $x\sqrt{2}$. This means that if one of the legs of the triangle measures 3, then the hypotenuse will be $3\sqrt{2}$.

This right triangle is important because it is half of a square. Understanding the 45°-45°-90° triangle will allow you to easily find the diagonal of a square from its side, or find the side of a square from its diagonal.

Here's an example.

7

In square *ABCD* above, what is the perimeter of triangle *ABC*?

A) $6\sqrt{2}$

B) 8

C) $12 + \sqrt{2}$

D) $12 + 6\sqrt{2}$

Here's How to Crack It
This question looks like a question about a square, and it certainly is in part, but it's really more about the two triangles formed by the diagonal.

In this square, we know that each of the triangles formed by the diagonal *AC* is a 45°-45°-90° right triangle. Since the square has a side of 6, using the 45°-45°-90° right triangle rule, each of the sides is 6 and the diagonal is $6\sqrt{2}$. Therefore, the perimeter of the triangle is $6 + 6 + 6\sqrt{2}$, or $12 + 6\sqrt{2}$ and the answer is (D).

The other important right triangle to understand is the 30°-60°-90° right triangle.

A 30°-60°-90° triangle with a short side of x will have a hypotenuse of $2x$ and a middle side of $x\sqrt{3}$. If the smallest side (the x side) of the triangle is 5, then the sides measure 5, $5\sqrt{3}$, and 10. This triangle is important because it is half of an equilateral triangle, and it allows us to find the height of an equilateral triangle, which is what we'll need to find the area of an equilateral triangle.

Try the following.

13

Triangle ABC above is equilateral, with sides of length 4. What is its area?

A) 3

B) $4\sqrt{2}$

C) $4\sqrt{3}$

D) 8

Triangle Tip
An easy way to figure out the height of an equilateral triangle is to take half of its side and multiply it by the square root of 3.

Here's How to Crack It

To find the area of the triangle, we need to know the base and the height. The question tells you that the base (line segment AC) is 4; now we need to find the height, which is *perpendicular* to the base. You can create the height by drawing a line from angle B straight down to the base, as you can see in the drawing above. Now you have two 30°-60°-90° triangles, and you can use the rules of 30-60-90 triangles to figure out the height. Half of the base would be 2, and that's the side across from the 30-degree angle, so you would multiply it by $\sqrt{3}$ to get the height.

Now we know that the base is 4 and the height is $2\sqrt{3}$, when we plug those numbers into the formula for area of a triangle, we get $A = \dfrac{1}{2} \times 4 \times 2\sqrt{3}$, which equals $4\sqrt{3}$. Thus, (C) is the correct answer.

SOHCAHTOA

Trigonometry will likely appear on your PSAT. But fear not! Many trigonometry questions you will see mostly require you to know the basic definitions of the three main trigonometric functions. SOHCAHTOA is a way to remember the three functions:

SOHCAHTOA stands for:

$$\text{sine} = \frac{opposite}{hypotenuse}$$

$$\text{cosine} = \frac{adjacent}{hypotenuse}$$

$$\text{tangent} = \frac{opposite}{adjacent}$$

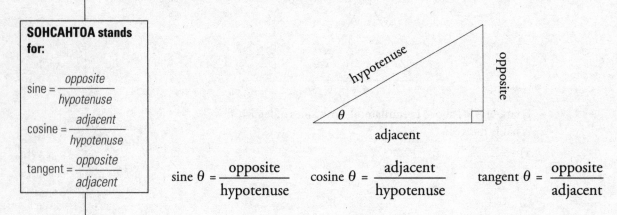

$$\text{sine } \theta = \frac{opposite}{hypotenuse} \qquad \text{cosine } \theta = \frac{adjacent}{hypotenuse} \qquad \text{tangent } \theta = \frac{opposite}{adjacent}$$

Let's see an example.

Which of the following gives the value of x?

A) $72 \sin 30°$

B) $\dfrac{72}{\sin 30°}$

C) $72 \cos 30°$

D) $72 \tan 30°$

Here's How to Crack It

You know the hypotenuse of the triangle, and you want to find the side opposite the angle. SOHCAHTOA tells you that sine is $\dfrac{\text{opposite}}{\text{hypotenuse}}$, so you want sine. You can eliminate (C) and (D), which do not contain sine. Next, set up the equation using the definition of sine: $\sin 30° = \dfrac{x}{72}$. To solve for x, multiply both sides by 72 and you get $72 \sin 30° = x$. This matches (A).

Similar Triangles

Similar triangles have the same shape, but they are not necessarily the same size. Having the same shape means that the angles of the triangles are identical and that the corresponding sides have the same ratio. Look at the following two similar triangles:

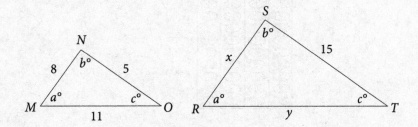

These two triangles both have the same set of angles, but they aren't the same size. Whenever this is true, the sides of one triangle are proportional to those of the other. Notice that sides NO and ST are both opposite the angle that is $a°$. These are called corresponding sides, because they correspond to the same angle. So the lengths of $\overline{NO}$ and $\overline{ST}$ are proportional to each other. In order to figure out the lengths of the other sides, set up a proportion: $\dfrac{MN}{RS} = \dfrac{NO}{ST}$. Now fill in the information that you know: $\dfrac{8}{x} = \dfrac{5}{15}$. Cross-multiply and you find that $x = 24$. You could also figure out the length of y: $\dfrac{NO}{ST} = \dfrac{MO}{RT}$. So, $\dfrac{5}{15} = \dfrac{11}{y}$, and $y = 33$. Whenever you have to deal with sides of similar triangles, just set up a proportion.

Give it a try.

9

Note: Figure not drawn to scale.

If the area of triangle ACE is 18, what is the area of triangle BCD?

Here's How to Crack It

The formula to find the area of a triangle is $A = \dfrac{1}{2}bh$. Plugging in the area and base of triangle *ACE* as given in the formula gives you the equation $18 = \dfrac{1}{2}(6)h$. Simplify the fraction and you will get $18 = 3h$. Divide both sides by 3 and you can see that the height of triangle *ACE* is 6. Because triangle *ACE* and triangle *BCD* have the same angle measures, they are similar. Therefore, you should create a proportion to find the length of $\overline{BD}$. The proportion should look like this: $\dfrac{4}{x} = \dfrac{6}{6}$, if *x* represents the length of $\overline{BD}$. Simplify your fractions and cross-multiply to see that $x = 4$. Plug the base and height of triangle *BCD* into the area formula: $A = \dfrac{1}{2}(4)(4)$. Simplify the equation and you will see that the area of triangle *BCD* is 8.

Drill 2

Answers can be found in Part III.

a. What is the area of triangle *XYZ* above? _____

b. What is the length of *YZ*? _____

c. What is the sine of ∠*Z*? _____

d. If the area of the triangle above is 400, what is the length of *AC*? _____

e. What is the length of *BC*? _____

f. What is the cosine of ∠*C*? _____

In the triangle above, $\tan a° = \dfrac{14}{15}$. What is the value of x?

Note: Figure not drawn to scale.

In triangle ABC above, if $AB = BC$, what is the value of x?

(Disregard the degree symbol when gridding your answer.)

Note: Figure not drawn to scale.

In the figure above, if triangle ABC is isosceles, what is the perimeter of the triangle?

A) 12.5

B) $10\sqrt{2}$

C) $10+5\sqrt{2}$

D) $15\sqrt{2}$

9

The owner of a barn needs to paint the front of the barn's roof. As shown in the figure above, the roof measures 8 m along the bottom, and the sides of the roof meet the bottom at a 30° angle. If one bucket of paint can cover 5 m², what is the minimum number of buckets the owner needs to purchase?

A) 1

B) 2

C) 3

D) 4

10

Note: Figure not drawn to scale.

In the figure above, if $AB = 5$, $AC = 13$, and $DE = 24$, what is the value of BD ?

A) 12

B) 10

C) 8

D) 5

13

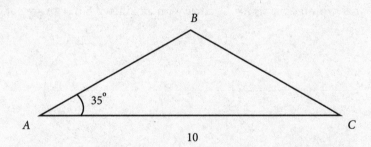

In the triangle above, $AB = BC$. Which of the following accurately expresses the perimeter of the triangle?

A) $10 + 10 \sin 55°$

B) $10 + 10 \cos 35°$

C) $10 + \dfrac{10}{\sin 55°}$

D) $25 \tan 35°$

CIRCLES

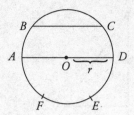

The **radius** of a circle is the distance from the center to the edge of the circle. In the figure above, *OD* is a radius. So is *OA*.

The **diameter** is the distance from one edge, through the center, to the other edge of the circle. The diameter will always be twice the measure of the radius and will always be the longest line you can draw through a circle. In the figure above, *AD* is a diameter.

A **chord** is any line drawn from one point on the edge of the circle to the other. In the figure above, *BC* is a chord. A diameter is the longest chord in a circle.

An **arc** is any section of the circumference (the edge) of the circle. *EF* is an arc in the figure above.

The **circumference** is the distance around the outside edge of the circle. The circumference of a circle with radius r is $2\pi r$. A circle with radius of 5 has a circumference of 10π.

The **area** of a circle with radius r is πr^2. A circle with a radius of 5 has an area of 25π.

Area = 9π

Circumference = 6π

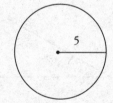

Area = 25π

Circumference = 10π

Quick Review
- An interior angle is an angle formed by two radii.
- A sector is the portion of the circle between the two radii.

Proportionality in a Circle

Here's another rule that plays a role in more advanced circle problems.

> Arc measure is proportional to interior angle measure, which is proportional to sector area.

This means that whatever fraction of the total degree measure is made up by the interior angle, the arc described by that angle is the same fraction of the circumference, and the pie piece created has the same fraction of the area.

Take a look at the figure below:

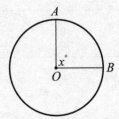

If angle *x* is equal to 90 degrees, which is one-quarter of 360 degrees, then the arc *AB* is equal to one-quarter of the circumference of the circle and the area of the sector of the circle enclosed by radii *OA* and *OB* is equal to one-quarter of the area of the circle.

To see how this works, try the following question.

6

The circle above with center *O* has a radius of 4. If *x* = 30, what is the length of arc *AB* ?

A) $\dfrac{\pi}{6}$

B) $\dfrac{2\pi}{3}$

C) 3

D) $\dfrac{3\pi}{2}$

Here's How to Crack It

Since the interior angle x is equal to 30 degrees, which is $\frac{1}{12}$ of 360 degrees, we know that the arc AB will be equal to $\frac{1}{12}$ of the circumference of the circle. Since the circle has radius 4, its circumference will be 8π. Therefore, arc AB will measure $\frac{1}{12} \times 8\pi$, or $\frac{2\pi}{3}$, (B).

11

Points A and B lie on a circle with center O such that the measure of $\angle OAB$ is 45°. If the area of the circle is 64π, what is the perimeter of $\triangle AOB$?

A) $8 + 8\sqrt{2}$

B) $16 + 8\sqrt{2}$

C) $16 + 16\sqrt{2}$

D) $32 + 16\sqrt{2}$

Here's How to Crack It

This time a diagram isn't given, so drawing the circle should be your first step. Since points A and B lie on the circle, $\overline{OA}$ and $\overline{OB}$ are both radii, and equal in length, making $\triangle AOB$ isosceles. The problem indicates that $\angle OAB$ is 45 degrees, which means that $\angle OBA$ is also 45 degrees, which makes $\triangle AOB$ a 45-45-90 triangle (remember those special right triangles?).

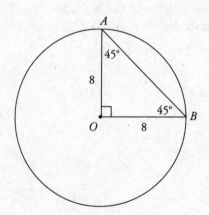

Given the circle's area of 64π, the radii of the circle (which are the legs of the isosceles right triangle) are 8, and the hypotenuse is $8\sqrt{2}$, making the perimeter $8 + 8 + 8\sqrt{2}$, or $16 + 8\sqrt{2}$, which is (B).

───────────○───────────

Tangents to a Circle

A tangent is a line that touches the edge of a circle at exactly one point. A radius drawn to the point of tangency forms a 90-degree angle with the tangent line. This comes up occasionally on hard problems, so take a look at the example below. As you work through this question, if you're thinking that you'd never know how to do it yourself, there's still a valuable lesson here, and it's that this question is not in your POOD, so you should look instead for a plug in or something you're more familiar with.

───────────○───────────

27

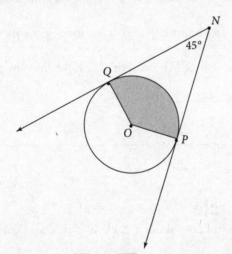

In the figure above, $\overline{NP}$ and $\overline{NQ}$ are tangent to the circle with center O at points P and Q, respectively. If the area of the shaded region is 24π, what is the circumference of the circle?

A) 8π

B) 12π

C) 16π

D) 40π

Here's How to Crack It

The key is remembering that any line or line segment drawn tangent to a circle is perpendicular to a radius drawn from the center of the circle to that tangent point; this means both $\angle OQN$ and $\angle OPN$ equal 90 degrees. With $\angle QNP$ given as 45 degrees, that leaves the central $\angle QOP$ of quadrilateral $QNPO$. Since all quadrilaterals contain 360 degrees and since 45 of the remaining 180 degrees are accounted for, that remaining angle must be 135 degrees. As all circles contain 360 degrees of arc, this means the shaded area represents $\frac{135}{360}$, or $\frac{3}{8}$, of the area of the entire circle.

Remember, we want to write down the formulas for quantities the question talks about, so that's $A = \pi r^2$ and $C = 2\pi r$. So far we don't have anything we can put directly into a formula, so what do we know? We're told that the area of the shaded sector is 24π, so we can use that to figure out the area of the whole circle, because we know it's proportional to the central angle. In fact, we've figured out that this part of the circle is $\frac{3}{8}$ of the whole, so the whole area must be $\frac{8}{3}$ times the sector, so $\left(\frac{8}{3}\right) \times 24\pi = 64\pi$ (this is a shortcut to using a proportion, which looks like this: $\frac{3}{8} = \frac{24\pi}{x}$, which if we cross-multiply and solve for x gives us 64π). Now we can use the first formula and solve for $r = 8$. We can put this right into the second formula and get $C = 16\pi$, so the answer is (C).

The Equation of a Circle

One last thing you may need to know about a circle is what the equation of a circle in the xy-plane looks like.

> The equation of a circle is as follows:
>
> $$(x - h)^2 + (y - k)^2 = r^2$$
>
> In the circle equation, the center of the circle is the point (h, k), and the radius of the circle is r.

Let's look at one.

13

What is the equation of a circle with center (2, 4) that passes through the point (–6, –2) ?

A) $(x + 2)^2 + (y + 4)^2 = 100$

B) $(x + 2)^2 + (y + 4)^2 = \sqrt{20}$

C) $(x - 2)^2 + (y - 4)^2 = 100$

D) $(x - 2)^2 + (y - 4)^2 = \sqrt{20}$

Here's How to Crack It

Take the given center and put it into the circle equation above. Plugging in $h = 2$ and $k = 4$, you get $(x - 2)^2 + (y - 4)^2 = r^2$. In the circle equation, x and y are the coordinates of a point on the circle. Plugging in the point (–6, –2), you get $(-6 - 2)^2 + (-2 - 4)^2 = r^2$, which simplifies to $(-8)^2 + (-6)^2 = r^2$, or $64 + 36 = r^2$. This means $r^2 = 100$, so the equation is $(x - 2)^2 + (y - 4)^2 = 100$. The correct answer is (C).

There is a chance that you might see a circle equation that is not in the form shown above. If this happens, you will need to complete the square to get the given equation into the proper form. Just follow the steps listed for completing the square in the Quadratic Equations section of the previous chapter. The only difference is that you'll have to do it twice—for the x terms and for the y terms. You may decide, however, that such a question is not worth your time. In that case, move on to something else!

Drill 3

Answers can be found in Part III.

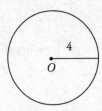

a. What is the area of the circle above with center *O*? _____

b. What is its circumference? _____

16

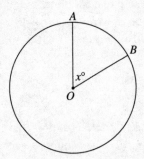

The circle shown above has its center at *O*. If *x* = 60 and the length of arc *AB* is 2π, what is the area of circle *O* ?

A) 36π

B) 12π

C) 6π

D) 6

18

A circle with center *O* has diameter $\overline{AB}$. Segment $\overline{AC}$ is tangent to the circle at point *A* and has a length of 5. If the area of the circle is 36π, what is the perimeter of triangle *ABC* ?

A) 15

B) 25

C) 30

D) 60

12

What is the center of a circle with equation
$x^2 + y^2 - 2x + 8y + 8 = 0$?

A) $(-1, 4)$

B) $(1, -4)$

C) $(-2, 8)$

D) $(2, -8)$

29

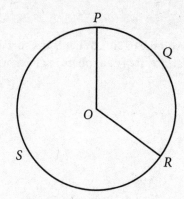

Note: Figure not drawn to scale.

Major arc *PSR* is $\dfrac{4}{3}$ the length of minor arc *PQR*. The length of major arc *PSR* is 6π units. What is the radius of the circle?

VOLUME

Volume questions on the PSAT can seem intimidating at times. The PSAT sometimes gives you questions featuring unusual shapes such as pyramids and spheres. Luckily, at the beginning of the Math sections (and the beginning of this chapter), you're given a reference information box with all the formulas you will ever need for volume questions on the PSAT.

Let's look at an example:

15

A sphere has a volume of 36π. What is the surface area of the sphere? (The surface area of a sphere is given by the formula $A = 4\pi r^2$.)

A) 3π

B) 9π

C) 27π

D) 36π

Here's How to Crack It

Start by writing down the formula for volume of a sphere from the beginning of the chapter: $V = \dfrac{4}{3}\pi r^3$. Put what you know into the equation: $36\pi = \dfrac{4}{3}\pi r^3$. From this you can solve for r. Divide both sides by π to get $36 = \dfrac{4}{3}r^3$. Multiply both sides by 3 to clear the fraction: $36(3) = 4r^3$. Note that we left 36 as 36 because the next step is to divide both sides by 4, and 36 divided by 4 is 9, so $9(3) = r^3$ or $27 = r^3$. Take the cube root of both sides to get $r = 3$. Now that you have the radius, use the formula provided to find the surface area: $A = 4\pi(3)^2$, which comes out to 36π, (D).

PLUGGING IN ON GEOMETRY

You can also Plug In on geometry questions, just as you can for algebra. Any time that you have variables in the answer choices or hidden variables, Plug In! As long as you follow all the rules of geometry while you solve, you'll get the answer.

Take a look at this problem.

In the figure above, what is the value of $x + y$?

A) 140

B) 180

C) 190

D) 210

Here's How to Crack It

You could solve this problem using algebra, but why? You can plug in whatever numbers you want for the other angles inside the triangle—as long as you make sure that all the angles in the triangle add up to 180 degrees. So plug in 60 and 90 for the other angles inside that triangle. Now you can solve for x and y: if the angle next to x is 60 degrees, then x will be equal to 120. If the angle next to y is equal to 90 degrees, then y will be equal to 90. This makes the sum $x + y$ equal to 120 + 90, or 210. No matter what numbers we pick for the angles inside the triangle, we'll always get the same answer, (D).

Drill 4

Try to use Plugging In on the following questions. Answers can be found in Part III.

3

In the figure above, what is the value of *b*, in terms of *a* ?

A) $30 - a$

B) $30 + a$

C) $60 + a$

D) $80 - a$

7

Cone *A* and Cone *B* are both right circular cones with the same height. If the radius of Cone *A* is $\frac{3}{4}$ of the radius of Cone *B*, which of the following is the ratio of the volume of Cone *A* to the volume of Cone *B* ?

A)   27:64

B)   9:16

C)   3:4

D)   4:3

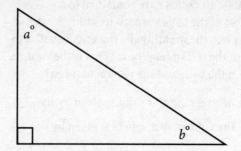

If sin $a° = x$, then cos $b° =$

A) x

B) $1 - x$

C) $\dfrac{1}{x}$

D) $x - 1$

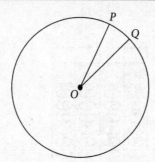

In the figure above, O is the center of the circle, the radius of the circle is x, and the length of minor arc PQ is $\dfrac{\pi x}{18}$. What is the area of sector POQ ?

A) $\dfrac{\pi x^2}{36}$

B) $\dfrac{\pi x^2}{18}$

C) $\dfrac{\pi x^2}{9}$

D) $\dfrac{\pi x^2}{3}$

Three spherical balls with radius r are contained in a rectangular box. Two of the balls are each touching 5 sides of the rectangular box and the middle ball. The middle ball also touches four sides of the rectangular box. What is the volume of the space between the balls and the rectangular box?

(Note: The volume of a rectangular solid is given by the equation $V = lwh$. The volume of a sphere is given by the equation $V = \frac{4}{3}\pi r^3$.)

A) $r^3(3 - 4\pi)$

B) $4r^2(14 - \pi)$

C) $4r^3(6 - \pi)$

D) $12r^2(r - \pi)$

A rectangular box is half as long as it is wide and one-third as wide as it is tall. If the volume of the box is 96, then what is its surface area? (Note: The formula for the volume of a rectangular solid is $V = lwh$).

IMAGINARY AND COMPLEX NUMBERS

So far you have been working with real numbers, which are any numbers that you can place on a number line. The PSAT may ask you to do mathematical operations with imaginary or complex numbers.

Imaginary Numbers

An imaginary number, very simply, is the square root of a negative number. Since there is no way to have a real number that is the square root of a negative number, mathematicians needed to come up with a way to represent this concept when writing equations. They use an italicized lowercase "I" to do that: $i = \sqrt{-1}$, and the PSAT will likely tell you that in any problem involving imaginary numbers.

Another common piece of information you will need to know about i is how it behaves when it is raised to a power. Here is i raised to the powers 1 through 8. Can you complete the next four values of i in the series?

$$i = \sqrt{-1} \qquad\qquad i^5 = \sqrt{-1} \qquad\qquad i^9 = ?$$

$$i^2 = -1 \qquad\qquad i^6 = -1 \qquad\qquad i^{10} = ?$$

$$i^3 = -\sqrt{-1} = -i \qquad i^7 = -\sqrt{-1} = -i \qquad i^{11} = ?$$

$$i^4 = 1 \qquad\qquad i^8 = 1 \qquad\qquad i^{12} = ?$$

Did you notice anything about the answer? If you said that there is a repeating pattern, then you are correct. This pattern will be helpful in answering questions containing imaginary and complex numbers.

Complex Numbers

Complex numbers are another way in which the PSAT may test the concept of imaginary numbers. A complex number is one that has a real component and an imaginary component connected by addition or subtraction. $8 + 7i$ and $3 - 4i$ are two examples of complex numbers.

You may be tested on complex numbers in a variety of ways. You may be asked to add or subtract the complex numbers. When you are completing these operations, you can treat i as a variable. Just combine the like terms in these expressions and then simplify. (Don't forget to distribute the subtraction sign.)

Here is an example:

---○---

7

If $i = \sqrt{-1}$, which of the following is equivalent to $(4 + 3i) - (2 - 2i)$?

A) 3

B) $2 + i$

C) $6 + i$

D) $2 + 5i$

Here's How to Crack It

Start by distributing the negative sign: $(4 + 3i) - (2 - 2i) = 4 + 3i - 2 + 2i$. Be careful with the negative signs, which are often the trickiest part of imaginary number questions. The real parts are 4 and -2, which can be added together to get 2. The imaginary parts are $3i$ and $2i$. These can also be added together to get $5i$. Note you cannot combine real parts and imaginary parts in a complex number, so the answer is simply (D).

The PSAT may also ask you to multiply complex numbers. Again, you can treat i as a variable as you work through the multiplication as if you were multiplying binominals. In other words, use FOIL to work through the problem. The only difference is that you substitute -1 for i^2.

Let's look at one.

10

If $i^2 = -1$ and $a = (i + 6)$, which of the following is the result of squaring a ?

A) $36i$

B) $i + 36$

C) $12i + 35$

D) $12i + 36$

Here's How to Crack It

The question states that $a = (i + 6)$, so the square of a must be $(i + 6)^2$. Expand the squared term using FOIL and you get $i^2 + 6i + 6i + 36$. Combine like terms to get $i^2 + 12i + 36$. Since $i^2 = -1$, you can simplify further to $(-1) + 12i + 36$, or $12i + 35$, which is (C).

Note that this question would appear in the calculator-allowed section. Your calculator has a handy i button, so feel free to use it when allowed if things get tricky.

Summary

- Be sure to review your basic geometry rules before the test; often, problems hinge on knowing that vertical angles are equal or that the sum of the angles in a quadrilateral is 360°.

- On all geometry problems, draw figures out and aggressively fill in everything you know.

- When two parallel lines are cut by a third line, the small angles are equal, the big angles are equal, and the sum of a big angle and a small angle is 180°.

- The perimeter of a rectangle is the sum of the lengths of its sides. The area of a rectangle is *length × width*.

- The perimeter of a triangle is the sum of the lengths of its sides. The area of a triangle is 1/2 *base × height*.

- Knowing the Pythagorean Theorem, common right triangles (such as 3-4-5 and 5-12-13), and special right triangles (45°-45°-90° and 30°-60°-90°) will help you figure out angles and lengths in a right triangle.

- For trigonometry questions, remember SOHCAHTOA:

  - $\text{sine} = \dfrac{opposite}{hypotenuse}$

  - $\text{cosine} = \dfrac{adjacent}{hypotenuse}$

  - $\text{tangent} = \dfrac{opposite}{adjacent}$

o   Similar triangles have the same angles and their lengths are proportional.

o   The circumference of a circle is $2\pi r$. The area of a circle is πr^2.

o   Circles that show an interior angle (an angle that extends from the center of the circle) have proportionality. The interior angle over the whole degree measure (360°) equals the same fraction as the arc enclosed by that angle over the circumference. Likewise, both of these fractions are equal to the area of the segment over the entire area of the circle.

o   When you see a line that is "tangent to" a circle, remember two things:
- The line touches the circle at exactly one point.
- The radius of the circle that intersects the tangent line is perpendicular (90°) to that tangent line.

o   The formulas to compute the volumes of many three-dimensional figures are supplied in the instructions at the front of both Math sections.

o   When plugging in on geometry problems, remember to use your knowledge of basic geometry rules; e.g., there are still 180° in a triangle when you're using Plugging In.

o   The imaginary number $i = \sqrt{-1}$, and there is a repeating pattern when you raise i to a power: i, −1, −i, 1. When doing algebra with i, treat it as a variable, unless you are able to substitute −1 for i^2 when appropriate.

Part III
Drill Answers
and
Explanations

CHAPTER 4

Dual-Passage Drill

38. **C** The author mentions *infections and cancers* as examples of the types of ailments that site-specific and conservative drug doses can more effectively help than other drug delivery systems that are not characterized by these attributes. The answer that best matches this description is (C). Choice (A) is not supported because the passage discusses treating these types of illnesses, not curing them. Choice (D) is also incorrect as it references vaccines, rather than treatments. Choice (B) is disproven by the passage; the paragraph clearly refers to drugs *used to predominately treat infections and cancers*. This implies that there are currently effective treatments for cancers, but there may be even better ones out there. The best answer is (C).

39. **D** The author states that the fibers range in size from nanometers to micrometers, which is an attribute that is intrinsically difficult to obtain from other fiber-fabrication processes. The only answer choice that matches this is (D). Choices (A) and (C) are not correct because precise fiber measurements and cellular measurements are not mentioned in the passage. Choice (B) is deceptively worded; the passage is describing the sizes of the fibers for the first time. Because there is no additional information being given about the size, (B) cannot be correct.

40. **B** In context, "residual" refers to the solvent that evaporates, as opposed to that which forms the collection of non-woven fibers, so it is the extra material that results from the electrospinning process. Therefore, the correct answer should match the meaning "extra." Because *durable, steadfast*, and *inhabiting* do not match this meaning, eliminate (A), (C), and (D). The remaining answer does match this meaning, making (B) the best answer.

41. **A** The author of Passage 1 prefers natural polymers to synthetic polymers because they possess lower levels of toxicity, immunogenicity, and improved biocompatibility as compared to synthetic polymers. This is best supported by (A). The author of Passage 1 does not discuss blending natural polymers with synthetic polymers—that's the author of Passage 2, so eliminate (B). Choice (D) is too extreme—while the author states that when combined, these polymers can have greater benefit; it does not go so far to say that when used individually, collagen and elastin are not effective. Choice (C) is not discussed in either passage, so it cannot be the correct answer.

42. **A** Passage 2 begins by discussing why there has been an increase in research and use of synthetic polymers as opposed to natural ones and reviews the positive attributes of synthetic. It then goes on to say in the second and final paragraph that researchers should not limit themselves to a purist approach, and a blend of polymer types may result in the most beneficial base yet of electrospun scaffolds. This best matches (A). Choice (C) is the opposite of this—the author does not think a purist approach is important to have. Choice (D) is too specific and does not address the connection between natural and synthetic polymers. Choice (B) goes too far; although the passage does

state that synthetic polymers can be created in laboratories, it does not say that they are easier to work with than natural fibers, only that many possible products can be made from them. The correct answer is (A).

43. **D** Although the author does state that synthetic polymers have clear benefits over natural ones, he goes on to urge that a blend of the two may create an even better option because they both have positive properties. Choice (D) is the only answer that matches the general point of the paragraph. Choice (A) is too specific because it addresses only the first line of the paragraph. Choice (B) is the opposite of what is stated in the paragraph; the author does not support the purist approach. Choice (C) is not addressed in the passage, so it is not correct. The best answer is (D).

44. **B** Don't forget to use POE! Passage 2 focuses on the positive aspects of synthetic polymers and the importance of keeping an open approach to building these drug delivery systems. Choice (B) is supported by the author's assertion that *because synthetic polymers can be created in laboratories...[they] can be engineered to address any particular clinical need*. Choice (A) is too vague and does not match the information presented in Passage 2 regarding synthetic polymers having many benefits over natural polymers. Eliminate (A). The passage states that the hydrophilicity and hydrophobicity of a polymer are related to its solubility, but it never states that one has more affect on solubility than the other. This makes (C) incorrect. Because there is no evidence from Passage 2 to support (D), the only possible answer is (B).

45. **C** Hydrophilicity and hydrophobicity are mentioned only in Passage 2, not in both passages. Therefore, eliminate (A). Differing electrical charges and viscosity are mentioned only in Passage 1, so (B) can be eliminated as well. The topics in (C) and (D) are addressed in both passages, but (D) goes too far. Passage 1 states that natural polymers *typically* possess positive aspects, not that they necessarily do, while Passage 2 argues for trying blended polymer bases. So eliminate (D). Passage 1 does state that site-specificity, stability, and dosage measurement all impact how well electrospun scaffolds work, while Passage 2 states that it is the aim of researchers to precisely fine-tune the properties of electrospun scaffolds. Choice (C) is the best-supported answer.

46. **B** Both passages discuss blended polymer bases: Passage 1 discusses the combination of collagen and elastin, while Passage 2 encourages research on synthetic and natural base blends, so eliminate (A). Choice (C) is incorrect because Passage 1 refers to both the efficacy of different drug delivery systems for cancers and infections, while Passage 2 does not refer to disease at all, just merely *medical applications*. Eliminate (C). Choice (D) is inaccurate for Passage 1 because the author of that passage clearly favors natural polymer bases. Only (B) matches both passages, as Passage 1 explains how electrospinning works, and Passage 2 discusses the need to look at combining polymer bases and continued interest in this field in the last paragraph.

47. **C** The tones differ in that Passage 1 strongly believes natural polymers are the best, while Passage 2 believes that, although synthetic polymers have more positive characteristics, both have benefits that should be utilized. This makes (C) the best answer. Choice (B) can be eliminated because *biased* and *subjective* mean the same thing. Choices (A) and (D) can be eliminated as the author of Passage 1 is neither belligerent nor pessimistic.

CHAPTER 5

Writing and Language Drill 1

1. Apostrophes; apostrophes and where they go

2. Verbs; verb tense and number

3. Words; transition words (direction)

4. Seem/Seems and their/its; verb number and pronoun number

5. Number of words; conciseness

CHAPTER 6

Writing and Language Drill 2

1.	B	7.	C
2.	D	8.	C
3.	C	9.	D
4.	D	10.	C
5.	B	11.	D
6.	A		

CHAPTER 7

Writing and Language Drill 3

1.	D	7.	A
2.	B	8.	C
3.	B	9.	B
4.	C	10.	D
5.	C	11.	C
6.	A		

CHAPTER 8

Writing and Language Drill 4

1. A
2. A
3. C
4. A
5. B
6. D
7. B
8. C
9. D
10. D
11. C

CHAPTER 9

Drill 1

1. **c** Examples: –7, 0, 1, 8

2. **d** Examples: .5, 2, 118

3. **g** Examples: –.5, –2, –118

4. **f** Examples: –4, 0, 10

5. **b** Examples: –5, 1, 17

6. **a** Examples: *Factors* of 12 are 1, 2, 3, 4, 6, and 12. Factors of 10 are 1, 2, 5, and 10.

7. **i** Examples: *Multiples* of 12 include –24, –12, 0, 12, 24, and so on. Multiples of 10 include –20, –10, 0, 10, 20, 30, and so on.

8. **h** Examples: 2, 3, 5, 7, 11, and so on. There are no negative *prime numbers*, and 1 is not prime.

9. **e** Examples: 3 and 4 are *distinct* numbers. –2 and 2 are also distinct.

10. **j** Examples: In the number 274, 2 is the *digit* in the hundreds place, 7 is the digit in the tens place, and 4 is the digit in the ones place.

11. **p** Examples: –1, 0, 1, and 2 are *consecutive* numbers. Be careful—sometimes you will be asked for *consecutive even* or *consecutive odd* numbers, in which case you would use just the odds or evens in a consecutive list of numbers.

12. **n** Examples: 6 is *divisible* by 2 and 3, but not by 4 or 5.

13. l Examples: When you divide 26 by 8, you get 3 with a *remainder* of 2 (2 is left over). When you divide 14 by 5, you get 2 with a remainder of 4 (4 is left over).

14. k Examples: When you add 2 and 3, you get a *sum* of 5. When you add −4 and 1, you get a sum of −3.

15. r Examples: When you multiply 2 and 3, you get a *product* of 6. When you multiply −4 and 1, you get a product of −4.

16. m Examples: When you subtract 2 from 3, you get a *difference* of 1. When you subtract −4 from 1, you get a difference of 5.

17. q Examples: When you divide 2 by 3, you get a quotient of $\frac{2}{3}$. When you divide −4 by 1, you get a quotient of −4.

18. o Examples: The absolute value of −3 is 3. The absolute value of 41 is 41.

Drill 2

a. 3^5
b. 3^1
c. 3^6
d. x^8
e. x^4
f. x^{12}
g. $2\sqrt{2}$
h. −4
i. $7\sqrt{3}$
j. $y\sqrt{y}$
k. $-y$
l. $6x\sqrt{y}$

3. A If $3^4 = 9^x$, then $81 = 9^x$. Therefore, $x = 2$. You could also rewrite 3^4 as $3 \times 3 \times 3 \times 3 = 9 \times 9$.

6. C Square both sides of the equation to get $m^2 + 39 = 64$. Solve for m to get $m^2 = 25$, so $m = \pm 5$. Therefore, one possible value for m is 5.

5. B If $(3^x)^3 = 3^{15}$, then by the rules of MADSPM, $3x = 15$, and $x = 5$.

8. D Take the two equations separately, using the rules of MADSPM. If $x^y \times x^6 = x^{54}$, then $y + 6 = 54$, and $y = 48$. If $(x^3)^z = x^9$, then $3z = 9$, and $z = 3$. Now you know that $y = 48$ and $z = 3$, so $y + z = 51$.

7. D Add 3 to both sides to get $\sqrt{s} = 12$. Square both sides of the equation to get $s = 144$.

8. **D** Since x^6 doesn't change form, eliminate (C). y^{-3} can be rewritten as $\dfrac{1}{y^3}$, so eliminate (A). $z^{\frac{1}{2}}$ can be rewritten as $\sqrt{z}$, so eliminate (B).

9. **A** Start with applying the root to the coefficient: $\sqrt[4]{81} = 3$. Therefore, eliminate (C) and (D) because these answer choices have the wrong coefficient. To find the fourth root of an exponent, divide the exponent by 4. Therefore, $\sqrt[4]{81b^3c} = 3b^{\frac{3}{4}}c^{\frac{1}{4}}$. The correct answer is (A).

9. **A** According to the question, the two functions are equal to each other. Therefore, $k^{0.3x} = k^{\frac{Bx}{9}}$, which means that $0.3x = \dfrac{Bx}{9}$. Multiply both sides by 9 to get $2.7x = Bx$. Solve for B to get $2.7 = B$. The correct answer is (A).

10. **B** When you simplify the fractional exponent, you get $\sqrt{x^5} = 8x$. Squaring both sides gives you $x^5 = 64x^2$. You can divide by x^2 on each side to get $x^3 = 64$ (remember your MADSPM rules!). Finally, taking the cube root of both sides gives you $x = 4$, which is (B).

11. **B** With a fractional exponent, the numerator is the power the number or variable is taken to and the denominator represents the root. Therefore, $(3m^2n^{-3})^{\frac{2}{3}} = \sqrt[3]{(3m^2n^{-3})^2}$. When taking a power to another power, multiply the exponents: $\sqrt[3]{(3m^2n^{-3})^2} = \sqrt[3]{9m^4n^{-6}}$. Note, only (B) has $\sqrt[3]{9}$ as part of its answers. Therefore, the correct answer must be (B). Another approach to these can be to plug in numbers for m and n and let the calculator do the hard work. See Chapter 10 for how to use this approach.

16. **D** Start with the left side. Take the cube root of 64 and rewrite: $b\sqrt[3]{64a^2} = 4b\sqrt[3]{a^2}$. Taking the cube root is the same as raising an expression to the $\dfrac{1}{3}$ power, so continue simplifying the left side: $4b\sqrt[3]{a^2} = 4b(a^2)^{\frac{1}{3}}$. Use the rules of MADSPM to multiply the exponents: $4b(a^2)^{\frac{1}{3}} = 4b(a^{\frac{b}{6}})$. Now that the left side is simplified, start working with the right side by squaring each term in the parentheses (be careful!): $(4\sqrt{3}a)^2 = 4^2 \times (\sqrt{3})^2 \times a^2 = 16 \times 3 \times a^2 = 48a^2$. When dealing with exponents, terms that have the same bases also have equal exponents, so set the terms with base a equal to each other to solve for the value of b: $a^{\frac{b}{6}} = a^2$. Solve for b by setting the exponents equal to each other: $\dfrac{b}{6} = 2$, and $b = 12$. An alternate final step could have been to set 48 equal to $4b$ and get $b = 12$.

23.　**A**　Remember MADSPM: when multiplying, add the exponents. Therefore, $16^{y+\frac{1}{2}}=16^y\times16^{\frac{1}{2}}$ and

the fraction is equivalent to $\dfrac{9\times8^y}{5\times16^y\times16^{\frac{1}{2}}}$. Taking a number to the $\dfrac{1}{2}$ power is the same as taking

the square root of the number. Therefore, $\dfrac{9\times8^y}{5\times16^y\times16^{\frac{1}{2}}}=\dfrac{9\times8^y}{5\times16^y\times4}$. Rewrite 16^y as $(2\times8)^y$ or

2^y8^y. Reduce the fraction to get $\dfrac{9}{5\times2^y\times4}$. Simplify the denominator to get $\dfrac{9}{20\times2^y}$. Separate

the fraction to get $\dfrac{9}{20\times2^y}=\dfrac{9}{20}\times\dfrac{1}{2^y}$. Only (A) includes the correct fractions. The correct answer

is (A).

Drill 3

3.　**C**　This is a translation question. Translate the English to math one step at a time to get $x = 3 + 7x$. Now you can subtract $7x$ from both sides to leave you with $-6x = 3$. Divide both sides by -6 and you find that x is equal to 3 divided by -6, which is (C).

2.　**B**　To start to solve the equation for y, cross-multiply to get $7y = (x + 4)(x + 3)$. Use FOIL on the right side to get $7y = x^2 + 3x + 4x + 12$ (the FOIL technique is discussed in Chapter 11). Combine like terms to get $7y = x^2 + 7x + 12$. Divide both sides by 7 to get $y = \dfrac{x^2 + 7x + 12}{7}$. The correct answer is (B).

5.　**D**　Currently Ann has $32 + 18 = 50$ recipes. Given that the book will include up to 90 recipes, Ann can include at most $98 - 50 = 48$ additional recipes. Therefore, $r \le 48$. Solve for r in (A) to get $r \ge 148$. Eliminate (A). Solve for r in (B) to get $r \le 148$. Eliminate (B). In (C), $98 - 50 - r \le 0$, so $48 - r \le 0$. Solve for r to get $-r \le -48$ or $r \ge 48$. Eliminate (C). In (D), $98 - 50 - r \ge 0$, so $48 - r \ge 0$. Solve for r to get $-r \ge -48$ or $r \le 48$. The correct answer is (D).

4.　**C**　Cross-multiply to get $3a \times 6d = 4b \times 5c$. Simplify both sides of the equation to get $18ad = 20bc$. Solve for bc to get $\dfrac{18ad}{20} = bc$. Reduce to get $\dfrac{9ad}{10} = bc$. The correct answer is (C).

28.　**6**　According to the question, Debbie's average daily miles walked are equal to one-hundredth of the square of the number of hours in one day. Given that there are 24 hours in a day, the calculation is $\dfrac{1}{100}(24)^2 = \dfrac{576}{100} = 5.76 \approx 6$. The correct answer is 6.

7. **A** Since the denominators on both sides of the equation are equal, set the numerators equal and solve for p. The equation becomes $2(p - 2) + 2(3 - p) = 2(3p - 6) + 3(6 - 2p)$. Distribute on both sides to get $2p - 4 + 6 - 2p = 6p - 12 + 18 - 6p$. Combine like terms to get $2 = 6$. All the p's disappeared, leaving a statement that is false. This means that there is no solution, and the correct answer is (A).

8. **C** Start with the easier equation and use Process of Elimination. The easier equation is related to the total number of skis and snowboards, $s + b$, the ski resort rented. According to the problem, the following number of skis and snowboards were rented:

	Total Skis and Snowboards rented
Friday	40
Saturday	55
Sunday	85
Total	**180**

Therefore, $s + b = 180$. Eliminate (A) and (D) because neither of these answers includes this equation. The other equation in the set is related to the amount of money the ski resort collected in rental fees. According to the question, the following amounts were collected:

	Rental Fees Collected
Friday	$1,100
Saturday	$1,400
Sunday	$2,100
Total	**$4,600**

Eliminate (B) because the total in the money equation is wrong. The correct answer is (C).

12. **B** First, get rid of the fractions by multiplying both sides of the equation by 21. The equation becomes $\frac{21(m + 9)}{3} + 21(2) = \frac{21(m - 2)}{7} + 21(3)$, which simplifies to $7(m + 9) + 42 = 3(m - 2) + 63$. Multiply it out to get $7m + 63 + 42 = 3m - 6 + 63$ or $7m + 105 = 3m + 57$. Subtract $3m$ and 105 from both sides, resulting in $4m = -48$; then divide both sides by 4. The result is $m = -12$, so the correct answer is (B).

9. **B** First, eliminate the parentheses by multiplying everything out. Be careful of the negative signs. The equation becomes $-4h - 20 = -6 + 3h + 14$. Combine like terms to get $-4h - 20 = 8 + 3h$. Subtract $3h$ from both sides, resulting in $-7h - 20 = 8$. Adding 20 to both sides turns the equation into $-7h = 28$. Divide both sides by -7 to find that $h = -4$; therefore, the correct answer is (B).

23. **C** Let s represent snickerdoodle cookies and c represent cinnamon cookies. Translate the two equations given in the problem as $2s + 7c = 14$ and $8s + 3c = 17.5$. To solve for one of the variables, try to make the coefficient for one of the variables the same and then add or subtract the two resulting

equations from each other to get rid of that variable. In this case, take the first equation and multiply it by -4 to get $-8s - 28c = -56$. Place the two equations on top of each other and add:

$$-8s - 28c = -56.00$$
$$+\ \underline{8s +\ \ 3c =\ \ \ 17.50}$$
$$-25c = -38.50$$

Solve for c to get $c = 1.54$. Plug 1.54 in for c in the first equation to get $2s + 7(1.54) = 14$. Solve for s to get $2s + 10.78 = 14$, or $2s = 3.22$, so $s = 1.61$. Plug 1.61 in for s and 1.54 in for c in the answers to see which answer works. Choice (A) becomes $2(1.61) + 3(1.54) = 8.00$. Solve the left side of the equation to get $3.22 + 4.62 = 8.00$ or $7.84 = 8.00$. This is not true, so eliminate (A). Choice (B) becomes $4(1.61) + 6(1.54) = 16.25$. Solve the left side of the equation to get $6.44 + 9.24 = 16.25$ or $15.68 = 16.25$. Eliminate (B). Choice (C) becomes $6(1.61) + 5(1.54) = 17.36$. Solve the left side of the equation to get $9.66 + 7.70 = 17.36$ or $17.36 = 17.36$. The correct answer is (C).

13.   **A**   The question states that there are infinitely many solutions to the equation. That means any real number should work for x, so plug in an easy number for every x in the equation. Avoid 0 in this case—it may make too many things disappear. If $x = 1$, the equation becomes $10[3(1) + a] - a[4(1) + 2] = 2a[(1) + 4]$. This simplifies to $10(3 + a) - a(4 + 2) = 2a(5)$ or $30 + 10a - 6a = 10a$. Combine like terms to get $30 + 4a = 10a$; then subtract $4a$ from both sides, resulting in $30 = 6a$. Therefore, $a = 5$, which matches (A).

25.   **A**   Let e = eggs and f = cups of flour. The two equations that are given in the problem are $5e + 4f = 5.50$ and $9e + 8f = 10.50$. Whenever there are two equations with the same two variables, think simultaneous equations. The goal with simultaneous equations is to create a common coefficient for one of the variables and then add or subtract the two equations from each other to get rid of that variable. In this case, multiply the first equation through by 2 to get $10e + 8f = 11.00$. Place the two equations on top of each other and subtract them:

$$10e + 8f = 11.00$$
$$-\ \underline{(9e + 8f = 10.50)}$$
$$e\ \ \ \ \ \ \ = 0.50$$

Therefore, $10e = 0.50 \times 10 = 5.00$. The correct answer is (A).

Drill 4

a.   6

b.   6

c. -1

d. -1

e.   1

f. $6\sqrt{2}$

g. $(0, 1)$

2. **B** The slope-intercept form of the equation of a line is $y = mx + b$, where m is the slope and b is the y-intercept. So the slope of the line given by the first equation is 6. To find the slope of a perpendicular line, you would take the negative reciprocal. So $c = -\dfrac{1}{6}$, which is (B).

6. **B** Parallel lines have equal slopes. Therefore, because the line in the graph has a negative slope, the correct answer will also have a negative slope. Eliminate (C) and (D) right away because they have positive slopes. Now find the exact slope of the line shown, and compare it with the remaining answers to see which line equation has the same slope. The slope of a line is determined by the equation $\dfrac{y_2 - y_1}{x_2 - x_1}$. Calculate the slope of the line shown to get $\dfrac{-1 - 0}{0 - (-3)} = \dfrac{-1}{3}$. The answers are all in the slope-intercept form of an equation, $y = mx + b$, where m = slope. Only (B) has a slope of $\dfrac{-1}{3}$, so the correct answer is (B).

3. **A** The slope-intercept form of the equation of a line is $y = mx + b$, where m is the slope and b is the y-intercept. So you would manipulate this equation to solve for y. Subtracting $2x$ from both sides of the equation and then dividing both sides by 3 gives you $y = -\dfrac{2}{3}x + 4$, so the y-intercept is 4.

12. **D** The x-intercept of a line is where the line crosses the x-axis. The line in the graph has a positive x-intercept, so you can eliminate (A) and (B). To find the x-intercept, first find the slope of the line and then use one of the points given to determine the value of x. The slope of a line is determined by the equation $\dfrac{y_2 - y_1}{x_2 - x_1}$. The slope of the line shown is $\dfrac{-4 - (-2)}{-6 - (-2)} = \dfrac{-2}{-4} = \dfrac{1}{2}$. At the x-intercept, $y = 0$, so the coordinates for the x-intercept are $(x, 0)$. To find x, plug point $(x, 0)$ and $(-2, -2)$ into the slope equation and solve for x: $\dfrac{-2 - 0}{-2 - x} = \dfrac{1}{2}$, so $\dfrac{-2}{-2 - x} = \dfrac{1}{2}$. Cross-multiply to get $-2 - x = -4$, or $-x = -2$. Therefore, $x = 2$, and the correct answer is (D).

7. **D** Look for an answer that has the same y-intercept and slope as the line shown in the graph. In the line shown, the point at which the line crosses the y-axis is 1, so the y-intercept is 1. Use the two points on the line—$(0, 1)$ and $(8, 0)$—to calculate the slope: $slope = \dfrac{y_2 - y_1}{x_2 - x_1} = \dfrac{0 - 1}{8 - 0} = -\dfrac{1}{8}$. Rewrite the answers in the slope-intercept form of the equations, $y = mx + b$, where m is the slope of the line and b is the y-intercept. In (A), the equation becomes $2y = x - 8$, or $y = \dfrac{1}{2}x - 4$. The slope of this line is $\dfrac{1}{2}$, and the y-intercept is -4, so eliminate (A). In (B), the equation becomes $4y = -x - 8$, or $y = -\dfrac{1}{4}x - 2$. The slope of this line is $-\dfrac{1}{4}$, and the y-intercept is -2, so eliminate (B).

In (C), the equation becomes $8y = 3x + 8$, or $y = \dfrac{3}{8}x + 1$. The slope of this line is $\dfrac{3}{8}$, and the y-intercept is 1, so eliminate (C). Choice (D) is the only one left, so it must be correct. In (D), the equation becomes $8y = -x + 8$, or $y = -\dfrac{1}{8}x + 1$. The slope of this line is $-\dfrac{1}{8}$ and the y-intercept is 1, which is the same as the slope and y-intercept of the line shown in the graph.

14   **B**   The slope of a line is determined by the equation $\dfrac{y_2 - y_1}{x_2 - x_1}$. Therefore, the slope of the line shown can be calculated as follows: $\dfrac{-\dfrac{17}{3} - \dfrac{16}{3}}{\dfrac{11}{2} - \left(-\dfrac{7}{2}\right)} = \dfrac{-\dfrac{33}{3}}{\dfrac{18}{2}} = \dfrac{-33}{3} \times \dfrac{2}{18} = -\dfrac{11}{9}$. The correct answer is (B).

15.   **A**   The line shown crosses the y-axis at -2; this point is also known as the y-intercept. The answers are all in the slope-intercept form, $y = mx + b$, where m is the slope and b is the y-intercept. You can eliminate (B) right away because the y-intercept in (B) is 2, not -2. Next, calculate the slope of the line with the two given points. The slope of a line is determined by the equation $\dfrac{y_2 - y_1}{x_2 - x_1}$. Therefore, the slope of the line shown can be calculated as follows: $\dfrac{2a - a}{\dfrac{9}{2}a - 3a} = \dfrac{a}{\dfrac{3}{2}a} = \dfrac{1}{\dfrac{3}{2}} = \dfrac{2}{3}$. The only remaining answer that has a slope equal to $\dfrac{2}{3}$ is (A), so that is the correct answer.

17.   **32**   Set the two equations equal to each other to get $4x^2 - 6x + 4 = 2x + 4$. Set the equation to 0 to get $4x^2 - 8x = 0$. Divide both sides of the equation by 4 to get $x^2 - 2x = 0$. Factor x out of the equation to get $x(x - 2) = 0$. Therefore, the two possible values for x are $x = 0$ and $x = 2$. Plug both of these values into the second equation to find the corresponding y-values. If $x = 0$, then $y = 2(0) + 4 = 4$. If $x = 2$, then $y = 2(2) + 4 = 8$. Therefore, the product of the two possible values of y is $4 \times 8 = 32$. The correct answer is 32.

Drill 5

28. 0.833 or $\dfrac{5}{6}$

        Take the number of contracted users, 225, and divide it by the total number of users in 2008, 270:

        $\dfrac{225}{270} = 0.8\overline{33}$ or $\dfrac{5}{6}$.

14. **625** Because $5x^2 = 125$, you know that $x^2 = 25$ and $x = -5$ or 5. Since you can grid in only positive numbers, assume $x = 5$. Therefore, $5x^3 = 5 \times 125 = 625$.

15. $\frac{5}{12}$ First, simplify inside the parentheses. Be careful with the negative signs: $z = 5 - 5(5z - 2 + 2z)$ becomes $z = 5 - 5(7z - 2)$. Multiply it out to get $z = 5 - 35z + 10$, or $z = 15 - 35z$. Adding $35z$ to both sides results in $36z = 15$, so $z = \frac{15}{36}$. This won't fit in the grid-in box, so reduce the fraction to make it is small enough to fit in the space provided. Divide the numerator and denominator of the fraction by 3. The correct answer is $\frac{5}{12}$.

29. 9   Start by squaring both sides of the equation to get $\left(5 - \sqrt{z}\right)\left(5 - \sqrt{z}\right) = z - 5$. Expand the left side of the equation to get $25 - 10\sqrt{z} + z = z - 5$. Subtract z from both sides to get $25 - 10\sqrt{z} = -5$. Solve for z to get $-10\sqrt{z} = -30$, so $\sqrt{z} = 3$. Square both sides of the equation to get $z = 9$. The correct answer is 9.

16. 6   Whenever you have two equations with the same two variables, think simultaneous equations. The goal with simultaneous equations is to create a common coefficient for one of the variables and then add or subtract the two equations from each other to get rid of that variable. To get rid of a, multiply the first equation by 7 to get $21a + 14b = 259$ and multiply the second equation by -3 to get $-21a - 12b = -255$. Place the two equations on top of each other and subtract them from each other.

$$
\begin{array}{r}
21a + 14b = 259 \\
\underline{-21a - 12b = -255} \\
2b = 4
\end{array}
$$

Solve for b to get $b = 2$. Therefore, $b^2 + 6b - 10 = 2^2 + 6(2) - 10 = 4 + 12 - 10 = 6$. The correct answer is 6.

30. 5   The conversion from Fahrenheit to Celsius on the first day can be calculated as follows: $\frac{5}{9}(95 - 32) = \frac{5}{9}(63) = 35$. The conversion from Fahrenheit to Celsius on the second day can be calculated as follows: $\frac{5}{9}(86 - 32) = \frac{5}{9}(54) = 30$. Therefore, the difference between the forecasted temperatures in degrees Celsius is $35 - 30 = 5$. The correct answer is 5.

31. 350   Set up an equation using the information from the question. Moriah's portion is compared with Mathew's portion, so call Mathew's portion m. Moriah's portion is 30 less than twice m, or $2m - 30$. Together, they paid \$540, so the equation is $m + 2m - 30 = 540$, or $3m - 30 = 540$. Add 30 to both sides to get $3m = 570$, so $m = 190$. That was Mathew's portion, and the question asks for Moriah's portion, which is $2(190) - 30 = 380 - 30 = 350$. The correct answer is 350.

17. 100   Let x be the amount of Solution 2 that Kimberly adds to Solution 1. Therefore, the total amount of Solution 3 Kimberly creates is $50 + x$. The amount of sugar in the portion of the mixture that came

from Solution 1 can be calculated as $50 \times 0.25 = 12.5$, and sugar from Solution 2 can be calculated as $x \times 0.10$. Therefore, the total amount of sugar in Solution 3 can be calculated as $12.5 + 0.1x$. Since Solution 3 has a 15% sugar content, this amount of sugar is equal to 15% of the ounces of Solution 3, or $0.15(50 + x)$. To solve for x, set up the following equation: $12.5 + 0.1x = 0.15(50 + x)$. Distribute the 0.15 on the right side of the equation to get $12.5 + 0.1x = 7.5 + 0.15x$, then $5 + 0.1x = 0.15x$, and finally $5 = 0.05x$. Therefore, $x = 100$ ounces of Solution 2, so the correct answer is 100.

CHAPTER 10

Drill 1

5. **B** Whenever the question includes variables, Plug In. If $m = 10$, then David pays $\$25 + \$0.05(10) = \$25.50$. Now plug in 10 for m in the answers to see which answer is equal to the target number of $\$25.50$. In (A), $25 + 1.05(10) = \$35.50$. Because this is not equal to the target number, eliminate (A). In (B), $25 + 0.05(10) = \$25.50$. This is equal to the target number. Leave (B), but check the remaining answers just in case. In (C), $0.05(25 + 10) = \$1.75$, and in (D), $1.05(25 + 10) = 36.75$. Neither of these is the target number, so eliminate (C) and (D). Therefore, the correct answer is (B).

4. **D** Pick numbers for a, b, and c such that $a = \dfrac{b}{c^2}$. If you pick $4 = \dfrac{16}{2^2}$, the question becomes, what is $\dfrac{1}{b^2}$ or $\dfrac{1}{16^2}$? The answer is $\dfrac{1}{256}$. When you work through all of the answer choices using $a = 4$, $b = 16$, and $c = 2$, which choice says this? Choice (D) does.

11. **D** Whenever there are variables in the problem and in the answer choices, Plug In. If $w = 20$, then Luciano's cup has $20 - 2 = 18$ ounces at the end of day 1. At the end of 7 days, Luciano's cup would have $18 - 8 = 10$ ounces. After 11 days, Luciano's cup would hold $10 - 5 = 5$ ounces. Plug in 20 for w in the answer choices to see which answer is equal to the target number of 5. Choice (A) becomes $\dfrac{20 - 2}{8} = \dfrac{18}{8} = 2.25$. This does not match the target number of 5, so eliminate (A). Choice (B) becomes $\dfrac{20 - 2}{2} - 10 = \dfrac{18}{2} - 10 = 9 - 10 = -1$. Eliminate (B). Choice (C) becomes $\left(\dfrac{1}{2}\right)(20) - 10 = 10 - 10 = 0$. Eliminate (C). Choice (D) becomes $\dfrac{20 - 10}{2} = \dfrac{10}{2} = 5$. This matches the target number; therefore, the correct answer is (D).

7. **A** Pick a number for p. How about 2? Now the problem reads $\dfrac{\frac{1}{8}}{2(2)} = \dfrac{1}{32}$. When you plug $p = 2$ into the answers, (A) turns out to be right.

9.　**C**　Whenever there are variables in the problem and in the answer choices, think Plugging In. Try using $c = 46$. This would mean the student got 46 questions correct and 4 questions wrong. The student's score would be $46(1) - 4\left(\dfrac{1}{4}\right) = 46 - 1 = 45$. Plug 46 in for c in the answer choices to see which answer equals 45, the target number. Choice (A) becomes $S = 50 - 0.25(46) = 50 - 11.5 = 38.5$. Eliminate (A). Choice (B) becomes $S = 50 - 0.75(46) = 50 - 34.5 = 15.5$. Eliminate (B). Choice (C) becomes $46 - 0.25(50 - 46) = 46 - 0.25(4) = 46 - 1 = 45$. Keep (C), but check (D) just in case it also works. Choice (D) becomes $46 - 0.75(50 - 46) = 46 - 0.75(4) = 46 - 3 = 43$. Eliminate (D). The correct answer is (C).

18.　**D**　Variables in the answer choices? Absolutely! So plug in your own numbers. For x (Jodi's account), plug in $18 (hey, who said Jodi had to be rich?). With $18 in her account, $\dfrac{1}{6}$ for rent is $3 and the car payment is also $3. Subtract that from the $18, and Jodi has $12 left in her account. Now plug in for y (the amount Jodi deposits); make that $8, bringing her account balance to $20. Well, she now purchases a set of knives for $10 ($\dfrac{1}{2}$ the amount in her account) and has $10 left. Go through all of the answer choices, using $x = 18$ and $y = 8$, and see which one gives you $10. The only one that works is (D).

12.　**B**　Inequalities with an absolute value can be tough to set up; there are two parts, and it's not always easy to remember how to deal with the negative values. Instead, try plugging in some easy numbers. Start with $y = 0$. The inequality becomes $2|0 - 5| < 24$ or $2(5) < 24$. That's true, so 0 works. Move up to $y = 1$, which results in $2|4 - 5| < 24$ or $2(1) < 24$. That's true, too, so keep going. Plugging in $y = 2$ results in $2(3) < 24$, $y = 3$ results in $2(7) < 24$, and $y = 4$ results in $2(9) < 24$. All these are true, but trying $y = 5$ results in $2(15) < 24$, which isn't true. So 4 is the greatest integer that works. Now try negative numbers. If $y = -1$, the inequality is $2(9) < 24$, which is true, but if $y = -2$, the inequality is $2(13) < 24$. Therefore, -1 is the smallest integer that works. The integers that satisfy the inequality are $-1, 0, 1, 2, 3$, and 4, and their sum is 9, (B).

29.　**92.3**　You don't know how many students are in the incoming freshman class, so Plug In. Because you're taking percentages of the class, make the total number of students 100. That means that there are 15 left-handed students in the class. There are also 65 female students and 35 male students. If $\dfrac{2}{3}$ of the left-handed students are male, then $\dfrac{2}{3} \times 15 = 10$ of the left-handed students are male, leaving 5 female left-handed students. If 5 of the 65 female students are left-handed, then the other 60 female students are right-handed. To find the percentage of female students who are right-handed, divide: $\frac{60}{65} = 0.923 = 92.3\%$. Remember to multiply a decimal by 100 to get the equivalent percentage.

Drill 2

3.   **D**   Start with (B). If $n = 3$, then the equation becomes $2(3 + 5) = 3(3 - 2) + 8$. Work the equation: $2(8) = 3(1) + 8$; $16 = 11$. This isn't true, so eliminate (B). You might not know whether you need a bigger or smaller number, so try a larger number. With (C), make $n = 4$. Now work the equation: $2(4 + 5) = 3(4 - 2) + 8$; $2(9) = 3(2) + 8$; $18 = 14$. Not quite; eliminate (C). Try (D): $2(8 + 5) = 3(8 - 2) + 8$; $2(13) = 3(6) + 8$; $26 = 26$. This works, so pick (D).

8.   **C**   Start by trying (C), 3, for x. Does $3^5 = 243$? Yes! So the answer is (C).

7.   **C**   Whenever there are numbers in the answer choices, think Plugging In the Answers. Start with one of the middle answers. Plug the numbers from (B) into the first equation to get $2(-3) - (-2) > -3$. Simplify the left side of the equation to get $-6 + 2 > -3$, or $-4 > -3$. Because this statement is not true, eliminate (B). It may not be clear which direction to go next; if so, just pick a direction. Plug the numbers from (C) into the first equation to get $2(-1) - (-1) > -3$. Simplify the left side of the equation to get $-2 + 1 > -3$, or $-1 > -3$. Because this is a true statement, plug the same numbers into the second equation to get $4(-1) + (-1) < 5$. Simplify the left side of the equation to get $-4 - 1 < 5$, or $-5 < 5$. Because this is a true statement, plug in the values from (C) into the last equation to get $-1 > -6$. Because the values given in (C) work in all three equations, the correct answer is (C).

10.   **D**   If you try plugging in (C), $\frac{1}{4}$, for x, the equation becomes $\frac{6}{4} + 4 = 5$, which is false. If you try plugging in (D), $\frac{1}{2}$, for x, the equation becomes $\frac{12}{4} + 2 = 5$, which is true. Therefore, the correct answer is (D).

20.   **A**   Whenever there are variables in the question and numbers in the answer choices, think Plugging In the Answers. Start with one of the middle answers. In (B), $v = -3$. Plug $v = -3$ into the second equation because it is the easier of the two equations, and solve for u. The resulting equation becomes $2(-3) = 7 + 5u$. Solve for u to get $-6 = 7 + 5u$, $-13 = 5u$, and $u = -\frac{13}{5}$. Now, use the same numbers for u and v in the first equation to see if that equation works. Plugging in $u = -\frac{13}{5}$ and $v = -3$, the first equation becomes $-\frac{5}{7} - \frac{11}{7}\left(-\frac{13}{5}\right) = -(-3)$. Solve both sides of the equation to get $-\frac{5}{7} + \frac{143}{35} = 3$. This is not true, so eliminate (B). It may not be clear which direction to go, so pick a direction. In (A), $v = -4$. Plug in $v = -4$ using the second equation and solve for u. The

resulting equation becomes $2(-4) = 7 + 5u$. Solve for u to get $-8 = 7 + 5u$, or $-15 = 5u$. Therefore, $u = -3$. Now, use the same numbers for u and v in the first equation to see if that equation works. Plugging in $u = -3$ and $v = -4$, the first equation becomes $-\frac{5}{7} - \frac{11}{7}(-3) = -(-4)$. Solve both sides of the equation to get $-\frac{5}{7} + \frac{33}{7} = 4$, or $\frac{28}{7} = 4$. Because this is a true statement, the correct answer is (A).

25. C Whenever the question includes variables and the answers are numbers, think Plugging In the Answers. According to the question, the alloy needs to contain between $10(0.1) = 1$ kg and $10(0.15) = 1.5$ kg of titanium. Choose an x-value that fits into the range of each of the answers to see which answer will create an alloy with an acceptable amount of titanium. Start with one of the answers in the middle. For (B), let $x = 3$. This means the resulting alloy would contain $10 - 3 = 7$ kg of 5% titanium alloy. The amount of titanium in the mixture can be calculated as $3(0.2) + 7(0.05) = 0.6 + 0.35 = 0.95$ kg, which is not enough titanium. Eliminate both (B) and (A), because (A) would give you an even smaller amount of titanium. For (C), let $x = 3.5$. This means the resulting alloy would contain $10 - 3.5 = 6.5$ kg of 5% titanium alloy. The amount of titanium in the mixture can be calculated as $3.5(0.2) + 6.5(0.05) = 0.7 + 0.325 = 1.025$ kg, which is an acceptable amount of titanium. The correct answer is (C).

Drill 3

a. 90

b. 320

c. 6

d. $x = 8$

e. 5

f. 3

g. 10

h. 120%

i. 108

j. 10%

k. $\frac{2,600}{18,600} =$ approximately 14%

The amount of money in a savings account after m months is modeled by the function $f(m) = 1,000(1.01)^m$.

l. $1,000

m. 1%

n. 40

o. 1.5

p. 5 kPa

2. **D** This question is asking us to compare pecks and bushels, so let's make a proportion: $\dfrac{10 \text{ pecks}}{2.5 \text{ bushels}} = \dfrac{x \text{ pecks}}{4 \text{ bushels}}$. Then we can cross-multiply and solve for x, which results in $x = 16$.

28. $\dfrac{5}{6}$ Probability is defined as $0 \le \dfrac{want}{total} \le 1$, so start by identifying the values for the numerator and denominator. The question is asking for the probability that a user in 2008 is a contracted user. Reference the 2-way table to find that, for 2008, there were 225 contracted users out of 270 total users. Set up the fraction and reduce: $\dfrac{225}{270} = \dfrac{5}{6} = 0.83$.

12. **B** Whenever there are variables in the question and answer choices, think Plugging In. If $t = 12$, then the air squad was able to reduce the size of the fire by $10 \times 0.07 = 0.7$ acres, and the area of the forest still on fire is $10 - 0.7 = 9.3$. Plug 12 in for t in the answer choices to see which answer equals the target number of 9.3. Choice (A) becomes $10 - (0.93)^{12 \times 12} = 10 - (0.93)^{144} \approx 10$. This does not match the target number, so eliminate (A). Choice (B) becomes $10 \times (1 - 0.07)^{\frac{12}{12}} = 10 \times (0.93)^{1} = 9.3$. Keep (B), but check the remaining answers just in case one of them works. Choice (C) becomes $10 - 93^{12 \times 12} = 10 - 93^{144}$, which is a very small negative number, and (D) becomes $(0.93)^{10 - 12(12)} = (0.93)^{10 - 144} = (0.93)^{-134} = 16,721.872$. Eliminate (C) and (D). The correct answer is (B).

15. **C** Consider each statement one at a time. The last two tests have an average of 90. If the student scored the same on both tests, his score would be 90 on each of those two tests. The two tests have a total of 180 points (2×90), so he could have also scored 0 on one test and 180 on the other test, or anything in between. No matter what, there's at least one test on which the student scored more than 85, so I must be true. Eliminate (B) and (D). Now you only need consider II (because there's no option remaining which includes III). You already determined that the last two tests have a total of 180 points. If the first three tests were an average of 80, then the total for those tests would be $3 \times 80 = 240$. The total points over all 5 tests would be $180 + 240 = 420$, and the average would be $420 \div 5 = 84$, which is less than 85. II is true, so choose (C).

19. **C** First, you need to calculate how far Maggie runs. For the first five minutes, she runs 1,200 meters before turning around and returning home. She then runs 2,100 more meters after retrieving her iPod. Therefore, she runs a total of 4,500 meters ($1,200 + 1,200 + 2,100$). Because she was at home for 3 minutes, the total time she spent running was 12 minutes. The question asks for speed in meters per second, so convert the 12 minutes to seconds by multiplying by 60. To find the speed, simply divide the 4,500 meters by the 720 seconds to get (C).

28. **45** If Marcia types 18 pages per hour, and David can type 14 pages per hour, then together they will be able to type $18 + 14$, or 32 pages per hour. To see what fraction of an hour it will take them to type 24 pages, set up a proportion: $\dfrac{32 \text{ pages}}{1 \text{ hour}} = \dfrac{24 \text{ pages}}{x \text{ hours}}$.

If you solve for x, you can see that they can type 24 pages in .75 of an hour. But that isn't the answer! The question asks for the answer in minutes. Three-quarters of an hour is equal to 45 minutes, so the answer is 45.

22. C To find percent difference, use the equation percent change = $\dfrac{\text{difference}}{\text{original}} \times 100$. Here, because you want to find what percent greater the number of registered Republicans who plan to vote for Candidate B is than the number of registered Democrats who plan to vote for Candidate B, the original will be the smaller number (the Democrats). This makes the equation: $\dfrac{70-56}{56} \times 100 =$ 25%, which matches (C).

25. C Whenever there are variables in the question and in the answer choices, think Plugging In.

Because the problem is dealing with percentages, make $x = 100$. Remember the distance formula,

distance = rate × time, or $d = r \times t$. Therefore, the time it takes Everett's parents can be calcu-

lated as $200 = 45 \times t$, so $t = 4.\overline{4}$. If Everett is driving at a speed 100% greater than his par-

ent's speed, then he is driving at 90 mph. Therefore, Everett's time can be calculated as follows:

$200 = 90 \times t$, so Everett's $t = 2.\overline{2}$. The difference in the amount of time it takes Everett versus his

parents is $4.\overline{4} - 2.\overline{2} = 2.\overline{2}$. Plug 100 in for x in each of the answers to see which one is equal to the

target of $2.\overline{2}$. Choice (A) becomes $\dfrac{-2(100)}{45\left(1+\dfrac{100}{100}\right)} = \dfrac{-200}{45(2)}$. Choice (A) is clearly a negative value, so

eliminate it. Choice (B) becomes $\dfrac{2(100)}{45\left(1-\dfrac{100}{100}\right)} = \dfrac{200}{45(0)}$. Because 0 cannot be in the denominator of

a fraction, (B) is impossible; eliminate it. Choice (C) becomes $\dfrac{2(100)}{45\left(1+\dfrac{100}{100}\right)} = \dfrac{200}{45(2)} = \dfrac{200}{90} = 2.\overline{2}$.

This matches the target so keep (C), but check (D) just in case it also works. Choice (D) becomes

$$\frac{45\left(\dfrac{100}{100}\right)}{200\left(1+\dfrac{100}{100}\right)} = \frac{45}{200(2)} = \frac{45}{400} = 0.1125.$$ Eliminate (D). The correct answer is (C).

27. **A** Start by examining (A). To determine how many people used both forms of transportation in each city, use the Group Equation: Total = Group 1 + Group 2 + Neither − Both. For Boston, this becomes 7,556 = 5,281 + 3,504 + 1,025 − B. Combine like terms: 7,556 = 9,810 − B. Subtract 9,810 from both sides: −2,254 = −B. Divide both sides by −1 to find that 2,254 people use both forms in Boston. Repeat the same for New York: 7,789 = 2,476 + 5,738 + 1,459 − B; 7,789 = 9,673 − B; −1,884 = −B, so 1,884 people in New York use both forms of public transportation. Finally, determine if 20% more people checked both in Boston by using the percent change formula: percent change = $\dfrac{\text{difference}}{\text{original}} \times 100$, so $\dfrac{2,254 - 1,884}{1,884} \times 100 = 19.7\%$. This is approximately 20%, so choose (A).

CHAPTER 11

Drill 1

3. **C** The x-intercepts are where the graph crosses the x-axis. At those points, the corresponding y-values are 0. To find the x-intercepts, factor the equation and set each factor equal to zero. In the answer choices, (C) is already fully factored such that it is easy to determine that the x-intercepts are at −3 and −5. Therefore, the correct answer is (C).

4. **C** Whenever there are variables in the question and in the answers, think Plugging In. If $m = 10$, then Monster Truck Inc. receives a down payment of $3,200 plus 10 months' worth of monthly payments. This can be calculated as 3,200 + 10(380) = 3,200 + 3,800 = $7,000. Plug in 10 for m in the answers to see which function equals 7,000. Choice (A) becomes $f(m) = 380 + 3,200(10) = 380 + 32,000 = 32,380$. Eliminate (A). Choice (B) becomes $f(m) = 3,200 + 36(10) = 3,200 + 360 = 3,560$. Eliminate (B). Choice (C) becomes $f(m) = 3,200 + 380(10) = 3,200 + 3,800 = 7,000$. Keep (C), but check (D) just in case it also works. Choice (D) becomes $f(m) = 10,480 − 380(10) = 10,480 − 3,800 = 6,680$. Eliminate (D). The correct answer is (C).

15. **3** Since the problem tells you that $f(a) = 10$, and that $f(x) = x^2 - x + 4$, you can plug a into the function for x so $f(a) = a^2 - a + 4$, and $10 = a^2 - a + 4$. Now you need to factor to solve for a. If you subtract 10 from both sides of the equation, you get $a^2 - a - 6 = 0$, which you can factor as $(a - 3)$ $(a + 2) = 0$. The value of a could be 3 or –2, but since the question tells you that a is non-negative, the value of a must be 3.

9. **C** The equation for the number of bonus points when the purchases are increased by 4 can be written as $a(p + 4) + 7$. According to the question, this sum will be 25 greater than $ap + 7$. Therefore, the following equation can be constructed to solve for a: $ap + 7 + 25 = a(p + 4) + 7$ or $ap + 32 = a(p + 4) + 7$. Distribute the a on the right side of the equation to get $ap + 32 = ap + 4a + 7$. Subtract ap from both sides of the equation to get $32 = 4a + 7$. Solve for a to get $25 = 4a$, so $6.25 = a$. The correct answer is (C).

21. **D** Negative exponents mean to take the reciprocal of the positive exponent. For example, $y^{-2} = \dfrac{1}{y^2}$, and $2^{-3} = \dfrac{1}{2^3}$. For fractional exponents, the denominator tells you what root of the number to take and the numerator acts as a normal exponent. So, $f(x)$ is $\dfrac{1}{\sqrt[3]{x^2}}$. First, find $f(8)$: $\dfrac{1}{\sqrt[3]{8^2}} = \dfrac{1}{\sqrt[3]{64}} = \dfrac{1}{4}$. Next, find $f(3)$: $\dfrac{1}{\sqrt[3]{3^2}} = \dfrac{1}{\sqrt[3]{9}}$. Put these values in for $\dfrac{f(8)}{f(3)}$. So, $\dfrac{\frac{1}{4}}{\frac{1}{\sqrt[3]{9}}} = \dfrac{1}{4} \div \dfrac{1}{\sqrt[3]{9}} = \dfrac{1}{4} \times \sqrt[3]{9} = \dfrac{\sqrt[3]{9}}{4}$. Remember to look at the answer choices so you don't keep trying to simplify when there's no need to.

23. **B** Set the more straightforward equation equal to 0 by subtracting 100 from each side to get $0 = x^2 - 24x + 44$. Factor the equation to get $0 = (x - 22)(x - 2)$. Solve for x to get $x = 2$ or 22. These numbers represent the hours since midnight, and 2 hours after midnight would be 2 A.M. That is not a choice. 22 hours after midnight is 10 P.M. Therefore, the correct answer is (B).

12. **B** Remember that the basic function equation states that $y = f(x)$. Given that the question states that f is a linear function, the table shows that 3 points on the line are $(-1, 2)$, (j, j), and $(5, -6)$. Use the slope formula to find the value of j. The slope formula states that given two points on a line $slope = \dfrac{y_2 - y_1}{x_2 - x_1}$. Given the two known points $(-1, 2)$ and $(5, -6)$, the slope can be calculated as follows: $\dfrac{-6 - 2}{5 - (-1)} = \dfrac{-8}{6} = \dfrac{-4}{3}$. Next plug the points (j, j) and $(-1, 2)$ into the slope formula to find

$j: \dfrac{2-j}{-1-j} = \dfrac{-4}{3}$. Cross-multiply to get $-4(-1 - j) = 3(2 - j)$. Distribute the -4 and the 3 to get

$4 + 4j = 6 - 3j$. Solve for j to get $4 + 7j = 6$, then $7j = 2$, and finally $j = \dfrac{2}{7}$. The correct answer is (B).

30. **148** Make $x = 12$ in each function: $f(12) = (12)^2 - 4 = 140$ and $g(12) = -\dfrac{1}{3}(12) - 4 = -8$. Subtract: $140 - (-8) = 148$.

31. **8** Perpendicular lines have negative reciprocal slopes, so the slope of $h(x)$ is 3. You can use the point $(-12, 0)$ to determine the y-intercept by first writing $h(x)$ in y-intercept form and solving for b: $h(x) = 3x + b$; plugging in $(-12, 0)$ gives you $0 = 3(-12) + b$. Multiply and you get $0 = -36 + b$. Add 36 to both sides and you find $b = 36$, so $h(x) = 3x + 36$. You want a point of intersection between $h(x)$ and $f(x)$, so put the functions equal to one another: $x^2 - 4 = 3x + 36$. This is a quadratic equation, so set it equal to zero: $x^2 - 3x - 40 = 0$. Factors of 40 that have a difference of 3 are 5 and 8, so this quadratic factors to $(x + 5)(x - 8) = 0$. The solutions are therefore $x = -5, 8$. Because you cannot input negative numbers into the grid, the answer is 8.

Drill 2

3. **A** The initial height of the projectile corresponds to the moment before it is launched. At that point, no time has passed, and so $t = 0$. Therefore, the correct answer is (A).

4. **B** You could solve this one by expanding the squared binomial, setting it equal to zero, factoring, and solving, but look for a faster way. When the question asks for a specific value and there are numbers in the answer choices, think Plugging In the Answers. In (A), if $t = -9$, the equation becomes $12 - (-9 + 2)^2 = 3$ or $12 - (-7)^2 = 3$. This becomes $12 - 49 = 3$, which is not true, so eliminate (A). In (B), if $t = -5$, $12 - (-5 + 2)^2 = 3$ or $12 - (-3)^2 = 3$. This becomes $12 - 9 = 3$, which is true, so (B) is the correct answer.

6. **B** The equations in the answer choices are factored, making it easy to see the roots. The correct answer will have roots at -3 and 1, as shown on the graph. For (A), the roots are $x - 3 = 0$ or $x = 3$ and $x + 1 = 0$ or $x = -1$, which are the right numbers but the wrong signs. For (B), though, the roots are -3 and 1, so (B) is the correct answer. Another approach would be to plug the given points into the answer choices to see which one works for both points.

9. **A** Whenever the question and the answers include variables, think Plugging In. If $x = 3$ and $y = 2$, then Aubri's score can be calculated as $3^4 - 2^4 = 81 - 16 = 65$. Plug 3 in for x and 2 in for y in the answers to see which answer equals the target number of 65. Choice (A) becomes $(3 + 2)(3 - 2)(3^2 + 2^2)(5)(1)(9 + 4) = (5)(1)(13) = 65$. Keep (A), but check the remaining answers just in case one of them also works. Choice (B) becomes $(3 + 2)^2(3^2 + 2^2) = (5)^2(9 + 4) = (25)(13) = 325$. Eliminate (B). Choice (C) becomes $(3 - 2)^2(3^2 + 2^2) = (1)^2(9 + 4) = (1)(13) = 13$. Eliminate (C). Choice (D) becomes $(3 + 2)(3 - 2)(3^2 - 2^2) = (5)(1)(9 - 4) = (5)(1)(5) = 25$. Eliminate (D). The correct answer is (A).

10. C   Plug –5 in for x and 2 in for y in the answers to see which equation contains the point (–5, 2). Choice (A) becomes $2 = (-5 + 5)^2 - 2$. Solve the right side of the equation to get $2 = (0)^2 - 2$, or $2 = 0 - 2$. Because this statement is not true, eliminate (A). Choice (B) becomes $2 = (-5 - 5)^2 - 2$. Solve the right side of the equation to get $2 = (-10)^2 - 2$, or $2 = 100 - 2$. Because this statement is not true, eliminate (B). Choice (C) becomes $2 = (-5 + 5)^2 + 2$. Solve the right side of the equation to get $2 = 2(0)^2 + 2$, or $2 = 0 + 2$. This statement is true so keep (C), but check (D) just in case. Choice (D) becomes $2 = 2(-5 - 5)^2 + 2$. Solve the right side of the equation to get $2 = 2(-10)^2 + 2$, then $2 = 2(100) + 2$, and finally $2 = 200 + 2$. This statement is not true, so eliminate (D). The correct answer is therefore (C).

14. 3   The maximum profit will occur at the vertex of the parabola. The equation is in vertex form, so the vertex is (3, 2,000). The x-coordinate is the price, so the shop should charge \$3. If you forget the form, you can use a sort of plugging in. To maximize its profit, the donut shop needs to make the negative part of the equation, $-4(x - 3)^2$, either positive or 0. Because $(x - 3)^2$ is always either positive or 0, it is not possible to make $-4(x - 3)^2$ positive. Therefore, the maximum profits will occur when $-4(x - 3)^2 = 0$. Solve for x by dividing both sides by -4 to get $(x - 3)^2 = 0$. Solve for x to get $x = 3$. The correct answer is 3.

23. B   Whenever there are variables in the question and numbers in the answers, think Plugging In the Answers. In (A), $c = 33$ and the equation becomes $x^2 + 24x + 33 = (x + 9)(x + p)$. This means that 33 would equal $9p$ once the right side was multiplied out. Eliminate (A) since 33 is not divisible by 9. In (B), $c = 135$ and the equation becomes $x^2 + 24x + 135 = (x + 9)(x + p)$. Divide 135 by 9 to get $x^2 + 24x + 135 = (x + 9)(x + 15)$. Test whether this is the right answer by using FOIL to expand $(x + 9)(x + 15)$ to get $x^2 + 24x + 135$. The middle term is in fact $24x$, and the correct answer is therefore (B).

26. B   Use Process of Elimination to solve this question. According to the question, the correct equation should be a parabola. Eliminate (D) because it represents the equation of a straight line. The water shoots up and then down, therefore eliminate (C), which is the equation of a parabola that is upward facing. Because the water shoots out from a spout that is 8 feet above the ground, the point (0, 8) must be on the graph. Plug this point into (A) to get $8 = -0^2 + 15$ and $8 = 15$. This is not true, so eliminate (A). Therefore, the correct answer is (B).

Drill 3

3. D   Whenever there are variables in the answer choices, think Plugging In. In the answers, plug in 15 for d to see which answer equals the corresponding oxygen concentration of 0.0022. Choice (A) becomes $\frac{1}{2} - \frac{1}{15^2} = \frac{1}{2} - \frac{1}{225} = 0.5 - 0.00\overline{4} \approx 0.496$. This does not match the target number, so eliminate (A). Choice (B) becomes $\frac{1}{100(15)} = \frac{1}{1500} = 0.000\overline{6}$. Eliminate (B). Choice (C) becomes $\frac{1}{15} = 0.0\overline{6}$. Eliminate (C). Therefore, the correct answer is (D).

6. **A** Notice that the 40 is being subtracted from the rest of the equation, which means that there is a $40 reduction in the driver's net pay. Look for other information in the question that suggests some type of reduction. The only information on any type of reduction is that the shipping company "deducts a separate fee daily for the use of the company's delivery truck." Therefore, it is reasonable to assume that the 40 represents this fee. The correct answer is (A).

9. **B** Focus only on the information that is needed to answer the question. The total number of customers is equal to the number of student customers, s, and the total number of non-student customers, n. Add these two groups together to get the overall total. The calculation for this is $s + n$. The correct answer is (B).

7. **B** Use Process of Elimination to solve this problem. According to the question, T represents temperature. Therefore, eliminate (A). Eliminate (C) because the question says nothing about Fahrenheit. According to the question, k represents the constant rate. Therefore, eliminate (D). The correct answer is (B).

10. **D** For this question, you have to find the slope of the best-fit line, which will represent the average yearly change. The formula for slope is $\dfrac{y_2 - y_1}{x_2 - x_1}$, so find two points to use. On the graph, the number of carp in 2010 was 25,000 and in 2011, the number of carp was 22,500. You can substitute these x- and y-values from the graph to get $\dfrac{25,000 - 22,500}{2010 - 2011}$. Simplify to get $\dfrac{2,500}{-1}$, or −2,500. Since the result is negative, it represents a decrease of 2,500. Therefore, the answer is (D).

8. **C** The equation includes a −0.40c. A minus sign indicates some type of reduction. According to the question, the only deduction to the net proceeds is the cost of paying for cleaning supplies. It is logical to assume that the students pay 0.40 in cleaning supplies for each car that they wash. Therefore, the correct answer is (C).

12. **C** Consider each answer and use Process of Elimination. Choice (A) is not supported by the graph because one employee had a linear decrease in energy, while the other employee's energy increased and decreased in an exponential fashion; eliminate (A). Choice (B) is also not supported; one employee had low energy after lunch (and may be drowsy), but the other employee had the highest energy level immediately after lunch. Eliminate (B). Choice (C) fits the employee who started with high energy and decreased throughout the afternoon; keep (C). Choice (D) fits neither employee: one employee decreased throughout the afternoon, and the other employee increased and then rapidly decreased. Eliminate (D) and choose (C).

11. **D** Whenever there are variables in the question and in the answer choices, think Plugging In. Plug in values that should work (those from 30–37) and values that shouldn't work (those outside of the given range) and use Process of Elimination. If $t = 37$, the correct answer will provide a statement that is true. Plug 37 in for t in the answers and eliminate any answers that are not true. Choice (A) becomes $|37 + 7| \leq 37$ or $|44| \leq 37$. Since this statement is false, eliminate (A).

Choice (B) becomes $|37 - 3.5| \leq 33.5$ or $|33.5| \leq 33.5$. Since this statement is true, keep (B). Choice (C) becomes $|37 - 30| \leq 7$, or $|7| \leq 7$. Since this statement is true, keep (C). Choice (D) becomes $|37 - 33.5| \leq 3.5$, or $|3.5| \leq 3.5$. Since this statement is true, keep (D). Next try a value that should not work, such as $t = 29$, in the remaining answer choices and eliminate any answers that provide a true statement. Choice (B) becomes $|29 - 3.5| \leq 33.5$ or $|25.5| \leq 33.5$. Since this statement is true, eliminate (B). Choice (C) becomes $|29 - 30| \leq 7$ or $|-1| \leq 7$. Since this statement is true eliminate (C). Therefore, the correct answer must be (D).

13. **B** Whenever there are variables in the question, think Plugging In. Plug in 2, 3, and 4 as the consecutive integers. In this case, $S = 2 + 3 + 4 = 9$ and $n = 3$. The equation becomes $9 = \left(\dfrac{a+k}{2}\right)(3)$. Divide both sides of the equation by 3 to get $3 = \left(\dfrac{a+k}{2}\right)$. Multiply both sides by 2 to get $a + k = 6$. Next, see which answer choice equals 6. Choice (A) becomes $2 + 3 = 5$, so eliminate (A). Choice (B) becomes $2 + 4 = 6$. Keep (B), but check the remaining answers just in case. Choice (C) doesn't work because there is only one middle integer, so eliminate (C). Choice (D) becomes $3 + 4 = 7$. Eliminate (D). Therefore, the correct answer must be (B).

23. **C** Use Process of Elimination to solve this question. Choices (A) and (B) are unlikely because $\dfrac{0.05}{12} \approx 0.004$, which is a much smaller amount than anyone could deposit into an account or could be in the account. According to the problem, the annual interest rate is 5%. Because $5\% = 0.05$, the fraction $\dfrac{0.05}{12}$ likely has something to do with the interest. So keep (C). Eliminate (D) because $\dfrac{0.05}{12}$ is too small to refer to a number of months. The correct answer is (C).

CHAPTER 12

Drill 1

a.   36
b.   24
c. $x = 10, y = 5$
d.   30
e.   22

4.   **D**   Because this is a square, the two sides are equal. Therefore, $2x + 1 = x + 3$. Solve for x, and you get that x must be 2. Therefore, a side equals $x + 3$ or $2x + 1 = 5$, so the area equals 25.

3. **D** Here are four lines; *a* and *b* are parallel, *d* intersects *a* and *b*, and *c* does not intersect both parallel lines. In statement I, angles 1 and 5 do not have to be equal because a side of angle 1 is line *c*, which has nothing to do with the parallel lines. Thus, the angles in statement I do not have to be equal, and you can eliminate (A). The angles in statement II have to be equal because angles 2 and 7 are opposite angles (two angles made up of the same two lines) and opposite angles must be equal. Eliminate (C). The angles in statement III must be equal because angles 3 and 9 are made up of the same line (line *d*) and one of the parallel lines. In fact, 3, 6, 5, and 9 are all the same "small angle," so eliminate (B). Therefore, statements II and III are true, and the correct answer is (D).

28. **60** Draw and label the diagonal of rectangle *ABCD*. Because you've made a right triangle, you can use the Pythagorean Theorem ($a^2 + b^2 = c^2$) to determine the length of $\overline{AB}$. One leg of the triangle is labeled 5, and the hypotenuse has a length of 13. Plug those values into the Pythagorean Theorem to get $5^2 + b^2 = 13^2$. Square everything that needs to be squared to get $25 + b^2 = 169$. Subtract 25 from both sides to get $b^2 = 144$. Because $\sqrt{144} = 12$, $\overline{AD}$ has a length of 12. Plug these values into the area formula for a rectangle ($A = lw$). The area of the rectangle is equal to 5×12. Because $5 \times 12 = 60$, the area of the square is 60.

9. **C** Because $\overline{BC}$ and $\overline{AD}$ are parallel, and $\overline{CD}$ is a transversal, $\angle ADC$ and $\angle BCD$ are supplementary interior angles. Therefore, their angle measures add up to 180°. Because $\angle ADC$ has a degree measure of 95°, $\angle BCD$ has a measure of 85°. Subtract 35 from 85 to see that $\angle ACD$ has a measure of 50°. This matches (C).

Drill 2

a. 24

b. 10

c. $\dfrac{6}{10}, \dfrac{3}{5}$, or 0.6

d. 20

e. $20\sqrt{5}$

f. $\dfrac{20}{20\sqrt{5}}, \dfrac{1}{\sqrt{5}}$, or $\dfrac{\sqrt{5}}{5}$

28. **7.5** SOHCAHTOA tells you that tangent is $\dfrac{\text{opposite}}{\text{adjacent}}$. You can set up a proportion: $\dfrac{14}{15} = \dfrac{7}{x}$. Cross-multiply: $14x = 105$. Divide both sides by 14: $x = 7.5$.

14. **100** Because the triangle is isosceles, with $AB = BC$, you know that angles *A* and *C* must have the same measure. So angle *A* must also be 40°. Angles *A* and *C* have a combined measure of 80°, and you need a total of 180° in the triangle. Therefore, *x* must measure 100°.

8. **C** The problem tells you that the triangle is isosceles, and you see there is a right angle present in the figure. This tells you that the base angles are 45° each. Since the length of side AB is 5, that means that the length of side BC is 5 as well. Using the relationships for a 45°-45°-90° right triangle, you can infer than the length of AC is $5\sqrt{2}$. To find the perimeter, add all three sides together: $5 + 5 + 5\sqrt{2} = 10 + 5\sqrt{2}$. The correct choice is (C).

9. **B** To find the answer, you need to know the total area. The formula for the area of a triangle is $A = \dfrac{bh}{2}$. To find the height, use a trigonometric ratio. Considering just the triangle on the right, you have a 30° angle. The adjacent side is 4, because it is half of the base. Because you have the adjacent side and need the opposite side, SOHCAHTOA tells you to use tan, which is $\dfrac{\text{opposite}}{\text{adjacent}}$. Therefore, $\tan 30° = \dfrac{h}{4}$. Multiplying both sides by 4 gives you $h = 4 \tan 30°$, or approximately 2.3. You can also use the special 30°-60°-90° triangle proportions. If the side opposite the 30° is s, the side opposite the 60° angle is $s\sqrt{3}$. Make $4 = s\sqrt{3}$ and solve for s, and you also get 2.3 for the height. Since 2.3 m is the height, the area of the entire triangle is $A = \dfrac{(8)(2.3)}{2}$, or approximately 9.2 m². To cover 9.2 m², the owner will need $\dfrac{9.2}{5}$ buckets, which is 1.84. Since 1 bucket is not enough, round up to 2, which is (B).

10. **D** Since these two triangles are right triangles and share the angle A, then all three angles must be congruent, and the triangles are therefore similar. You need to determine which sides correspond in order to set up a proportion. Since the only value given in the large triangle is the base, you need to determine the base of the smaller triangle in order to form your proportion. You may recognize the smaller triangle as a Pythagorean triple (5-12-13), but if you do not, you can use the Pythagorean Theorem to solve for the base, which is 12. Using this value, you can then set up a proportion: $\dfrac{5}{12} = \dfrac{x}{24}$. Solving this for x will yield 10. Be careful though, the question did not ask for AD; it asked for BD. So you need to subtract 5 (the length of AB) from this to get $BD = 5$, which is (D).

13. **C** If $AB = BC$, then $\angle BCA = \angle BAC = 35°$. Indicate that in the diagram and draw a line from point B to AC to create two right triangles:

AB and BC are equal hypotenuses of the right triangles. You know the side adjacent to the 35° angle, so you want cosine: $\cos 35° = \dfrac{5}{AB}$. Solving this for AB, you get $AB = \dfrac{5}{\cos 35°}$. Multiply that by 2 and add that to 10 and you get $10 + \dfrac{10}{\cos 35°}$ for the perimeter, but that's not an answer. However, (C) is $10 + \dfrac{10}{\sin 55°}$. Remember that $\sin x = \cos(90 - x)$, so $\sin 55° = \cos 35°$. Therefore, the answer is (C).

Drill 3

a.   16π
b.   8π

16. **A** Angle AOB is 60 degrees, which is $\dfrac{1}{6}$ of 360 degrees. Since arc AB is 2π, it is $\dfrac{1}{6}$ of the total circumference. The circumference then is $6 \times 2\pi$, which comes to 12π. The diameter of the circle is 12, making the radius 6. The area of the circle then is 36π, (A).

18. **C** Since there is no figure given, you should draw one according to the directions. The figure should look like the following:

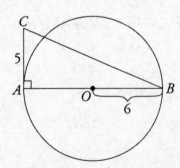

Given that the area of the circle is 36π, the radius is 6. That means that the diameter is 12. The point where a tangent hits the circle makes a 90-degree angle, so angle OAC is 90 degrees. Now that you have a right triangle, you can use the Pythagorean Theorem to find that the length of BC is 13. Adding $5 + 12 + 13$ gives you 30, (C).

12. **B** The equation of a circle with its center at (h, k) is $(x - h)^2 + (y - k)^2 = r^2$. To convert the given equation into this form, you must create two expressions that are perfect squares. Given $x^2 - 2x$, you can create a perfect square by "completing the square." Take half of 2, which is 1, and square it to get 1. Finally, add and subtract this number. This gives you $x^2 - 2x + 1 - 1$. The expression $x^2 - 2x + 1$ is a perfect square, giving you $(x - 1)^2 - 1$. Do the same with $y^2 + 8y$ to get $y^2 + 8y + 16 - 16$, which equals $(y + 4)^2 - 16$. Now you have $(x - 1)^2 - 1 + (y + 4)^2 - 16 + 8 = 0$. Rearranging, you get $(x - 1)^2 + (y + 4)^2 = 9$. Because $h = 1$ and $k = -4$, you have a center of $(1, -4)$, which is (B).

29. **5.25** Start by translating English to math. "Major arc PSR is $\frac{4}{3}$ the length of minor arc PQR" becomes $PSR = \frac{4}{3} PQR$. Because $PSR = 6\pi$, you can substitute and then solve for PQR: $6\pi = \frac{4}{3} PQR$; $18\pi = 4PSR$; $\frac{9}{2}\pi = PSR$. Because major arc PSR and minor arc PQR make up the entire circumference of the circle, $PRS + PQR$ is the circumference of the circle: $6\pi + \frac{9}{2}\pi = \frac{21}{2}\pi$. The formula for circumference is $2\pi r$, so you can solve for r: $2\pi r = \frac{21}{2}\pi$; $4r = 21$; $r = \frac{21}{4}$, or 5.25.

Drill 4

3. **B** There are variables in the answer choices, so plug in a number for a. How about 90, just to make the math easy? If $a = 90$, then the other angle inside the triangle must be equal to 60. Therefore, b must be equal to 120. What choice says 120, remembering that $a = 90$? Choice (B) does.

7. **B** This is another great example of Plugging In. Make 3 the radius of Cone A and 4 the radius of Cone B. Set the height to 3. The volume of Cone A is therefore 9π, and the volume of Cone B is 16π. Divide both sides by π to get a ratio of 9:16. Choice (B) is correct.

5. **A** Plug In! You are given a right triangle, so plug in for the sides of the right triangle. Make the triangle a Pythagorean triplet. Make the side opposite the angle with measure $a°$ equal to 3, the side opposite the angle with measure $b°$ equal to 4, and the hypotenuse equal to 5. SOHCAHTOA tells you that sine is $\frac{\text{opposite}}{\text{hypotenuse}}$, so $\sin a° = \frac{3}{5}$ and $x = \frac{3}{5}$. Cosine is $\frac{\text{adjacent}}{\text{hypotenuse}}$, so $\cos b° = \frac{3}{5}$. Make $x = \frac{3}{5}$ in each answer choice, and look for what equals $\frac{3}{5}$. Only (A) works.

22. **A** Plug in for x, choosing 18 to make the math easier. Since $A = \pi r^2$ and $r = 18$, the total area is 324π.

Since $C = 2\pi r$, the total circumference is 36π. Minor arc PQ takes up $\frac{\pi x}{18}$ or π of 36π, which is

$\dfrac{1}{36}$. Sector *POQ* must therefore take up $\dfrac{1}{36}$ of the area, which is $\left(\dfrac{1}{36}\right)324\pi = 9\pi$. This is the tar-

get answer, so plug $x = 18$ into the answer choices to see which one equals 9π. Choice (A) becomes

$\dfrac{\pi(18)^2}{36} = \dfrac{324\pi}{36} = 9\pi$. This matches the target. Since all the other answers have the same numera-

tor and different denominators, only (A) will work.

26.   C   Start by drawing a rectangular box with three spheres in a row:

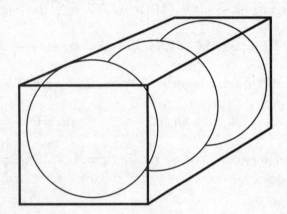

Next, plug in for the variable. Make $r = 2$. To find the volume between the box and the spheres, find the volume of the box and subtract the volume of the three spheres. If the radius of each sphere is 2, then the square faces on either end must have sides double the radius, or 4, The long dimension of the box will be 3 times 4, or 12. Therefore, the volume of the box is $V = (4)(4)(12) = 192$. To find the volume of one sphere, use the formula: $V = \dfrac{4}{3}\pi(2)^3 = \dfrac{32\pi}{3}$. Because there are three spheres, multiply this by three; the total volume of the three spheres is 32π. Therefore, the volume between the box and the spheres is $192 - 32\pi$. This is your target; circle it. Make $r = 2$ in each answer and eliminate any choice that does not equal your target. The only choice that works is (C).

29.   160   According to the problem, $\dfrac{1}{2}w = l$ and $3w = h$. Since you know that volume equals *lwh*, you can form an equation: $(\dfrac{1}{2}w)(w)(3w) = 96$. Now you know that $\dfrac{3}{2}w^3 = 96$. Solving this equation for *w* yields $w = 4$. From this, you can calculate that $l = 2$ and $h = 12$. The formula for surface area is Surface Area $= 2lw + 2lh + 2hw$. Plug in your values for *l*, *w*, and *h* into the equation to get surface area $= 160$.

Part IV
Practice Tests

Chapter 13
Practice Test 1

Reading Test

60 MINUTES, 47 QUESTIONS

Turn to Section 1 of your answer sheet to answer the questions in this section.

DIRECTIONS

Each passage or pair of passages below is followed by a number of questions. After reading each passage or pair, choose the best answer to each question based on what is stated or implied in the passage or passages and in any accompanying graphics (such as a table or graph).

Questions 1–9 are based on the following passage.

The following is an excerpt from a novel by Thomas Hardy published in 1878. This portion speaks about a man named Clym Yeobright who has recently returned to his hometown, Egdon Heath.

In Clym Yeobright's face could be dimly seen the typical countenance of the future. The observer's eye was arrested, not by his face as a picture, but by his face
Line as a page; not by what it was, but by what it recorded.
5 His features were attractive in the light of symbols, as sounds intrinsically common become attractive in language, and as shapes intrinsically simple become interesting in writing.

He had been a lad of whom something was
10 expected. Beyond this all had been chaos. That he would be successful in an original way, or that he would go to the dogs in an original way, seemed equally probable. The only absolute certainty about him was that he would not stand still in the
15 circumstances amid which he was born.

Hence, when his name was casually mentioned by neighbouring yeomen, the listener said, "Ah, Clym Yeobright—what is he doing now?" When the instinctive question about a person is, What is
20 he doing? it is felt that he will be found to be, like most of us, doing nothing in particular. There is an indefinite sense that he must be invading some region of singularity, good or bad. The devout hope is that he is doing well. The secret faith is that he is making
25 a mess of it. Half a dozen comfortable market-men, who were habitual callers at the Quiet Woman as they passed by in their carts, were partial to the topic. In

fact, though they were not Egdon men, they could hardly avoid it while they sucked their long clay tubes
30 and regarded the heath through the window. Clym had been so inwoven with the heath in his boyhood that hardly anybody could look upon it without thinking of him. So the subject recurred: if he were making a fortune and a name, so much the better for him; if he
35 were making a tragical figure in the world, so much the better for a narrative.

The fact was that Yeobright's fame had spread to an awkward extent before he left home. "It is bad when your fame outruns your means," said the Spanish Jesuit
40 Gracian. At the age of six he had asked a Scripture riddle: "Who was the first man known to wear breeches?" and applause had resounded from the very verge of the heath. At seven he painted the Battle of Waterloo with tiger-lily pollen and black-currant juice,
45 in the absence of water-colours. By the time he reached twelve he had in this manner been heard of as artist and scholar for at least two miles round. An individual whose fame spreads three or four thousand yards in the time taken by the fame of others similarly situated
50 to travel six or eight hundred, must of necessity have something in him. Possibly Clym's fame, like Homer's, owed something to the accidents of his situation; nevertheless famous he was. He grew up and went to London; and thence, shortly after, to Paris, where he
55 had remained till now.

Something being expected of him, he had not been at home many days before a great curiosity as to why he stayed on so long began to arise in the heath.

CONTINUE ▶

The natural term of a holiday had passed, yet he still
60　remained.

Was Yeobright's mind well-proportioned? No.
A well-proportioned mind is one which shows no
particular bias; its usual blessings are happiness and
mediocrity. It enables its possessors to find their way
65　to wealth, to wind up well, to step with dignity off the
stage, to die comfortably in their beds, and to get the
decent monument which, in many cases, they deserve.
It never would have allowed Yeobright to do such a
ridiculous thing as throw up his business to benefit his
70　fellow-creatures.

He walked along towards home without attending
to paths. If anyone knew the heath well it was Clym.
He was permeated with its scenes, with its substance,
and with its odours. He might be said to be its product.
75　His eyes had first opened thereon; with its appearance
all the first images of his memory were mingled, his
estimate of life had been coloured by it: his toys had
been the flint knives and arrow-heads which he found
there, wondering why stones should "grow" to such
80　odd shapes; his flowers, the purple bells and yellow
furze: his animal kingdom, the snakes and croppers;
his society, its human haunters. He gazed upon the
wide prospect as he walked, and was glad.

1

The passage most strongly suggests that which of the
following is true of Clym?

A) The locals support him, which has bolstered his
achievement.

B) He is not going to return to Paris because his fame
was all accidental.

C) His religious upbringing prepared him well for
prosperity.

D) He was expected to either prosper or fail but not
to be mired in anything banal.

2

Which choice provides the best evidence for the
answer to the previous question?

A) Lines 10–15 ("That he . . . born")

B) Lines 40–43 ("At the age . . . heath")

C) Lines 51–55 ("Possibly . . . now")

D) Lines 61–64 ("Was . . . mediocrity")

3

As used in line 3, "arrested" most nearly means

A) indicted.

B) engaged.

C) forced.

D) charged.

4

The author uses the quote ("It is bad . . . your means")
in lines 38–39 primarily to suggest that

A) Clym may not live up to the people of his
hometown's expectations, despite relatively
widespread fame.

B) Clym has used his fame to his advantage for too
long and now people are beginning to bore of
him.

C) Clym has run out of money and can no longer
support his luxurious European lifestyle.

D) Clym can never live up to his own notoriety.

5

The fifth paragraph (lines 56–60) primarily serves to

A) show the townspeople's frustration that Clym
won't go back to Paris.

B) underscore that Clym's extended return is
incongruous with someone of his potential.

C) provide an example of the locals' intrusive
presence in Clym's life.

D) prove that Clym's illustriousness has spread to an
awkward extent.

6

As used in line 52, "accidents" most nearly means

A) crashes.

B) slips.

C) chance.

D) trauma.

CONTINUE ➔

7

Based on the information in the passage, Yeobright is known chiefly for his

A) vast wealth and reputation overseas.

B) sweeping acclaim and abundant promise.

C) unique aesthetic features and tragic circumstances.

D) aptitude as a scholar and preacher.

8

Which choice provides the best evidence for the answer to the previous question?

A) Lines 1–4 ("In Clym . . . recorded")

B) Lines 45–47 ("By the time . . . round")

C) Lines 47–51 ("An individual . . . in him")

D) Lines 53–55 ("He grew . . . now")

9

The comparison in lines 6–8 ("as sounds . . . writing") is most similar to which of the following?

A) The allure of the color yellow becoming stronger in a painting of a sunrise versus on the palette

B) A beautiful dress that looks beautiful worn and on the hanger

C) A phrase in another language causing confusion until it is translated

D) Diamond rings that are more attractive than ruby rings

CONTINUE

Questions 10–18 are based on the following passage.

This passage is adapted from Michael Pollan, *The Botany of Desire*. © 2001 by Michael Pollan.

The modern tulip has become such a cheap and ubiquitous commodity that it's hard for us to recover a sense of the glamour that once surrounded the
Line flower. That glamour surely had something to do with
5 its roots in the Orient—Anna Pavord speaks of the "intoxicating aura of the infidels" that surrounded the tulip. There was, too, the preciousness of the early tulips, the supply of which could be increased only very slowly through offsets, a quirk of biology that kept
10 supply well behind demand. In France in 1608, a miller exchanged his mill for a bulb of Mère Brune. Around the same time a bridegroom accepted a single tulip as the whole of his dowry—happily, we are told; the variety became known as "Marriage de ma fille."
15 Yet tulipomania in France and England never reached the pitch it would in Holland. How can the mad embrace of these particular people and this particular flower be explained?

For good reason, the Dutch have never been
20 content to accept nature as they found it. Lacking in conventional charms and variety, the landscape of the Low Countries is spectacularly flat, monotonous, and swampy. "An universal quagmire" is how one Englishman described the place; "the buttock of
25 the world." What beauty there is in the Netherlands is largely the result of human effort: the dikes and canals built to drain the land, the windmills erected to interrupt the unbroken sweep of wind across it. In his famous essay on tulipomania, "The Bitter Smell of
30 Tulips," the poet Zbigniew Herbert suggests that the "monotony of the Dutch landscape gave rise to dreams of multifarious, colorful, and unusual flora."

Such dreams could be indulged as never before in seventeenth-century Holland, as Dutch traders
35 and plant explorers returned home with a parade of exotic new plant species. Botany became a national pastime followed as closely and avidly as we follow sports today. This was a nation, and a time, in which a botanical treatise could become a best-seller and a
40 plantsman like Clusius a celebrity.

Land in Holland being so scarce and expensive, Dutch gardens were miniatures, measured in square feet rather than acres and frequently augmented with mirrors. The Dutch thought of their gardens as jewel

45 boxes, and in such a space even a single flower—and especially one as erect, singular, and strikingly colored as a tulip—could make a powerful statement.

To make such statements—about one's sophistication, about one's wealth—has always been
50 one of the reasons people plant gardens. In the seventeenth century the Dutch were the richest people in Europe and, as the historian Simon Schama shows in *The Embarrassment of Riches*, their Calvinist faith did not keep them from indulging in the pleasures of
55 conspicuous display. The exoticism and expense of tulips certainly recommended them for this purpose, but so did the fact that, among flowers, the tulip is one of the most extravagantly useless. Up until the Renaissance, most of the flowers in cultivation had
60 been useful as well as beautiful; they were sources of medicine, perfume, or even food. In the West flowers have often come under attack from various Puritans, and what has always saved them has been their practical uses. It was utility, not beauty, that earned the
65 rose and lily, the peony and all the rest a spot in the gardens of monks and Shakers and colonial Americans who would otherwise have had nothing to do with them.

When the tulip first arrived in Europe, people
70 set about fashioning some utilitarian purpose for it. The Germans boiled and sugared the bulbs and, unconvincingly, declared them a delicacy; the English tried serving them up with oil and vinegar. Pharmacists proposed the tulip as a remedy for
75 flatulence. None of these uses caught on, however. "The tulip remained itself," Herbert writes, "the poetry of Nature to which vulgar utilitarianism is foreign." The tulip was a thing of beauty, no more, no less.

10

The passage suggests that in seventeenth-century Europe, tulips were prized primarily for their

A) intoxicating scent.

B) exotic botany.

C) extravagant beauty.

D) medicinal qualities.

CONTINUE

11

Which choice provides the best evidence for the answer to the previous question?

A) Lines 4–7 ("That glamour . . . tulip")

B) Lines 33–36 ("Such dreams . . . species")

C) Lines 74–75 ("Pharmacists . . . flatulence")

D) Lines 77–78 ("The tulip . . . less")

12

As used in line 16, "pitch" most nearly means

A) throw.

B) angle.

C) level.

D) promotion.

13

The author uses the word "spectacularly" (line 22) in order to

A) emphasize the beauty to be found in the flat landscape of the Low Countries.

B) highlight the monotonous nature of the Dutch landscape.

C) maintain the tone of irony used to describe the Dutch attitude toward their land.

D) underscore the importance of human efforts to make the Low Countries beautiful.

14

The primary purpose of the fourth paragraph (lines 33–40) is to

A) illustrate the widespread popularity of botany in seventeenth-century Holland.

B) indicate that the Dutch landscape is as flat as a baseball field.

C) provide an example to show the relative lack of fame of Dutch traders and plantsmen.

D) introduce a metaphor supporting the idea that the Dutch obsession for tulips was unusually strong.

15

It can be inferred from the passage that seventeenth-century Dutch gardens were

A) as small as jewel boxes.

B) indicators of wealth and sophistication.

C) full of exotic and expensive flowers.

D) often adorned by only a single flower.

16

Which choice provides the best evidence for the answer to the previous question?

A) Lines 41–44 ("Land . . . mirrors")

B) Lines 48–50 ("To make . . . gardens")

C) Lines 69–71 ("When . . . it")

D) Lines 74–75 ("Pharmacists . . . however")

17

As used in line 70, "utilitarian" most nearly means

A) practical.

B) industrial.

C) culinary.

D) decorative.

18

It can reasonably be inferred from the passage that the characteristic that makes the tulip most different from a rose or a lily is its

A) price.

B) exoticism.

C) beauty.

D) uselessness.

CONTINUE

Questions 19–28 are based on the following passage and supplementary material.

This passage is adapted from Harriet H. Robinson, "Early Factory Labor in New England," in Massachusetts Bureau of Statistics of Labor, *Fourteenth Annual Report* (Boston: Wright & Potter, 1883). Robinson was a mill-worker, writer, and social activist who played a prominent role in the labor and women's suffrage movements in the United States.

In 1832, Lowell was little more than a factory village. Five "corporations" were started, and the cotton mills belonging to them were building. Help was in great demand and stories were told all over the country of the new factory place, and the high wages that were offered to all classes of workpeople; stories that reached the ears of mechanics' and farmers' sons and gave new life to lonely and dependent women in distant towns and farmhouses. Troops of young girls came from different parts of New England, and from Canada, and men were employed to collect them at so much a head, and deliver them at the factories.

At the time the Lowell cotton mills were started, the caste of the factory girl was the lowest among the employments of women. In England and in France, particularly, great injustice had been done to her real character. She was represented as subjected to influences that must destroy her purity and self-respect. In the eyes of her overseer she was but a brute, a slave, to be beaten, pinched and pushed about. It was to overcome this prejudice that such high wages had been offered to women that they might be induced to become millgirls, in spite of the opprobrium that still clung to this degrading occupation.

The early millgirls were of different ages. Some were not over ten years old; a few were in middle life, but the majority were between the ages of sixteen and twenty-five. The very young girls were called "doffers." They "doffed," or took off, the full bobbins from the spinningframes, and replaced them with empty ones. These mites worked about fifteen minutes every hour and the rest of the time was their own. When the overseer was kind they were allowed to read, knit, or go outside the millyard to play. They were paid two dollars a week. The working hours of all the girls extended from five o'clock in the morning until seven in the evening, with one halfhour each, for breakfast and dinner. Even the doffers were forced to be on duty nearly fourteen hours a day. This was the greatest hardship in the lives of these children. Several years later a tenhour law was passed, but not until long after some of these little doffers were old enough to appear before the legislative committee on the subject, and plead, by their presence, for a reduction of the hours of labor.

Those of the millgirls who had homes generally worked from eight to ten months in the year; the rest of the time was spent with parents or friends. A few taught school during the summer months. Their life in the factory was made pleasant to them. In those days there was no need of advocating the doctrine of the proper relation between employer and employed. Help was too valuable to be ill-treated.

The most prevailing incentive to labor was to secure the means of education for some male member of the family. To make a gentleman of a brother or a son, to give him a college education, was the dominant thought in the minds of a great many of the better class of millgirls. I have known more than one to give every cent of her wages, month after month, to her brother, that he might get the education necessary to enter some profession. I have known a mother to work years in this way for her boy. I have known women to educate young men by their earnings, who were not sons or relatives. There are many men now living who were helped to an education by the wages of the early millgirls.

CONTINUE

The table below shows the daily schedule for workers at the Lowell Mills in 1851.

	From 1st to 10th inclusive				From 11th to 20th inclusive				From 21st to last day of month			
	1st Bell	2d Bell	3d Bell	Eve. Bell	1st Bell	2d Bell	3d Bell	Eve. Bell	1st Bell	2d Bell	3d Bell	Eve. Bell
January	5.00	6.00	6.50	*7.30	5.00	6.00	6.50	*7.30	5.00	6.00	6.50	*7.30
February	4.30	5.30	6.40	*7.30	4.30	5.30	6.25	*7.30	4.30	5.30	6.15	*7.30
March	5.40	6.00		*7.30	5.20	5.40		*7.30	5.05	5.25		6.35
April	4.45	5.05		6.45	4.30	4.50		6.55	4.30	4.50		7.00
May	4.30	4.50		7.00	4.30	4.50		7.00	4.30	4.50		7.00
June												
July												
August												
September	4.40	5.00		6.45	4.50	5.10		6.30	5.00	5.20		*7.30
October	5.10	5.30		*7.30	5.20	5.40		*7.30	5.35	5.55		*7.30
November	4.30	5.30	6.10	*7.30	4.30	5.30	6.20	*7.30	5.00	6.00	6.35	*7.30
December	5.00	6.00	6.45	*7.30	5.00	6.00	6.50	*7.30	5.00	6.00	6.50	*7.30

TIME TABLE OF THE LOWELL MILLS,
To take effect on and after October 21st, 1851.

The Standard time being that of the meridian of Lowell, as shown by the regulator clock of JOSEPH RAYNES, 43 Central Street

*Expecting on Saturdays from Sept. 21st to March 20th inclusive, when it is rung at 20 minutes after sunset.

19

The perspective from which Robinson writes is best described as that of

A) a disinterested observer.

B) a passionate advocate.

C) an irate troublemaker.

D) a carefree eyewitness.

20

In lines 3–12 ("Help . . . factories"), Robinson explicitly cites which of the following as a reason that women moved to Lowell to work in the cotton mills?

A) The opportunity to live in a more appealing climate

B) The appeal of generous vacation time

C) The chance to enjoy the company of a diverse array of coworkers

D) The promise of attractive remuneration

21

In the context of the passage as a whole, the author most likely mentions the working conditions of England and France (beginning in line 15) in order to

A) demonstrate the superiority of European factory work.

B) provide a historical overview of the Industrial Revolution.

C) draw a contrast between those conditions and the conditions promised to workers in the Lowell mills.

D) argue that American factories should follow the European model.

22

Which choice provides the best evidence for the answer to the previous question?

A) Lines 1–2 ("In . . . village")

B) Lines 9–12 ("Troops . . . factories")

C) Lines 20–24 ("It . . . occupation")

D) Lines 46–48 ("Those . . . friends")

CONTINUE

23

As used in line 23, "opprobrium" most nearly means

A) disgrace.

B) praise.

C) benevolence.

D) trauma.

24

The passage suggests which of the following about the youngest girls employed at the Lowell mills?

A) They had complete freedom to spend their time as they chose.

B) They spent the majority of their time in educational settings.

C) They ranged in age from 10–16 years old.

D) They were afforded more leisure time than were the older girls and adult women.

25

Which choice provides the best evidence for the answer to the previous question?

A) Lines 29–30 ("They . . . ones")

B) Lines 31–34 ("These . . . play")

C) Lines 48–49 ("A few . . . months")

D) Lines 54–56 ("The most . . . family")

26

The information in the table provided most supports which of the following claims made in the passage?

A) Women working in the mills were forced to be on duty nearly fourteen hours per day.

B) There were five growing corporations in Lowell in 1832.

C) Many of the millgirls gave some or all of the wages that they earned to male family members.

D) The idea of working in the mills gave new life to girls and women living in isolated towns across North America.

27

As used in line 54, "prevailing" most nearly means

A) conquering.

B) current.

C) predominant.

D) rare.

28

Which of the following best represents the main idea of the last paragraph (lines 54–67)?

A) The early female mill-workers in Lowell were universally contemptuous of their male relatives.

B) Providing financial resources for their male relatives' education was commonplace among the early female mill-workers in Lowell.

C) A college education is the surest way to achieve the status of a gentleman.

D) The primary reason that middle-aged women worked in the Lowell mills was to provide financial resources for their daughters.

CONTINUE

Questions 29–37 are based on the following passage and supplementary material.

This passage is adapted from Laurel Woodruff and George Bedinger, "Titanium: Light, Strong, and White" in the U.S. Geological Survey's 2013 Fact Sheet.

Titanium (Ti) is a strong silver-gray metal that is highly resistant to corrosion and is chemically inert. It is as strong as steel but 45 percent lighter, and it
Line is twice as strong as aluminum but only 60 percent
5 heavier. Titanium dioxide (TiO_2) has a very high refractive index, which means that it has high light-scattering ability. As a result, TiO_2 imparts whiteness, opacity, and brightness to many products.

Titanium was first discovered in 1791 by the British
10 clergyman and amateur geologist William Gregor, who produced a white metallic oxide from black magnetic sands. In 1795, the German chemist Martin Klaproth named the oxide "titanium" after the Greek *Titans*, a mythical race of immortal giants with incredible
15 strength and stamina. Pure titanium metal was first isolated in 1910 by chemist Matthew Hunter. Hunter's difficult isolation process made titanium metal mainly a laboratory curiosity until 1938 when William Kroll developed a method (known as the Kroll method)
20 to produce titanium metal in commercial quantities. Because of the unique physical properties of titanium metal and the whiteness provided by TiO_2, titanium is now used widely in modern industrial societies.

Most titanium ore is refined into TiO_2 to impart a
25 durable white color to paint, paper, rubber, wallboard, and plastic. The paint industry began using TiO_2 because of concerns about the environmental hazards related to the use of lead in paint. Because TiO_2 is relatively inert, it can also be used as coloring in
30 such products as toothpaste, skim milk, candy, and sunscreen.

Only about 5 percent of the world's annual production of titanium minerals goes to make titanium metal. The high strength-to-weight ratio and corrosion
35 resistance of titanium metal and its alloys make them particularly valuable to the aerospace industry. Because titanium metal is nonreactive in the human body, it is also used to make artificial hip joints, pins for setting bones, and other types of biological implants.

40 Titanium is the ninth most abundant element in the Earth's crust and can be found in nearly all rocks. The economic viability of a titanium deposit is determined by the grade and available tonnage, as well as the deposit type and titanium mineralogy.

45 The most economically important titanium minerals are ilmenite (which is a titanium-iron oxide that crystallizes at high temperatures from magma) and two TiO_2 polymorphs, rutile and anatase (which have the same chemical composition but different
50 crystal structures). Ninety percent of the world's titanium is accounted for by ilmenite, but because rutile has a very high index of refraction, it is the most desirable mineral for the pigment industry.

Economic high-grade magmatic ilmenite
55 deposits are found in particular rock types. These deposits develop by crystallization of ilmenite from titanium- and iron-enriched magmas. Segregation and emplacement of these early ilmenite-laden liquids are likely related to dynamic magmatic processes
60 accompanying the emplacement of anorthosite (a plagioclase-rich rock) and related mafic rocks. Magmatic ilmenite is currently being mined at the Lac Tio mine in Quebec, Canada, and at Tellnes, a large open pit mine in southern Norway.

The table below shows the percent distribution of titanium pigment in various U.S. industries.

Estimated U.S. Distribution of Titanium Pigment Shipments, Titanium Dioxide Content, by Industry[1] (Percent)		
Industry	**2011**	**2012**
Paint, varnish, lacquer	58.5	59.8
Paper	8.6	10.6
Plastics and rubber	27.9	24.6
Other[2]	5.0	5.0
Total	100.0	100.0

[1] Excludes exports.

[2] Includes agricultural, building materials, ceramics, coated fabrics and textiles, cosmetics, food, and printing ink. Also includes shipments to distributors.

CONTINUE

29

The authors state that which of the following characteristics of titanium accounts for its ability to impart white coloring and brightness to objects?

A) Its resistance to corrosion

B) Its relatively light weight

C) Its natural abundance

D) Its high refractive index

30

Which choice provides the best evidence for the answer to the previous question?

A) Lines 5–8 ("Titanium . . . products")

B) Lines 15–20 ("Pure . . . quantities")

C) Lines 32–36 ("Only . . . industry")

D) Lines 40–44 ("Titanium . . . mineralogy")

31

As used in line 18, "curiosity" most nearly means

A) oddity.

B) inquisitiveness.

C) eagerness.

D) desire.

32

The information presented in the table above supports which of the following claims made in the passage?

A) High-grade magmatic ilmenite deposits are developed by magma crystallization in particular rock types.

B) Titanium dioxide imparts opacity and brightness to many products.

C) Most titanium dioxide is used in products such as paint, paper, rubber, wallboard, and plastic.

D) The economic viability of a titanium deposit is determined primarily by quality and weight.

33

The authors claim that the use of titanium in certain products is preferable to that of lead because of lead's dangerous health effects. Do the authors support the idea that titanium is safe for human use with specific reasons and/or examples?

A) Yes, because the authors note that titanium was first discovered in 1791 and that pure titanium metal was first isolated in 1901.

B) Yes, because the authors note that titanium's relative inertness makes it safe for use in toothpaste, milk, and sunscreen and that its non-reactiveness in the human body makes it safe for use in medical procedures.

C) No, because the authors describe a large open pit mine in Norway and imply that mining titanium in such conditions is potentially hazardous to human health.

D) No, because the authors claim that titanium is safe for use in certain products used by humans but do not support that claim with any reasons or examples.

34

As used in line 35, "resistance" most nearly means

A) safeguard.

B) support.

C) blocking.

D) struggle.

35

The authors compare titanium metal to steel and aluminum in order to

A) show a specific way in which titanium imparts brightness and opacity to objects.

B) prove that titanium is stronger than all other metals.

C) provide an illustration of titanium's strength and lightness relative to certain other metals.

D) highlight the particularly abundant nature of titanium as a renewable resource that can be easily mined.

CONTINUE

36

It can be inferred from the passage that the form of titanium most useful to the manufacturing of paint products is

A) rutile.

B) ilmenite.

C) anatase.

D) titanium metal.

37

Which choice provides the best evidence for the answer to the previous question?

A) Lines 1–5 ("Titanium . . . heavier")

B) Lines 50–53 ("Ninety . . . industry")

C) Lines 54–55 ("Economic . . . types")

D) Lines 62–64 ("Magmatic . . . Norway")

CONTINUE

Questions 38–47 are based on the following passages.

Passage 1 is adapted from "A Wandering Mind Reveals Mental Processes and Priorities." Copyright, University of Wisconsin-Madison. March 2012. Reprinted with permission. Passage 2 is excerpted from Josie Glausiusz, "Living in an Imaginary World." Reproduced with permission. Copyright © 2014 Scientific American, a division of Nature America, Inc. All rights reserved.

Passage 1

In an experiment—designed and executed by Prof. Bar's post-doctoral researcher Dr. Vadim Axelrod—participants were treated with transcranial direct current stimulation (tDCS), a procedure that uses low-
Line
5   level electricity to stimulate specific brain regions. "We focused tDCS stimulation on the frontal lobes because this brain region has been previously implicated in mind wandering, and also because it is a central locus of the executive control network that allows us to
10 organize and plan for the future," Bar explains.

The researchers used tDCS to stimulate the occipital cortex—the visual processing center in the back of the brain. They also conducted control studies where no tDCS was used.

15 While the self-reported incidence of mind wandering was unchanged in the case of occipital and sham stimulation, it rose considerably when this stimulation was applied to the frontal lobes. "Our results demonstrate that the frontal lobes play a causal
20 role in the production of mind wandering behavior."

In an unanticipated finding, the present study demonstrated how the increased mind wandering behavior produced by external stimulation not only does not harm subjects' ability to succeed at an
25 appointed task, it actually helps. Bar believes that this surprising result might stem from the convergence, within a single brain region, of both the "thought controlling" mechanisms of executive function and the "thought freeing" activity of spontaneous, self-directed
30 daydreams.

"Over the last 15 or 20 years, scientists have shown that mind wandering involves the activation of a gigantic default network involving many parts of the brain," Bar says. "This cross-brain involvement may
35 be involved in behavioral outcomes such as creativity and mood, and may also contribute to the ability to stay successfully on-task while the mind goes off on its merry mental way."

While it is commonly assumed that people have a
40 finite cognitive capacity for paying attention, Bar says that the present study suggests that the truth may be more complicated. "Interestingly, while our study's external stimulation increased the incidence of mind wandering, rather than reducing the subjects' ability
45 to complete the task, it caused task performance to become slightly improved. The external stimulation actually enhanced the subjects' cognitive capacity."

Passage 2

Some researchers believe that increasing the amount of imaginative daydreaming we do or
50 replaying variants of the millions of events we store in our brain can be beneficial. A painful procedure in a doctor's office, for example, can be made less distressing by visualizations of soothing scenes from childhood.

55 Yet to enhance creativity, it is important to pay attention to daydreams. Psychologist Jonathan W. Schooler of the University of California, Santa Barbara calls this "tuning out" or deliberate "off-task thinking." In an as yet unpublished study, he
60 and his colleague Jonathan Smallwood asked 122 undergraduates at the University of British Columbia to read a children's story and press a button each time they caught themselves tuning out. The researchers also periodically interrupted the students as they were
65 reading and asked them if they were "zoning out" or drifting off without being aware of it. "What we find is that the people who regularly catch themselves—who notice when they're doing it—seem to be the most creative," Schooler says. Such subjects score higher on
70 a standard test of creativity, in which they are asked to describe all the uses of a common object, such as a brick; high scorers compile a longer and more creative list. "You need to have the mind-wandering process," he explains, "but you also need to have meta-awareness
75 to say, 'That's a creative idea that popped into my mind.'"

The mind's freedom to wander during a period of deliberate tuning out could also explain the flash of insight that may pop into a person's head when he
80 or she takes a break from an unsolved problem. Ut Na Sio and Thomas Ormerod, two researchers at the University of Lancaster in England, conducted a recent meta-analysis of studies of these brief reveries. They

CONTINUE ▶

found that people who engaged in a mildly demanding
85 task, such as reading, during a break from, say, a visual
assignment, such as the hat-rack problem—in which
participants have to construct a sturdy hat rack using
two boards and a clamp—did better on that problem
than those who did nothing at all. They also scored
90 higher than those engaged in a highly demanding
task—such as mentally rotating shapes—during
the interval. Allowing our mind to ramble during a
moderately challenging task, it seems, enables us to
access ideas not easily available to our conscious mind
95 or to combine these insights in original ways. Our
ability to do so is now known to depend on the normal
functioning of a dedicated daydreaming network deep
in our brain.

38

Based on the information in Passage 1, it can be
reasonably inferred that mind wandering

A) is caused by the occipital lobes.

B) depends on interaction among all parts of the
brain.

C) reacts to a sham stimulation.

D) is initiated by the frontal lobes.

39

Which choice provides the best evidence for the
answer to the previous question?

A) Lines 1–5 ("In an . . . regions")

B) Lines 11–13 ("The researchers . . . brain")

C) Lines 18–20 ("'Our . . . behavior'")

D) Lines 25–30 ("Bar . . . daydreams")

40

As used in line 26, "stem" most nearly means

A) branch.

B) originate.

C) contain.

D) restrain.

41

The author of Passage 2 mentions "a painful
procedure in a doctor's office" in lines 51–52 in order
to

A) provide a personal example to illustrate an
abstract concept.

B) trigger a certain memory for her readers.

C) suggest a location for enhancing creativity.

D) offer a specific illustration of a general statement.

42

As used in line 63, "caught" most nearly means

A) detected.

B) entangled.

C) developed.

D) overtook.

43

Passage 2 most clearly suggests that daydreaming

A) is the only way to solve a difficult problem.

B) often occurs during visits to the doctor's office.

C) can enhance creativity if an individual is aware
of it.

D) has no discernible benefits.

44

Which choice provides the best evidence for the
answer to the previous question?

A) Lines 48–51 ("Some researchers . . . beneficial")

B) Lines 56–59 ("Psychologist . . . off-task thinking")

C) Lines 66–69 ("What we . . . creative")

D) Lines 77–80 ("The mind's . . . problem")

CONTINUE

45

Which specific point is made in Passage 1 but not in Passage 2? Passage 1

A) correlates mind wandering with intelligence.

B) lists everyday activities that people do while experiencing mind wandering.

C) delineates the regions of the brain activated during mind wandering.

D) describes specific details of mind wandering research.

46

The authors of both passages would most likely agree with which of the following?

A) Outside stimuli inevitably lead to mind wandering.

B) Mind wandering does not impede the completion of certain tasks.

C) Mind wandering elicits creativity and passion.

D) Intelligent people have exclusively internally-driven thoughts.

47

In which lines does the author of Passage 2 most directly corroborate the conclusion about external stimulation on concentration as presented in Passage 1?

A) Lines 51–54 ("A painful . . . childhood")

B) Lines 59–63 ("In an . . . tuning out")

C) Lines 73–76 ("You need . . . mind")

D) Lines 83–89 ("They found . . . all")

STOP

**If you finish before time is called, you may check your work on this section only.
Do not turn to any other section.**

Writing and Language Test

35 MINUTES, 44 QUESTIONS

Turn to Section 2 of your answer sheet to answer the questions in this section.

DIRECTIONS

Each passage below is accompanied by a number of questions. For some questions, you will consider how the passage might be revised to improve the expression of ideas. For other questions, you will consider how the passage might be edited to correct errors in sentence structure, usage, or punctuation. A passage or a question may be accompanied by one or more graphics (such as a table or graph) that you will consider as you make revising and editing decisions.

Some questions will direct you to an underlined portion of a passage. Other questions will direct you to a location in a passage or ask you to think about the passage as a whole.

After reading each passage, choose the answer to each question that most effectively improves the quality of writing in the passage or that makes the passage conform to the conventions of standard written English. Many questions include a "NO CHANGE" option. Choose that option if you think the best choice is to leave the relevant portion of the passage as it is.

Questions 1–11 are based on the following passage and supplementary material.

Supply and Demand

Many parents and students have become concerned that exorbitant college university tuitions are not worth the investment. [A] In response, colleges have not lowered tuitions (quite the contrary), but they have become more sensitive to the connection between university education and eventual employment. **1** Schools are beginning to answer the call for job skills and hirability rather than the traditional hallmarks of university education.

1

If the writer were to delete the parenthetical phrase *quite the contrary* from the previous sentence, the sentence would primarily lose

A) an indication on the part of the author that his college tuition was relatively low.

B) a reminder that college tuitions have in fact been rising.

C) a troubling reminder that college is simply too expensive for many who want to go.

D) nothing at all, because the information is given elsewhere in the paragraph.

CONTINUE ➡

Graphs like the one shown below measure college success by the attainment of employment, and **2** Business majors are over 10% more likely to have jobs that require college degrees after college than are Humanities majors. As a result, **3** there have been a sharp rise in more practical majors, like SCM, or supply-chain management.

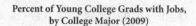

Percent of Young College Grads with Jobs, by College Major (2009)

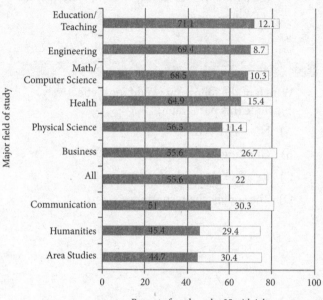

Percent of grads under 25 with jobs

■ percent in jobs that require college degrees
□ percent in jobs that don't require college degrees

The term "supply chain management" was coined by Keith Oliver in a 1982 interview. **4** However it happened, when the term began to take hold, the practice of supply-chain management came to be more and more clearly defined. [B] The most general definition holds that SCM is the strategic, systematic coordination of how a business works. For **5** instants, when you buy a new car, your purchase comes at the end of a complex supply chain—the last step of which is the factory sending **6** they're road-ready vehicle to the dealership.

2

Which of the following gives information consistent with the chart?

A) NO CHANGE

B) less than 50% of those with Area Studies majors are currently employed.

C) the Health Professions provide the safest bet for those entering college now.

D) the national average shows that only about 50% of all college grads are currently employed.

3

A) NO CHANGE

B) there've been

C) there has been

D) they're has been

4

Which of the following would best maintain the focus established in the first sentence of this paragraph?

A) NO CHANGE

B) By the mid-1990s,

C) One afternoon,

D) To get down to "business,"

5

A) NO CHANGE

B) instant's,

C) instances,

D) instance,

6

A) NO CHANGE

B) it's

C) its

D) their

CONTINUE

Before this step, however, hundreds or thousands of other, smaller processes have to take place first. [C] Each of these has to be imported from other suppliers, 7 which is one could say a process from mining to recycling of the vehicle or its decomposition in the process. After all, when you're done with your car, it doesn't just disappear. [D] You might sell it to someone else, back to a dealer, or to a junkyard for parts. 8 Make sure you get a good price!

7

A) NO CHANGE

B) a process that one could say goes all the way from the mining of natural resources to the eventual decomposition or recycling of the vehicle.

C) from natural resources mining to the decomposition of vehicle recycling in the process one could say.

D) in the life cycle of the car one could say it's both the natural resources and decomposition of the recycling.

8

Which of the following would most effectively conclude this paragraph?

A) NO CHANGE

B) Goodnight, sweet prince!

C) It's all so interesting!

D) The supply chain continues!

CONTINUE ➡

A supply-chain manager can't manage every single step of this process, but he or she can oversee the supply-chain for a specific company. A supply-chain manager, then, can provide a major financial benefit to the company for which he or she works. Efficient processes are generally cheaper **9** processes—and not just for manufacturing. SCM practices can also be applied to customer-service, especially to experiences that involve a number of employees. In **10** this way, like any college major, SCM is narrow enough to be an actual major but broad enough to be applicable to a number of industries and actual jobs.

Question 11 asks about the previous passage as a whole.

9

A) NO CHANGE

B) processes; and not

C) processes. And not

D) processes—and, not

10

A) NO CHANGE

B) this way, like any college major

C) this way, like, any college major,

D) this way like any college major

Think about the previous passage as a whole as you answer question 11.

11

Upon reviewing the essay and concluding that some information has been left out, the author composes the following sentence:

> The automaker doesn't make the metals that go into the car, or the fluids that power its various functions, or the rubber on the tires.

The best placement for this sentence would be at point

A) A in paragraph 1.

B) B in paragraph 2.

C) C in paragraph 3.

D) D in paragraph 3.

Questions 12–22 are based on the following passage.

Millard Fillmore's Presidency: Feel More Strongly About It?

Everyone knows who the first President of the United States was, but it takes a real expert to know that the thirteenth was Millard Fillmore. **12** As Zachary Taylor's Vice President, Fillmore took over in 1850 after Taylor's sudden death. Fillmore belonged to the Whig party. With Fillmore's departure in 1853, the Whig party fell out of national politics, **13** but make no mistake, a lot of old guys were wearing wigs back then. If the American people have forgotten that there ever was a true third party, that is likely because **14** they simply faded away at a time when the national conversation was more concerned with the events that would lead up to the Civil War. Millard Fillmore, however, is more than just **15** a funny name that can make us chuckle—like all presidents, he had some influence on life as we live it today.

12

At this point in the essay, the writer is considering adding the following true statement:

> Rutherford B. Hayes, born in 1822, was the nineteenth.

Should the writer make the addition here?

A) Yes, because it provides another obscure fact that readers might like to know.

B) Yes, because more readers have heard of Hayes than of Millard Fillmore.

C) No, because it does not advance the main point that this paragraph is making.

D) No, because Hayes's presidency was far too controversial to deserve mention here.

13

Which of the following would best support the statement made in the first part of this sentence?

A) NO CHANGE

B) though the party's life span in England followed a different trajectory.

C) but Fillmore came back again in 1856 as the candidate for the Know-Nothing party.

D) and every president has been a Democrat or a Republican ever since.

14

A) NO CHANGE

B) they all

C) we

D) the Whig party

15

A) NO CHANGE

B) a funny name that can wash away all our tears—

C) a guffaw-inducing handle, or sobriquet,

D) a funny name—

CONTINUE

Fillmore's influence has been especially strong in international affairs. Relations between Japan and the United States began to open up around this time, after Japan's long history of **16** isolating. **17** After the British opened relations with China, Fillmore and his cabinet took inspiration in trying to open relations with Japan. This was an early step in the productive (and often fraught) relationship between the two nations.

A) NO CHANGE

B) isolationism.

C) isolation of itself.

D) isolationism of the nation.

Which of the following would best explain the use of the word *inspiration* in the later part of this sentence?

A) NO CHANGE

B) While there were plenty of other things to do at the White House,

C) In the land that would eventually produce Toyota and Nintendo,

D) Totally unrelated to the conflicts the nations would have in World War II,

CONTINUE

The best-known, and perhaps most-reviled, of Fillmore's "accomplishments" is his passing of the Fugitive Slave Act in 1851. This Act made slavery a national, **18** the whole United States, problem, as it forbade those in non-slave states from protecting escaped slaves. An escaped slave, because he was considered "property," was committing an act of theft by escaping, and the person who harbored that escapee **19** will be then considered an accessory to that crime. The Fugitive Slave Act is a major scar on American **20** history, nevertheless, it is at least partly responsible for spurring the Civil War. The Fugitive Slave Act held back civil rights **21** forever because it demonstrated that the American government was not the progressive force, especially for African-Americans, that its constitution promised it would be.

Millard Fillmore was at the center of many of these things. While it may not be time to list him among our greatest presidents (in fact, he is routinely listed among the worst), Fillmore certainly provides the essential reminder that history is complex and the **22** presidency, even in its worst form, is a uniquely influential position in the history of the contemporary world.

18

Which of the following would best maintain the focus of this sentence by contributing to the main idea of the paragraph?

A) NO CHANGE

B) like as it related to everyone,

C) rather than merely a southern,

D) and at times international,

19

A) NO CHANGE

B) was

C) is

D) could of been

20

A) NO CHANGE

B) history, therefore,

C) history, and

D) history, but

21

A) NO CHANGE

B) for many years

C) for an eternity

D) for too darn long

22

A) NO CHANGE

B) presidency. Even in its worst form is a uniquely influential position in the history of the contemporary world.

C) presidency: even in its worst form, is a uniquely influential position in the history of the contemporary world.

D) presidency, even in its worst form, is a, uniquely, influential position, in the history of the contemporary world.

CONTINUE ➡

Questions 23–33 are based on the following passage.

The _Noir_ Side of Classic American Literature

[1] Film director Robert Siodmak once said, "Hollywood has given the world two kinds of motion pictures which are typically American. [2] They are the western and the gangster film." [3] In 23 that way, Dashiell Hammett and Raymond Chandler are considered the gold standard for great hardboiled fiction by authors from many nations. [4] The same might be said for American literary contributions. [5] With such fantastic authors working in the genre of detective 24 fiction, we can begin to see how these mystery novels come to be so much more than mere entertainment. [6] As Siodmak's quote implies, there is more than meets the eye to certain works in the "entertainment" genres. 25

23

A) NO CHANGE
B) those,
C) genres,
D) the "gangster" genre,

24

A) NO CHANGE
B) fiction. We can
C) fiction we can
D) fiction: we can

25

The best placement for sentence 4 would be

A) where it is now.
B) after sentence 2.
C) after sentence 5.
D) after sentence 6.

26 No one can match the intricacy and cleverness of Raymond Chandler's great novels. Macdonald was born Kenneth Millar in Canada in 1915, and he spent most of his formative years there. In his 20s, Millar attended the University of **27** Michigan, when he earned a Ph.D. in English literature, writing a dissertation on the works of Romantic poet Samuel Taylor Coleridge. Millar finished the degree in 1946, but in 1944, he published his first novel, *The Dark Tunnel*. While it may seem that Millar was being pulled in two different directions— **28** toward the "high" Coleridge and the "low" detective novel—Millar's later work under the pseudonym Ross Macdonald shows that he never took the separation very seriously.

26

Which of the following would most effectively introduce this paragraph by linking it to the previous paragraph?

A) NO CHANGE

B) Robert Siodmak had finished most of his career before Ross MacDonald became famous.

C) One proponent of this high-end of crime fiction is Ross Macdonald.

D) This is not to say, however, that there isn't a lot of garbage out there too.

27

A) NO CHANGE

B) Michigan, which

C) Michigan, where

D) Michigan which

28

Which of the following choices would best maintain the focus of this sentence?

A) NO CHANGE

B) Samuel Taylor Coleridge was most famous for his poem "The Rime of the Ancient Mariner"

C) toward movies and toward books, which both placed demands on his time

D) as to whether he liked Raymond Chandler or Dashiell Hammett better

CONTINUE

It is, after all, Macdonald's **29** superciliousness that puts his work in a category separate from that of his "pulp" contemporaries. While studying literature, Millar engaged closely not only with words but also with ideas, and the emergent discourses of psychoanalysis and Marxist economics did a good deal to inform how his characters operated. After all, **30** Macdonalds texts remind us that even the foulest murders are committed by **31** people who have a very human motivation. Macdonald was able to get inside the heads of his characters and to humanize some of the most horrendous and inhumane activities. No one is ever forgiven or rewarded for doing bad in a Macdonald novel, but neither is anyone ever portrayed as a purely evil monster.

Although murders, **32** thefts, and kidnappings may propel the plots of his books as they would in less self-conscious works, Macdonald treats them with a literary touch and uses the mystery form to show the depths of life's very mysteriousness. Following **33** to the detective novel in the footsteps of Hammett and Chandler, Macdonald brings something that literary fiction has known all along: human beings are the greatest mystery of all.

29

A) NO CHANGE
B) smartness
C) know-how
D) sophistication

30

A) NO CHANGE
B) Macdonald's
C) Macdonalds's
D) Macdonalds'

31

A) NO CHANGE
B) those who have a very human motivation.
C) someone who has a very human motivation.
D) people who have very human motivations.

32

A) NO CHANGE
B) thefts and kidnappings
C) thefts and, kidnappings
D) thefts, and kidnappings,

33

The best placement for the underlined portion would be

A) where it is now.
B) after the word *Chandler* (and before the comma).
C) after the word *brings*.
D) after the word *are*.

CONTINUE

Questions 34–44 are based on the following passage and supplementary material.

Space: The Next Dimension (of Natural Resources)

At a time when the scientific community the world over 34 do all they can to warn the public about the effects of global warming, the idea of "resources" can get 35 lost in the big message. The contemporary dialogue is much more concerned with use and effectiveness than with 36 resourcefulness. We should not forget, however, the age-old concern that resources will, at some point, simply run out. There have been many alternatives presented: solar, wind, and hydrogen power are the day's particularly hot topics. It has become clear, though, that these new resources will not cure us fully of energy dependency, especially with as large as that dependency is on fossil fuels. 37

34

A) NO CHANGE

B) does all it can

C) do all it can

D) does all they can

35

A) NO CHANGE

B) lost in the mix.

C) lost amid the noise.

D) lost.

36

A) NO CHANGE

B) themselves.

C) the resources themselves.

D) them.

37

Which of the following, if added here, would provide the most effective conclusion to this paragraph and the most effective transition to the next?

A) The solution to Earth's problems may finally have come, however, from a seemingly unlikely source: space.

B) World leaders are finally starting to take seriously the idea that there is a climate-change problem.

C) Some believe that climate change is either not happening or not caused by human activity.

D) Space, the final frontier, has captured the hearts and minds of Americans since the early twentieth century.

CONTINUE

The new, and currently hypothetical, solution to the problem is called "asteroid mining." As **38** wonderful as it may sound, asteroid mining is exactly what it sounds like. It refers to mining asteroids and other near-Earth objects for their raw materials, as these materials dwindle on Earth. Mining data show that **39** discoveries of new nickel sources in 2009 were less than half of what they were only ten years before. Scientists believe that the asteroids could contain a variety of minerals—including iron, nickel, and titanium. The practice may also enable astronauts to gather supplies for space journeys without overstocking or **40** getting new supplies on Earth. This practice, called "in-situ resource utilization," could change both space travel and exploration to be much safer and much more predictable **41** than currently.

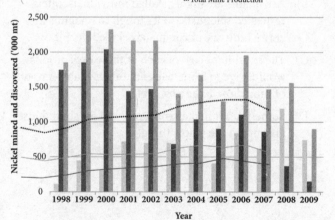

Potential Production from New Discoveries Relative to World Nickel Production, 1998-2009

Legend:
- Sulfide Discovered (3-yr Avg)
- — Sulfide Production
- Laterite Discovered (3-yr Avg)
- — Laterite Production
- Total Nickel in New Discoveries (3-yr Avg)
- ··· Total Mine Production

Note: Potential production in new discoveries is calculated using a 75% resources-to-reserves conversion rate and subtracting 10% for sulfide processing losses and 25% for laterite processing losses; a running three-year average of the annual totals is shown.

Data source: MEG's Strategies for Nickel Reserves Replacement study.

38

A) NO CHANGE
B) outlandish
C) wacky
D) idiosyncratic

39

Which of the following choices gives information consistent with the graph?

A) NO CHANGE
B) sulfide production, from 1998 to 2009, was consistently lower than laterite production.
C) for the first time in history, total nickel production in 2009 was lower than the three-year average of total nickel in new discoveries.
D) the total nickel found in new discoveries has decreased steadily since 1998.

40

A) NO CHANGE
B) getting supplies a second time
C) resupplying
D) having resupplied

41

A) NO CHANGE
B) than now.
C) than in the present.
D) than they currently are.

CONTINUE ▶

Scientists are confident in the potential results of asteroid mining precisely because they do not consider it all that distinct from Earth-bound mining. In fact, many resources exist in their relative abundance on Earth because of the rain of asteroids that hit the Earth after its surface [42] cooled, although the Earth and many of the asteroids were formed from similar proto-planetary material, Earth was much larger and pulled the many smaller asteroids into [43] its orbit and eventually onto its surface billions of years ago. Therefore, despite the obvious difficulty of capturing an in-flight asteroid, scientists are fairly certain of what they will find on these asteroids if and when they do.

Still, many are concerned that the infinitude of space may be a stopgap solution. First and foremost, the cost of extracting minerals from asteroids and then returning those minerals to Earth far outstrips the value of the minerals themselves. [44] Then, obviously, if we have depleted the vast (and once seemingly infinite) resources of Earth, there is no reason to believe that we will not deplete those of space as well. As a result, asteroid mining may have to remain "a" solution rather than "the" solution to our current energy woes.

42

A) NO CHANGE
B) cooled; although
C) cooled, although,
D) cooled although

43

A) NO CHANGE
B) their
C) it's
D) one's

44

At this point, the author wants to add a detail that will support the claim made in the previous sentence. Which of the following would most effectively achieve that goal?

A) NASA already uses a large amount of public funds, so the venture would have to be privately funded.

B) Astronauts are highly skilled individuals, often respected scientists, so it's tough to imagine an entire industry of adequately skilled people.

C) The exorbitant cost of each of these expeditions would have to bring back an unreasonable amount of mined ore to be profitable.

D) Sometimes it makes you wonder if we should just give up on the whole thing.

STOP
**If you finish before time is called, you may check your work on this section only.
Do not turn to any other section.**

No Test Material On This Page

Math Test – No Calculator

25 MINUTES, 17 QUESTIONS

Turn to Section 3 of your answer sheet to answer the questions in this section.

$A = \pi r^2$
$C = 2\pi r$

$A = \ell w$

$A = \frac{1}{2} bh$

$c^2 = a^2 + b^2$

Special Right Triangles

$V = \ell w h$

$V = \pi r^2 h$

$V = \frac{4}{3} \pi r^3$

$V = \frac{1}{3} \pi r^2 h$

$V = \frac{1}{3} \ell w h$

The number of degrees of arc in a circle is 360.
The number of radians of arc in a circle is 2π.
The sum of the measures in degrees of the angles of a triangle is 180.

CONTINUE ➡

1

Which of the following functions is represented in the graph above?

A) $y = (x - 3)^2$

B) $y = (x + 3)^2$

C) $y = x - 3$

D) $y = x^2 + 3$

2

If $b < 0$, which of the following could be the graph of $y = 3x + b$?

A)

B)

C)

D)

CONTINUE

3

If $\dfrac{x^2 - 4x + 3}{3} = 2(x - 1)$, what is one possible value of x?

A) 3

B) 5

C) 6

D) 9

4

From January of 1993 to January of 1999, the median income of U.S. households rose from 49,000 to 57,000. If this trend had continued linearly, which of the following equations could have been used to predict the median income, in thousands, in the United States x years after January 1999?

A) $I = 49 + 8x$

B) $I = 57 + 8x$

C) $I = 57 + \dfrac{4}{3}x$

D) $I = 49 + \dfrac{4}{3}x$

5

If $\dfrac{3(z + 3)}{4} - \dfrac{2(z - 2)}{3} = 2$, what is the value of z?

A) −19

B) 13

C) 19

D) 41

6

Medical researchers measured the populations of bacteria in a petri dish after treatment with the new antibiotic as well as in a petri dish that was untreated. The graph above plots the populations of bacteria in both dishes. Which of the following expressions shows the difference in population between the treated petri dish and the control dish t hours after treatment?

A) $5{,}000(0.95)^t - 4{,}000(0.9)^t$

B) $4{,}000(0.95)t - 5{,}000(0.9)t$

C) $5{,}000(0.9)^t - 4{,}000(0.95)^t$

D) $5{,}000(1.1)^t - 4{,}000(1.05)^t$

CONTINUE

7

If $\dfrac{a^3}{\sqrt{ab}} = b$ and $ab > 0$, which of the following

statements must be true?

A) $a = b^3$

B) $a^5 = b^3$

C) $a^2 = b^2$

D) $a^2 = b$

8

At the farmer's market, a bag of apples and 3 cartons of strawberries cost $18 total. If a bag of apples costs 50% more than a carton of strawberries, how much does a bag of apples cost?

A) $4.00

B) $4.50

C) $5.13

D) $6.00

9

The number of visitors, V, a website receives doubles every 3 months. If 6 months ago the website received 24,500 visitors, how many visitors, in thousands, will it receive t years from now?

A) $V = 24.5(2^{4t})$

B) $V = 98(2^t)$

C) $V = 98(2^{4t})$

D) $V = 49\left(2^{\frac{t}{3}}\right)$

10

At a store the cost of a shirt and two pairs of equally priced socks is $24, and the cost for three of the same shirt and two pairs of the same socks is $32. What is the cost of the shirt and one pair of socks?

A) 4

B) 10

C) 14

D) 56

CONTINUE

11

David is a criminology student and wants to determine the effect of several population parameters on the murder rate in a city. He collects data from hundreds of U.S. cities and determines that the number of murders can be approximated with a formula: $M = P\left(\dfrac{51 - I\sqrt{L}}{25}\right)$, in which P is the population in thousands, I is the median income, and L is the literacy rate expressed as a decimal. Which of the following expresses I in terms of M, P, and L?

A) $\dfrac{1}{\sqrt{L}}\left(51 - \dfrac{25M}{P}\right)$

B) $\dfrac{1}{\sqrt{L}}\left(\dfrac{25M}{P} - 49\right)$

C) $\dfrac{M}{P} - \dfrac{51}{25} + \sqrt{L}$

D) $\sqrt{L}\left(51 - \dfrac{25M}{P}\right)$

12

The radius of circle O (not shown) is 4, and the radian measure of central angle AOB is between $\dfrac{3\pi}{4}$ and $\dfrac{5\pi}{4}$. Which of the following could be the length of the arc AB ?

A) 3π

B) 4π

C) 5π

D) 8π

13

The value of John's baseball card collection decreases exponentially over time, and the value of his silver collection increases exponentially over time. If the value of John's two collections combined t years from now is given by the function $V = 500(1.05)^t + 600(0.95)^{\frac{t}{2}}$, which of the following statements must be true?

A) John's silver collection is more valuable currently than his baseball collection.

B) The value of John's silver collection changes at a faster rate than the value of John's baseball card collection.

C) John's baseball card collection decreases in value by 10% every six months.

D) The total value of the two collections remains constant over time.

CONTINUE

DIRECTIONS

For questions 14–17, solve the problem and enter your answer in the grid, as described below, on the answer sheet.

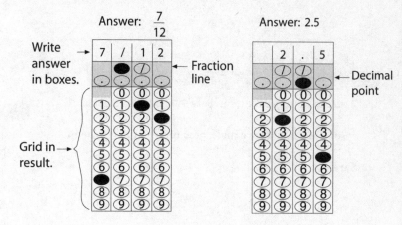

Answer: $\frac{7}{12}$

Write answer in boxes.

Fraction line

Grid in result.

Answer: 2.5

Decimal point

1. Although not required, it is suggested that you write your answer in the boxes at the top of the columns to help you fill in the circles accurately. You will receive credit only if the circles are filled in correctly.

2. Mark no more than one circle in any column.

3. No question has a negative answer.

4. Some problems may have more than one correct answer. In such cases, grid only one answer.

5. **Mixed numbers** such as $3\frac{1}{2}$ must be gridded as 3.5 or 7/2. (If is entered into the grid, it will be interpreted as $\frac{31}{2}$, not as $3\frac{1}{2}$.)

6. **Decimal Answers:** If you obtain a decimal answer with more digits than the grid can accommodate, it may be either rounded or truncated, but it must fill the entire grid.

Acceptable ways to grid $\frac{2}{3}$ are:

Answer: 201 – either position is correct

NOTE: You may start your answers in any column, space permitting. Columns you don't need to use should be left blank.

CONTINUE ▶

14

If $f(x) = 3x$ and $g(x) = x - 3$, what is the value of $f(4) - g(2)$?

15

There are 8 more males in Sara's class than females. If $\frac{3}{5}$ of the students are male, how many students are in Sara's class?

16

For positive integers c and d, the value of c is at least 3 times the value of d. If the difference between c and d is no more than 8, what is the largest possible value of d ?

17

The distance an object in motion travels is given by the following equation: $Displacement = V_i t + 0.5at^2$, in which V_i, a, and t represent initial velocity, acceleration, and time, respectively. The final velocity of the object is calculated with the equation $V_f = V_i + at$. How long does an object travel, in seconds, if it has a displacement of 22 meters, an initial velocity of 15 meters per seconds, and a final velocity of 5 meters per second?

STOP
**If you finish before time is called, you may check your work on this section only.
Do not turn to any other section.**

No Test Material On This Page

Math Test – Calculator

45 MINUTES, 31 QUESTIONS

Turn to Section 4 of your answer sheet to answer the questions in this section.

DIRECTIONS

For questions 1–27, solve each problem, choose the best answer from the choices provided, and fill in the corresponding circle on your answer sheet. **For questions 28–31,** solve the problem and enter your answer in the grid on the answer sheet. Please refer to the directions before question 28 on how to enter your answers in the grid. You may use any available space in your test booklet for scratch work.

NOTES

1. The use of a calculator **is permitted**.

2. All variables and expressions used represent real numbers unless otherwise indicated.

3. Figures provided in this test are drawn to scale unless otherwise indicated.

4. All figures lie in a plane unless otherwise indicated.

5. Unless otherwise indicated, the domain of a given function f is the set of all real numbers x for which $f(x)$ is a real number.

REFERENCE

$A = \pi r^2$
$C = 2\pi r$

$A = \ell w$

$A = \frac{1}{2} bh$

$c^2 = a^2 + b^2$

Special Right Triangles

$V = \ell wh$

$V = \pi r^2 h$

$V = \frac{4}{3}\pi r^3$

$V = \frac{1}{3}\pi r^2 h$

$V = \frac{1}{3}\ell wh$

The number of degrees of arc in a circle is 360.
The number of radians of arc in a circle is 2π.
The sum of the measures in degrees of the angles of a triangle is 180.

CONTINUE

1

A proton fired through medium *B* travels at half the velocity of a proton fired through medium *A*. If the proton in medium *A* travels 100,000 meters in 5 milliseconds, what is the velocity of the proton in medium *B* ?

A) 10,000 meters per millisecond

B) 20,000 meters per millisecond

C) 40,000 meters per millisecond

D) 50,000 meters per millisecond

2

Which of the following values is a solution of $6x - 5 > 2 + 15x$?

A) $-\dfrac{8}{9}$

B) $-\dfrac{5}{9}$

C) $-\dfrac{2}{7}$

D) 0

3

Which of the following values of *r* is a solution for the equation $r + 22 = 3r - 26 + r^2$?

A) −8

B) −6

C) 4

D) 8

4

To be eligible for Spartanville's Super Service Award, a resident must complete at least 2,000 hours of community service through a designated program. There are two designated programs this year: volunteering at the Community Center for 7.5 hours per day and removing street litter for 4 hours per day. Which of the following inequalities represents the possible number of days spent volunteering at the Community Center *c* and days removing street litter *l* needed to be eligible for this year's Spartanville Super Service Award?

A) $\dfrac{7.5}{c} + \dfrac{4}{l} > 2{,}000$

B) $\dfrac{7.5}{c} + \dfrac{4}{l} \geq 2{,}000$

C) $7.5c + 4l > 2{,}000$

D) $7.5c + 4l \geq 2{,}000$

CONTINUE

5

Lengths of Fish (inches)
6
9
9
36
39
x

The table above shows the lengths, in inches, of all the fish caught by a fisherman in one day. If the median length was 15, then what was the mean length?

A) 15

B) 16.5

C) 19

D) 20

6

A certain gold coin has a volume of 5 cubic centimeters. The density of gold is 19.3 grams per cubic centimeter. If 1 ounce is equal to 28.3 grams, what is the approximate mass of the coin in ounces? (Note: Density is mass divided by volume.)

A)   3.41

B)   7.33

C)   32.16

D)   2,730.95

7

Dr. Seeker, a noted paleontologist, polls colleagues around the world asking for the their theory on what caused the mass extinction of most dinosaur species and brought about the end of the Cretaceous Period. After polling 200,000 of his colleagues, 151,394 of them reply that they believe the mass extinction to be caused by the Chicxulub Asteroid impact. The remaining 48,606 reply with alternative theories. From this data, which is the best conclusion that Dr. Seeker could make?

A) Approximately 10% of all scientists polled believe the mass extinction to be caused by the Chicxulub Asteroid impact.

B) Approximately 25% of all scientists polled believe the mass extinction to be caused by the Chicxulub Asteroid impact.

C) Approximately 50% of all scientists polled believe the mass extinction to be caused by the Chicxulub Asteroid impact.

D) Approximately 75% of all scientists polled believe the mass extinction to be caused by the Chicxulub Asteroid impact.

8

A computer chip factory currently has 50 employees and has an output of 385 computer chips per day. A manager determined that for each additional employee hired, the output of the factory would increase by 42 computer chips. Which of the following functions, $C(x)$, expresses the total output of the factory for x employees when $x \geq 50$?

A) $C(x) = 42^{(x-50)} + 385$

B) $C(x) = (x)^{42} + 385$

C) $C(x) = 42x + 385$

D) $C(x) = 385 + 42(x - 50)$

CONTINUE

9

$$\frac{3(t + 2)}{4} = \frac{100 - 5t + 44}{8}$$

In the equation above, what is the value of t ?

A) −69

B) 4

C) 12

D) 36

10

In the xy-plane, the graph of $y = (3x - 6)(x - 6)$ represents a parabola. If the x- and y-coordinates of the parabola's vertex are to be expressed as constants or coefficients, which of the following forms of the equation is appropriate?

A) $y = (3x - 6)(x - 6)$

B) $y = 3(x - 4)^2 + (-12)$

C) $y = 3(x^2 - 8x + 12)$

D) $y = 3x^2 - 24x + 36$

11

Taylor is preparing to write his next novel, which will be 700 pages long. While typing, Taylor types at a constant rate of 23 words per minute. If each page contains 800 words, which of the following functions p models the number of pages Taylor has left to type after typing for m minutes?

A) $p(m) = \dfrac{700 - 800m}{23}$

B) $p(m) = \dfrac{700 - 23m}{800}$

C) $p(m) = 700 - \dfrac{23m}{800}$

D) $p(m) = 700 - \dfrac{800}{23m}$

CONTINUE

12

Line *b* is shown above. Line *c* is parallel to line *b* and contains the point (3, –2). Which of the following could be the equation of line *c* ?

A) $y = 2x - 8$

B) $y = \dfrac{1}{2}x - \dfrac{7}{2}$

C) $y = \dfrac{1}{2}x - \dfrac{1}{2}$

D) $y = -\dfrac{1}{2}x - \dfrac{7}{2}$

13

In State Q, the number of people in poverty halved each year from 2008 to 2012. There were 50,000 people in poverty in State Q in 2008, and *m* represents the number of months since January 2008, where $0 \le m \le 48$. Which of the following functions $f(m)$ could be used to estimate the number of people in poverty in State Q *m* months after January 2008 ?

A) $f(m) = 50{,}000 - \left(\dfrac{1}{2}\right)m$

B) $f(m) = 50{,}000 - \left(\dfrac{1}{2}\right)\left(\dfrac{m}{12}\right)$

C) $f(m) = 50{,}000 \times \left(\dfrac{1^{\frac{m}{12}}}{2}\right)$

D) $f(m) = 50{,}000 - m^{\frac{1}{2}}$

CONTINUE ▶

14

Days worked

In the graph above, x represents the number of days Chris has worked his part-time job and y represents the total amount of money in his bank account. If the graph has a slope of 40, what is the value of b, assuming Chris deposits all his earnings and does not spend any of the money in his bank account?

A) 117

B) 77

C) 40

D) 37

15

If $y = x^2 + x - 20$ and $z = x^2 + 10x + 25$, what is $\dfrac{y^2}{z}$, in terms of x ?

A) $\dfrac{x^4 - 8}{10x}$

B) $\dfrac{x^4 + x^2 - 400}{x^2 + 10x + 25}$

C) $x^2 - 8x - 15$

D) $x^2 - 8x + 16$

CONTINUE

16

The Squared Up framing store charges $61 to frame a customer's picture. The owner of the store calculated that the cost to frame each picture is $38 in materials plus $5 in the labor cost. The store must also pay $720 each month in general operating costs. Squared Up is profitable when the income from framing a customer's picture exceeds the total cost of framing the picture plus the general operating cost. If p is the number of pictures framed in a month, which of the following gives all possible values of p for which Squared Up is profitable during that month?

A) $p > 40$

B) $p < 40$

C) $p > 12$

D) $p < 12$

Questions 17–18 refer to the following information.

A nonprofit group wanted to determine whether there is an association between a household's income and the amount of money spent on groceries. After surveying 800 randomly selected households in Florida, the nonprofit found that as the household's income increased, its spending on groceries decreased.

17

If the nonprofit wanted to determine whether an association exists between a household's income and the average amount of money spent on groceries per person, which of the following changes to the survey would be most appropriate?

A) Determine the number of people per household who earn income.

B) Determine the total number of people per household.

C) Increase the number of households surveyed in Florida.

D) Survey households in additional states.

18

Which of the following conclusions is supported by the data?

A) As a household's income increases, the more it spends at restaurants.

B) A household's income is inversely proportional to the amount of money spent on groceries in Florida.

C) Having a lower household income causes the household to spend more on groceries.

D) There is a positive correlation between a household's income and the amount of money spent on groceries in the United States.

CONTINUE

19

$$2x - 96 = 4y - x$$
$$3y + 10x = y + 90$$

Based on the system of equations above, what is the value of $\dfrac{x}{y}$?

A) $-\dfrac{4}{5}$

B) $-\dfrac{3}{4}$

C) $-\dfrac{1}{5}$

D) $\dfrac{4}{3}$

20

Larissa uploaded 40,000 songs from her computer to her web storage. The mean file size of a song is 0.022 gigabytes, and the total time to upload all the files was 7.5 hours. If 1 gigabyte is equal to 1,024 megabytes, what is the upload rate for the files in megabytes per second, rounded to the nearest hundredth?

A)   1.48

B)   3.00

C)   33.37

D)   250.28

21

As part of her research into the social behaviors of felines, Dr. Ivask begins to observe the cheetah population near a noted watering hole in Namibia at the start of the year 2012. After years of observing the cheetahs, she constructs the equation $c(y) = 17y + 112$, in which y represents the number of years since the start of 2012 and c represents the cheetah population at the start of that given year. Dr. Ivask notes that after the start of 2015, an additional 20 cheetahs from a different region of Namibia join her cheetah population. Which of the following would be the number of cheetahs in the population that Dr. Ivask is observing after the additional 20 cheetahs joined?

A)   132

B)   163

C)   166

D)   183

CONTINUE

22

Number of Cars	Bronx	Brooklyn	Manhattan	Queens	Staten Island
Zero	960	1,120	1,280	720	80
One	640	560	480	600	40
Two	320	160	320	240	100
Three	0	160	80	80	60

The New York City Department of Motor Vehicles compiled the data for the number of cars owned in each of the city's five boroughs. There are 8 million residents in all five boroughs. The table above shows the number of residents, in thousands, from each of the five boroughs who own the specified number of cars. What percent of the New York City residents own more than the median number of cars per person and live in Manhattan?

A) 5%

B) 11%

C) 27%

D) 48%

23

If $8s = 4t + 17$ and $6t - 5s = 4$, what is the value of $6s + 4t$?

A) 13

B) 15

C) 21

D) 42

24

Circle C is defined by the equation $x^2 + y^2 - 8x + ky = 172$, and parabola P is defined by the equation $y = x^2 - 8x + 22$. For which value of k will circle C be centered at the vertex of parabola P ?

A) −12

B) −4

C) 6

D) 8

25

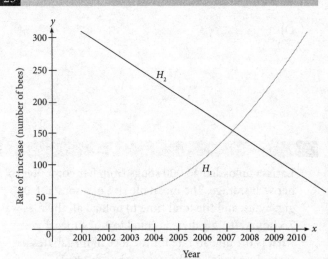

An entomologist analyzed the populations of two bee colonies, H_1 and H_2. She documented the rate of increase, which is the number of bees added to a colony in that year, for each colony over a 10-year period starting in the year 2000. The findings are modeled in the graph above. Which of the following conclusions can be drawn based on the entomologist's findings?

A) The population of H_2 decreased at a constant rate for each of the 10 years.

B) In 2008, the populations of H_1 and H_2 were equal.

C) In 2005, the population of H_2 was increasing at a faster rate than was the population of H_1.

D) The population of H_1 doubled from 2001 to 2005.

CONTINUE

26

In 2007, a biologist introduced a colony of phytoplankton into Great Blue Fish Lake, which had never contained phytoplankton before. The number of phytoplankton y in Great Blue Fish Lake can be estimated using the equation $y = \left(6.23^{\frac{k}{12}}\right)$, where k represents the number of months since the population was introduced. Which of the following is a proper interpretation of the elements of the equation?

A) 8,564,600 represents the number of phytoplankton after 1 year.

B) 8,564,600 represents the number of phytoplankton prior to 2007.

C) 6.23 represents the rate of increase on phytoplankton each month.

D) 6.23 represents the rate of increase on phytoplankton each year.

27

The scatterplot above show the size of the Arctic Ice Cap as observed from 1920 to 2015. Which of the following is the closest approximation of the average annual decrease in the area of the Arctic Ice Cap as indicated by the line of best fit?

A) 1 square kilometer

B) 6.6 square kilometers

C) 100,000 square kilometers

D) 66,000 square kilometers

DIRECTIONS

For questions 28–31, solve the problem and enter your answer in the grid, as described below, on the answer sheet.

1. Although not required, it is suggested that you write your answer in the boxes at the top of the columns to help you fill in the circles accurately. You will receive credit only if the circles are filled in correctly.

2. Mark no more than one circle in any column.

3. No question has a negative answer.

4. Some problems may have more than one correct answer. In such cases, grid only one answer.

5. **Mixed numbers** such as $3\frac{1}{2}$ must be gridded as 3.5 or 7/2. (If ⬚ is entered into the grid, it will be interpreted as $\frac{31}{2}$, not as $3\frac{1}{2}$.)

6. **Decimal Answers:** If you obtain a decimal answer with more digits than the grid can accommodate, it may be either rounded or truncated, but it must fill the entire grid.

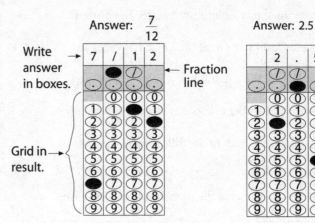

Answer: $\frac{7}{12}$ Answer: 2.5

Write answer in boxes. ← Fraction line

Grid in result. Decimal point ←

Acceptable ways to grid $\frac{2}{3}$ are:

Answer: 201 – either position is correct

NOTE: You may start your answers in any column, space permitting. Columns you don't need to use should be left blank.

CONTINUE ▶

28

$$(x - 2)^2 + (y + 8)^2 = 144$$

The equation of a circle in the xy-plane is shown above. What is the length of the diameter of the circle?

29

$$p(x) = \frac{(x + 4)(x - 4)(\sqrt{-x})}{x + 4}$$

For how many values of x does $p(x) = 0$?

Questions 30–31 refer to the following information.

A new car dealership offers a choice of two different compensation packages to its salespeople. With Package A, a salesperson is paid an annual salary of $10,000 plus a commission as a percentage of the sale price of each car sold that year. With Package B, a salesperson is not paid any salary but earns a fixed fee for each car sold that year. A salesperson must choose one of the packages at the time of hire and has the option to switch packages only on January 1 of each year.

30

On January 1, 2003, Jason chose compensation Package A. Jason sold 110 cars with a mean sales price of $30,000 that year. If Jason had chosen compensation Package B, his total compensation for the year would have been $1,550 more. If the commission percentage of Package A was 1%, what was the fixed fee per car, in dollars, for compensation Package B in 2003 ?

31

In 2005, the commission percentage of Package A was 1.5%, and the fixed fee per car of Package B was $725. Jason sold 80 cars that year and determined that his total compensation would be the same under both Package A and Package B. What is the mean price, in thousands of dollars, of the cars that Jason sold in 2005 ?

STOP

If you finish before time is called, you may check your work on this section only.
Do not turn to any other section.

The Princeton Review®

COMPLETE MARK ●	**EXAMPLES OF** **INCOMPLETE MARKS**	It is recommended that you use a No. 2 pencil. It is very important that you fill in the entire circle darkly and completely. If you change your response, erase as completely as possible. Incomplete marks or erasures may affect your score.

■ TEST NUMBER

ENTER TEST NUMBER
For instance, for Practice Test #1, fill in the circle for 0 in the first column and for 1 in the second column.

0	○ ○
1	○ ○
2	○ ○
3	○ ○
4	○ ○
5	○ ○
6	○ ○
7	○ ○
8	○ ○
9	○ ○

■ SECTION 1

COMPLETE MARK ● **EXAMPLES OF INCOMPLETE MARKS**

It is recommended that you use a No. 2 pencil. It is very important that you fill in the entire circle darkly and completely. If you change your response, erase as completely as possible. Incomplete marks or erasures may affect your score.

■ SECTION 2

	A B C D		A B C D		A B C D		A B C D		A B C D
1	○○○○	10	○○○○	19	○○○○	28	○○○○	37	○○○○
2	○○○○	11	○○○○	20	○○○○	29	○○○○	38	○○○○
3	○○○○	12	○○○○	21	○○○○	30	○○○○	39	○○○○
4	○○○○	13	○○○○	22	○○○○	31	○○○○	40	○○○○
5	○○○○	14	○○○○	23	○○○○	32	○○○○	41	○○○○
6	○○○○	15	○○○○	24	○○○○	33	○○○○	42	○○○○
7	○○○○	16	○○○○	25	○○○○	34	○○○○	43	○○○○
8	○○○○	17	○○○○	26	○○○○	35	○○○○	44	○○○○
9	○○○○	18	○○○○	27	○○○○	36	○○○○		

| COMPLETE MARK ● | EXAMPLES OF INCOMPLETE MARKS ○⊗⊖◉ ●🖐◑◐ | It is recommended that you use a No. 2 pencil. It is very important that you fill in the entire circle darkly and completely. If you change your response, erase as completely as possible. Incomplete marks or erasures may affect your score. |

■ SECTION 3

1 A B C D ○○○○   4 A B C D ○○○○   7 A B C D ○○○○   10 A B C D ○○○○   13 A B C D ○○○○

2 A B C D ○○○○   5 A B C D ○○○○   8 A B C D ○○○○   11 A B C D ○○○○

3 A B C D ○○○○   6 A B C D ○○○○   9 A B C D ○○○○   12 A B C D ○○○○

Only answers that are gridded will be scored. You will not receive any credit for anything written in the boxes.

14

/ ○○
· ○○○○
0 ○○○○
1 ○○○○
2 ○○○○
3 ○○○○
4 ○○○○
5 ○○○○
6 ○○○○
7 ○○○○
8 ○○○○
9 ○○○○

15

/ ○○
· ○○○○
0 ○○○○
1 ○○○○
2 ○○○○
3 ○○○○
4 ○○○○
5 ○○○○
6 ○○○○
7 ○○○○
8 ○○○○
9 ○○○○

16

/ ○○
· ○○○○
0 ○○○○
1 ○○○○
2 ○○○○
3 ○○○○
4 ○○○○
5 ○○○○
6 ○○○○
7 ○○○○
8 ○○○○
9 ○○○○

17

/ ○○
· ○○○○
0 ○○○○
1 ○○○○
2 ○○○○
3 ○○○○
4 ○○○○
5 ○○○○
6 ○○○○
7 ○○○○
8 ○○○○
9 ○○○○

NO CALCULATOR ALLOWED

PSAT/NMSQT PRACTICE TEST ANSWER SHEET

| COMPLETE MARK ● | EXAMPLES OF INCOMPLETE MARKS | It is recommended that you use a No. 2 pencil. It is very important that you fill in the entire circle darkly and completely. If you change your response, erase as completely as possible. Incomplete marks or erasures may affect your score. |

■ SECTION 4

	A B C D		A B C D		A B C D		A B C D		A B C D
1	○○○○	7	○○○○	13	○○○○	19	○○○○	25	○○○○
2	○○○○	8	○○○○	14	○○○○	20	○○○○	26	○○○○
3	○○○○	9	○○○○	15	○○○○	21	○○○○	27	○○○○
4	○○○○	10	○○○○	16	○○○○	22	○○○○		
5	○○○○	11	○○○○	17	○○○○	23	○○○○		
6	○○○○	12	○○○○	18	○○○○	24	○○○○		

Only answers that are gridded will be scored. You will not receive any credit for anything written in the boxes.

28   **19**   **30**   **31**

CALCULATOR ALLOWED

Chapter 14
Practice Test 1:
Answers and
Explanations

PRACTICE TEST 1 ANSWER KEY

Section 1: Reading

1.	D	25.	B
2.	A	26.	A
3.	B	27.	C
4.	A	28.	B
5.	B	29.	D
6.	C	30.	A
7.	B	31.	A
8.	C	32.	C
9.	A	33.	B
10.	C	34.	C
11.	D	35.	C
12.	C	36.	A
13.	B	37.	B
14.	A	38.	D
15.	B	39.	C
16.	B	40.	B
17.	A	41.	D
18.	D	42.	A
19.	B	43.	C
20.	D	44.	C
21.	C	45.	C
22.	C	46.	B
23.	A	47.	D
24.	D		

Section 2: Writing and Language

1.	B	23.	D
2.	A	24.	A
3.	C	25.	B
4.	B	26.	C
5.	D	27.	C
6.	C	28.	A
7.	B	29.	D
8.	D	30.	B
9.	A	31.	D
10.	A	32.	A
11.	C	33.	C
12.	C	34.	B
13.	D	35.	D
14.	D	36.	C
15.	D	37.	A
16.	B	38.	B
17.	A	39.	A
18.	C	40.	C
19.	B	41.	D
20.	C	42.	B
21.	B	43.	A
22.	A	44.	C

Section 3: Math (No Calculator)

1.	A	11.	A
2.	D	12.	B
3.	D	13.	B
4.	C	14.	13
5.	A	15.	40
6.	C	16.	4
7.	B	17.	2.2
8.	D		
9.	C		
10.	C		

Section 4: Math (Calculator)

1.	A	16.	A
2.	A	17.	B
3.	A	18.	B
4.	D	19.	A
5.	D	20.	C
6.	A	21.	D
7.	D	22.	B
8.	D	23.	D
9.	C	24.	A
10.	B	25.	C
11.	C	26.	D
12.	B	27.	D
13.	C	28.	24
14.	B	29.	1
15.	D	30.	405
		31.	40

PRACTICE TEST 1 EXPLANATIONS

Section 1—Reading

1. **D** Use POE! Although there doesn't seem to be any animosity, there is no evidence of the townspeople supporting Clym, so eliminate (A). Choice (B) can be eliminated because it is not supported in the passage. Clym's fame was built over years in his youth, and there is no reason given for why he is not going to return to Paris. You don't even know for sure whether he will return or not. Choice (C) is not stated in the passage, which mentions Clym telling a *Scripture riddle*, but this does not mean his upbringing was religious. Choice (D) is correct because the passage states that *the only absolute certainty about him was that he would not stand still in the circumstances amid which he was born.*

2. **A** The answer to question 1 is best supported by (A) because this portion of the passage discusses that something was expected of Clym regardless of whether it was good or bad, and he would not simply stagnate.

3. **B** The *observer's eye* is being *arrested* by Clym's face, which is later described as *attractive*. This is obviously not a criminal type of arrest, so (A) and (D) can be eliminated. This sentence is discussing an onlooker's glance being captured by Clym's features, so (C) doesn't make sense because nothing is forcing this. Choice (B) is the correct answer.

4. **A** Use POE! Choice (B) can be eliminated because there is no support that people are beginning to bore of him. Choice (C) can be eliminated because the passage doesn't say anything about the state of Clym's finances or how fancy his lifestyle is. Choice (D) can be eliminated because you don't know for sure that he never could live up to his renown. You don't know precisely if the quote was originally about Clym, but it doesn't matter. The author uses this quote to plant the idea of disappointment. Later in the passage, suspicions continue when a *curiosity as to why he stayed on so long* arises. You know that Clym went off to London and Paris, but now he is back and for longer than a holiday.

5. **B** This paragraph suggests that Clym has stayed in town longer than a normal vacation, which causes *curiosity* because he is someone who has *something being expected of him*. These two ideas seem to be at odds with each other, which is best summarized in (B). There is no evidence to support the idea that the townspeople want him to return to Paris or that they are intrusive in his life, so (A) and (C) can be eliminated. The word *prove* in (D) is too strong because this paragraph doesn't even discuss awkward spreading of Clym's fame, so (D) can be eliminated as well. Choice (B) is the correct answer.

6. **C** This sentence is contrasting the idea that comes before it, which says that Clym *must of necessity have something in him* by saying that it is possible his fame *owed something to the accidents of his situation*. In context, the word *accidents* means "luck" or "happenstance." The answer that best summarizes this is (C). Choice (A) is incorrect because no literal crashes are mentioned. Choice (B) is also too literal a definition of *accidents* and does not relate to luck. Choice (D) plays off the idea of an accident like a car accident, but it is incorrect in this context.

7. **B** Use POE! The passage doesn't say anything about Clym being wealthy or having reputation overseas, so eliminate (A). The passage does mention his facial features but not any sort of tragic circumstances, so eliminate (C). Clym is never said to have any skill as a preacher, so eliminate (D). Only (B) correctly characterizes him because he is known to be *famous* and *a lad of whom something was expected*.

8. **C** The answer to the previous question is best supported by (C). In these lines, Clym is described as *An individual whose fame has spread* and therefore must *have something in him*. None of the other answer choices support this idea of fame and potential.

9. **A** The comparison being made in the first paragraph is one of something prosaic (sounds and shapes) becoming *attractive* and *interesting* when used in conjunction with others to create language or writing. This relationship is best mirrored in (A). The color yellow by itself on the palette is commonplace, but painted with other colors into something such as a sunrise makes it more appealing. Choice (B) describes two things as equally appealing. Choice (C) is about something not being beautiful until it is understood. Choice (D) is comparing two different types of gems.

10. **C** The passage says that the tulip was useless but beautiful. The passage makes no mention of the tulip's scent, so eliminate (A). Though the tulip is called exotic, the author does not ascribe the flower's popularity to its exotic botany; eliminate (B). Because (C) mentions the flower's beauty, (C) is the best answer. The passage specifically states that the tulip had no medicinal qualities, so eliminate (D).

11. **D** Only (D) mentions the tulip's beauty, the answer to the previous question.

12. **C** In context, the word *pitch* refers to the *mad embrace* of the tulip by the Dutch. Therefore, the correct answer should mean something like "frenzy." *Throw, angle,* and *promotion* mean completely different things, while *level* can mean "intensity," which most closely matches the meaning of *pitch*. Therefore, (C) is correct.

13. **B** In context, the word *spectacularly* emphasizes how very flat, monotonous, and swampy Holland is. Eliminate (A) because the Low Countries are never described as beautiful. Choice (B) is correct because the Dutch landscape is described as monotonous. Get rid of (C) because there is no tone of irony in the passage. Eliminate (D) because the efforts to make the Low Countries beautiful are not mentioned until later in the paragraph.

14. **A** The fourth paragraph describes the popularity of botany in 17th-century Holland. This matches (A). Choice (B) is incorrect because there is no mention of a baseball field. Choice (C) contradicts the passage, which says that Dutch botanists were extremely famous. Choice (D) is incorrect because there is nothing that says the Dutch obsession was unusually strong.

15. **B** The passage states that Dutch gardens were used to make statements about one's sophistication and wealth. Choice (A) is incorrect because it takes an overly literal interpretation of the statement that the Dutch saw their gardens as being like jewel boxes. Choice (B) is correct because the passage states that flowers were a status symbol for the Dutch. Choice (C) says that all Dutch gardens were full of exotic and expensive flowers, which is not supported by the text. Choice (D) says that Dutch

gardens had only one flower in them; this is also not supported by the text, which states only that that one flower could make a powerful statement.

16. **B** The answer to the previous question states that the flowers were used as a status symbol for the Dutch. Choice (A) is incorrect because it emphasizes how tiny and prized Dutch gardens were, but it does not mention social status. Choice (B) is correct because it states "*To make such statements—about one's sophistication, about one's wealth—has always been one of the reasons people plant gardens,*" which matches question 15. Choices (C) and (D) are incorrect because they do not discuss status or wealth in relation to the flower.

17. **A** In context, *utilitarian* means "useful." Only *practical* matches this meaning. The best answer is (A).

18. **D** The passage contrasts the useful rose and lily with the useless tulip. There is no indication of the price of roses or lilies; therefore, eliminate (A). There is no indication of whether or not roses or lilies are exotic, so eliminate (B). There is no indication that roses and lilies are not beautiful, so eliminate (C). Choice (D) is supported by the text's claim that roses and lilies were originally prized for how useful they are, but that the tulip is *extraordinarily useless*.

19. **B** The blurb indicates that the author of this passage *was a mill-worker, writer, and social activist* and played an important role in *the labor and women's suffrage movements*. Therefore, *disinterested* would not describe Robinson's perspective, so (A) can be eliminated. Choice (B) is a good match because she is a social activist, and the final sentence of the passage expresses her strong belief that *many men...were helped to an education by the wages of the early millgirls*. Choice (C) is incorrect because Robinson never expresses anger nor is she trying to cause trouble. Choice (D) is incorrect because *carefree* does not capture the way she proudly and positively portrays the hard work of the women she describes in this passage. Therefore, (B) is the best answer.

20. **D** In the first paragraph, the author states that *women* and *troops of young girls* came from all over to take advantage of the cotton mills that were looking for help and the *high wages that were offered to all classes of work-people*. Therefore, women moved to Lowell because they wanted these jobs with high wages. Choices (A) and (B) are incorrect because the author does not discuss the climate or any vacation time in this paragraph. Choice (C) is tempting because the women and girls were coming from *distant towns*, *different parts of New England*, and *Canada*. However, the author does cite working in a diverse atmosphere as the reason for them wanting to work in the cotton mills. This leaves (D). Even if you're unsure about what *remuneration* means, you can confidently pick (D) because of POE. However, if you do know what *remuneration* means (money paid for work or service), then (D) is clearly the correct answer.

21. **C** This question is really asking, "Why does the author mention the working conditions of England and France?" In the second paragraph, the author states that, at the time, being a factory girl was the lowest employment position a woman could hold. This view—that working as a millgirl was a *degrading occupation*—was established due to the treatment of women in factories in countries like England and France. In order to overcome this prejudice, high wages were offered to entice

women to work as millgirls. Thus, the author refers to working conditions in England and France to illustrate how the working conditions at the Lowell mills would be different. Choice (C) is a good match. Eliminate (A) and (D) because the author says exactly the opposite. The conditions in these two European countries were neither superior nor were they a model that the author was advocating for the United States. The author gave an example of working conditions elsewhere during this time period but did not provide a historical overview of the Industrial Revolution, so (B) is incorrect. The best answer is (C).

22. **C** The answer to the previous question was that the working conditions in England and France were mentioned in order to *draw a contrast between those conditions and the conditions promised to workers in the Lowell mills.* Because being a factory girl was a *degrading occupation*, the corporations in Lowell needed a way to convince women to take these positions, so they offered high wages. The lines that best support this answer are lines 20–24, (C). Eliminate (A) and (B) because neither choice offers a contrast between the conditions in European factories to those in the Lowell mills. Choice (D) provides information about working conditions only in the Lowell mills but provides no information about the working conditions in England and France. Therefore, (C) is the best answer.

23. **A** The corporations were trying to find ways to *overcome a prejudice* by offering them high wages to work in a role that had a negative association still clinging to *this degrading occupation.* Work that is degrading would cause humiliation or shame, so *opprobrium* means something similar to "shame." Eliminate (B) and (C) because those choices have positive meanings. Choice (D) is a possibility because *trauma* (a disturbing or distressing event) could cause shame; however, the word itself does not mean "shame," so this answer should be eliminated. Choice (A) is *disgrace*, which is a synonym for "shame." Therefore, the best answer is (A).

24. **D** In the third paragraph, the author describes the youngest girls employed at the Lowell mills. While they might have some free time, they were responsible for taking off the *full bobbins from the spinning-frames* and replacing *them with empty ones*, so they did not have "complete freedom," which makes (A) incorrect. There is no mention of the youngest girls spending their time in an educational setting in this paragraph or the passage, so (B) is not correct. Choice (C) is incorrect because the doffers were aged under 10 years old. This leaves (D), which can be supported by information earlier in the third paragraph. In lines 31–34, the author lists activities that the girls might occupy their free time with when they weren't replacing empty bobbins. The correct answer is (D).

25. **B** The answer to the previous question was that the youngest girls were afforded more leisure time than were the older girls and adult women. The best evidence for this answer is found in lines 31–34, (B). Choice (A) is incorrect because these lines describe only what the youngest girls were called and what they did in the mills, not that they had more leisure time than the older girls and women. Choice (C) is incorrect because those lines are not specifically referring to the youngest girls. Choice (D) includes lines that make no mention of the youngest girls working in the mills, so it cannot provide supporting evidence for the previous question. The correct answer is (B).

26. **A**   The table provided in this passage *shows the daily schedule for the workers at the Lowell Mills in 1851.* Choice (A) is a good match because this answer references the amount of time the women were required to be at the mills, and the table contains the daily schedule for the year. The table does not indicate that there are five corporations or how the millgirls spent their wages, so eliminate (B) and (C). Choice (D) is incorrect because the daily schedule provided in the table in no way connects to (D)'s claim. Choice (A) is the best answer.

27. **C**   In the last paragraph, the author explains that the main incentive for women who wanted these jobs was to *secure the means of education for some male member of the family.* The money for the men's education was the most important reason to take these jobs. In context, *prevailing* means something similar to "main" or "most important." Eliminate (A), (B), and (D) because they do not mean the same thing as "main" or "most important." *Predominant* does mean the same thing as "main" or "most important," so (C) is the best answer.

28. **B**   The fifth paragraph discusses the idea that the money the millgirls earned often went to *secure the means of education for some male member of the family.* Lines 56–59 indicate that the importance of a college education for the men was a *dominant thought* in the minds of many of the millgirls. The author also gives examples of women who provided men the means to earn their education. The author never indicates that the women were *contemptuous* (scornful) of the men, so (A) should be eliminated. Choice (B) is a good match because it was common for the women to use their earnings to pay for their male relatives' education, and the author gives examples of women who did so. Choice (C) could be true, but that claim is never directly made in the passage, and more importantly, it is not the main idea of the fifth paragraph. Choice (D) is incorrect because the women were not earning money for their daughters; they were using the money to pay for the male relatives' education. Therefore, the best answer is (B).

29. **D**   The first paragraph mentions titanium's ability to impart white coloring and brightness to objects. Lines 5–7 state that the *very high refractive index* of titanium dioxide means that it *has high light-scattering ability.* The phrase *as a result* lets the reader know that this quality is what allows titanium dioxide to impart *whiteness, opacity, and brightness to many products.* While the authors do state in the first paragraph that titanium is *highly resistant to corrosion,* (A), and *45% lighter than steel,* (B), these facts are not mentioned in relation to titanium's ability to impart whiteness and brightness to objects. Choice (C) is mentioned in lines 40–41, but there is no reference to whiteness or brightness in this paragraph. Therefore, the correct answer is (D).

30. **A**   The answer to the previous question was that titanium's *high refractive index* accounts for its ability to impart white coloring and brightness to objects. Lines 5–8 directly state this, so (A) provides the best evidence for the answer to the previous question and is the correct answer. Eliminate (B) and (C) because they do not refer to titanium's ability to impart whiteness and brightness to objects. The fact titanium is naturally abundant does not account for its ability to impart whiteness or brightness to objects, so eliminate (D).

31. **A** Matthew Hunter was the first person to isolate titanium metal. However, because the process was so difficult, the metal was considered a laboratory *curiosity*. Once William Kroll developed a method to produce the metal in commercial quantities, titanium was used more widely. In context, the word *curiosity* means something similar to "peculiar" or "unusual" because, at first, it could not be made into commercial quantities due to the difficult isolation process—it was something found only in a laboratory. Choices (C) and (D) do not mean "peculiar" or "unusual," so eliminate them. Choice (B) is often associated with *curiosity*; however, it does not match "unusual" and does not make sense in context because the metal itself cannot be inquisitive, so eliminate (B). Only *oddity* in (A) has a meaning similar to "peculiar" or "unusual" and is the best answer.

32. **C** Use POE! The table presents the percentage of titanium dioxide and the distribution by industry for 2011 and 2012. Choice (A) does not contain any information that is listed in the table, so get rid of (A). The table does not include information about opacity and brightness, so eliminate (B). Choice (C) could work because the products listed are found in the table and would account for more than 75% of titanium dioxide's distribution, which supports the idea that *most* titanium dioxide is used in these products. The table does not provide information on quality or weight, so eliminate (D). The best answer is (C).

33. **B** Lines 26–28 mention that the paint industry began using titanium dioxide because of the environmental hazards associated with lead paint. Then, lines 28–31 list several products that titanium is used in for coloring because it is *relatively inert*. Lines 36–39 mention that titanium is also used in biological implants because the metal is *nonreactive in the human body*. The authors do support the idea that titanium is safe for human use and give specific examples and reasons, so (C) and (D) can be eliminated. Choice (A) is incorrect because it does not provide the correct reasons/examples to answer this question. The correct answer is (B) because it includes the information from lines 28–31 and lines 36–39.

34. **C** The text says that the *corrosion resistance of titanium metal and its alloys make them particularly valuable*. Therefore, *resistance* must mean something like "prevention." *Safeguard* means "protect," so eliminate (A). *Support* means "help" or "hold up," so eliminate (B). *Blocking* matches "prevention," so keep (C). *Struggle* means "fight" or "effort," so eliminate (D). The correct answer is (C).

35. **C** The authors mention steel and aluminum in the first paragraph. Titanium is compared with steel— *It is as strong as steel but 45 percent lighter*—and aluminum—*it is twice as strong as aluminum but only 60 percent heavier*. So the authors are comparing the three metals to give the reader a sense of titanium's strength and weight compared with those qualities in steel and aluminum. Choice (C) is a good match. The authors discuss titanium's ability to impart brightness and opacity to objects later in this paragraph but not compared in any way to steel or aluminum, so eliminate (A). While titanium is stronger than aluminum, it is only as strong as steel, so titanium is not *stronger than all other metals*. Eliminate (B). The natural abundance of titanium is never mentioned in this paragraph. When it is mentioned later in the passage, steel and aluminum are not, so eliminate (D). Therefore, the best answer is (C).

36. **A** In lines 52–53, the authors state that *rutile has a very high index of refraction* and *is the most desirable in the pigment industry*. Because *rutile* is the most desirable form of titanium for the pigment industry, it is likely the most useful for manufacturing paint products, (A). *Ilmenite* accounts for 90% of the world's titanium, but the authors do not state that it is used by the pigment industry or for paint products; eliminate (B). The specific economic importance of *anatase* is never directly stated, so eliminate (C). *Titanium metal* was mentioned earlier in the passage as being useful for biological implants and to the aerospace industry, not to the pigment industry; eliminate (D). The correct answer is (A).

37. **B** Because the answer to the previous question was *rutile*, (B), lines 50–53, would best support this answer. The lines in (A) make no reference to *rutile*. Choices (C) and (D) discuss ilmenite, which is not the correct answer to the previous question. Therefore, the answer that provides the best evidence for the answer to the previous question is (B).

38. **D** This question asks what can be inferred about *mind wandering* in Passage 1. Notice that this is the first question in a paired set, so it can be done in tandem with question 39. Consider the answers to question 39 first. The lines for (39A) simply describe the experiment of Dr. Axelrod, but don't give any specifics about mind wandering. Eliminate (39A). The lines for (39B) continue with a direct description of the experiment. Again, there is no discussion of mind wandering, so these lines don't support any of the answers for question 38. Eliminate (39B). The lines for (39C) say that experiment showed that *frontal lobes play a causal role in the production of mind wandering behavior*. These lines support (38D), so draw a line connecting those two answers. The lines for (39D) do not mention mind wandering, so eliminate that answer. Without support from question 39, (38A), (38B), and (38C) can be eliminated. The correct answers are (38D) and (39C).

39. **C** (See explanation above)

40. **B** This question asks what the word *stem* most nearly means in line 26. Go back to the text, find the word *stem*, and cross it out. Then read the window carefully, using context clues to determine another word that would fit in the text. The text says that *Bar believes that this surprising result might stem from the convergence*. Therefore, *stem* must mean something like "come from." *Branch* means "divide from," so eliminate (A). *Originate* means "come from," so keep (B). *Contain* means "hold in," so eliminate (C). *Restrain* means "hold back," so eliminate (D). The correct answer is (B).

41. **D** This question asks why the author mentions "a painful procedure in a doctor's office." Carefully read the window to figure out why the author would use that phrase. The author mentions that *increasing the amount...of daydreaming we do...can be beneficial*. She then goes on to say that the doctor's visit can be *made less distressing by visualizations of soothing scenes*. The mention of the doctor's office is included as an example of her previous statement. Eliminate any answers that aren't consistent with this prediction. Choice (A) might initially look attractive because the author does provide an example, but there's no evidence the example is a *personal example*. Additionally, the concept is not an abstract one. Eliminate (A). Choice (B) can be eliminated because the author is not attempting to *trigger a...memory*. She is simply using the doctor's office as an example. Eliminate (B). Choice (C) can be eliminated because it has nothing to do with the window or the prediction. Choice (D) is a clear paraphrase of the prediction and the correct answer.

42. **A** This question asks what the word *caught* most nearly means in line 63. Go back to the text, find the word *caught*, and cross it out. Then read the window carefully, using context clues to determine another word that would fit in the text. The text says that the researchers *asked 122 undergraduates at the University of British Columbia to read a children's story and press a button each time they caught themselves tuning out.* The missing word must mean something like "noticed" or "became aware of." *Detected* means "noticed," so keep (A). *Entangled* means "intertwined" or "ensnared," so eliminate (B). *Developed* means "to make more advanced," so eliminate (C). *Overtook* means "to move ahead of," so eliminate (D). Although *entangled* and *overtook* are both possible definitions of *caught*, neither of them is consistent with the prediction. The correct answer is (A).

43. **C** This question asks what the passage most clearly suggests about daydreaming. Notice that this is the first question in a paired set, so it can be done in tandem with question 44. Look at the answers for question 44 first. The lines for (44A) say that *increasing the amount of...daydreaming... can be beneficial.* These lines don't support any of the answers for question 43, so eliminate (44A). The lines for (44B) simply define daydreaming as *tuning out or off-task thinking.* These lines don't support any of the answers for question 43, so eliminate (44B). Choice (44C) says that people *who notice when they're [tuning out]...seem to be the most creative.* These lines support (43C), so draw a line connecting these two answers. Choice (44D) mentions a *flash of insight* about an *unsolved problem.* These lines might initially seem to support (43A), but there's no indication in the text that daydreaming is the *only way* to solve a difficult problem. Eliminate (44D). Without support from question 44, (43A), (43B), and (43D) can be eliminated. The correct answers are (43C) and (44C).

44. **C** (See explanation above)

45. **C** This question asks for a point made in Passage 1, but not in Passage 2. Since this is a question about both passages, it should be done after the questions about an individual passage. Passage 1 does not mention a correlation between mind wandering and intelligence, so eliminate (A). Passage 2 mentions everyday activities (*reading, visit to the doctor's office*), so eliminate (B). Passage 1 mentions *the frontal lobes* and *occipital cortex* when discussing the study by *Dr. Vadim Axelrod,* but there are no brain regions mentioned in Passage 2, so keep (C). Passage 2 discusses details about a study in which *people who engaged in a mildly demanding task, such as reading, during a break from, say, a visual assignment, such as the hat-rack problem—in which participants have to construct a sturdy hat rack using two boards and a clamp—did better on that problem than those who did nothing at all.* Eliminate (D). The correct answer is (C).

46. **B** This question asks for something the authors of Passage 1 and Passage 2 would both agree with. Since this is a question about both passages, it should be done after the questions about an individual passage. While Passage 1 says that *our study's external stimulation increased the incidence of mind wandering,* it does not say it's *inevitable,* which is too extreme, so eliminate (A). Passage 1 says that mind wandering did not reduce *the subjects' ability to complete the task* and *it caused task performance to become slightly improved* and Passage 2 says that mind wandering *could also explain [a] flash of insight,* so keep (B). Passage 2 does not mention *passion,* so eliminate (C). Passage 1 does not talk about *intelligent people,* so eliminate (D). The correct answer is (B).

47.   **D**   This question asks which lines in Passage 2 *most directly corroborate the conclusion about external stimulation on concentration as presented in Passage 1*. Look for a conclusion about *external stimulation* in Passage 1, and then check each set of lines in the answer choices. The last paragraph in Passage 1 says that *external stimulation increased the incidence of mind wandering* and *the external stimulation actually enhanced the subjects' cognitive capacity*. The lines for (A) say that daydreaming can help relieve stressful experiences, but there is no connection to cognitive capacity. Eliminate (A). The lines for (B) simply describe an experiment, but don't address the results of the experiment. Eliminate (B). The lines for (C) say that mind wandering is important, but meta-awareness is also needed. There is no mention of cognitive capacity, so eliminate (C). The lines for (D) say that researchers *found that people who engaged in a mildly demanding task, such as reading…did better on that problem than those who did nothing at all*. This supports the idea that external stimulation enhanced cognitive capacity. The correct answer is (D).

Section 2—Writing and Language

1.   **B**   The phrase *quite the contrary* is meant to emphasize that tuition costs are not only not decreasing, they are increasing. The answer that best matches this is (B). Choice (A) is not supported by the text—the author does not mention his or her tuition costs. Choice (C) goes too far; although the phrase does indicate that tuition costs have increased, it does not support the claim that it is too expensive for many who wish to attend college. There is no indication elsewhere in the paragraph that tuition has increased, so (D) is not correct. The best answer is (B).

2.   **A**   The sentence in question states that *Business majors are over 10% more likely to have jobs that require college degrees…than are Humanities majors*. According to the graphic, this statement is true. Business majors holding jobs that require college degrees are counted at 55.6%, while Humanities majors holding jobs that require college degrees are counted at 45.4%. Choice (B) is incorrect; more than 50% of Area Studies majors are employed in both jobs that do and do not require a college degree. Choice (C) is not supported by the graphic, as it demonstrates only the current rate of employment for certain areas of studies by college degree requirement; it does not indicate future trends. Choice (D) is not relevant to the point being made in the paragraph. Also, because the focus is on specific types of majors that are more likely to lead to employment for graduates, (D) is too vague. The only answer that is supported by the graphic and expresses this point is (A).

3.   **C**   The underlined portion *there have been* refers to the *sharp rise* later in the sentence. Because a *sharp rise* is a singular subject, it needs to have a singular verb. Because both (A) and (B) are plural (and they have the exact same meaning), they can be eliminated. Choice (D) corrects the agreement error between the subject and verb but includes an apostrophe error with "they're." The correct answer is (C), as it corrects the agreement error with the word "has" and does not contain any additional errors.

4.   **B**   The first sentence of this paragraph describes when the phrase "supply-chain management" was introduced. The second sentence describes the progression of how that term and practice became defined. The choice that stresses this progression over time is (B), as it clearly establishes a timeline

by referencing a specific era. Choice (C) references time but is too vague. Choices (A) and (D) are both awkward and are not related to the progression of the term. The best answer is (B).

5. **D** In this sentence, the author is introducing an example to support his or her argument. The idiomatic phrase used should be "For instance." The only choice that contains the correct phrasing is (D).

6. **C** Expand out the contraction. *They're* is the same as *they are*, which is not correct in this context. Eliminate (A). The remaining answer choices contain both plural and singular pronouns. Because the noun earlier in the sentence that is being replaced is *factory*, which is singular, a singular pronoun is needed. Eliminate (D) as well. Expanding (B) results in "it is," which is incorrect. The *its* in (C) is singular and demonstrates the factory's possession of the *road-ready vehicles*, so it is the correct answer.

7. **B** As it is currently written, the sentence is very awkward. Because the introductory phrase is describing the process of supply-chain management, that process needs to be placed closely to that phrase in the sentence. Only (B) does this. Choice (C) has *natural resources* being described by the introductory phrase and is also awkward. Choice (D) has *the life cycle of the car* being described by the introductory phrase rather than the process and would create a comma splice. Choice (B) is the best answer.

8. **D** The central idea of this paragraph is the multi-step process that supply-chain management goes through. The most effective conclusion to the paragraph will relate to that process in some way or other. Choice (A) refers to making personal profit, which is not directly related to the process. Choice (B) refers to a prince, which does not make sense with the topic of this paragraph. Choice (C) indicates that the topic of the paragraph is interesting but does not refer to it directly. Rather, *it* could refer back to a number of singular pronouns used in the previous sentence. Because this answer would create ambiguity, (C) is not a very effective conclusion. Choice (D) directly refers to the supply chain mentioned in the paragraph, which makes it the most effective conclusion to this paragraph.

9. **A** Punctuation is what is changing in the answer choices. As the sentence is written in the passage, a complete idea comes before the single dash. As long as a complete idea comes before a single dash, it is grammatically correct, regardless of what comes after. Keep (A). Because the second part of the sentence is not a complete idea, neither a period nor a semicolon can be used, so eliminate both (B) and (C). In (D), the use of the single dash is grammatically correct, but the comma is unnecessary. Therefore, the best answer is (A).

10. **A** Two commas should be used around unnecessary information. Because the phrase *like any college major* is not necessary in this sentence, the two commas are correct as written. Eliminate (B) and (D). Choice (C) should be eliminated because it adds an extra comma after *like*, which is not needed. Therefore, the correct answer is (A).

11. **C** The additional sentence refers to aspects of manufacturing a car. Because the only parts of the passage that discussed car manufacturing are paragraphs 2 and 3, eliminate (A). Choice (B) places the discussion of different aspects of car manufacturing before the example of car manufacturing is mentioned, so it is not the best answer. Choice (C) places the additional sentence after a reference to *hundreds or thousands of other, smaller processes* and before *Each of these has to be....* Because there

is nothing mentioned in the first sentence of paragraph 3 that *Each* is clearly referring to, the additional sentence not only connects these two ideas but also corrects that ambiguity error. Choice (D) would place the additional sentence later in the paragraph, where the discussion is focused on the selling of the car rather than the manufacturing of it. The best answer is (C).

12. **C** The central idea of the first paragraph is who Millard Fillmore is and the background of his presidency. Because the addition is referring to a completely unrelated president who took office years after Fillmore and does not relate to Fillmore or his presidency directly, the best answer is (C). Choice (D) is not supported by the text. Choices (A) and (B) are incorrect because the addition would take the focus away from the topic being discussed rather than bring any benefit to the reader.

13. **D** As written, the second part of the sentence does not support the first part, which indicates that Fillmore's presidency marked the end of the Whig Party's popularity in the United States. Currently, the sentence is about wigs, not the Whig Party. Eliminate (A). Of the remaining choices, the only one that references the lack of the Whig Party in presidential politics is (D). Choice (B) refers to England, which is not relevant. Choice (C) focuses on Fillmore rather than the absence of the Whig Party.

14. **D** The pronoun *they* in the underlined portion is plural. The previous sentence mentions that the *Whig party fell out of national politics,* so *they* is referring to the Whig Party, which is singular. Eliminate (A) and (B) because both contain plural pronouns. Between (C) and (D), only (D) clearly indicates what noun is being discussed and is therefore the correct answer.

15. **D** Because there is nothing grammatically incorrect with any of the answer choices, the most concise choice that maintains the meaning of the sentence will be the best answer. Choices (A), (B), and (C) all contain superfluous information. The most concise answer is (D).

16. **B** This sentence is discussing the growing relationship between the United States and Japan. The underlined portion is referring to the previous approach taken by Japan to foreign relations. Japan's approach would be better described by a noun rather than a verb, so (A) is incorrect. *Itself* is redundant in (C); the sentence refers to Japan's own history of isolation. Choice (D) is both wordy and ambiguous; the word *nation* could refer to either of the nations listed at the beginning of the sentence. The most concise and grammatically correct answer is (B).

17. **A** The second part of this sentence states that the *inspiration* led Fillmore and others to try to *open relations with Japan.* The word *inspiration* should therefore refer to a similar instance of this happening. Choice (A) gives the example of the British and Chinese opening relations, which is similar to what happened with the United States and Japan. Choice (B) refers to an aspect only of American life, not two countries increasing relations. Similarly, (C) refers to aspects only of Japan, so it too can be eliminated. Choice (D) is completely off topic, discussing conflicts that would come later in history rather than an opening up of relations. The best answer is (A).

18. **C** The sentence discusses slavery as a national problem. As written, the phrase *the whole United States* is redundant with the word *national*. Eliminate (A). Choice (B) is awkward and contains redundant language with the word *everyone*. The sentence refers to *non-slave states*, which indicates the different approaches taken by the North and the South toward slavery. Choice (C) indicates the shift that was made by Fillmore to making slavery a national concern, rather than just a southern one. As there is no evidence that slavery was an international concern, (D) cannot be correct. The best answer is (C).

19. **B** This question is testing verb tense. Because both the non-underlined portion of the sentence and the underlined portion are discussing how the Fugitive Slave Act worked when it was enacted, both portions should be in the past tense. Choice (A) should be eliminated because it uses the future tense. Choice (C) is in the present tense and can also be eliminated. Choice (D) incorrectly uses the word *of* instead of *have* after *could* and should be eliminated. The only answer choice that correctly contains the past tense is (B).

20. **C** The answer choices contain various conjunctions, which are meant to link ideas. Since STOP punctuation is used in the answer choices, use the Vertical Line Test. Both ideas are complete, so (A) and (B) should be eliminated since *nevertheless* and *therefore* are not FANBOYS (a semicolon would be needed in place of the first comma to be correct punctuation). The difference between (C) and (D) is the type of FANBOYS used. The first part of the sentence discusses the negative side of the Fugitive Slave Act, and the second part of the sentence discusses how it helped spur—or cause—the Civil War. Therefore, a word that indicates a similarity in thought should be used, which makes (C) the best answer.

21. **B** The word *forever* is not accurate, as civil rights began to be addressed in the mid-20th century in the United States. Furthermore, *forever* and *eternity* are synonyms. Both (A) and (C) cannot be correct, so eliminate them. Between (B) and (D), (B) is the factually accurate and less opinionated choice, whereas (D) is informal and doesn't match the academic tone of this passage (nor does the author state his or her personal opinion about how long civil rights were held back). Choice (B) is the correct answer.

22. **A** Because STOP punctuation appears in the answer choices, use the Vertical Line Test. Because the part before the punctuation is incomplete and the part after the punctuation is incomplete, (B) and (C) can be eliminated. Choice (D) adds unnecessary commas around *uniquely* and after *position*, so this choice is incorrect. This leaves (A), which correctly places commas around *even in its worst form* and is therefore the correct answer.

23. **D** It is unclear what the phrase *that way* at the beginning of the sentence is referring to. Choice (B) switches from *that way* to "those," which does not make anything clearer in the sentence. Choice (C) replaces *that way* with "genres." Although "genres" is more specific than (A) and (B), it does not refer to any specific type or types and so is still highly vague. Choice (D) provides the most detailed answer "the 'gangster' genre," which not only makes the underlined portion clearer, but also matches the topic of the paragraph and passage. Therefore, the best answer is (D).

24. **A** This question is testing punctuation. The first part of the sentence is an incomplete idea, while the second part is a complete idea. Because a period can link only two complete ideas, (B) cannot be correct. Also, because a complete idea must come before a colon, (D) is wrong. Compare (A) and (C). Because the first part of the sentence constitutes an introductory phrase, a comma should follow the phrase. Choice (A) is the best answer.

25. **B** Pay attention to where there is a shift in the paragraph that seems out of place. The first two sentences give a quote from a film director about American film, while the remainder of the paragraph discusses American literature. As this shift comes between sentences 2 and 3, moving sentence 4 between those two would provide a link between the discussion of American film and literary genres. All other answer choices place this sentence between sentences discussing American literature, which do not need to be linked. The correct answer is (B).

26. **C** The second paragraph discusses the background and work of Ross Macdonald. The best introduction to this paragraph is one that is focused on Ross Macdonald specifically. Eliminate (A) and (B), which are focused on different authors. Choice (C) introduces Ross Macdonald, and therefore the subject of the paragraph. Choice (D) does not mention authors at all but rather is merely negative about writing in general. The best answer is (C).

27. **C** The answer choices are switching which "wh" word is used: "when," "which," and "where." *When* is used to refer to time; *which* is used to refer to things other than people, places, and time; and *where* is used to refer to places. In this sentence, the thing being referred to is *University of Michigan*. Because the University of Michigan is a place, the correct answer should have "where." Choice (C) is the correct answer.

28. **A** The first part of the sentence discusses the two different directions it appeared that Millar was being pulled in, so the best choice to maintain the focus of the sentence will relate that topic. As written, the underlined portion gives an example of those two directions. Choice (B) discusses the most famous work of Coleridge, which does not maintain the focus of the sentence since the sentence is about Millar. Choice (C) mentions both movies and books, but there is no indication in this sentence or paragraph that Millar was at all involved with movies. Choice (D) discusses Millar's preference between two different writers, but the authors are not *directions* he was being pulled in. The only answer that maintains the focus of this sentence is (A).

29. **D** The latter part of the sentence refers to Macdonald's work as *separate from that of his "pulp" contemporaries,* so the correct answer must mean the opposite of "lowly" or "cheap." *Superciliousness* means "haughtily disdainful." This is not the opposite of "lowly," so eliminate (A). *Smartness* can mean "cleverness" or "sassiness." Cleverness might work, so keep (B). *Know-how* means "practical skill," which is quite casual and not exactly the opposite of "lowly," so eliminate (C). *Sophistication* means "educated" or "refinement." This is the opposite of "low" or "cheap," so keep (D). The rest of the paragraph talks about Millar *studying literature,* being *engaged...with ideas,* and being *able to get inside the heads of his characters.* These ideas are more consistent with sophistication than smartness, so eliminate (B). The correct answer is (D).

30. **B** Based on the answer choices, this question is testing apostrophe usage. The text refers to the text of Macdonald, which indicates possession, so eliminate (A). Because Macdonald does not end in an "s," eliminate (C) and (D). To show possession, an apostrophe + "s" should be added to the end of the name. The only choice that contains this correct construction is (B).

31. **D** As written, the underlined portion contains a noun agreement error. Many *people* cannot have a single *motivation* between them all. Eliminate (A). Choice (B) repeats this error, as "those" is plural and "motivation" is singular. Choice (C) corrects the agreement error by replacing *people* with "someone," but this creates a new agreement error with the *murders* earlier in the sentence. Choice (D) correctly addresses the noun agreement error by retaining "people" and changing "motivation" to "motivations," while not creating any new errors.

32. **A** The sentence contains a list: *murders, thefts,* and *kidnappings.* All items in a list must be separated by a comma. As there is a comma after *thefts* in the underlined portion, this sentence is correct as written. Choice (B) omits the comma after *thefts,* which is incorrect (remember to include the comma before the word "and"). Choice (C) omits the comma after *thefts* but includes a comma after *and,* which is also incorrect. Choice (D) adds a comma after the last item in the list *kidnapping,* so it is also incorrect.

33. **C** The current placement of the underlined phrase creates an error since the underlined portion separates the correct idiomatic phrase: *Following in the footsteps of….* Eliminate (A). Choice (B) creates a sentence that sounds as though Hammett and Chandler are literally walking toward the detective novel; eliminate (B). Choice (D) does not make sense, as humans are not anything *to* the detective novel. Only (C) expresses the author's intended meaning—that it is Macdonald who is bringing something to the detective novel.

34. **B** There are verb changes in the answer choices, so the first thing to do is to check if the subject and verb are consistent. The subject earlier in the sentence is *the scientific community,* which is singular. The verb in the underlined portion is *do,* which is plural. Eliminate both (A) and (C). Choices (B) and (D) both correct the subject-verb agreement error with "does" but contain different pronouns. Because *the scientific community* is singular, it must be replaced by a singular pronoun. Because (D) contains "they," which is plural, it can be eliminated. The correct answer is (B).

35. **D** Choices (A), (B), and (C) are all very similar as they include extraneous words. Choice (D) is the most concise answer which also maintains the meaning of the sentence. Therefore, (D) is the best answer.

36. **C** There are pronoun and noun changes in the answer choices, so the first thing to do is check what noun these pronouns are replacing. There is some ambiguity in the passage as to the original word, so using a noun is the safer choice. Choices (B) and (D) can be eliminated. *Resources* makes sense in the context of the passage, while *resourcefulness* does not. Choice (C) is the correct answer.

37. **A** This paragraph ends by mentioning a problem: *that these new resources will not cure us fully of energy dependency.* The next paragraph introduces a solution to the problem: "asteroid mining" in space. To conclude this paragraph and introduce the next paragraph, the best choice will connect these

two ideas. Choice (A) is a good match. Choices (B) and (C) can be eliminated because neither answer mentions space. Choice (D) can be eliminated because it doesn't reference the problem discussed in the first paragraph. Therefore, the best answer is (A).

38. **B** The previous sentence refers to a *new, and currently hypothetical, solution.* The latter part of the sentence with the underlined portion says the method is *exactly what it sounds like,* and this is contrasted to how *it may sound.* The underlined portion must mean something like "weird" or "unusual." *Wonderful* means "amazing," which is not consistent. Eliminate (A). *Outlandish* means "strange." This is consistent, so keep (B). *Wacky* also means "strange," but it is more casual than "outlandish." Eliminate (C). *Idiosyncratic* means "a peculiarity of temperament" and is generally used to describe people. This is not consistent, so eliminate (D). The correct answer is (B).

39. **A** Compare the answer choices with the provided graphic. Choice (A) is true based on the graph; new nickel discoveries in 2009 were under 1,000 mt, while new nickel discoveries in 1999 were over 2,000 mt. Choice (B) is incorrect; sulfide production was consistently higher than laterite production from 1998 to 2009. Choice (C) is also incorrect, as total nickel production was lower than the three-year average of total nickel in new discoveries from 1998 to 2004, 2006, and 2008. Choice (D) is also incorrect; according to the graphic, the total nickel found since 1998 has fluctuated over time. The only possible answer is (A).

40. **C** The point of the underlined portion of the sentence is that the ship will not need to restock supplies. The most concise way of saying this while maintaining the meaning of the sentence is (C), *resupplying.* Choices (A), (B), and (D) all say the same thing but are wordier.

41. **D** The underlined portion refers to both *space travel* and *exploration,* but that is not clear as the sentence is currently written. Choices (A), (B), and (C) are all ambiguous; they do not directly refer to *space travel* and *exploration,* so none completes the comparison being made. Choice (D) corrects this error by including the pronoun "they" to refer to the subjects earlier in the sentence, which completes the comparison, making (D) the best answer.

42. **B** The answer choices contain changes in punctuation. Using the Vertical Line Test, it is apparent that both the first part and the second part of the sentence are complete ideas. Because a comma by itself cannot link two complete ideas together, (A) and (C) are incorrect. Two complete ideas also cannot be linked without punctuation, so (D) is incorrect. Because two complete ideas can be linked by a semicolon, (B) is the correct answer.

43. **A** There are apostrophes in the answer choices, so check for the need of an apostrophe first. The word *its* refers to the Earth, which is correct without the apostrophe (*it's* is the contraction form of "it is"), so (C) can be eliminated. Because the Earth is a singular object, (B) can be eliminated as it is a plural pronoun. Because there is no reason to change from "it" to "one" when referring to the Earth, eliminate (D) and choose (A).

44. **C** The claim in the previous statement focuses on the belief that the cost of asteroid mining is far greater than the worth of what is being mined. The question asks for an addition that best supports

this claim, so eliminate any answer choices that do not relate to this topic. Choice (B) is focused on the skill of astronauts, not on the cost of asteroid mining. Choice (D) is too general of a statement and does not relate specifically to the cost of asteroid mining. Choice (A) refers to money by noting the types of funding NASA receives but does not specifically relate that funding to asteroid mining. Choice (C) brings up the exorbitant costs of "these expeditions," which is a direct reference to the mining in the previous sentence. Therefore, (C) is the only answer that supports the previous sentence.

Section 3—Math (No Calculator)

1. **A** Use POE to eliminate (C) because the equation in (C) is a straight line. Remember the rules of graph transformations. If the number is inside the parentheses, the graph moves left or right in the opposite direction of the sign. In this case, the graph has been moved 3 units in the positive direction and therefore the correct answer is (A). An alternate way to approach this question is to plug in the point (0, 3) into each of the equations to see which equation works.

2. **D** The equation of a line is $y = mx + b$ where m stands for slope and b stands for the y-intercept. In the given equation the slope is a positive 3. Use POE to eliminate (B) and (C) since both of these lines have a negative slope. According to the question, the y-intercept is negative. Use this information to eliminate (A), which has a positive y-intercept. The correct answer is (D).

3. **D** Whenever there are variables in the question and numbers in the answers think Plugging In the Answers. Start with (B). If $x = 5$, then the equation becomes $\dfrac{5^2 - (4)(5) + 3}{3} = 2(5-1)$. Solve both sides of the equation to get $\dfrac{25 - 20 + 3}{3} = 2(4)$, $\dfrac{8}{3} = 8$. Because this is not a true statement, eliminate (B). It may not be clear which direction to go, so just pick a direction. Choice (C) becomes $\dfrac{6^2 - (4)(6) + 3}{3} = 2(6-1)$. Solve both sides of the equation to get $\dfrac{36 - 24 + 3}{3} = 2(5)$, $\dfrac{15}{3} = 10$, and $5 = 10$. Eliminate (C). Choice (D) becomes $\dfrac{9^2 - (4)(9) + 3}{3} = 2(9-1)$. Solve both sides of the equation to get $\dfrac{81 - 36 + 3}{3} = 2(8)$, $\dfrac{48}{3} = 16$, and $16 = 16$. Therefore, the correct answer is (D).

4. **C** According to the question, the median income rose $8,000 in a 6-year period. If the trend continues linearly, then the median income would rise again in 6 years. Whenever there are variables in the question, think Plugging In. If $x = 6$, then the median income would be $57,000 + 8,000 = 65,000$. Plug in 6 for x in the answer choices to see which answer equals 65. Choice (A) becomes $I = 49 + (8)(6) = 97$. Eliminate (A). Choice (B) becomes $I = 57 + (8)(6) = 105$. Eliminate (B). Choice (C) becomes $I = 57 + \left(\dfrac{4}{3}\right)(6) = 57 + 8 = 65$. Keep (C), but check (D) just in case. Choice (D) becomes $I = 49 + \left(\dfrac{4}{3}\right)(6) = 49 + 8 = 57$. Eliminate (D). Therefore, the correct answer is (C).

5.   **A**   Whenever there are variables in the question and numbers in the answer choices, think Plugging In the Answers. Start with (B). If $z = 13$, the equation becomes $\frac{3(13+3)}{4} - \frac{2(13-2)}{3} = 2$. Simplify the left side of the equation to get $\frac{3(16)}{4} - \frac{2(11)}{3} = 2$, $12 - 7.\overline{3} = 2$, and $4.\overline{6} = 2$. Eliminate (B). It may not be clear which direction to go from here, so just pick a direction. If you try (A), $z = -19$, then the equation becomes $\frac{3(-19+3)}{4} - \frac{2(-19-2)}{3} = 2$. Simplify the right side of the equation to get $\frac{3(-16)}{4} - \frac{2(-21)}{3} = 2$, $3(-4) - \left[2(-7)\right] = 2$, $-12 - [-14] = 2$, $-12 + 14 = 2$, and $2 = 2$. Therefore, the correct answer is (A).

6.   **C**   The decay rate is not linear; therefore, you can eliminate (B). Because the percentages in (D) are increasing (greater than 1), you can eliminate (D). The black line starts at a count of 5,000 and is decreasing at a higher rate than the grey line. Therefore, the black decay rate (starting at 5,000) must be higher. Therefore, the answer is (C) because it is decreasing at a rate of 10% (0.9 = 1.0 – 0.1), and the grey would be decreasing at a lower rate of 5% (0.95 = 1.0 – 0.05).

7.   **B**   Start by multiplying both sides of the equation by $\sqrt{ab}$ to get $a^3 = b \times \sqrt{ab}$. Square both sides of the equation to get $a^6 = b^2 \times ab$. Combine like terms to get $a^6 = ab^3$ and $a^5 = b^3$. Therefore, the correct answer is (B).

8.   **D**   According to the question, a bag of apples and 3 cartons of strawberries cost \$18. If a = a bag of apples and c = a carton of strawberries, then $a + 3c = 18$. According to the question, a bag of apples cost 50% more than a carton of strawberries, which can be written as $a = 1.5c$. Substitute this into the first equation to get $1.5c + 3c = 18$. Solve for c to get $4.5c = 18$, and $c = 4$. Therefore, $a = 1.5(4) = 6$. The correct answer is (D).

9.   **C**   If the website received 24,500 visitors 6 months ago, then three months ago the website received $24,500 \times 2 = 49,000$ visitors, and today the website is receiving $49,000 \times 2 = 98,000$ visitors. Whenever there are variables in the question and in the answers, think Plugging In. Every year the number of visitors will increase by a factor of $2^4 = 16$. So, if $t = 2$, then the population would increase $16 \times 16 = 2^8$. Therefore, in 2 years the population would be $98,000 \times 2^8$, which, when expressed in thousands, would simply be 98×2^8. Eliminate (A) and (D) because neither of these answers includes 98. In (B), the equation becomes $V = 98(2^2)$. Eliminate (B). The correct answer is therefore (C).

10.   **C**   If x is the cost of a shirt and y is the cost of a pair of socks, then $x + 2y = 24$ and $3x + 2y = 32$. Whenever there are two equations with the same variables, think simultaneous equations. Stack the two equations on top of each other and subtract them to get:

$$
\begin{array}{rl}
3x + 2y &= 32 \\
-(\ x + 2y &= 24) \\
\hline
2x \quad\ \ &= 8
\end{array}
$$

Solve for x to get $x = 4$. Plug this value of x back into the bottom equation to get $4 + 2y = 24$. Solve for y to get $2y = 20$ and $y = 10$. Therefore, the cost of a shirt and a pair of socks is $4 + 10 = 14$. The correct answer is (C).

11. **A** Use Bite-Sized Pieces and POE to solve this problem. Multiply both sides by 25 to get $25M = P\left(51 - I\sqrt{L}\right)$. Because M is now multiplied by 25, eliminate (C). The correct answer will include 51 in it, so eliminate (B). Divide both sides by P to get $\dfrac{25M}{P} = 51 - I\sqrt{L}$. Subtract 51 from both sides to get $\dfrac{25M}{P} - 51 = -I\sqrt{L}$. In order to isolate I, both sides will need to be divided by $\sqrt{L}$. Choice (D) multiplies by $\sqrt{L}$ instead. Eliminate (D). The correct answer is (A).

12. **B** Start by converting the radians to degrees by multiplying the radian values by $\dfrac{180}{\pi}$: $\dfrac{3\pi}{4} \times \dfrac{180}{\pi} = 135$ and $\dfrac{5\pi}{4} \times \dfrac{180}{\pi} = 225$. Therefore, the central angle AOB is between 135 and 225 degrees. The value of 180 degrees, which is half the circle, is between these two values, so calculate the arc length if the central angle is 180 degrees. The formula for the circumference of a circle is $C = 2\pi r$. Therefore, the full circumference of circle O can be calculated as $C = 2\pi(4) = 8\pi$. If the central angle were 180 degrees, then the length of arc AB would be half that, or 4π. The correct answer is (B).

13. **B** Because John's baseball card collection decreases in value over time, and his silver collection increases over time, the $500(1.05)^t$ of the equation must be related to his silver collection, and the $600(0.95)^{\frac{t}{2}}$ part of the equation must be related to his baseball card collection. Use POE to find the answer. The current value of his silver collection, at $t = 0$, is 500, and the current value of his baseball card collection is $600(0.95)^{\frac{t}{2}}$. For this reason, eliminate (A). Given that t is time in years, the baseball card collection is losing 5% in value every 2 years. Eliminate (C) for this reason. According to the equation, the silver collection gains 5% every year, and the baseball collection loses 5% every 2 years, so eliminate (D). Therefore, the total value of the baseball and silver collection will not remain constant over time. The correct answer is therefore (B).

14. **13** Plug in the numbers given in the function to get $f(4) = 3(4) = 12$ and $g(2) = 2 - 3 = -1$. Therefore, $f(4) - g(2) = 12 - (-1) = 13$. The correct answer is 13.

15. **40** According to the question, males make up $\dfrac{3}{5}$ of the class, which means that females make up $\dfrac{2}{5}$ of the class. The difference between males and females is 8, which is equal to $\dfrac{3}{5} - \dfrac{2}{5} = \dfrac{1}{5}$ of the class. Therefore, the number of students in the class can be calculated as $\dfrac{1}{5}(\text{total}) = 8$. Solve for the total to get a total of 40 students. The correct answer is 40.

16. **4** According to the question, c is at least 3 times the value of d. This can be translated as $c \geq 3d$, and the difference between c and d is no more than 8, which can be translated as $c - d \leq 8$. To find the greatest value of d, plug in values for d. It may help to create a chart like the following:

d	$c \geq 3d$	$c - d \leq 8$ (plug in the smallest value of c).
1	$c \geq 3$	$3 - 1 = 2$
2	$c \geq 6$	$6 - 2 = 4$
3	$c \geq 9$	$9 - 3 = 6$
4	$c \geq 12$	$12 - 4 = 8$

Therefore, the smallest possible value of d is 4. The correct answer is 4.

17. **2.2** First, put the values given in the problem into the equations. Because displacement is 22 meters and initial velocity is 5 meters, the first equation becomes $22 = 15t + 0.5at^2$. The second equation becomes $5 = 15 + at$. Working with the second equation, subtract 15 from both sides to get $-10 = at$, which means that $a = \dfrac{-10}{t}$. Next, substitute this value for a into the first equation to get $22 = 15t + 0.5\left(\dfrac{-10}{t}\right)\left(t^2\right)$. Simplify the equation to get $22 = 15t + 0.5(-10t)$. Distribute the 0.5 to get $22 = 15t - 5t$. Solve for t to get $22 = 10t$ *and* $t = 2.2$. The correct answer is 2.2.

Section 4—Math (Calculator Allowed)

1. **A** According to the question, the proton traveled through medium A at 100,000 meters in 5 milliseconds, which is equal to a velocity of 20,000 meters per millisecond. Therefore, the velocity through medium B can be calculated as $20{,}000 \div 2 = 10{,}000$ meters per millisecond. The correct answer is therefore (A).

2. **A** Plugging In the Answers with negative fractions could take awhile, so solve the inequality. Add 5 to both sides to get $6x < 7 + 15x$. Subtract $15x$ from both sides to get $-9x < 7$. Remember when dividing by a negative number, flip the inequality sign. Solve for x to get $x > -\dfrac{7}{9}$. The only value that is less than this is $-\dfrac{8}{9}$. The correct answer is (A).

3. **A** Whenever the question includes variables and the answers are numbers, think Plugging In the Answers. Start with (B). If $r = -6$, the equation becomes $-6 + 22 = 3(-6) - 26 + 6^2$. Simplify the equation to get $16 = -18 - 26 + 36$ and $16 = -8$. Eliminate (B). It may not be clear which direction to go, so just pick one. In (A), $r = -8$ and the equation becomes $-8 + 22 = 3(-8) - 26 + (-8)^2$. Simplify the equation to get $14 = -24 - 26 + 64$ and $14 = 14$. The correct answer is (A).

4. **D** Use POE. The term *at least* means $\geq$. On this basis, eliminate (A) and (C). To calculate the total number of hours worked at the community center, multiply the number of hours worked per day by the number of days. This calculation is $7.5c$. Likewise, to calculate the total number of hours spent removing street litter, multiply the number of hours worked per day by the number of days. This calculation is $4l$. Therefore, eliminate (B). The correct answer is (D).

5. **D** The median is the middle number when the numbers are listed in order from low to high. In order for the median length to be 15, x must be in the middle of the list of numbers. So, lined up from low to high, the numbers are 6, 9, 9, x, 36, and 39. There is no one middle number, so the median is the average of the middle two. Therefore, $\frac{9+x}{2} = 15$. Solve for x to get $9 + x = 30$ and $x = 21$. To find the mean length, add all of the numbers together and divide by 6: $\frac{6+9+9+21+36+39}{6} = 20$. The correct answer is (D).

6. **A** According to the question, density $= \frac{\text{mass}}{\text{volume}}$. Substitute the numbers given into the equation to get $19.3 = \frac{\text{mass}}{5}$. Solve for mass and get 96.5 grams. Use the following proportion to convert mass into ounces: $\frac{1}{28.3} = \frac{x}{96.5}$. Cross-multiply to get $28.3x = 96.5$. Solve for x to get $x \approx 3.41$. The correct answer is (A).

7. **D** Use POE to solve this question. In (A), $0.10 \times 200{,}000 = 20{,}000$. However, you know from the information given that far more scientists believe the mass extinction to be caused by the Chicxulub Asteroid. Therefore, eliminate (A). In (B), $0.25 \times 200{,}000 = 50{,}000$. Again, far more scientists believe the mass extinction to be caused by the Chicxulub Asteroid. Eliminate (B). In (C), $0.50 \times 200{,}000 = 100{,}000$. Again, the number of scientists who believe the mass extinction to be caused by the Chicxulub Asteroid is much higher. Therefore, the answer must be (D).

8. **D** Whenever there are variables in the question and in the answer choices, think Plugging In. If $x = 52$, then the output is $385 + 2(42) = 385 + 84 = 469$ computer chips. Plug 52 in for x in the answers to see which answer equals 469. Choice (A) becomes $C(52) = 42^{(52-50)} + 385 = 42^2 + 385 = 2{,}149$. Eliminate (A). Choice (B) becomes $C(52) = 52^{42} + 385$. This number is huge! Eliminate (B). Choice (C) becomes $C(52) = 42(52) + 385 = 2{,}184 + 385 = 2{,}569$. Eliminate (C). Therefore, the answer must be (D).

9. **C** Multiply the right side of the equation by $\frac{2}{2}$ to get $\frac{6(t+2)}{8} = \frac{100 - 5t + 44}{8}$. Because the denominators are now the same, $6(t + 2) = 100 - 5t + 44$. Distribute the 6 to get $6t + 12 = 100 - 5t + 44$. Combine like terms to get $6t + 12 = 144 - 5t$ and $11t + 12 = 144$. Solve for t to get $11t = 132$ and $t = 12$. The correct answer is (C).

10. **B** The question is asking about changing the format of the equation for a parabola to the vertex form of the equation. The vertex form of a parabola is $y = a(x - h)^2 + k$, where (h, k) denotes the vertex of the parabola. Only (B) is written in this format.

11. **C** Whenever there are variables in the question and in the answers, think Plugging In. If $m = 2$, then Taylor has written $23 \times 2 = 46$ words. Given that each page has 800 words, Taylor has written far less than a page, which means he has 699 pages plus a fraction of a page left.

Plug in 2 for m in the answers to see which answer yields 699 plus a fraction. Choice (A) becomes $p(m) = \dfrac{700 - 800(2)}{23} = \dfrac{700 - 1600}{23} = \dfrac{-900}{23}$. Eliminate (A). Choice (B) becomes $p(m) = \dfrac{700 - 23(2)}{800} = \dfrac{700 - 46}{800} = \dfrac{654}{800}$, which is less than a page. Eliminate (B). Choice (C) becomes $p(m) = 700 - \dfrac{23(2)}{800} = 700 - \dfrac{46}{800} = 699.9425$. This is possible. Keep (C), but check (D) just in case. Choice (D) becomes $p(m) = 700 - \dfrac{800}{23(2)} = 700 - \dfrac{800}{46} \approx 700 - 17.39 \approx 682.61$. Eliminate (D), and you're left with (C).

12. **B** The line shown includes the points $(-3, 1)$ and $(-1, 2)$. The equation for the slope of a line is $m = \dfrac{y_2 - y_1}{x_2 - x_1}$, which for the line shown can be calculated as $m = \dfrac{1 - 2}{-3 - (-1)} = \dfrac{-1}{-3 + 1} = \dfrac{-1}{-2} = \dfrac{1}{2}$. Parallel lines have the same slope, so eliminate (A) and (D), which do not have a slope of $\dfrac{1}{2}$. Plug the point $(3, -2)$ into the remaining answer choices to see which one works. Choice (B) becomes $-2 = \dfrac{1}{2}(3) - \dfrac{7}{2}$, or $-2 = \dfrac{3}{2} - \dfrac{7}{2}$. This becomes $-2 = -\dfrac{4}{2}$, which is true.

13. **C** A quick look at the answer choices shows that the population of people in poverty in 2008 must have been 50,000. Whenever there are variables in the question and in the answers, think Plugging In. If $m = 12$, then the population of those in poverty should be $50{,}000 \div 2 = 25{,}000$. Plug 12 in for m in the answers to see which answer equals 25,000. Choice (A) becomes $f(m) = 50{,}000 - \dfrac{1}{2}(12) = 50{,}000 - 6 = 49{,}994$. Eliminate (A). Choice (B) becomes $f(m) = 50{,}000 - \left(\dfrac{1}{2}\right)\left(\dfrac{12}{12}\right) = 50{,}000 - 0.5 = 49{,}999.5$. Eliminate (B). Choice (C) becomes $f(m) = 50{,}000\left(\dfrac{1^{\frac{12}{12}}}{2}\right) = 50{,}000\left(\dfrac{1}{2}\right) = 25{,}000$. Keep (C), but check (D) just in case. Choice (D) becomes $f(m) = 50{,}000 - 12^{\frac{1}{2}} \approx 50{,}000 - 3.45 = 49{,}996.55$. Eliminate (D), and you're left with (C).

14. **B** The equation to find the slope of a line is $m = \dfrac{y_2 - y_1}{x_2 - x_1}$. The slope for the line shown can be calculated as $40 = \dfrac{277 - b}{5 - 0}$. Simplify the fraction to get $40 = \dfrac{277 - b}{5}$. Multiply both sides of the equation by 5 to get $200 = 277 - b$. Solve for b to get $-77 = -b$ and $77 = b$. The correct answer is (B).

15. **D** Whenever there are variables in the question and in the answers, think Plugging In. If $x = 4$, then $y = 4^2 + 4 - 20 = 16 + 4 - 20 = 0$ and $\dfrac{y^2}{z} = \dfrac{0^2}{z} = 0$. Plug 4 in for x in the answers to see which answer equals 0. Choice (A) becomes $\dfrac{4^4 - 8}{10(4)} = \dfrac{256 - 8}{40} = \dfrac{248}{40}$. Eliminate (A). Choice (B) becomes $\dfrac{4^4 + 4^2 - 400}{4^2 + 10(4) + 25} = \dfrac{256 + 16 - 400}{16 + 40 + 25} = \dfrac{-128}{81}$. Eliminate (B). Choice (C) becomes $4^2 - (8)(4) - 15 = 16 - 32 - 15 = -31$. Eliminate (C), and you're left with (D).

16. **A** Start by using POE. The more pictures Squared Up frames, the greater its profits will be. Therefore, the correct answer must include a > symbol. Eliminate (B) and (D). Start with the remaining answers. According to (C), Squared Up would turn a profit if it framed 13 pictures. Profit = Revenue – Expenses. On 13 pictures, Squared Up would make $13 \times 61 = 793$ in revenue. The expenses to frame these pictures can be calculated as $13(38 + 5) + 720 = 13(43) + 720 = 559 + 720 = 1{,}279$. Because expenses exceed revenues, Squared Up will not make a profit if it framed only 13 pictures. Eliminate (C), and you're left with (A).

17. **B** The average amount spent per person in a household can be calculated as the total amount spent on groceries divided by the number of people in the household. The survey provided no data on the number of people in each household. Therefore, the correct answer is (B).

18. **B** Use POE to solve. Because no data is provided on meals had at restaurants, eliminate (A). According to the question, as household income increased, grocery spending decreased. Therefore, (B) is a possible answer. While there is a connection between household income and grocery spending, it is not clear from the data that it is a causal connection. Therefore, eliminate (C). The data focuses just on Florida and therefore no inferences can be made about grocery spending in the United States. Eliminate (D), and you're left with (B).

19. **A** Whenever there are two equations with the same variables, think simultaneous equations. First, rewrite both equations so that the variables are on one side of the equation. The first equation becomes $3x - 96 = 4y$ and $3x - 4y = 96$. The second equation becomes $10x + 2y = 90$. Multiply this second equation by 2 to get $20x + 4y = 180$. Place the two equations on top of each other and add them:

$$\begin{array}{r} 20x + 4y = 180 \\ + \ \ 3x - 4y = 96 \\ \hline 23x \qquad = 276 \end{array}$$

Solve for x to get $x = 12$. Plug 12 in for x in the second equation to get $3(12) - 4y = 96$. Solve for y to get $36 - 4y = 96$, $-4y = 60$, and $y = -15$. Therefore, $\dfrac{x}{y} = -\dfrac{12}{15} = -\dfrac{4}{5}$. The correct answer is (A).

20. **C** The mean file size of a single song is $0.022 \times 1{,}024 = 22.528$ megabytes. The file size of all the songs Larissa uploaded is $40{,}000 \times 22.528 = 901{,}120$ megabytes. The upload time in seconds is

$7.5 \times 60 \times 60 = 27,000$ seconds. Therefore, the upload time in megabytes per second is $\frac{901,120}{27,000} \approx 33.37$. The correct answer is (C).

21. **D** 2015 is 3 years after 2012. Therefore, $y = 3$, and the function becomes $c(3) = 17(3) + 112 = 51 + 112 = 163$. Given that 20 additional cheetahs joined, the total population is $163 + 20 = 183$. The correct answer is (D).

22. **B** Start by figuring out the median number of cars owned in all 5 boroughs. To do this, find the total number of cars and then see where the middle of the list is:

Number of Cars	Total in All 5 Boroughs
Zero	4,160
One	2,320
Two	1,140
Three	380

The median number is at 4 million cars, which is 0 cars. Next, add up the number of residents who live in Manhattan and own more than 0 cars:

Number of Cars	Manhattan
One	480
Two	320
Three	80
Total	**880**

The question can be translated as 880,000 is what percent of 8,000,000? Do math translation to get the following equation: $880,000 = \frac{x}{100} \times 8,000,000$. Solve for x to get $x = 11$. The correct answer is (B).

23. **D** Whenever there are two equations with two variables, think simultaneous equations. Rewrite the first equation as $8s - 4t = 17$ and the second equation as $-5s + 6t = 4$. Stack the two equations on top of each other and add them:

$$8s - 4t = 17$$
$$\underline{+(-5s + 6t = 4)}$$
$$3s + 2t = 21$$

Multiply the entire equation by 2 to get $6s + 4t = 42$. The correct answer is (D).

24. **A** The vertex form of a parabola is $y = a(x - h)^2 + k$, where (h, k) stands for the vertex. Start by converting the parabola equation into its vertex form by completing the square. The equation becomes $y - 6 = x^2 - 8x + 22 - 6$. Simplify the equation to get $y - 6 = x^2 - 8x + 16$. Factor the right side of the equation to get $y - 6 = (x - 4)^2$. Move the 6 over to get $y = (x - 4)^2 + 6$. Therefore, the vertex of the parabola is $(4, 6)$. The equation of a circle is $(x - h)^2 + (y - k)^2 = r^2$, where

the center of the circle is (h, k). Therefore, the equation of a circle centered at $(4, 6)$ is $(x - 4)^2 + (y - 6)^2 = r^2$. Expand the circle equation to get $x^2 - 8x + 16 + y^2 - 12y + 36 = r^2$. Rewrite the equation of the circle given in the problem as $x^2 - 8x + y^2 + ky = 172$. Therefore, $ky = -12y$ and $k = -12$. The correct answer is (A).

25. **C** Use POE. Be careful in reading the y-axis. The information provided is related to the rate of increase not the population. Given that no information on the actual population is given, eliminate (B) and (D). According to the graph, the population of H_2 increased by 300 bees in 2001, but only increased by 250 bees in 2003. In other words, the population increased albeit at a slower rate during the 10 years. For this reason eliminate (A). The correct answer is (C).

26. **D** Use POE to solve this question. Given that y is the number of phytoplankton over time, eliminate (A). According to the question, prior to 2007 there were no phytoplankton in the lake, so eliminate (B). According to the problem, k represents the number of months the population was introduced. Therefore, the rate of increase in a month would be equal to $6.23^{\frac{1}{12}}$. Eliminate (C). The correct answer is (D).

27. **D** Look for years where the line of best fit gives an easy-to-approximate number for the area of square miles. 1970 correlates with approximately 12 million for the decrease in area of square miles, and 2000 correlates with 10 million. Subtract these values for a difference of 2 million. Then divide by 30, because there is a 30-year difference between 1970 and 2000. The answer is roughly 66,000, which is (D).

28. **24** In a circle equation in the form $(x - h)^2 + (y - k)^2 = r^2$, the center is (h, k) and the radius is r. In the given equation, $r^2 = 144$. Take the square root of both sides to get $r = 12$. The diameter equals $2r$, so the diameter is $2(12) = 24$. The correct answer is 24.

29. **1** In order for $p(x)$ to equal 0, the numerator must equal 0. If $(x + 4) = 0$ or $(x - 4) = 0$, then $x = \pm 4$. However, x cannot equal -4 because that would make the denominator 0. Therefore, the only value that will make the function 0 is when $x = 4$. The correct answer is 1.

30. **405** Under Package A, Jason earned $\$10,000 + (.01)(110)(30,000) = \$43,000$. The question states that had Jason chosen Package B, he would have earned $43,000 + 1,550 = 44,550$. Given that Package B is comprised of a fixed price per car $\times$ the number of cars sold, and Jason sold 110 cars, the fixed amount earned for each car can be calculated as $44,500 \div 110 = 405$. The correct answer is 405.

31. **40** There is enough information given to see how much Jason would earn with Package B. Multiply the amount he earns per car by the number of cars: $725 \times 80 = 58,000$. Now write an equation for Package A: $A = \$10,000 + (.015)(80)x$, where x is the mean sales price of the cars sold. You can set this equation equal to 60,000 because Package A equals Package B. The answer is $\$40,000$. Since the question is asking for thousands, 40 should be gridded in.

Raw Score (# of correct answers)	Reading Test Score	Writing and Language Test Score	Math Section Score	Raw Score (# of correct answers)	Reading Test Score	Writing and Language Test Score	Math Section Score
0	8	8	160	25	22	26	510
1	9	8	180	26	23	26	520
2	10	9	200	27	23	27	530
3	11	9	210	28	24	28	540
4	12	10	220	29	24	28	550
5	12	10	240	30	25	29	560
6	13	11	260	31	26	29	570
7	13	11	280	32	26	30	580
8	14	12	300	33	27	30	590
9	14	13	320	34	28	31	600
10	15	14	330	35	28	32	610
11	15	15	350	36	29	33	620
12	16	15	370	37	30	33	630
13	16	16	380	38	30	34	640
14	17	17	400	39	31	34	650
15	17	17	410	40	32	35	660
16	18	18	420	41	33	36	670
17	18	19	430	42	33	37	680
18	19	20	440	43	34	37	690
19	19	21	450	44	35	38	700
20	20	22	460	45	36		710
21	20	22	470	46	37		730
22	21	23	480	47	38		740
23	21	24	490	48			760
24	22	25	500				

CONVERSION EQUATION SECTION AND TEST SCORES

Chapter 15
Practice Test 2

Reading Test

60 MINUTES, 47 QUESTIONS

Turn to Section 1 of your answer sheet to answer the questions in this section.

DIRECTIONS

Each passage or pair of passages below is followed by a number of questions. After reading each passage or pair, choose the best answer to each question based on what is stated or implied in the passage or passages and in any accompanying graphics (such as a table or graph).

Questions 1–9 are based on the following passage.

This passage is adapted from Henry James, "The Beast in the Jungle," originally published in 1903. The passage describes the meeting, after many years, of John Marcher and May Bertram.

"You know you told me something I've never forgotten and that again and again has made me think of you since; it was that tremendously hot day when we
Line went to Sorrento, across the bay, for the breeze. What I
5 allude to was what you said me, on the way back, as we sat under the awning of the boat enjoying the cool. Have you forgotten?"

He had forgotten and was even more surprised than ashamed. But the great thing was that he saw
10 in this no vulgar reminder of any "sweet" speech. The vanity of women had long memories, but she was making no claim on him of a compliment or a mistake. With another woman, a totally different one, he might have feared the recall possibly even of some
15 imbecile "offer." So, in having to say that he had indeed forgotten, he was conscious rather of a loss than of a gain; he already saw an interest in the matter of her mention. "I try to think—but I give up. Yet I remember that Sorrento day."

20 "I'm not very sure you do," May Bertram after a moment said; "and I'm not very sure I ought to want you to. It's dreadful to bring a person back at any time to what he was ten years before. If you've lived away from it," she smiled, "so much the better."

25 "Ah, if *you* haven't why should I?" he asked.

"Lived away, you mean, from what I myself was?"

"From what *I* was. I was of course [a boor],"

Marcher went on; "but I would rather know from you just the sort of [boor] I was than—from the
30 moment you have something in your mind—not know anything."

Still, however, she hesitated. "But if you've completely ceased to be that sort—?"

"Why I can then all the more bear to know. Besides,
35 perhaps I haven't."

"Perhaps. Yet if you haven't," she added, "I should suppose you'd remember. Not indeed that *I* in the least connect with my impression the invidious name you use. If I had only thought you foolish," she explained,
40 "the thing I speak of wouldn't so have remained with me. It was about yourself." She waited as if it might come to him; but as, only meeting her eyes in wonder, he gave no sign, she burnt her ships. "Has it ever happened?"

45 Then it was that, while he continued to stare, a light broke for him and the blood slowly came to his face, which began to burn with recognition. "Do you mean I told you—?" But he faltered, lest what came to him shouldn't be right, lest he should only give himself
50 away.

"It was something about yourself that it was natural one shouldn't forget—that is if one remembered you at all. That's why I ask you," she smiled, "if the thing you then spoke of has ever come to pass?"

55 Oh then he saw, but he was lost in wonder and found himself embarrassed. This, he also saw, made her sorry for him, as if her allusion had been a mistake. It took him but a moment, however, to feel it hadn't

CONTINUE ▶

been, much as it had been a surprise. After the first
60 little shock of it her knowledge on the contrary began,
even if rather strangely, to taste sweet to him. She was
the only other person in the world then who would
have it, and she had had it all these years, while the fact
of his having so breathed his secret had unaccountably
65 faded from him. No wonder they couldn't have met
as if nothing had happened. "I judge," he finally said,
"that I know what you mean. Only I had strangely
enough lost any sense of having taken you so far into
my confidence."

1

The point of view from which the passage is written
can best be described as

A) a first-person narrator telling his life story.

B) a disinterested reporter listing objective facts.

C) a critical observer who judges Marcher's actions.

D) a sympathetic chronicler who relates to Marcher's
feelings.

2

Over the course of the passage, the emotions of John
Marcher shift from

A) incredulity to begrudging acceptance.

B) confusion to disconcerted recognition.

C) disdain to unrequited love.

D) amazement to painful embarrassment.

3

Information in the passage suggests that John
Marcher and May Bertram are

A) comforting one another over mistakes made
during the previous ten years.

B) trusting one another with sensitive personal
information.

C) reminiscing about former times and
conversations.

D) expressing their true feelings for one another.

4

Which choice provides the best evidence for the
answer to the previous question?

A) Lines 1–6 ("You know . . . cool")

B) Lines 22–24 ("It's dreadful . . . better")

C) Lines 55–57 ("Oh then . . . mistake")

D) Lines 61–65 ("She was . . . him")

5

As used in line 12, "claim" most nearly means

A) application.

B) remark.

C) appeal.

D) demand.

6

In the second paragraph, the "loss" (line 16) Marcher
feels most likely refers to

A) a connection over an interest he has in common
with May.

B) a missed opportunity to compliment May.

C) his longing to return to the warm weather in
Sorrento.

D) May's rejection of his speech declaring love for
her.

7

The conversation between Marcher and May Bertram
suggests that Marcher had previously told May about
which of the following?

A) A troublesome puzzle

B) A romantic confession

C) A forgotten trifle

D) A personal belief

CONTINUE

8

Which choice provides the best evidence for the answer to the previous question?

A) Lines 1–4 ("You know . . . breeze")

B) Lines 11–13 ("The vanity . . . mistake")

C) Lines 20–22 ("I'm not . . . to")

D) Lines 67–69 ("Only I . . . confidence")

9

As used in line 57, "allusion" most nearly means

A) reference.

B) image.

C) quotation.

D) apparition.

CONTINUE

Questions 10–18 are based on the following passage.

This passage is adapted from a speech delivered by Winston Churchill on May 13, 1940. Churchill became Prime Minister of Britain on May 10. This speech was his first address to the House of Commons, in which he asks the House to support his new administration.

I beg to move,

That this House welcomes the formation of a Government representing the united and inflexible
Line resolve of the nation to prosecute the war with
5 Germany to a victorious conclusion.

On Friday evening last I received His Majesty's commission to form a new Administration. It [w]as the evident wish and will of Parliament and the nation that this should be conceived on the broadest possible basis
10 and that it should include all parties, both those who supported the late Government and also the parties of the Opposition. I have completed the most important part of this task. A War Cabinet has been formed of five Members, representing, with the Opposition
15 Liberals, the unity of the nation. The three party Leaders have agreed to serve, either in the War Cabinet or in high executive office. The three Fighting Services have been filled. It was necessary that this should be done in one single day, on account of the extreme
20 urgency and rigour of events. A number of other positions, key positions, were filled yesterday, and I am submitting a further list to His Majesty to-night. I hope to complete the appointment of the principal Ministers during to-morrow. The appointment of the
25 other Ministers usually takes a little longer, but I trust that, when Parliament meets again, this part of my task will be completed, and that the administration will be complete in all respects.

I considered it in the public interest to suggest
30 that the House should be summoned to meet today. Mr. Speaker agreed, and took the necessary steps, in accordance with the powers conferred upon him by the Resolution of the House. At the end of the proceedings today, the Adjournment of the House will
35 be proposed until Tuesday, 21st May, with, of course, provision for earlier meeting, if need be. The business to be considered during that week will be notified to Members at the earliest opportunity. I now invite the House, by the Motion which stands in my name, to
40 record its approval of the steps taken and to declare its confidence in the new Government.

To form an Administration of this scale and complexity is a serious undertaking in itself, but it must be remembered that we are in the preliminary
45 stage of one of the greatest battles in history, that we are in action at many other points in Norway and in Holland, that we have to be prepared in the Mediterranean, that the air battle is continuous and that many preparations, such as have been indicated
50 by my hon. Friend below the Gangway, have to be made here at home. In this crisis I hope I may be pardoned if I do not address the House at any length today. I hope that any of my friends and colleagues, or former colleagues, who are affected by the political
55 reconstruction, will make allowance, all allowance, for any lack of ceremony with which it has been necessary to act. I would say to the House, as I said to those who have joined this government: "I have nothing to offer but blood, toil, tears and sweat."

60 We have before us an ordeal of the most grievous kind. We have before us many, many long months of struggle and of suffering. You ask, what is our policy? I can say: It is to wage war, by sea, land and air, with all our might and with all the strength that God can
65 give us; to wage war against a monstrous tyranny, never surpassed in the dark, lamentable catalogue of human crime. That is our policy. You ask, what is our aim? I can answer in one word: It is victory, victory at all costs, victory in spite of all terror, victory, however
70 long and hard the road may be; for without victory, there is no survival. Let that be realised; no survival for the British Empire, no survival for all that the British Empire has stood for, no survival for the urge and impulse of the ages, that mankind will move forward
75 towards its goal. But I take up my task with buoyancy and hope. I feel sure that our cause will not be suffered to fail among men. At this time I feel entitled to claim the aid of all, and I say, "come then, let us go forward together with our united strength."

CONTINUE ▶

10

Over the course of the speech, Churchill's focus shifts from

A) defeating Germany to reconstructing the government.

B) forming a War Cabinet to establishing war policy.

C) appointing an Administration to bolstering spirits.

D) reconciling differences to accepting defeat.

11

As used in line 4, "prosecute" most nearly means

A) fight.

B) litigate.

C) accuse.

D) enforce.

12

In the speech, Churchill claims that his administration must be formed more quickly than usual because

A) the king has told him to act with haste.

B) Parliament has been united under three party leaders.

C) the British Empire is in danger of losing the war.

D) the international political situation requires unusual measures.

13

Which choice provides the best evidence for the answer to the previous question?

A) Lines 6–7 ("On Friday . . . Administration")

B) Lines 18–20 ("It was . . . events")

C) Lines 53–57 ("I hope . . . to act")

D) Lines 71–75 ("Let that . . . goal")

14

It can be inferred from the passage that Churchill's administration

A) is likely to be controversial.

B) will meet with approval from all members of the House of Commons.

C) is dominated by Opposition Liberals.

D) has some unfilled positions.

15

Which choice provides the best evidence for the answer to the previous question?

A) Lines 13–15 ("A war . . . nation")

B) Lines 24–28 ("The appointment . . . respects")

C) Lines 31–33 ("Mr. Speaker . . . House")

D) Lines 60–62 ("We have . . . suffering")

16

Churchill makes the statement "I have nothing to offer but blood, toil, tears and sweat" (lines 58–59) primarily to

A) convey his deep level of commitment to the war effort.

B) indicate that he believes Britain has little hope of winning the war.

C) suggest that there is not much he can offer in support of the military.

D) offer evidence of his dedication to a governing coalition.

CONTINUE ▶

17

The primary rhetorical effect of the repetition of the words "victory" and "no survival" in the last paragraph is to

A) emphasize the hopeless nature of Britain's struggle.

B) clarify the administration's war strategy.

C) underscore the long-term implications of the outcome of the war.

D) maintain the sense of optimism introduced earlier in the speech.

18

As used in line 76, "suffered" most nearly means

A) endured.

B) allowed.

C) tolerated.

D) endorsed.

CONTINUE

Questions 19–28 are based on the following passage and supplementary material.

This passage is adapted from Alex Kotlowitz, *Never a City So Real.* © 2004 by Alex Kotlowitz.

Fourteen miles southeast of the Loop, at the base of Lake Michigan, the city's easternmost corner, one finds a fistful of neighborhoods with hearty names
Line like Irondale, Hegewisch, The Bush, and Slag Valley.
5 This is South Chicago. Apart from Altgeld Gardens—a vast public housing complex virtually hidden from the rest of the world by towering mountains of garbage and often referred to as Chicago's Soweto—South Chicago is the city's most isolated community, its most
10 removed. The labor lawyer and author Tom Geoghegan has called it "a secret city." The vast majority of Chicagoans have never set foot here, and as if to ensure such detachment, above the compact redbrick bungalows with postage-stamp-size yards looms the
15 Chicago Skyway, a highway on stilts, which takes the prosperous to their cottages along the Indiana and Michigan shorelines. The neighborhoods below are modest in appearance, a collection of small homes and small taverns and diners with simple names like Steve's,
20 Pete's Hideaway, Who Cares?, Small World Inn, and Maria's Den. There's nothing fanciful about this area. As one observer wrote: "Streets named Commercial and Exchange offer testimony that people came here to make a buck, not admire the scenery."
25 And yet the scenery, so to speak, is awe-inspiring, the man-made equivalent of the Rockies. Dark, low-to-the-ground muscular structures, some three times the size of a football field, sprawl across the landscape, sprouting chimneys so tall that they're equipped
30 with blinking lights to alert wayward aircraft. These chimneys shoot full-bodied flames thirty feet into the sky; at night they appear almost magical, like giant torches heating the moon. Billows of smoke linger in the air like phantom dirges. It used to be, when the
35 steel mills were going strong, that these smokestacks spat out particles of graphite that would dust the streets and cars and rooftops like snow, catching the sun and setting the neighborhood aglitter. Suspended conveyor belts, pipes, and railroad overpasses weave in, out, and
40 over the behemoth buildings. The noise is crushing, the stench of sulfur so powerful that not even a closed car window can keep it at bay. Had Rube Goldberg lost his sense of humor, this is, I imagine, what he would have produced.

45 This is the heart of American industrial might, or what's left of it. The first of the mills was built in the 1850s, and within a hundred years more steel was produced in this stretch of land than anywhere else in the world. The freighters delivered iron ore
50 from Minnesota's Mesabi Range, and the mills turned the mineral into steel, shipping it west by rail and eventually east by the St. Lawrence Seaway. By the 1960s, the mills employed eighty thousand men and women; they cascaded in from Poland, from
55 Yugoslavia, from Mexico, and from the American South. Steel mills and refineries lined up along the dredged Calumet River and along the Lake Michigan shoreline, extending twenty-two miles from South Chicago to Gary, Indiana. This stretch of boiling steel
60 was the equivalent of an industrial mountain stream, the source for can openers and knives, refrigerators and cars, bridges and skyscrapers. It fed this country's insatiable hunger for consumption and comfort. It was, in short, the nation's lifeblood.
65 The local population is still so dependent on the mills that the daily newspaper in Hammond, Indiana, which is just over the Chicago border, runs a box score every Wednesday of the region's steel tonnage and capacity. Nonetheless, there are only fifteen
70 thousand working in the mills now; the owners grew complacent, so accustomed to their oligopoly that they forgot how to compete. Between the mills that still roll steel, there are hundreds of acres of vacant land littered with abandoned factory buildings stripped
75 of their exteriors, brick coke houses collapsing in on themselves, and railroad tracks and bridges that have turned a muddy brown from rust.

Domestic Steel Production, 1950-2000

Source: American Iron and Steel Institute

CONTINUE ▶

19

The author of the passage most likely believes South Chicago

A) should be a more popular vacation destination.

B) will soon have no working steel mills.

C) is isolated from the rest of the city.

D) embodies the dirty, smelly nature of American industry.

20

Which choice provides the best evidence for the answer to the previous question?

A) Lines 5–10 ("Apart . . . removed")

B) Lines 25–26 ("And yet . . . Rockies")

C) Lines 40–42 ("The noise . . . bay")

D) Lines 45–46 ("This is . . . of it")

21

The author includes a list of restaurant names (lines 19–21) primarily to

A) emphasize the modest nature of the neighborhood.

B) recommend places for visitors to have a meal.

C) suggest that there is little variety in the eating establishments.

D) explain why most people never visit South Chicago.

22

As used in line 38, "suspended" most nearly means

A) drooping.

B) hanging.

C) slumbering.

D) fixed.

23

In the context of the passage, steel mills are compared to

A) the Rockies.

B) wayward aircraft.

C) a football field.

D) phantom dirges.

24

Which choice provides the best evidence for the answer to the previous question?

A) Lines 1–4 ("Fourteen . . . Valley")

B) Lines 11–17 ("The vast . . . shorelines")

C) Lines 26–30 ("Dark . . . aircraft")

D) Lines 49–52 ("The freighters . . . Seaway")

25

As used in line 63, "consumption" most nearly means

A) eating.

B) expenditure.

C) corrosion.

D) burning.

26

In the context of the passage as a whole, the primary purpose the last paragraph is to

A) criticize the steel mill owners.

B) lament the state of abandoned property.

C) explain the current status of the steel mills.

D) suggest changes to the steel industry.

CONTINUE

Which claim about domestic steel production is supported by the graph?

A) Production increased only from 1950 to 2000.

B) Production was stagnant between 1950 and 2000.

C) Production peaked in the 1960s, followed by a steep decline in the 1970s.

D) Net production increased slightly from 1950 to 2000.

28

It can reasonably be inferred from the passage and the graph that

A) U.S. steel mills reached their greatest productivity in the mid-1970s.

B) U.S. steel production in areas other than South Chicago has increased since the 1960s.

C) all domestic steel mills cut their workforces by over 75% between 1950 and 2000.

D) air pollution in communities surrounding steel mills was worse in the 1970s than in 2000.

CONTINUE

Questions 29-37 are based on the following passage and supplementary material.

This passage is adapted from E. Gene Towne and Joseph M. Craine, "Ecological Consequences of Shifting the Timing of Burning Tallgrass Prairie." © 2014 by E. Gene Towne and Joseph M. Craine. A forb is an herbaceous flowering plant.

Periodic burning is required for the maintenance of tallgrass prairie. The responses of prairie vegetation to fire, however, can vary widely depending upon
Line when the fires occur. Management and conservation
5 objectives such as biomass production, livestock performance, wildlife habitat, and control of specific plant species, often influence when grasslands are burned. In some prairie regions, timing of seasonal burns have been used to manipulate the balance of C_3
10 and C_4 species, control woody species, stimulate grass flowering, and alter the proportion of plant functional groups. Most grassland fire research, however, has focused on either burn frequency or comparing growing season burns with dormant season burns,
15 and there are few studies that differentiate effects from seasonal burning within the dormant season. In the Kansas Flint Hills, when prairies are burned is an important management issue, but the ecological consequences of burning at different times are poorly
20 understood.

The Flint Hills are one of the last remaining regions supporting extensive native tallgrass prairie in North America and frequent burning is integral to its preservation and economic utilization. Since
25 the early 1970's, recommendations have been to burn Kansas Flint Hills grasslands annually in late spring, typically once the dominant grasses have emerged 1.25–5 cm above the soil surface. Although frequent late-spring burning has maintained the Flint Hills
30 grassland, the resultant smoke plumes from en masse burning often leads to air quality issues in nearby cities. Concentrated smoke from grass fires produces airborne particulates, volatile organic compounds, and nitrogen oxides that facilitate tropospheric ozone
35 production. Burning in late spring also generates more ozone than burning in winter or early spring due to the higher air temperatures and insolation.

If the Flint Hills tallgrass prairie, its economic utilization, and high air quality are all to be
40 maintained, a good understanding of the consequences of burning at different times of the year is necessary. Burning earlier in spring has been regarded as undesirable because it putatively reduces total biomass production, increases cool-season [grasses] and
45 undesirable forbs, is ineffective in controlling woody species, and lowers monthly weight gains of steers compared to burning in late spring. Consequently, burning exclusively in late spring has become ingrained in the cultural practices of grassland
50 management in the Flint Hills, and local ranchers often burn in unison when weather conditions are favorable.

Despite long-standing recommendations that tallgrass prairie be burned only in late spring, the data supporting this policy is equivocal. Total biomass
55 production was lower in plots burned in early spring than plots burned in late spring, but the weights included grasses, forbs, and shrubs. It was not known if [grass] biomass was reduced by early-spring burning or if the differences were a site effect rather than a
60 treatment effect. Burning in early spring also shifted community composition in a perceived negative pattern because it favored cool-season grasses and forbs. This shift in community composition, however, may actually be desirable because many cool-season
65 grasses have higher production and nutritional quality than warm-season grasses at certain times of the year, and many forb species are beneficial to the diet of grazers. Burning in late spring has been considered the most effective time to control invasive shrubs,
70 but *Symphoricarpos orbiculatus* was the only woody species that declined with repeated late spring burning. Finally, average weight gain of steers was lower in an unburned pasture than in burned pastures, but there was no significant difference in monthly weight gain
75 among cattle grazing in early-, mid-, or late-spring burned pastures.

The historical studies that formed the foundation for time of burning recommendations in tallgrass prairie are inconclusive because none had
80 experimental replications and most were spatially limited to small plots. All of these studies were interpreted as suggesting that shifting the time of burning by only a few weeks would negatively influence the plant community. A more recent large-
85 scale replicated study that compared the effects of annual burning in autumn, winter, and late spring found that the timing of burning had no significant effect on grass production and no reductions in the composition of desirable warm-season grasses.

CONTINUE ➡

Grass

Forb

Changes in Upland and Lowland Grass (a) and Forb (b) Productivity Over Time for Autumn-, Winter-, and Spring-Burned Watersheds

29

The authors of the passage most likely believe that

A) burning should be done on a semiannual basis.

B) no burning should happen in the late spring.

C) late spring may not be the best time for burning.

D) changing burning schedules will negatively influence plants.

30

According to the passage, which of the following does NOT influence decisions on the timing of seasonal burns?

A) Biomass production

B) Control of specific plant species

C) Tropospheric ozone production

D) Weather

31

The passage suggests that the Kansas Flint Hills

A) are an ecologically sensitive area that must be treated with extreme caution.

B) must be regularly burned to remain economically viable.

C) have a unique composition of grasses and forbs that must be studied further.

D) will not support healthy livestock if the burning schedule changes.

32

Which choice provides the best evidence for the answer to the previous question?

A) Lines 21–24 ("The Flint . . . utilization")

B) Lines 38–41 ("If the Flint . . . necessary")

C) Lines 42–47 ("Burning . . . spring")

D) Lines 54–57 ("Total biomass . . . shrubs")

33

As used in line 49, "practices" most nearly means

A) traditions.

B) rehearsals.

C) accomplishments.

D) chores.

34

As used in line 54, "equivocal" most nearly means

A) wrong.

B) misleading.

C) ambivalent.

D) unclear.

CONTINUE ➤

Based on the passage, it can be inferred that *Symphoricarpos orbiculatus* is

A) a forb species beneficial to grazers.

B) an invasive shrub.

C) a woody warm-season grass.

D) a late spring grass.

Which choice provides the best evidence for the answer to the previous question?

A) Lines 52–54 ("Despite . . . is equivocal")

B) Lines 60–63 ("Burning in . . . forbs")

C) Lines 63–68 ("This . . . of grazers")

D) Lines 68–71 ("Burning . . . spring burning")

Which claim about grasses is supported by the graph?

A) Spring burning always results in higher biomass than does autumn or winter burning.

B) Over time, biomass will increase only in prairies burned in spring.

C) The timing of burning does not significantly affect biomass.

D) Biomass declined sharply in 2012 due to drastically lower rainfall.

CONTINUE

Questions 38–47 are based on the following passages.

These passages are adapted from KU Leuven, "Bacterium counteracts 'coffee ring effect.'" © 2013 and University of Pennsylvania, "Physicists undo the 'coffee ring effect.'" © 2011 Science Daily.

Passage 1

A team of University of Pennsylvania physicists has shown how to disrupt the "coffee ring effect"— the ring-shaped stain of particles leftover after coffee
Line drops evaporate—by changing the particle shape. The
5 discovery provides new tools for engineers to deposit uniform coatings.

The research was conducted by professor Arjun Yodh, director of the Laboratory for Research on the Structure of Matter; doctoral candidates Peter Yunker
10 and Matthew Lohr; and postdoctoral fellow Tim Still.

"The coffee ring effect is very common in everyday experience," Yunker said. "To avoid it, scientists have gone to great lengths designing paints and inks that produce an even coating upon evaporation. We found
15 that the effect can be eliminated simply by changing the shape of the particle."

University of Chicago physicists Sidney Nagel, Thomas Witten and their colleagues wrote an influential paper about this process in 1997, which
20 focused mainly on suspended spherical particles, but it was not until the Yodh team's recent experiments that the surprising role played by suspended particle shape was discovered.

Yodh's team used uniformly sized plastic particles
25 in their experiments. These particles were initially spherical but could be stretched into varying degrees of eccentricity, to ensure the experiments only tested the effect of the particle's shape on the drying pattern. The researchers were surprised at how big an effect particle
30 shape had on the drying phenomenon.

"Different particle geometries change the nature of the membrane at the air-water interface," Yodh said. "And that has big consequences." Spherical particles easily detach from the interface, and they flow past one
35 another easily because the spheres do not substantially deform the air-water interface. Ellipsoid particles, however, cause substantial undulation of the air-water interface that in turn induces very strong attractions between the ellipsoids. Thus the ellipsoids tend to get
40 stuck on the surface, and, while the stuck particles can continue to flow towards the drop's edges during

evaporation, they increasingly block each other, creating a traffic jam of particles that eventually covers the drop's surface.

45   After experimenting with suspended particle shape, the researchers added a surfactant, essentially soap, into the drops to show that interactions on the drop's surface were responsible for the effect. With the surfactant lowering the drop's surface tension, ellipsoid
50 particles did not get stuck at the interface and flowed freely to the edge.

"We were thinking it would be useful if you could just sprinkle in a few of these ellipsoid particles to remove the coffee ring effect," Yodh said, "and we
55 found that sometimes this idea works and sometimes it doesn't."

Passage 2

Researchers from the Departments of Chemical Engineering and Chemistry at KU Leuven have now discovered how to counteract coffee rings with
60 'surfactants', i.e., soap. The key to the discovery was not a kitchen towel, but a bacterium that counteracts the coffee ring effect at the microscopic level.

When a coffee ring dries, its edges become noticeably darker and thicker. This occurs because the
65 coffee particles move toward the edge of the stain while the water in the liquid evaporates. At a microscopic level, this coffee ring effect can also be seen in liquids with particles of other materials such as plastic and wood.

70   In various industrial applications—applying an even coat of paint or varnish, for example—the coffee ring effect can be particularly troublesome and scientists have long been seeking ways to counteract it. Raf De Dier and Wouter Sempels (Departments
75 of Chemical Engineering and Chemistry) have now described a solution based on examples found in nature. De Dier and Sempels carried out experiments and calculations on nanomaterials as well as on a particularly promising bacterium, *Pseudomonas*
80 *aeruginosa*.

Pseudomonas aeruginosa is a dangerous bacterium that can cause infections in open wounds. "A *Pseudomonas aeruginosa* bacteria colony wants to find as large a breeding ground as possible. To avoid
85 overconcentration on the edges of a wound when spreading itself during the drying-out process, the

CONTINUE

bacterium produces substances that counteract the coffee ring effect."

These surface-tension-disrupting substances are
90 called surfactants. Detergents such as soap are also surfactants. "Add soap to a stain—a coffee stain or any other stain—and you will still get a coffee ring effect. But at the same time the soap causes a counterflow from the edge back towards the centre of the stain
95 in such a way that the small particles—material or bacteria—end up in a kind of whirlwind. In this way, you get a more uniform distribution of particles as evaporation occurs."

38

Passage 1 most strongly suggests that Professor Yodh's team at the University of Pennsylvania assumed which of the following before their experiments?

A) The shape of the particles leads to detachment from the interface.

B) The shape of the particles has a minimal effect on drying patterns.

C) The shape of a spherical particle can't be changed to ellipsoid.

D) The shape of the particles is the only factor that affects the membrane.

39

The author of Passage 1 refers to a paper by University of Chicago physicists Sidney Nagel and Thomas Witten (lines 17–23) primarily to

A) imply that Nagel and Witten could have discovered the impact of ellipsoid particles.

B) describe an impediment to research on suspended spherical particles.

C) suggest that the study done by Nagel and Witten influenced the research by Yodh's team.

D) contrast the results of earlier, flawed research with the useful data obtained more recently.

40

Based on the passage, which choice best describes the relationship between Nagel and Witten's and Yodh's research?

A) Yodh's research challenges Nagel and Witten's.

B) Yodh's research builds on Nagel and Witten's.

C) Nagel and Witten's research contradicts Yodh's.

D) Nagel and Witten's research supports Yodh's.

41

As used in line 37, "undulation" most nearly means

A) attraction.

B) evaporation.

C) undertow.

D) ripple.

42

In lines 84–90 ("To avoid . . . surfactants"), what is the most likely reason the author of Passage 2 compares detergents and bacterium?

A) To justify research into surfactants from bacterium, since the surfactants in soap may not serve industrial needs

B) To alert companies that want surfactants for paint and varnish to the dangers of bacterium

C) To show that soap can help reduce the movement of particles to the edge of a stain, but can't stop it

D) To contend that soap is a better surfactant so it's best to avoid using *Pseudomonas aeruginosa* until further studies have been done

43

What does Passage 2 most strongly suggest about the coffee ring effect?

A) It generates many studies on ways to thwart it.

B) It sends microscopic particles into a whirlwind.

C) It can be eliminated with the use of surfactants.

D) It has various industrial applications.

CONTINUE

44

Which choice provides the best evidence for the answer to the previous question?

A) Lines 57–60 ("Researchers . . . soap")

B) Lines 60–62 ("The key . . . level")

C) Lines 66–69 ("At a . . . wood")

D) Lines 70–74 ("In various . . . counteract it")

45

As used in line 97, "uniform" most nearly means

A) spread thin.

B) similarly shaped.

C) evenly distributed.

D) wiped clean.

46

Is the main conclusion presented by the author of Passage 2 consistent with the properties of the coffee ring effect, as described in Passage 1?

A) No, since Passage 1 shows that surfactants can increase the coffee ring effect if ellipsoids are present.

B) No, since the study in Passage 1 describes how oblong spheres diminish the coffee ring effect.

C) Yes, since the study in Passage 2 explains that surfactants have an effect on the movement of particles.

D) Yes, since the study in Passage 2 concludes that bacteria can be genetically modified in order to produce surfactants.

47

One difference between the studies described in the two passages is that unlike the researchers discussed in Passage 1, the researchers in Passage 2

A) stretch the *Pseudomonas aeruginosa* until they become surfactants.

B) utilize biological organisms to disrupt the surface tension.

C) experiment on nanomaterials in order to breed *Pseudomonas aeruginosa*.

D) explore ways to increase evaporation speed and particle flow.

STOP

**If you finish before time is called, you may check your work on this section only.
Do not turn to any other section.**

No Test Material On This Page

Writing and Language Test

35 MINUTES, 44 QUESTIONS

Turn to Section 2 of your answer sheet to answer the questions in this section.

DIRECTIONS

Each passage below is accompanied by a number of questions. For some questions, you will consider how the passage might be revised to improve the expression of ideas. For other questions, you will consider how the passage might be edited to correct errors in sentence structure, usage, or punctuation. A passage or a question may be accompanied by one or more graphics (such as a table or graph) that you will consider as you make revising and editing decisions.

Some questions will direct you to an underlined portion of a passage. Other questions will direct you to a location in a passage or ask you to think about the passage as a whole.

After reading each passage, choose the answer to each question that most effectively improves the quality of writing in the passage or that makes the passage conform to the conventions of standard written English. Many questions include a "NO CHANGE" option. Choose that option if you think the best choice is to leave the relevant portion of the passage as it is.

Questions 1–11 are based on the following passage.

Getting a CLOe

Imagine you go to a restaurant you've never tried before. Now, let's say you **1** had a bad experience. What next? For many, the answer is **2** simple, get on social media and tell the world. Aside from telling all your

1
A) NO CHANGE
B) have had
C) were having
D) have

2
A) NO CHANGE
B) simple get on
C) simple: get on
D) simple, hop on

CONTINUE

friends and followers about the experience on Twitter and Facebook, **3** you would probably decide not to return to that restaurant. In fact, you might have used these services to find the restaurant in the first place. And really, if a place has two out of five stars on Yelp when you look it up, what's the chance you'll go there in the first place?

Companies, not just restaurants, are starting to see that their biggest business generators are not TV or Internet ads anymore. **4** Today, "buzz" gets created on social media, and it is more important than ever for companies to **5** insure that they are showing the best possible face to the world on social media. Maintaining that public face has created a new job: Chief Listening Officer. Where a Social Media Manager might be in charge of a **6** companies output on Facebook and other sites, a Chief Listening Officer is on the other side. A CLO scours blogs, Pinterest, tumblr, Facebook, Twitter, Google, Yelp, and whatever new site will be hot when you read this to make sure that a company's public image is under control.

3

Which of the following would best maintain the focus of this sentence and paragraph?

A) NO CHANGE

B) you might also go to a consumer-review site, such as Yelp, to tell future patrons.

C) it might make you feel better to tell your friends and relatives about the experience over the phone.

D) you could take the edge off by watching videos of animals doing funny stuff.

4

The author is considering deleting the phrase *not just restaurants* from the preceding sentence and adjusting the punctuation accordingly. Should the phrase be kept or deleted?

A) Kept, because it clarifies that the practice described in the essay is not limited to one industry.

B) Kept, because it encourages companies other than restaurants to hire Chief Listening Officers.

C) Deleted, because it incorrectly implies that patrons of other businesses discuss their experiences on social media.

D) Deleted, because the previous paragraph is all about restaurants, and this one is not.

5

A) NO CHANGE

B) assure the public

C) ensure

D) make insurance

6

A) NO CHANGE

B) companies'

C) company's

D) companys'

CONTINUE ➔

If a CLO sees a bad review on someone's blog, for instance, the CLO might contact a customer-service representative **7** and make it better to see if the situation can be remedied. On the other hand, if a company **8** unfurls a new advertising campaign and the ads are getting buzz on Twitter or many views on YouTube, the CLO might tell his marketing team to keep up the good work. The incredible **9** thing about this is that it is more detailed than market research has ever been before. People share their entire lives on social media, and a single post can reveal not only someone's positive or negative reaction but also **10** their age, gender, location, social status, friends, and so on.

7

A) NO CHANGE
B) and improve things
C) and say, "Get on it!",
D) DELETE the underlined portion.

8

A) NO CHANGE
B) rolls out
C) unrolls
D) roles out

9

A) NO CHANGE
B) thing about this kind of "market research"
C) thing
D) reality

10

A) NO CHANGE
B) they're
C) your
D) his or her

CONTINUE

Some criticize the CLO position as a fad, suggesting that companies are overreacting to the power of social media. **11** The fact of the matter is, however, CLOs will be needed as long as social media are around. After all, consumers are realizing that social-media reviews are often the purest of the pure—neither that of an overrefined food critic or tech geek nor that of someone in the pay of this or that company. The people are talking, and companies have at last made their "listening" official.

11

Which of the following most directly answers the criticism presented in the previous sentence?

A) NO CHANGE

B) They see social media as temporarily popular but not likely to endure.

C) Teachers say that students spend too much time on social media.

D) They say that some social media outlets are more effective than others.

Questions 12–22 are based on the following passage and supplementary material.

Gimme Fever…Actually, Please Don't

Medical science has created some modern miracles, but it can be difficult to appreciate just how miraculous some of them are. The Spanish Flu hit the United States in the 1910s, and **12** polio rocked the foundations of America in the 1930s and 1940s, but it is difficult to imagine an epidemic like the Philadelphia Yellow Fever Epidemic of 1793. The official register listed over 5,000 deaths between August 1st and November 9th of that year. These figures are staggering when we consider that Philadelphia city, **13** the largest city in the country today, had a population of over 1.5 million, and its surrounding areas had only about 50,000.

Rank	Place	Population
1	New York city, NY *	33,131
2	Philadelphia city, PA*	28,522
3	Boston town, MA*	18,320
4	Charleston city, SC	16,359
5	Baltimore town, MD	13,503
6	Northern Liberties township, PA*	9,913
7	Salem town, MA	7,921
8	Newport town, RI	6,716
9	Providence town, RI*	6,380
10	Marblehead town, MA	5,661
10	Southwark district, PA*	5,661
12	Gloucester town, MA	5,317
13	Newbury town, MA	4,837
14	Portsmouth town, NH	4,720
15	Sherburne town (Nantucket), MA*	4,620
16	Middleborough town, MA	4,526
17	New Haven city, CT*	4,487
18	Richmond city, VA	3,761
19	Albany city, NY	3,498
20	Norfolk borough, VA	2,959
21	Petersburg town, VA	2,828
22	Alexandria town, VA*	2,748
23	Hartford city, CT*	2,683
24	Hudson city, NY	2,584
* See Notes for Individual Places.		
Source: U.S. Bureau of the Census Internet Release date: June 15, 1998		

Population of the 24 Urban Places: 1790

12

Which of the following would provide a detail that would best maintain the focus of this paragraph?

A) NO CHANGE

B) many people died from this flu, especially soldiers in World War I,

C) it's possible to get flu vaccinations at your local drug store now,

D) it just faded away even though doctors could never cure it,

13

Which of the following gives information consistent with the chart?

A) NO CHANGE

B) the second largest city in the country at that time, had a population of only about 28,000,

C) second only to New York and Boston, had a population of over 28,000 at the time,

D) was larger than its neighboring New York City by nearly 10,000 people,

CONTINUE ▶

It was not ultimately medical science that saved the day during this epidemic. Doctors tried various **14** things, but they were stalled by their inability to figure out both how the disease originated and how **15** it was spreading. It therefore seemed a godsend when the frost came in November, and the number of deaths tapered off. Medical historians now know that the disease was spread by mosquitoes, but this was **16** pretty shady until nearly a century after the disease had come and gone.

14

A) NO CHANGE

B) options

C) management models

D) treatment approaches

15

A) NO CHANGE

B) it spread.

C) it had been spread.

D) its spread.

16

A) NO CHANGE

B) stupid idiocy

C) not verified

D) downright wrong

CONTINUE

[1] In 1793, Philadelphia was the second largest city in the new nation of the United States. [2] As a result, all of the quarantine and curfew measures that **17** they tried to impose had failed. [3] Panicked politicians blamed immigration. [4] The city's College of Physicians published a letter in the city newspapers that spoke to the confusion. [5] They recognized the epidemic for what it was, but their eleven measures for prevention were haphazard and confused and included the avoidance of **18** alcohol, hot sun, and night air. [6] Philadelphia didn't know what had hit it. [7] Dr. Benjamin Rush, one of the earliest and most brilliant physicians in all of American history, blamed a rotten shipment of coffee that had come into Philadelphia's port. **19**

17

A) NO CHANGE
B) one
C) city authorities
D) some

18

A) NO CHANGE
B) alcohol, hot sun and night air.
C) alcohol, hot sun, and also night air.
D) alcohol, hot sun, and the air of the night.

19

The best placement for sentence 7 would be

A) where it is now.
B) at the beginning of the paragraph.
C) after sentence 1.
D) after sentence 3.

CONTINUE →

It's difficult to imagine an epidemic on this kind of scale today. Moreover, Philadelphia's relative prominence and sophistication in that era should give us pause. The medical establishment sat [20] back helplessly: as the disease ravaged the city. The recent outbreak of [21] the Ebola virus, in West Africa, provides a terrifying reminder, of just how deadly certain diseases can be, when they are unchecked or inadequately understood. [22] By the same token, the Yellow Fever Epidemic provides a remarkable instance of a city's resilience in the face of adversity. As the population of the city was literally decimated, and other yellow-fever epidemics continued to ravage the city, Philadelphia persisted, and with it, the new nation grew stronger, just as it has in the face of crisis ever since.

20

A) NO CHANGE
B) back helplessly, as the disease
C) back helplessly as the disease
D) back helplessly; as the disease

21

A) NO CHANGE
B) the Ebola virus in West Africa provides a terrifying reminder of just how deadly certain diseases can be when
C) the Ebola virus, in West Africa provides a terrifying reminder, of just how deadly certain diseases can be when
D) the Ebola virus, in West Africa, provides a terrifying reminder of just how deadly certain diseases can be, when

22

A) NO CHANGE
B) On the other hand,
C) Therefore,
D) Thus,

CONTINUE

Questions 23–33 are based on the following passage.

The Singing Brakeman

— 1 —

The early days of recorded music can be hazy. Many people find it difficult to believe that artists recording before the radio boom in the 1940s, or even before the rock and roll boom in the 1950s, could have had any success at all **23** seems doubtful. Despite this misconception, there is a treasure trove of recorded music from that era, and not only by the greats of bebop and swing. **24**

— 2 —

The circumstances of **25** Rodgers's birth is obscure, but legend has it that he was born in Meridian, Mississippi in 1897. Little is known **26** for sure, but his father was a foreman on the Mobile and Ohio Railroad in Meridian. Jimmie eventually became a brakeman, but **27** a health issue cut his career short. He stayed alive for a few years after his dismissal in 1927, but he could no longer work the rails.

23

A) NO CHANGE

B) strikes us as odd.

C) appears improbable.

D) DELETE the underlined portion and end the sentence with a period.

24

Which of the following would most effectively conclude this paragraph by introducing the main subject of the essay as a whole?

A) It takes a real music connoisseur to know who was famous before Elvis Presley.

B) Most of the best-known names from the 1930s and 1940s are those of jazz singers.

C) One of these greats was Jimmie Rodgers, one of the first megastars of country music.

D) Some of the greats were Robert Johnson, Mississippi John Hurt, and Jimmie Rodgers.

25

A) NO CHANGE

B) Rodgers's birth are

C) Rodgers's birth has been

D) Rodgers's birth was

26

A) NO CHANGE

B) for certain,

C) for sure about his family,

D) for sure about his mother, father, and siblings,

27

At this point, the writer wants to include a detail that provides specific information about Rodgers's illness. Which of the following would best fulfill that goal?

A) NO CHANGE

B) problems with his health

C) a bout of tuberculosis

D) one of the current diseases

CONTINUE ➤

— 3 —

The recording had moderate success, and it sparked Rodgers to pursue his music career in earnest. In October of that year, after Rodgers chased his dream, Victor released "Blue Yodel," better known as "T for Texas," which sold **28** all the way to New York City half a million copies. Rodgers quickly became a household name, and his trademark yodel would be known the world over. By this **29** time, Rodgers had become the famous "Singing Brakeman," and his influence would be felt for many generations to come.

— 4 —

This influence would not be felt only in country music either: blues singer Howlin' Wolf cited Rodgers as an early **30** influence, like Elvis Presley. Ultimately losing his battle with tuberculosis at age 33, Rodgers may have lived a short life, but if the history of American music is an indication, his influence is still alive and well.

28

If the punctuation were to be adjusted accordingly, the best placement for the underlined portion would be

A) where it is now.

B) after the word *year*.

C) after the word *dream*.

D) after the word *copies*.

29

A) NO CHANGE

B) time, when Rodgers

C) time, as Rodgers

D) time: Rodgers

30

A) NO CHANGE

B) influence, as did Elvis Presley.

C) influence, similar to Elvis Presley.

D) influence, much like that of Elvis Presley.

CONTINUE

— 5 —

This inability to work, however, proved to be **31** fortuitous for Rodgers's great passion—music. At age 13, Rodgers had already secretly organized two traveling shows, only to be recovered and brought back to Meridian by his father. Once Jimmie could no longer work the **32** rails, however, he pursued his musical career in earnest. In Bristol, Tennessee, Rodgers organized his first band. That same year, the band was asked to record some songs for Ralph Peer of the Victor Talking Machine Company. The recordings survive today, though they feature a solo Jimmie Rodgers rather than his whole band, as a pre-recording quarrel led them to break up. **33**

31

A) NO CHANGE

B) chancy

C) blessed

D) charmed

32

A) NO CHANGE

B) rails however he

C) rails; however, he

D) rails, however he

33

The best placement for paragraph 5 would be

A) where it is now.

B) before paragraph 1.

C) before paragraph 2.

D) before paragraph 3.

CONTINUE

Questions 34–44 are based on the following passage and supplementary material.

Whale Grandmothers Know Best

We don't often think to apply gender differences to the animal kingdom. Certainly, males and females have <u>**34** a distinct role,</u> but these seem to be largely determined by biology and by the propagation of the species. As a result, many females do not live much beyond menopause, the phase after which females can no longer reproduce. The data below show that <u>**35** only a handful of animals, such as the black-tailed prairie dog, have any post-reproductive life span at all.</u> Some species, however, like humans, short-finned pilot whales, and killer whales, have females who typically live two or more decades after

34

A) NO CHANGE

B) a distinction,

C) a role that is distinct,

D) distinct roles,

35

Which of the following gives accurate data based on the graph?

A) NO CHANGE

B) most animals, including homo sapiens, tend to have some post-reproductive life span.

C) the common bottlenose dolphin has one of the shortest pre-reproductive life spans relative to other animals.

D) no rodent species has any post-reproductive life span at all.

Relationship Between Reproductive Phase and Life Span Across Species

Before reproduction   Reproductive life span

Post reproductive life span   Record of longevity

CONTINUE ▶

menopause. Scientists have long wondered why evolution has determined [36] they should live so much longer, sometimes to be as old as 90, than their counterparts in other species.

[37] It seems that the social forces that define gender may apply to the animal kingdom as well, even though we consider animal behavior to be determined almost entirely by nature rather than nurture. After watching over 750 hours of video and observing the behaviors of pods of whales, [38] whale grandmothers were observed to have teaching behaviors by the scientists.

36

A) NO CHANGE
B) any of them
C) themselves
D) the female whales

37

Which of the following would provide the most effective transition from the previous paragraph to this paragraph?

A) The answer may have come from a recent study of killer whales.
B) Killer whales are some of the most fascinating marine species.
C) Pretty much everyone knows by now that whales are mammals, not fish.
D) Scientists will experiment and try new things until they find something interesting.

38

A) NO CHANGE
B) scientists observed that many of the teaching behaviors were performed by whale grandmothers.
C) whale grandmothers were the most likely to exhibit teaching behaviors.
D) teaching behaviors were observed from whale grandmothers that were shown to scientists.

CONTINUE

39 This knowledge is particularly useful for whale pods because the abundance of salmon is typically what determines whale life-cycles, both reproduction and mortality.

The scientists ascribe this behavior to what they refer to as the grandmothers' roles as "repositories of ecological **40** knowledge" in other words. Sharpened memories and long experience of learned behaviors make the older females extremely valuable to future generations. Without this knowledge, the younger whales would not be able to make the transition to maturity, and the species would not continue to propagate. The elder females have evolved this longevity because the species, simply put, needs it. **41**

39

At this point, the writer is considering adding the following true statement:

> The older female whales were the most likely to lead younger whales to salmon feeding grounds, particularly in the periods where the usually plentiful salmon were sparse.

Should the writer make this addition here?

A) Yes, because it clarifies some of the teaching behaviors mentioned in the previous sentence.

B) Yes, because it gives some credit to older whales, who were otherwise ignored in the study.

C) No, because the information conflicts with other information given later in the passage.

D) No, because the scientists' observations are not given as conclusive.

40

A) NO CHANGE

B) knowledge" in other words; sharpened

C) knowledge," in other words, sharpened

D) knowledge." In other words, sharpened

41

The writer is considering replacing the word *longevity* with the word *life* in the previous sentence. Should the writer make the change or keep the sentence as it is?

A) Keep the sentence as is, because "longevity" provides a more formal way of saying the same thing.

B) Keep the sentence as is, because the sentence refers to the length of whale life, not only the life itself.

C) Make the change, because "life" provides a more general way of articulating the point.

D) Make the change, because readers may not know the meaning of the word "longevity."

42 From a gender perspective, these findings further break down the idea that gender roles are biologically determined. From an age perspective, the findings also show that societies that value youth and middle age to the detriment of old age may do so at **43** there own peril. Anyone with grandparents knows that these older relatives have experienced enough of life to know a thing or two. In whale pods as well as human communities, it seems, life may depend on the accrued knowledge **44** about the secrets of life that have been gathered by the old people who know about it.

42

Which of the following choices would introduce this paragraph most effectively?

A) Gender discrimination does not really exist in whale communities.

B) Whale grandmothers know things other than where to find the salmon.

C) There is a beautiful scene in Herman Melville's *Moby Dick* featuring whale families.

D) The findings are interesting to non-scientists as well.

43

A) NO CHANGE

B) their

C) it's

D) its

44

A) NO CHANGE

B) of some of the secret-knowing people whose long lives are long enough.

C) of those who have lived long enough to know the secrets of long life.

D) the longer-lived people who are more secret oriented.

STOP
If you finish before time is called, you may check your work on this section only.
Do not turn to any other section.

No Test Material On This Page

Math Test – No Calculator

25 MINUTES, 17 QUESTIONS

Turn to Section 3 of your answer sheet to answer the questions in this section.

DIRECTIONS

For questions 1–13, solve each problem, choose the best answer from the choices provided, and fill in the corresponding circle on your answer sheet. **For questions 14–17,** solve the problem and enter your answer in the grid on the answer sheet. Please refer to the directions before question 14 on how to enter your answers in the grid. You may use any available space in your test booklet for scratch work.

NOTES

1. The use of a calculator **is not permitted**.
2. All variables and expressions used represent real numbers unless otherwise indicated.
3. Figures provided in this test are drawn to scale unless otherwise indicated.
4. All figures lie in a plane unless otherwise indicated.
5. Unless otherwise indicated, the domain of a given function f is the set of all real numbers x for which $f(x)$ is a real number.

REFERENCE

$A = \pi r^2$
$C = 2\pi r$

$A = \ell w$

$A = \frac{1}{2} bh$

$c^2 = a^2 + b^2$

Special Right Triangles

$V = \ell wh$

$V = \pi r^2 h$

$V = \frac{4}{3}\pi r^3$

$V = \frac{1}{3}\pi r^2 h$

$V = \frac{1}{3}\ell wh$

The number of degrees of arc in a circle is 360.
The number of radians of arc in a circle is 2π.
The sum of the measures in degrees of the angles of a triangle is 180.

CONTINUE

1

Which of the following ordered pairs (x, y) satisfies both equations $x = \frac{1}{2}y + 3$ and $y = x^2 - 5x + 6$?

A) $(0, 3)$

B) $(2, -2)$

C) $(4, 2)$

D) $(6, 12)$

2

Which of the following is an equivalent form of the expression $30y - 12cy$?

A) $(5 - 2c)y$

B) $(30 - 12c)y$

C) $18(c - 2y)$

D) $18cy^2$

3

The formula $F = ma$ is used to calculate the force on an object with a mass, m, and an acceleration, a. Based on this formula, what is the acceleration, a, in terms of F and m ?

A) $a = Fm$

B) $a = F + m$

C) $a = \dfrac{F}{m}$

D) $a = \dfrac{m}{F}$

4

$$-4j - 10k = 50$$
$$j - 3k = 4$$

If (j, k) is the solution to the system of equations above, what is the value of j ?

A) 13

B) −5

C) −7

D) −10

CONTINUE

5

The equation $y = 3{,}100x + 105$ models the relationship between the weight, y, in grams, of an average giant panda and the number of months, x, after it was born. If the equation is graphed in the xy-plane, what is indicated by the slope of the graph?

A) The weight, in grams, of an average giant panda at birth

B) The number of months it takes an average giant panda to gain weight

C) The age, in months, of an average giant panda when it is fully matured

D) The weight, in grams, that an average giant panda gains each month

6

Which of the following is a solution to the equation $3b^2 - 6b = 5 + 4b^2$?

A) -5

B) 0

C) 1

D) 3

7

A line is graphed in the xy-plane. If the line has an x-intercept of 4 and contains the point $(-2, 6)$, which of the following cannot be true?

A) The point $(-10, -6)$ is on the line.

B) The slope of the line is negative.

C) The y-intercept is positive.

D) The point $(10, -6)$ is on the line.

8

A patterned quilt uses 16 different squares of fabric. Each square of fabric must have an area of at least 340 square inches and no more than 360 square inches. What inequality represents all possible values of the total area of fabric, f, in square inches needed for the quilt?

A) $5{,}740 \le f \le 5{,}760$

B) $5{,}440 \le f \le 5{,}760$

C) $5{,}440 \le f \le 5{,}460$

D) $340 \le f \le 360$

CONTINUE

9

Christen wants to buy dishes that cost \$17.30 each and bowls that cost \$14.90 each. A 15% discount will be applied to the entire purchase and no tax is charged. If Christen buys 3 dishes, which equation relates the number of bowls purchased, n, and the total cost in dollars, x?

A) $51.90 + 14.90n = 1.15x$

B) $51.90 + 14.90n = 0.85x$

C) $1.15(51.90 + 14.90n) = x$

D) $0.85(51.90 + 14.90n) = x$

10

$$\left(a^{\frac{1}{3}}b^{\frac{1}{4}}\right)^{3}\left(a^{\frac{1}{3}}b^{\frac{1}{4}}\right)^{4} = a^{\frac{k}{3}}b^{\frac{k}{4}}$$

If the equation above, where k is a constant, is true for all positive values of a and b, what is the value of k?

A) 3

B) 4

C) 7

D) 10

11

A baker has \$75 with which to purchase ingredients. The baker needs to buy at least 2 containers of flour and at least 3 containers of cocoa powder. Flour costs \$3.99 per container, and cocoa powder costs \$5.99 per container. If f represents the number of containers of flour and c represents the number of containers of cocoa powder, which of the following systems of inequalities models this situation?

A) $\begin{cases} f \geq 2 \\ c \geq 3 \\ 3.99f + 5.99c \geq 75 \end{cases}$

B) $\begin{cases} f + c \geq 5 \\ 3.99f + 5.99c \geq 75 \end{cases}$

C) $\begin{cases} f \geq 2 \\ c \geq 3 \\ 3.99f + 5.99c \leq 75 \end{cases}$

D) $\begin{cases} f + c \geq 5 \\ 3.99f + 5.99c \leq 75 \end{cases}$

12

If the equation $x = (y + 5)(y - 15)$ is graphed in the xy-plane, what is the y-coordinate of the parabola's vertex?

A) 5

B) 10

C) 25

D) 100

CONTINUE

13

In the figure above, the ratio $\dfrac{FJ}{FH}$ has the same value as the ratio $\dfrac{FG}{GH}$. Which of the following angle measures must be congruent?

A) $\angle FGH$ and $\angle FHJ$

B) $\angle FJG$ and $\angle FJH$

C) $\angle GFJ$ and $\angle HFJ$

D) $\angle GFH$ and $\angle FJH$

CONTINUE

DIRECTIONS

For questions 14–17, solve the problem and enter your answer in the grid, as described below, on the answer sheet.

1. Although not required, it is suggested that you write your answer in the boxes at the top of the columns to help you fill in the circles accurately. You will receive credit only if the circles are filled in correctly.

2. Mark no more than one circle in any column.

3. No question has a negative answer.

4. Some problems may have more than one correct answer. In such cases, grid only one answer.

5. **Mixed numbers** such as $3\frac{1}{2}$ must be gridded as 3.5 or 7/2. (If is entered into the grid, it will be interpreted as $\frac{31}{2}$, not as $3\frac{1}{2}$.)

6. **Decimal Answers:** If you obtain a decimal answer with more digits than the grid can accommodate, it may be either rounded or truncated, but it must fill the entire grid.

Acceptable ways to grid $\frac{2}{3}$ are:

Answer: 201 – either position is correct

NOTE: You may start your answers in any column, space permitting. Columns you don't need to use should be left blank.

14

Monica sells home-made jams and she made half as many ounces of jam on Wednesday as she did on Thursday. She made a total of 3 pounds and 6 ounces of jam on those two days. How many ounces of jam did Monica make on Thursday? (Note: 16 ounces = 1 pound)

15

$$6(2y + z) = 12y + 18$$

In the equation above, z is a constant. For what value of z does the equation have an infinite number of solutions?

16

$$(gx^2 - 4y^2)(6x^2 + hy^2)$$

In the expression above, g and h are non-zero constants with a difference of 5. If the value of the coefficient on the x^2y^2 term is zero when the expression is multiplied out and the like terms are collected, what is the value of gh ?

17

$$8y^2 - dy - 15$$

If $2y - 3$ is a factor of the expression above, in which d is an integer, what is the value of d ?

STOP
**If you finish before time is called, you may check your work on this section only.
Do not turn to any other section.**

No Test Material On This Page

Math Test – Calculator

45 MINUTES, 31 QUESTIONS

Turn to Section 4 of your answer sheet to answer the questions in this section.

DIRECTIONS

For questions 1–27, solve each problem, choose the best answer from the choices provided, and fill in the corresponding circle on your answer sheet. **For questions 28–31,** solve the problem and enter your answer in the grid on the answer sheet. Please refer to the directions before question 28 on how to enter your answers in the grid. You may use any available space in your test booklet for scratch work.

NOTES

1. The use of a calculator **is permitted**.

2. All variables and expressions used represent real numbers unless otherwise indicated.

3. Figures provided in this test are drawn to scale unless otherwise indicated.

4. All figures lie in a plane unless otherwise indicated.

5. Unless otherwise indicated, the domain of a given function f is the set of all real numbers x for which $f(x)$ is a real number.

REFERENCE

$A = \pi r^2$
$C = 2\pi r$

$A = \ell w$

$A = \frac{1}{2}bh$

$c^2 = a^2 + b^2$

Special Right Triangles

$V = \ell wh$

$V = \pi r^2 h$

$V = \frac{4}{3}\pi r^3$

$V = \frac{1}{3}\pi r^2 h$

$V = \frac{1}{3}\ell wh$

The number of degrees of arc in a circle is 360.
The number of radians of arc in a circle is 2π.
The sum of the measures in degrees of the angles of a triangle is 180.

CONTINUE

1

A college bookstore makes a profit of $0.75 for every 12 pencils it sells. Which of the following is the profit that the store makes for selling 20 pencils?

A) $0.75

B) $0.95

C) $1.25

D) $2.22

2

A student planned to finish her summer reading assignment over the course of a 20-day portion of her summer vacation. Each day, she recorded the percent of her assignment she had left to read. The graph below shows the data for each day of the 20-day portion of her summer vacation.

Percent of Summer Reading Assignment Remaining

During which of the following periods is the decrease in the percent of her remaining summer reading the least?

A) Days 1 though 5

B) Days 3 through 8

C) Days 7 through 12

D) Days 13 through 17

3

Sydney borrowed money from a friend and is paying back the loan. The remaining amount she owes, A, can be calculated by the equation $A = 870 - 30w$, where w represents the number of weeks since she took the loan. What does the number 870 represent?

A) The total amount of money Sydney has repaid

B) The amount of money Sydney repays each week

C) The number of weeks Sydney has been paying back the loan

D) The original amount that Sydney borrowed

CONTINUE

Questions 4 and 5 refer to the following information.

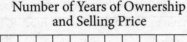

Number of Years of Ownership
and Selling Price

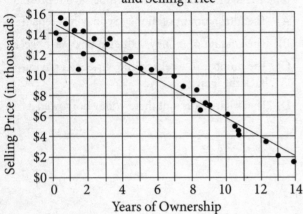

For 32 cars that were identical when new, the scatterplot above shows the number of years of ownership and the selling price when the first owner sold the car. The line of best fit is also shown.

4

Which of the following statements about the relationship between years of ownership and selling price is true?

A) As the number of years of ownership increases, the selling price decreases.

B) As the number of years of ownership decreases, the selling price decreases.

C) As the number of years of ownership increases, the selling price increases.

D) As the number of years of ownership decreases, the selling price remains constant.

5

For the car that was sold after exactly 7 years of ownership, the actual selling price of the car was approximately how much more than the selling price predicted by the line of best fit?

A) $650

B) $1,250

C) $2,150

D) $3,350

6

When the equation $y = 2x - b$, where b is a constant, is graphed in the xy-plane, the line passes through the point $(3, -1)$. What is the value of b ?

A)   −5

B)   −3

C)   1

D)   7

CONTINUE

7

Month	Balance
0	$1,400
1	$1,344
2	$1,290
3	$1,239
4	$1,189
5	$1,142

The table above shows the balance, in dollars, of a bank account. Which of the following best describes the model that fits the data?

A) Exponential, decreasing by approximately 4% per month

B) Exponential, decreasing by approximately 8% per month

C) Linear, decreasing by approximately $47 per month

D) Linear, decreasing by approximately $56 per month

8

A team of scientists is tracking a snail moving at a rate of 700 millimeters per minute. If there are 10 millimeters in a centimeter, at what rate does that snail move in <u>centimeters per hour</u>?

A)   4,200

B)   7,000

C)   42,000

D)   420,000

9

$$5\left(\frac{y}{2} + 5\right) = 2y + \frac{1}{2}y + 25$$

Which of the following describes the solution to the equation shown above?

A) The only solution is $y = 1\frac{1}{2}$.

B) The only solution is $y = 10$.

C) The equation has infinitely many solutions.

D) The equation has no solutions.

10

$$(2ab^2 + 5a^2 - 7a^2b) - (2ab^2 + 7a^2b - 3a^2)$$

Which of the following is equivalent to the expression above?

A) $4a^2b^4 - 21a^2b + 35a^2b$

B) $4ab^2 + 8a^2 - 14a^2b$

C) $2a^2 + 4ab^2$

D) $8a^2 - 14a^2b$

CONTINUE ➡

11

Athletes in a School

	Left-Handed	Right-Handed
Varsity	11	98
Junior Varsity	17	144

The table above provides data about the 270 athletes in a particular high school. Approximately what percent of the athletes in the school are right-handed varsity athletes?

A) 6 percent

B) 36 percent

C) 53 percent

D) 98 percent

12

The table below shows the maximum weights that each of eight people at a gym can bench press.

Bench Press Weights

Person	Pounds
Aaron	40
Beth	30
Carey	110
Donna	230
Ethan	130
Fay	70
Gino	60
Helen	170

What is the difference between the maximum weight, in pounds, that Helen can bench press and the median weight, in pounds, of all eight people?

A) 10

B) 65

C) 70

D) 80

13

The table below shows the daily attendance of a Physics and a Biology class each day of a particular week.

Daily Attendance

Day	Physics	Biology
Monday	25	32
Tuesday	27	25
Wednesday	23	32
Thursday	31	21
Friday	25	28

Based on the information in the table, which of the following statements is true?

A) Both the mode and the range for the Physics class are less than the mode and range for the Biology class.

B) Both the mode and the range for the Physics class are greater than the mode and range for the Biology class.

C) The mode for the Physics class is less than the mode for the Biology class, but the range for the Physics class is greater than the mode for the Biology class.

D) The mode for the Physics class is greater than the mode for the Biology class, but the range for the Physics class is less than the mode for the Biology class.

14

A car company produces a particular model of car one at a time in its factories. If it takes one of the company's factories a total of 1,080 minutes to produce a single car, how many cars of that particular model can be produced by that particular factory in 540 <u>hours</u>?

A) 20

B) 25

C) 30

D) 35

CONTINUE

Questions 15–17 refer to the following information.

A major hospital conducted a study on a new experimental physical therapy method for some of its patients recovering from knee-replacement surgery. At the beginning of the study, 485 patients who had just had knee-replacement surgery were selected for the study; 194 of the patients were given the experimental physical therapy, and the remaining patients were put into conventional physical therapy. A summary of the recovery times for the patients who were in the study is shown in the table below.

Recovery Time for 485 Patients in the Study

Recovery Time	Experimental Therapy	Conventional Therapy
6 months or less	82	151
More than 6 months	112	140

15

What is the difference, to the nearest whole percent, between the percentage of patients in the experimental physical therapy with a recovery time of more than 6 months and the percentage of patients in the conventional physical therapy who had a recovery time of more than 6 months?

A) 10%

B) 8%

C) 6%

D) 4%

16

Of the patients in the conventional physical therapy, the ratio of those who had one knee replaced to those who had both knees replaced is approximately 3:7. Which of the following is the best approximation for the number of patients in the conventional physical therapy who had both knees replaced?

A) 58

B) 87

C) 125

D) 204

17

If a patient in the study is selected at random, which of the following is closest to the probability that the patient will have a recovery time of more than 6 months?

A) 0.28

B) 0.40

C) 0.52

D) 0.81

CONTINUE

18

A circle is graphed in the *xy*-plane. If a circle has center (–3, 5) and a radius of 4, which of the following could be an equation of the circle?

A) $(x - 3)^2 - (y - 5)^2 = 4$

B) $(x - 3)^2 + (y - 5)^2 = 4$

C) $(x + 3)^2 - (y - 5)^2 = 16$

D) $(x + 3)^2 + (y - 5)^2 = 16$

19

A piano player charges a flat fee for an appearance plus an hourly rate based on the length of the performance. The equation $C = 100t + 50$ will relate the total charge *C*, in dollars, for a performance to the time *t*, in hours, of a performance. Based on this equation, how many additional hours will the length of the performance need to be for the piano player to charge an additional dollar?

A) $\dfrac{1}{100}$

B) $\dfrac{1}{50}$

C) 50

D) 100

20

Equal amounts of fencing are used to surround both an octagonal area and a square area. If each side of the octagon is 5 yards shorter than each side of the square, how many yards of fencing are needed to surround each area?

A) 20

B) 40

C) 60

D) 80

21

In the *xy*-plane, the graph of the function *f* is a parabola. If the graph of *f* intersects the *x*-axis at (*k*, 0) and (3, 0), and the vertex of *f* is at (5, –3), what is the value of *k* ?

A) 9

B) 7

C) 5

D) 1

CONTINUE

22

$$g(x) = \frac{3x + 9}{3x^2 - 3x - 18}$$

Which of the following is an equivalent form of rational function *g* that displays as constants or coefficients values that are not part of the domain?

A) $g(x) = \dfrac{1}{3x^2}$

B) $g(x) = \dfrac{1}{x - 2}$

C) $g(x) = \dfrac{x + 3}{x^2 - x - 6}$

D) $g(x) = \dfrac{3(x + 3)}{3(x - 3)(x + 2)}$

23

$$SA = 4\pi r^2$$

The formula for the surface area of a sphere with radius *r* is shown above. The radius of a volleyball is about 3 times the radius of a tennis ball. If a volleyball and a tennis ball are spherical, approximately how many times larger is the surface area of a volleyball than the surface area of a tennis ball?

A) 3

B) 9

C) 27

D) 36

24

A particle accelerates at a constant rate from a velocity of 20 meters per second to a velocity of 50 meters per second in 10 seconds. Which of the following expresses the velocity *V*, in meters per second, in terms of the time *t*, in seconds, after the acceleration began, for $0 \le t \le 10$?

A) $V = -50 + 3t$

B) $V = 20 + 3t$

C) $V = -20 - 3t$

D) $V = 50 - 3t$

25

If the function *h* is defined by $h(x) = 2x^2 - 7x - 3$, what is $h(x + 3)$?

A) $h(x + 3) = 2x^2 - 7x$

B) $h(x + 3) = 2x^2 - 7x - 6$

C) $h(x + 3) = 2x^2 + 5x - 6$

D) $h(x + 3) = 2x^2 - 23x + 15$

CONTINUE

26

$$10x - 62 = 9y$$
$$\frac{1}{4}x = y$$

The equations of two lines are shown above. If the lines are graphed on the *xy*-plane, which of the following ordered pairs represents the point of intersection of the two lines?

A) (8, 2)

B) (16, 4)

C) (24, 6)

D) (32, 8)

27

The amount of carbon-14 in a sample halves every 5,730 years. Which of the following best describes the type of decay that models the relationship between amount of carbon-14 and time?

A) Linear decay, because the amount of carbon-14 decreases by the same factor every 5,730-year period

B) Linear decay, because the amount of carbon-14 decreases by the same amount every 5,730-year period

C) Exponential decay, because the amount of carbon-14 decreases by the same factor every 5,730-year period

D) Exponential decay, because the amount of carbon-14 decreases by the same amount every 5,730-year period

CONTINUE

DIRECTIONS

For questions 28–31, solve the problem and enter your answer in the grid, as described below, on the answer sheet.

1. Although not required, it is suggested that you write your answer in the boxes at the top of the columns to help you fill in the circles accurately. You will receive credit only if the circles are filled in correctly.

2. Mark no more than one circle in any column.

3. No question has a negative answer.

4. Some problems may have more than one correct answer. In such cases, grid only one answer.

5. **Mixed numbers** such as $3\frac{1}{2}$ must be gridded as 3.5 or 7/2. (If $\boxed{3\ 1\ /\ 2}$ is entered into the grid, it will be interpreted as $\frac{31}{2}$, not as $3\frac{1}{2}$.)

6. **Decimal Answers:** If you obtain a decimal answer with more digits than the grid can accommodate, it may be either rounded or truncated, but it must fill the entire grid.

Answer: $\frac{7}{12}$ Answer: 2.5

Write answer in boxes.
Fraction line
Grid in result.
Decimal point

Acceptable ways to grid $\frac{2}{3}$ are:

Answer: 201 – either position is correct

NOTE: You may start your answers in any column, space permitting. Columns you don't need to use should be left blank.

28

$$y = x + 8$$
$$y = x^2 - x - 7$$

If (x, y) is a solution to the equation above, what is one possible value for the sum x and y ?

29

Type of Metal	Weight (ounces)	Price ($)
Gold	2	2,500
Platinum	5	7,500

A jewelry supply store sells boxes of sheet metal for gold and platinum at the weights and prices listed in the table above. A jeweler wants to purchase at least 90 ounces of metal and plans to spend at least $170,000. If she has already ordered 10 boxes of gold, what is the minimum number of boxes of platinum she can order to satisfy the requirements?

CONTINUE

Questions 30 and 31 refer to the following information.

Hours Spent Jogging

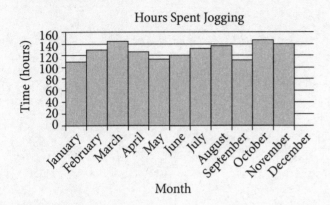

Month

The graph above shows the amount of time, in hours, that Robert spend jogging in each month through a particular year. The information for the month of December is not included in the graph.

30

In November, Robert jogged at an average pace of 8 miles per hour. In December, Robert ran for *h* hours at an average pace of 7 miles per hour. If the total distance that Robert jogged each of the two months was the same, what is the value of *h* ?

31

In June, Robert ran at a pace of 5 miles per hour at the beginning of the month before he increased in pace to 6 miles per hour toward the end of the month. If he spent 70% of this jogging time at the slower pace, and the rest at the faster pace, what is the total distance, in miles that Robert jogged during the month of June?

STOP

If you finish before time is called, you may check your work on this section only.
Do not turn to any other section.

PSAT/NMSQT PRACTICE TEST ANSWER SHEET

	EXAMPLES OF	It is recommended that you use a No. 2 pencil. It is very important that you fill in the entire circle darkly and completely. If you change your response, erase as completely as possible. Incomplete marks or erasures may affect your score.
COMPLETE MARK ●	**INCOMPLETE MARKS** 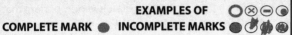	

■ **TEST NUMBER**

ENTER TEST NUMBER
For instance, for Practice Test #1, fill in the circle for 0 in the first column and for 1 in the second column.

0 ◯◯
1 ◯◯
2 ◯◯
3 ◯◯
4 ◯◯
5 ◯◯
6 ◯◯
7 ◯◯
8 ◯◯
9 ◯◯

■ **SECTION 1**

	A B C D		A B C D		A B C D		A B C D
1	◯◯◯◯	13	◯◯◯◯	25	◯◯◯◯	37	◯◯◯◯
2	◯◯◯◯	14	◯◯◯◯	26	◯◯◯◯	38	◯◯◯◯
3	◯◯◯◯	15	◯◯◯◯	27	◯◯◯◯	39	◯◯◯◯
4	◯◯◯◯	16	◯◯◯◯	28	◯◯◯◯	40	◯◯◯◯
5	◯◯◯◯	17	◯◯◯◯	29	◯◯◯◯	41	◯◯◯◯
6	◯◯◯◯	18	◯◯◯◯	30	◯◯◯◯	42	◯◯◯◯
7	◯◯◯◯	19	◯◯◯◯	31	◯◯◯◯	43	◯◯◯◯
8	◯◯◯◯	20	◯◯◯◯	32	◯◯◯◯	44	◯◯◯◯
9	◯◯◯◯	21	◯◯◯◯	33	◯◯◯◯	45	◯◯◯◯
10	◯◯◯◯	22	◯◯◯◯	34	◯◯◯◯	46	◯◯◯◯
11	◯◯◯◯	23	◯◯◯◯	35	◯◯◯◯	47	◯◯◯◯
12	◯◯◯◯	24	◯◯◯◯	36	◯◯◯◯		

The
Princeton
Review®

PSAT/NMSQT PRACTICE TEST ANSWER SHEET

COMPLETE MARK ● **EXAMPLES OF** **INCOMPLETE MARKS**	It is recommended that you use a No. 2 pencil. It is very important that you fill in the entire circle darkly and completely. If you change your response, erase as completely as possible. Incomplete marks or erasures may affect your score.

■ SECTION 2

1 A B C D   10 A B C D   19 A B C D   28 A B C D   37 A B C D

2 A B C D   11 A B C D   20 A B C D   29 A B C D   38 A B C D

3 A B C D   12 A B C D   21 A B C D   30 A B C D   39 A B C D

4 A B C D   13 A B C D   22 A B C D   31 A B C D   40 A B C D

5 A B C D   14 A B C D   23 A B C D   32 A B C D   41 A B C D

6 A B C D   15 A B C D   24 A B C D   33 A B C D   42 A B C D

7 A B C D   16 A B C D   25 A B C D   34 A B C D   43 A B C D

8 A B C D   17 A B C D   26 A B C D   35 A B C D   44 A B C D

9 A B C D   18 A B C D   27 A B C D   36 A B C D

PSAT/NMSQT PRACTICE TEST ANSWER SHEET

| COMPLETE MARK ● | EXAMPLES OF INCOMPLETE MARKS | | It is recommended that you use a No. 2 pencil. It is very important that you fill in the entire circle darkly and completely. If you change your response, erase as completely as possible. Incomplete marks or erasures may affect your score. |

■ SECTION 3

1 A B C D ○○○○
2 A B C D ○○○○
3 A B C D ○○○○

4 A B C D ○○○○
5 A B C D ○○○○
6 A B C D ○○○○

7 A B C D ○○○○
8 A B C D ○○○○
9 A B C D ○○○○

10 A B C D ○○○○
11 A B C D ○○○○
12 A B C D ○○○○

13 A B C D ○○○○

Only answers that are gridded will be scored. You will not receive any credit for anything written in the boxes.

14

/ ○○
· ○○○○
0 ○○○○○
1 ○○○○○
2 ○○○○○
3 ○○○○○
4 ○○○○○
5 ○○○○○
6 ○○○○○
7 ○○○○○
8 ○○○○○
9 ○○○○○

15

/ ○○
· ○○○○
0 ○○○○○
1 ○○○○○
2 ○○○○○
3 ○○○○○
4 ○○○○○
5 ○○○○○
6 ○○○○○
7 ○○○○○
8 ○○○○○
9 ○○○○○

16

/ ○○
· ○○○○
0 ○○○○○
1 ○○○○○
2 ○○○○○
3 ○○○○○
4 ○○○○○
5 ○○○○○
6 ○○○○○
7 ○○○○○
8 ○○○○○
9 ○○○○○

17

/ ○○
· ○○○○
0 ○○○○○
1 ○○○○○
2 ○○○○○
3 ○○○○○
4 ○○○○○
5 ○○○○○
6 ○○○○○
7 ○○○○○
8 ○○○○○
9 ○○○○○

NO CALCULATOR ALLOWED

| COMPLETE MARK ● | EXAMPLES OF INCOMPLETE MARKS | | It is recommended that you use a No. 2 pencil. It is very important that you fill in the entire circle darkly and completely. If you change your response, erase as completely as possible. Incomplete marks or erasures may affect your score. |

■ **SECTION 4**

1 A B C D
2 A B C D
3 A B C D
4 A B C D
5 A B C D
6 A B C D

7 A B C D
8 A B C D
9 A B C D
10 A B C D
11 A B C D
12 A B C D

13 A B C D
14 A B C D
15 A B C D
16 A B C D
17 A B C D
18 A B C D

19 A B C D
20 A B C D
21 A B C D
22 A B C D
23 A B C D
24 A B C D

25 A B C D
26 A B C D
27 A B C D

Only answers that are gridded will be scored. You will not receive any credit for anything written in the boxes.

28

/ ○○
· ○○○○
0 ○○○○○
1 ○○○○○
2 ○○○○○
3 ○○○○○
4 ○○○○○
5 ○○○○○
6 ○○○○○
7 ○○○○○
8 ○○○○○
9 ○○○○○

19

/ ○○
· ○○○○
0 ○○○○○
1 ○○○○○
2 ○○○○○
3 ○○○○○
4 ○○○○○
5 ○○○○○
6 ○○○○○
7 ○○○○○
8 ○○○○○
9 ○○○○○

30

/ ○○
· ○○○○
0 ○○○○○
1 ○○○○○
2 ○○○○○
3 ○○○○○
4 ○○○○○
5 ○○○○○
6 ○○○○○
7 ○○○○○
8 ○○○○○
9 ○○○○○

31

/ ○○
· ○○○○
0 ○○○○○
1 ○○○○○
2 ○○○○○
3 ○○○○○
4 ○○○○○
5 ○○○○○
6 ○○○○○
7 ○○○○○
8 ○○○○○
9 ○○○○○

CALCULATOR ALLOWED

Chapter 16
Practice Test 2:
Answers and
Explanations

PRACTICE TEST 2 ANSWER KEY

Section 1: Reading		Section 2: Writing and Language		Section 3: Math (No Calculator)		Section 4: Math (Calculator)	
1. D	25. B	1. D	23. D	1. C	11. C	1. C	16. D
2. B	26. C	2. C	24. C	2. B	12. A	2. A	17. C
3. C	27. D	3. B	25. B	3. C	13. D	3. D	18. D
4. A	28. B	4. A	26. C	4. B	14. 36	4. A	19. A
5. C	29. C	5. C	27. C	5. D	15. 3	5. B	20. B
6. A	30. C	6. C	28. C	6. A	16. 24	6. D	21. B
7. D	31. B	7. D	29. A	7. A	17. 2	7. A	22. D
8. B	32. A	8. B	30. B	8. B		8. A	23. B
9. A	33. A	9. B	31. A	9. D		9. C	24. B
10. C	34. D	10. D	32. A	10. C		10. D	25. C
11. A	35. B	11. A	33. D			11. B	26. A
12. D	36. D	12. A	34. D			12. D	27. C
13. B	37. C	13. B	35. A			13. A	28. 2 or 18
14. D	38. B	14. D	36. D			14. C	29. 20
15. B	39. C	15. B	37. A			15. A	30. 160
16. A	40. B	16. C	38. B				31. 636
17. C	41. D	17. C	39. A				
18. B	42. A	18. A	40. D				
19. C	43. A	19. D	41. B				
20. A	44. D	20. C	42. D				
21. A	45. C	21. B	43. B				
22. B	46. C	22. A	44. C				
23. A	47. B						
24. C							

PRACTICE TEST 2 EXPLANATIONS

Section 1—Reading

1. **D** Throughout the passage, the reader is presented with John Marcher's inner thoughts as he tries to remember the comment he made to May Bertram many years ago. The narrator describes John in the second paragraph as being *even more surprised than ashamed* and more *conscious of a loss than a gain*. In the eighth paragraph, the narrator says that *the blood slowly came to his face...[and] began to burn with recognition*. Later in the last paragraph, John is described as *embarrassed*. The narrator is not judging him but rather describing his emotions through the course of this interchange with May, so eliminate (C). Choice (D) is a good match. This passage is not told from a first-person perspective, so (A) cannot be the correct answer. The first-person pronouns are used when one of the characters is speaking. The information presented to the reader is not a list of facts but rather details about John's emotions and various questions the two characters ask each other, making (B) incorrect. Therefore, the best answer is (D).

2. **B** In lines 45–47 (*Then it was that...a light broke for him...which began to burn with recognition.*), there is a shift in the emotions of John Marcher. Before this point in the passage, he is not sure what comment he made to May Bertram and is trying to remember. His emotions in this part of the passage can be described as unsure, which matches well with *confusion* in (B). Once the *light broke for him*, he falters and is hesitant to *give himself away* and later feels *embarrassed*. So while he has remembered the comment, he is uncomfortable about the fact that she has known his secret for all these years. This feeling of discomfort and realization matches well with the second part of (B)—*disconcerted recognition*. *Begrudging* in (A) doesn't match John's emotions at the end of the passage. *Amazement* in (D) is not a good match for John's emotions at the beginning of the passage—he was surprised that he had forgotten what she said but not "amazed" by that fact. Neither part in (C) can be supported by the passage. Therefore, (B) is the best answer.

3. **C** This passage is primarily centered on a secret that John told May long ago, but nothing indicates that mistakes were made in the past. Eliminate (A). Only John shared a secret with May; both did not share secrets with each other, so (B) is incorrect. They are discussing only this past secret, not their feelings, so (D) is also incorrect. In the first paragraph of the passage, May references a previous outing on a boat, during which John said something that has always remained in her memory. This supports (C) in which they are discussing a former time and conversation.

4. **A** Work both this question and the previous question together by matching answer choices to one another. If you cannot find a match for an answer in question 3, then that cannot be the correct answer. Choice (A) describes a discussion of conversation that took place on a boat ride sometime in the past. This best matches (C) in question 3, so keep it. Choice (B) contains the advice that one should not be reminded of what they were ten years ago. While it seems like this may match with (A) in question 3, there is not actual mention of mistakes that were made. Eliminate (B).

Choice (C) describes a reaction both of the characters have to one character remembering something from the past, which does not match any answers in question 3. Choice (D) refers to May knowing a secret of John's, which appears to match (B) in question 3. But read carefully! It is only John who trusted May with a secret, not that they both trusted each other. The best match and only pair that is supported by the passage is (A).

5. **C**   The sentence in question describes how John Marcher realized that May Bertram was not asking him to remember *a compliment* he had given her nor was she asking him to admit to *a mistake*. May was not making any request of him. In context, *claim* means something similar to "request." Choices (A), (B), and (D) do not mean "request," which leaves (C). *Appeal* in (C) is the most similar word to "request," so it is the best answer.

6. **A**   In the first part of the sentence, the author reveals that John Marcher feels that by not remembering what he said to May Bertram, he's lost something rather than gained something. After the semicolon in this sentence, the author writes *he already saw an interest in the matter of her mention.* Therefore, he, too, is interested in learning what May remembers just as she is interested in discovering if he does remember. The two have a shared concern (does he remember what he said), so the *loss* that John feels is referring to this concern that has brought them together; keep (A). Earlier in the paragraph, John realized that she was not asking him for a compliment or to acknowledge a mistake, so eliminate (B). Sorrento and its weather were mentioned in the first paragraph, but John makes no indication that he wishes to return there, so (C) is incorrect. Neither May nor John have expressed a declaration of love for each other, so he has not rejected anything from her—he realized earlier that she was not asking him to admit a mistake, so (D) is also incorrect. The best answer is (A).

7. **D**   In the passage, May says, *"It was about yourself"* and, *"Has it ever happened?"* Later in the passage, she asks, *"if the thing you then spoke of has ever come to pass?"* There is no indication that they talked about a *puzzle,* so eliminate (A). When May first brings up the conversation, the passage says *but the great thing was that he saw in this no vulgar reminder of any "sweet" speech,* so there was no *romantic confession.* Eliminate (B). While John did initially forget what he said to May, it is not a *trifle.* When he remembers, the passage says that *he was lost in wonder and found himself embarrassed,* so eliminate (C). It is a *personal belief.* The correct answer is (D).

8. **B**   This question asks for the best evidence that *John doesn't believe he's made any declarations of love to May.* Check the lines in each answer choice to see whether they support John's belief. May speaks in the lines for (A) and nothing is revealed about John's thoughts, so eliminate (A). The lines for (B) say that *she was making no claim on him of a compliment or a mistake,* which supports John's belief that he did not declare his love. Keep (B). In the lines for (C), May questions whether he does remember, but there is no mention of a declaration of love, so eliminate (C). In the lines for (D), John says that he *lost any sense of having taken [her] so far into [his] confidence,* which is not about love, so eliminate (D). The correct answer is (B).

9. **A** The sentence in question describes John Marcher noticing that his reaction to May Bertram's last question has *made her feel sorry for him*. Because he became embarrassed, he believes that she feels it was a mistake to give him hints about what he said. In context, *allusion* means something similar to "hints" about what he said. Choices (B), (C), and (D) do not mean "hints," which leaves (A). *Reference* in (A) is the word most similar to "hint" and is, therefore, the best answer.

10. **C** The passage begins with an explanation of why and how Churchill formed a new government and the bodies and appointments therein. The passage then transitions to speaking of *one of the greatest battles in history* and that the aim of the new government and the country is *victory*, and he urges the new government and country to *go forward together with…united strength*. This best supports (C) because the passage first discusses formation of a new government through appointments and then goes on to rally that government to the shared cause of defeating Germany. Choice (A) also references both of these topics but lists them in the opposite order that they appear in the passage. Choice (B) is too narrow because it focuses only on the formation of the War Cabinet, as opposed to the government as a whole. Choice (D) is incorrect because the passage does not encourage an acceptance of defeat but rather urges a policy dedicated to victory. The best answer is (C).

11. **A** As used in this context, the word *prosecute* is used to mean "pursue" the war with Germany. Choices (B) and (C) are deceptive; they are both words that can be used in the same situation that prosecute is used as it relates to the law, but that is not how prosecute is being used in this context. Eliminate both choices. Between *fight* and *enforce*, "fight" more accurately matches the meaning of pursuing a way. Therefore, (A) is the best answer.

12. **D** After describing the positions in the government that had been filled, Churchill states that *it was necessary that this should be done in one single day, on account of the extreme urgency and rigour of events*. These events, as referenced throughout the passage, are the war-related interactions with Germany. The answer that best matches this statement is (D). Choice (A) is too narrow, and there is no indication in the passage why the King asked for the formation of the new administration or that it had to be hasty. The previous leadership of Parliament and the number of parties had nothing to do with why a new government needed to be formed quickly, so (B) can be eliminated. Choice (C) is too extreme; although the war is the reason the new government must be formed so quickly, the war has only just begun. There is no indication that the British Empire is about to lose the war, only that it needs to become better enabled to fight the war effectively. The best answer is (D).

13. **B** As the correct answer to the previous question was (D), the choice that best supports that answer will reference the international political situation. Choice (A) references only the King's orders to form a new government, not why that government needed to be formed, so it is incorrect. Choice (C) references the political reconstruction of parliament and that Churchill hopes those affected by his quick actions will *make allowances…for any lack of ceremony*. However, these lines do not explain *why* his actions had to be quick, so (C) is incorrect as well. Finally, (D) discusses only the need of the British to prevail in their fight, not why Churchill needed to form his administration with haste. The best supported answer is (B)—that line specifically references the larger *events* that prompted the formation of the new government.

14. **D** The passage provides a great deal of information regarding Churchill's administration, so approach this question with POE. At no point does Churchill indicate that he believes the new government will be controversial, and he even invites the body before him to *record its approval of the steps taken and to declare its confidence in the new Government.* Because it seems unlikely that Churchill would invite such an action if he believed the majority would not agree, (A) is not a supported answer based on the text. However, despite the fact that Churchill seems confident by calling a vote of approval, (B) is extreme in saying that *all* the members of the House of Commons will approve it. Choice (C) is discredited by the several references made throughout the third paragraph to the various party members appointed to positions of leadership and to the united representation of the country through the new government. At the end of the third paragraph, Churchill does state that not all of the Minister positions have been appointed because they will take longer, but he hopes that task will be soon completed. This supports (D), which mentions that there are some unfilled positions in the government.

15. **B** Work both this question and the previous question together in a pair to see if any match, because these answer choices are the references for justifying the answer to question 14. Use Parallel POE to find the answer to both questions. Beginning with the answer choices for question 15, (A) contains a description of the formation of a war cabinet that represents the *unity of the nation.* This matches (B) in question 14 because both reference unity, but that answer for question 14 contains extreme language *(all).* Choice (B) refers to the fact that some minister positions are still unfilled, which best matches (D) in question 14. Choice (C) refers to Mr. Speaker and the steps he has taken, which does not match any choices in question 14. Choice (C) can be eliminated. Choice (D) refers to suffering in the time ahead, which also does not match any choices in question 14, so it can be eliminated as well. The only choices left that match choices from question 14 are (A) and (B). Because this question is open-ended, use your POE rules. While (A) does match an answer in question 14, (B) in question 14 is too extreme and not fully supported by the passage. Because (B) in question 15 matches (A) in question 14 and both are explicitly supported by the passage, it is the correct answer.

16. **A** This question asks why Churchill makes the statement that he has *nothing to offer but blood, toil, tears, and sweat.* His use of physical imagery serves to show the amount of exertion Churchill is willing to expend on accomplishing the task at hand. The best match to this description is (A)— this statement is meant to convey Churchill's deep level of commitment to the war effort. Choice (B) is refuted by the remainder of the passage, as Churchill strongly speaks of victory, so it cannot be correct. Choice (D) goes against common sense—his statement is a list of what he is ready to offer. This list does not count as "evidence" of his dedication but more as a description of the intense level of dedication he intends to offer. The best answer is (A).

17. **C** Churchill repetitively uses the phrases *victory* and *no survival* to stress the importance of these aspects to the battle. Without victory, the British Empire will fundamentally change from what it currently is, or so Churchill believes. His repetitive use of the phrases serves to emphasize that point. Choice (A) cannot be correct because Churchill is urging the country to future victory; eliminate it. Because these words are used for emphasis rather than to describe any specific

strategy, (B) is not supported by the text of the passage and can be eliminated. Although the use of the phrase victory is optimistic, Churchill declares that there would be no survival for the British Empire without victory to stress the importance of what is at stake, so optimism is an overly positive word in (D). The answer that is best supported by the passage is (C); both these terms are used to stress the importance of the outcome of the war for the British Empire.

18. **B** As used in this context, the word *suffered* means "to permit"—Churchill believes that mankind will not permit their cause (victory over tyranny) to fail. Choices (A) and (C) are synonyms—if people endure or tolerate something, they "deal with" it. To not "deal with" their cause (failing) is not as precise as the prediction: to not "permit" their cause to fail. Additionally, there cannot be two correct answers, so examine the other two answers. Eliminate (D) because *endorsed* means *approved*, which would go against what Churchill is saying in this context. Choice (B) is a synonym for "permit," so it would work in this context. Churchill is certain that their cause will not be allowed to fail among men. The best answer is (B).

19. **C** The author discusses quite a bit about South Chicago in this passage, so the best approach to this question is POE. The author does not discuss anything about vacation destinations or tourism and references a quote that says no one goes there to admire the scenery, so (A) is not supported by the passage. The author does address the decrease of workers in the steel mills but also states that the local population is still highly dependent on the mills. It says nothing that would indicate all the mills will soon close, so (B) can be eliminated. In the first paragraph, the author describes South Chicago as *isolated, removed, and detached,* which strongly supports (C). Choice (D) is highly negative, and while the author does refer to the unattractive appearances of some buildings and reference ashes from chimneys, this is too sweeping a statement to refer to South Chicago as a whole. The best answer is (C).

20. **A** Because the correct answer to the previous question says that the author believes South Chicago is very isolated from the rest of the city, the correct answer to this question must support that answer. The only answer that does this is (A) because that line refers to South Chicago as the *most isolated community…most removed.* Choice (B) discusses the aesthetics of South Chicago, (C) refers to the noise and smell of South Chicago, and (D) contains a reference to American industry. Because these last three choices do not contain any information related to isolation, (A) is the best answer.

21. **A** The author mentions the names of the restaurants while describing what South Chicago is like. He refers to the appearance of these neighborhoods as *modest* and says the names of the restaurants are *simple.* The point the author is making will match the *modest* and *simple* nature of the area in general. The answer that is best supported by this is (A) because it says that it is the modest aspect of the neighborhood that the author is trying to emphasize.

22. **B** In this sentence, *suspended* is used to describe the *belts, pipes, and railroad* as being up in the air. The answer must therefore match the meaning of "up in the air." The only answer that matches this is (B), *hanging.* Neither (C) nor (D) has any relation to being up in the air, so they can be eliminated. Although the word *drooping* can mean "hanging," it refers to a certain way something hangs that is not supported by the sentence, so (A) is also wrong. The best answer is (B).

23. **A** This question is asking for a direct comparison being made in the passage, so look back to the second paragraph to find the answer. The first sentence of the second paragraph states that the scenery of South Chicago is *the man-made equivalent of the Rockies*. Because the scenery in South Chicago is comprised of the steel mills, the comparison is likening those mills to the Rockies. This supports (A). Choice (B) refers to why the lights are on the chimneys, (C) refers to the size of some of the structures, and (D) gives a description of the smoke. The best answer is (A).

24. **C** Work both this question and the previous question together to see if any match; these answer choices are the references for justifying the answer to question 23. You can then use Parallel POE to find the answers to both questions. Beginning with the answer choices in question 24, (A) contains a description of neighborhoods that does not match any of the choices in question 23. Choice (A) can be eliminated. Choice (B) describes a highway and also does not match any of the choices in question 23, so it can be eliminated as well. Choice (C) contains words that match three choices in question 23, so be careful! Although the lines reference *football fields* and *aircrafts*, these are descriptions that are part of the larger comparison that the steel mills are like the Rockies. This best matches (A) in question 23. Choice (D) describes the function of the steel mills and does not match any choice in question 23. Therefore, (C) is the correct answer.

25. **B** In this sentence, *consumption* is referring to all of the things American's consume or purchase, such as the items listed in the previous sentence. The closest thing to the meaning of consume or purchase in the answers is (B). Choice (A) is an alternate definition of consumption that does not work in the context of this sentence, so it is not correct. Neither corrosion nor burning matches the meaning of purchase at all, so (C) and (D) cannot be correct. The best answer is (B).

26. **C** Pay close attention to what this question is asking: it asks not only for the primary purpose of the last paragraph but also how that relates to the whole passage. The last paragraph is focused on the current state of the steel mills of South Chicago and the decrease in production from the mills. This fits with the descriptive approach the passage has taken as a whole to illustrate this area of a city for the reader. Although the author does take a critical view of the owners of mills, (A) is too specific and does not touch on how this paragraph relates to the passage as a whole. Choice (B) goes too far in saying that the author is lamenting the state of South Chicago; the author is only describing the state of that area, not sharing his personal feelings about it. Choice (D) has the same issue; the author is not suggesting changes, only reviewing changes that have taken place. The best answer is (C)—that the author is explaining the current state of the steel mills—this matches the descriptive nature of the last paragraph and the passage as a whole.

27. **D** Compare each answer against the data provided in the graph. Choice (A) can be eliminated because domestic steel production did not increase only from 1950 to 2000. Choice (B) can also be eliminated because the domestic steel production did not remain stagnant during that time period; it fluctuated. Eliminate (C), as the peak of domestic steel production occurred in the 1970s, not the 1960s. Choice (D) is supported by the graph: the domestic steel production was just under 100 million tons in 1950 and just over 100 million tons in 2000, so the net production had only slightly increased from where it started. The correct answer is (D).

28. **B** This question is asking for a synthesis of information between the graph and the passage. Choice (A) could be true, but nowhere on the graph is it indicated that this data represents only South Chicago's steel mill production. Furthermore, the passage does not explicitly state that the mills reached their greatest productivity in the mid-1970s. Eliminate (A). Choice (C) is extreme by saying that *all* domestic steel mills cut their workforces, which is not supported by either the passage or the graph. Choice (D) references air pollution, which is mentioned in the passage but is in no way addressed by the graph, so eliminate it. Choice (B) states that U.S. steel production has increased in areas other than South Chicago. This is supported by the graph in that there has been a general increase in steel production domestically and is also supported by the passage in the last paragraph—there has not been an increase in South Chicago's steel production.

29. **C** In the second paragraph, the authors state that the grasslands are burned *annually in late spring* and then mention some of the air quality issues that have resulted from late spring burning. They acknowledge that *late spring burning has maintained* the grassland, but it comes at a price, which makes (C) a possible answer. The authors never state that burning should be done twice a year, so (A) should be eliminated. Late spring burning has been the recommendation since the early 1970s and does maintain the grassland, so the authors would not agree with (B). The authors discuss the consequences of burning during different times of the year in the following paragraph, and in the last paragraph they include information from historical studies claiming that shifting the burning time *would negatively impact the plant community*. However, they also mention that a recent study *found that the time of burning had no significant effect* and believe the recommendations are *inconclusive*, so (D) is incorrect. The best answer is (C).

30. **C** Pay attention to the word *NOT* in the question. Use POE to eliminate three answer choices that do influence decisions on the timing of seasonal burning. Choices (A) and (B) are found in lines 4–8 (the second sentence of the first paragraph: *Management...are burned*), so eliminate those two choices because they *do* influence decisions. Lines 47–51 (the last sentence in paragraph 3: *Consequently...are favorable.*) indicate that weather influences the timing of seasonal burns, so (D) should be eliminated. This leaves (C). *Tropospheric ozone production* is mentioned as a consequence of late spring burning not as something that influences when burning happens. Therefore, (C) is the correct answer.

31. **B** The authors describe the Kansas Flint Hills at the beginning of the second paragraph as *one of the last remaining regions supporting extensive native tallgrass prairie in North America, and frequent burning is integral to its preservation and economic utilization*. Choice (B) is a good paraphrase of this sentence. The authors never directly say in this paragraph or elsewhere in the passage that this area is *sensitive* or that *extreme caution* be used when dealing with this area, so eliminate (A). While the passage implies that the Flint Hills are a special grassland, one might assume that they are composed of a unique composition of grasses and shrubs. However, there is no evidence to support that it requires more study, so eliminate (C). Choice (D) is not the best answer, even though it seems feasible at first glance. The article discusses how early spring burning leads to lower weight gain in cattle. However, the passage does not deem the weight gain as being unhealthy. In addition, this option goes against the main idea of the passage. The best answer is (B).

32. **A** The answer to the previous question was that burning the Kansas Flint Hills regularly is essential to keep the area economically useful. The best support for this answer can be found in first sentence of the second paragraph (A). The remaining choices can be eliminated because none of these lines mention that the burning must happen regularly—each focuses on the time of the season when the burning occurs. Therefore, (A) is the correct answer.

33. **A** For the sentence in question, the word *practices* is used to refer to something that is done so much that it has become *ingrained* into the culture—*burning exclusively in late spring has become ingrained in the cultural practices.* Thus, burning in late spring has become a custom, so the correct answer should mean something similar to "customs." Eliminate (B), (C), and (D) because they don't have the same meaning as "customs." *Traditions* in (A) is most similar to "customs," so it is the best answer.

34. **D** For the sentence in question, the word *equivocal* is used to describe the data supporting the policy that *tallgrass prairie be burned only in late spring.* The rest of the paragraph details the data and reveals results (many which were conflicting or unknown) about burning during various parts of the spring. At the beginning of the last paragraph, the authors state, *The historical studies…for time of burning recommendations in tallgrass prairie are inconclusive.* So *equivocal* should mean something similar to "uncertain." Eliminate (A), (B), and (C) because they don't have the same meaning as uncertain." *Unclear* in (D) is most similar to "uncertain," so it is the best answer.

35. **B** This sentence is discussing burning to control *invasive shrubs*. The conjunction *but* lets the reader know that *Symphoricarpos orbiculatus* is in contrast to the first part of the sentence: while *burning in late spring* has been an effective way to control the shrubs, the only wooded species to decline was this species. Therefore, *Symphoricarpos orbiculatus* is a wooded species of invasive shrub, so (B) is the answer. Forbs and grasses are mentioned earlier in the paragraph as part of early spring burning, so (A), (C), and (D) can be eliminated. The best answer is (B).

36. **D** This question is the best evidence question in a paired set. Because the previous was a specific question, simply look at the lines used to answer the previous question. The lines used in the prediction were *burning in late spring has been considered the most effective time to control invasive shrubs, but Symphoricarpos orbiculatus was the only woody species that declined with repeated late spring burning.* The correct answer is (D).

37. **C** Use POE to check each answer against the graph. Choice (A) is incorrect because spring burning does not always have a higher biomass than that of other seasons. There is not enough information provided in the graph to support (B) or (D)—prairies and rainfall are not represented in the graph. This leaves (C), which can be supported by the figure because the three lines are generally rising and falling together: regardless of the time of year, there isn't a significant change in biomass. Therefore, the best answer is (C).

38. **B** The passage states that the *researchers were surprised at how big an effect particle shape had on the drying phenomenon.* Thus, (B) is correct because they had assumed shape wouldn't have a major effect. Choice (A) is incorrect because the detachment from the interface happens when

surfactants are added. Choice (C) is the opposite of what they did in the experiment, which is stretch the spheres, so that's incorrect. Choice (D) is incorrect because Passage 1 describes how surfactants affect the membrane, not just the particles.

39.　**C**　The passage states that *University of Chicago physicists Sidney Nagel, Thomas Witten, and their colleagues wrote an influential paper about this process in 1997, which focused mainly on suspended spherical particles, but it was not until the Yodh team's recent experiments that the surprising role played by suspended particle shape was discovered.* It's clear that their paper was influential and that they used spherical particles, but Passage 1 gives no other information about their work. Thus, (C) is correct. There's no reason given for why Nagel and Witten didn't experiment with ellipsoid particles, so (A) is incorrect. Passage 1 doesn't state whether Nagel and Witten's work in any way limited other studies, nor does the passage state that their research was flawed, so (B) and (D) are incorrect.

40.　**B**　The passage states that *Sidney Nagel, Thomas Witten, and their colleagues wrote an influential paper,* and Yodh's team starts off working with spherical particles, so it's clear that Yodh's research builds on Nagel and Witten's. Choice (B) is the best answer. Choices (C) and (D) are impossible because Nagel and Witten came first. Choice (A) is too strong because it's unclear that Yodh's work in any way proved Nagel and Witten's work wrong. Rather, it appears that Yodh's team tried things that the earlier team had not.

41.　**D**　The passage states that *spherical particles easily detach from the interface, and they flow past one another easily because the spheres do not substantially deform the air-water interface. Ellipsoid particles, however, cause substantial undulation of the air-water interface that in turn induces very strong attractions between the ellipsoids.* Because the spheres do not deform the interface, and the ellipsoids behave differently, they must cause the interface to change shape or "ripple." Thus, (D) is correct. For (A), the *attraction* of the ellipsoids causes the undulation, so this answer is incorrect. *Evaporation* happens much later in the process, so (B) is incorrect. The word *undertow* could possibly address the movement of the ellipsoid particles, but it does not mean the same as undulation in this context, so (C) is incorrect.

42.　**A**　Passage 2 mentions that surfactants are in soap and that surfactants can reduce the coffee ring effect, but the passage also states that scientists have been working for many years to find surfactants for industrial applications, so there must be a need for surfactants in forms other than those in soap. Thus, (A) is the best answer for why the author of Passage 2 compares detergents and bacterium. Choice (B) is incorrect because the passage doesn't address the dangers of using the bacterium, nor does the passage state that soap is a better surfactant, so (D) is incorrect as well. Choice (C) is mentioned in the passage, but it doesn't explain why the author of Passage 2 discusses detergents and bacterium together.

43.　**A**　Passage 2 states that *the coffee ring effect can be particularly troublesome and scientists have long been seeking ways to counteract it.* Thus, (A) is correct. Choice (B) is incorrect because that's the effect of surfactants. Choice (C) is incorrect because the passage states that the effect can be reduced, but not completely eliminated—*Add soap to a stain—a coffee stain or any other stain—and you will still* *get a coffee ring effect.* Choice (D) is incorrect because the coffee ring effect actually hinders industrial applications.

44. **D** Choice (D) explains why the coffee ring effect generates many studies on ways to thwart it: *In various industrial applications—applying an even coat of paint or varnish, for example—the coffee ring effect can be particularly troublesome and scientists have long been seeking ways to counteract it.* Thus, (A), (B), and (C) are incorrect.

45. **C** In the beginning of Passage 2, the author explains how the coffee ring effect works: *The coffee particles move toward the edge of the stain while the water in the liquid evaporates.* When surfactants are added to the particles, *the soap causes a counterflow from the edge back towards the centre of the stain in such a way that the small particles—material or bacteria—end up in a kind of whirlwind.* Thus, the particles are more evenly distributed, so (C) is the best answer. For (A), it's not clear whether they're spread thin or thick, so this is incorrect. Choice (B) doesn't make sense in the context of *distribution of particles as evaporation occurs.* Choice (D) also doesn't address the way the particles are distributed, so it is incorrect.

46. **C** Both passages describe the properties of the coffee ring effect similarly, and both studies look at how to diminish the effect. They have different solutions, but both passages address how surfactants cause particles to move away from the edge of a fluid, thus reducing the coffee ring effect. This makes (C) the best answer. Choice (A) is incorrect because it says the opposite of what the passage says, and (B) is not correct because the results of the study in Passage 1 don't prove that the conclusion of Passage 2 is inconsistent with the properties of the coffee ring effect. Choice (D) is incorrect because the fact that bacteria can be genetically modified to not produce surfactants doesn't change the fact that when the bacteria have surfactants, they react as the scientists would expect.

47. **B** In Passage 2, the researchers use a bacterium to counteract the coffee ring effect, so (B) is correct. They do not stretch the *Pseudomonas aeruginosa* bacterium, so (A) is incorrect. They also do not experiment on nanomaterials in order to breed *Pseudomonas aeruginosa.* They more likely breed *Pseudomonas aeruginosa* in order to experiment on nanomaterials, so (C) is incorrect. Choice (D) is true of both studies, so it is not the best answer.

Section 2—Writing and Language

1. **D** The answer choices indicate that verb tense is being tested, so let the non-underlined portions guide your choice of verb. Present tense is seen in the first part of this sentence: *Imagine you go….* Eliminate (A) and (B) because both use *had,* which is the wrong tense. Choice (C) is also incorrect since *were having* is not consistent with the verbs in the non-underlined portion: *Imagine* or *go.* Choice (D) uses a present tense verb that is consistent with the verbs in rest of the sentence, so it is the best answer.

2. **C** Look at the answers to see that comma usage is being tested. First, check to see if *For many, the answer is simple* is an introductory idea. Because it is a complete idea and the idea after the comma

is a complete idea (in this case, a command), a comma should not be used. Eliminate (A) and (D). Compare (B) and (C). Choice (C) has a colon, and (B) has no punctuation. Because the two ideas are complete, punctuation is needed. Therefore, the correct answer is (C).

3. **B** Notice the question, and use POE to find the best answer that maintains the focus of the sentence and paragraph. The focus of the paragraph is on the relationship between social media and restaurants. As written, the sentence is not focused on social media, but on the decision to not return to a restaurant. Eliminate (A). Choice (B) mentions Yelp, a consumer review website that is mentioned later in the paragraph. Therefore, (B) is a good answer. Choice (C) makes no mention of social media, so eliminate it. Choice (D) mentions neither social media nor restaurants, so eliminate (D). The best answer is (B).

4. **A** Whenever you are given the option to delete, determine whether the portion in question serves a precise role within the passage. In this case, *not just restaurants*, transitions between the first paragraph, which is all about restaurants, and the second paragraph, which is about the behavior of companies in general. This matches (A). Eliminate (B) because the phrase *just restaurants* does not encourage anyone to hire CLOs. Eliminate (C) because this phrase itself does not imply anything about the patrons' discussions. Eliminate (D) because the fact that the previous paragraph is all about restaurants and the current one is in support of keeping the phrase, not eliminating it. Therefore, the best answer is (A).

5. **C** Look at the answers to see that the word *insure* is being tested. *Insure* describes what companies should do, and the next sentence says that companies should maintain public face. Therefore, the best answer will mean something like "make sure." Because *insure* means to arrange for compensation in the event of damage, (A) and (D) can be eliminated. Because *assure* means to dispel doubts, (B) can also be eliminated. Because *ensure* means to make it certain that something will happen, (C) is the best answer.

6. **C** Look at the answers to see that apostrophes are being tested. First, look immediately after the word in question to see if it (*company*) should be possessive. Because the Social Media Manager is in charge of the output of a company, the word is possessive and requires an apostrophe. Eliminate (A). Because *companys'* is not a word, eliminate (D). A difference between (B) and (C) is the placement of the apostrophe. Because the word immediately preceding the underlined word is *a*, the underlined word should be singular. Therefore, the apostrophe must come before the *s*, as is the case in (C). Thus, (C) is the best answer.

7. **D** Whenever you are given the option to delete, determine whether the portion in question serves a precise role within the passage. The sentence ends with the phrase *to see if the situation can be remedied*, so the underlined portion is redundant, as are the options in (B) and (C). Therefore, the best answer is (D).

8. **B** Look at the answers to see that the word *unfurls* is being tested. Because the advertising campaign is described as *new*, the underlined word should mean something like introduces. *Unfurls* means

"unfolds," so (A) is not the correct answer. *Rolls out* means introduces, so (B) is a good answer. *Unrolls* means flatten out from a roll, so (C) is not the best answer. A *role* is a part that an actor plays or a position that someone assumes in a certain situation, so (D) should be eliminated. The correct answer is (B).

9. **B** The underlined portion of this sentence contains a pronoun *(this)*, so make sure it is consistent with the non-underlined portion by finding the other pronouns and nouns. The partner noun is *market research*, but *this* could partner with any of the singular nouns in the previous sentence. Therefore, *this* is an ambiguous pronoun. Eliminate (A). Next, compare (B) and (C). Whenever you are given the option to be more concise, determine whether the portion in question serves a precise role within the passage. The phrase *about this kind of "market research"* does play a precise role in the passage. It provides a partner noun for the pronoun *it* in the same sentence. Without *this kind of market research, it* would be an ambiguous pronoun. Though they are more concise, (C) and (D) do not provide the clarity that (B) does. Therefore, (B) is the best answer.

10. **D** The underlined portion of this sentence is a pronoun, so make sure it is consistent with the non-underlined portion by finding the other pronouns and nouns. The partner noun is *someone*, which is singular. Therefore, the underlined pronoun must also be singular. Eliminate (A) and (B). Because *your* cannot partner with anything other than other forms of *you*, eliminate (C). Choice (D) is correct.

11. **A** The criticism in the previous sentence is that the CLO position is not going to last for long. (A fad is anything that is fashionable for a short amount of time.) Choice (A) directly answers the criticism and is therefore a good answer. Choice (B) agrees with the criticism, so it can be eliminated. Choice (C) has nothing to do with the CLO position, so it too can be eliminated. Choice (D) is also not the best answer, as it makes no mention of how long social media will last.

12. **A** Because the paragraph is contrasting the scale of the Yellow Fever Epidemic with that of other diseases, keep (A). Choice (B) provides unnecessary information, namely World War I, so eliminate (B). Choice (C) makes no mention of other diseases, so eliminate (C). Choice (D) does not support the paragraph's main idea that the Yellow Fever Epidemic was worse than the others mentioned; eliminate (D). Therefore, (A) is the best answer.

13. **B** The chart provides census data from 1790. The underlined portion discusses the population of cities today; eliminate (A). The chart indicates that Philadelphia was the second largest city in the country and had a population of 28,522. Therefore, (B) is consistent with the chart, so you can keep it. Choice (C) states that Philadelphia was smaller than Boston and is therefore not consistent with the chart, so eliminate (C). Choice (D) is also inconsistent with the chart, as it states that Philadelphia was larger than New York. Choice (B) is the best answer.

14. **D** The sentence describes what *doctors tried*. The words *things* and *options* could each refer to anything, so they are not precise; eliminate (A) and (B). While *management models* might work, that is not precisely what doctors do. *Treatment approaches* better fits what the *doctors tried*. The correct answer is (D).

15. **B** The answer choices indicate that verb tense is being tested, so let the non-underlined portions guide your choice of verb. Past tense is seen in *how the disease originated*, so (B) is consistent. Choice (A) uses an *-ing* verb, which is not consistent with *originated*. Choice (C) uses *had been,* which is not consistent with *originated*, so eliminate it. Choice (D) uses *spread* as a noun, so eliminate it as well. The correct answer is (B).

16. **C** Of the four choices, (A), (B), and (D) are too informal to match the academic tone of the rest of the paper. Choice (C) is the best answer.

17. **C** The underlined portion of this sentence is a pronoun, so make sure it is consistent with the non-underlined portion by finding the other pronouns and nouns. There are multiple potential partner nouns in the previous sentence, including *Philadelphia* and *nation*. Therefore, the correct answer should not contain a pronoun. Because (A), (B), and (D) contain pronouns, (C) is the best answer because it clearly specifies who tried to impose quarantine and curfew measures.

18. **A** Look at the answers to see that comma usage is being tested. Because the underlined portion is a list, there must be a comma placed after each item on the list. Choice (B) omits the comma after *hot sun*, so it is incorrect. Choices (C) and (D) add unnecessary words and are therefore not the best answers. The best and most concise answer is (A).

19. **D** Sentence 7 provides an account of the confusion that accompanied the arrival of Yellow Fever in Philadelphia by providing a prominent physician's theory regarding the cause of the disease. Therefore, it should not follow an account of the eleven measures for prevention, so (A) is not the best answer. In addition, such an account should not introduce the paragraph. Therefore, (B) is incorrect. Sentence 7 is too specific to follow a general sentence like sentence 2, so (C) is incorrect. Sentence 3 mentions another party's theory regarding the cause of the disease. Therefore, (D) is the best answer.

20. **C** Look at the answers to see that STOP punctuation is being tested. Perform the Vertical Line Test to see that the semicolon in (D) separates a complete idea from an incomplete idea, so eliminate it. While a comma and a colon can separate a complete idea from an incomplete idea, there is no reason to pause/interrupt the sentence in this case, so eliminate (A) and (B). Because no punctuation is needed, (C) is the best answer.

21. **B** Look at the answers to see that comma usage is being tested. Check to see if the phrases *in West Africa, provides a terrifying reminder,* and *of just how deadly certain diseases can be,* are necessary or unnecessary information. If any are removed from the sentence, it does not make sense. Therefore, they are all necessary and should not be set off by commas. Choice (B) is the best answer.

22. **A** *By the same token* means something like "for the same reason" or "in the same way." Because both ideas have to do with the effects of an epidemic, (A) is an appropriate introduction to this sentence. Because (B) indicates that the Yellow Fever Epidemic and the Ebola Virus are somehow opposites, (B) is not the best answer. Eliminate (C) and (D), which indicate that the final sentence is the last logical step in an argument. Choice (A) is the best answer.

23. **D** Whenever you are given the option to delete, determine whether the underlined portion serves a precise role within the passage. The sentence has already said that *Many people find it hard to believe*, so the phrase *seems doubtful* is redundant. Eliminate (A). Eliminate (B) and (C) as well because they express the same idea as *seems doubtful*. Choice (D) is the best answer.

24. **C** The main subject of the passage as a whole is a musician named *Rodgers*. The best answer will introduce Rodgers, so (A) and (B) should be eliminated. Choice (D) introduces Jimmie Rodgers, but it also introduces two other musicians who are not mentioned again in the passage. Therefore, (C) is the best answer.

25. **B** The underlined portion of this sentence includes a verb, so find the subject to check whether it agrees with the verb. The subject of *is* is *circumstances*, which is plural. Therefore, the verb must be plural. Eliminate (A), (C), and (D). Choice (B) is correct.

26. **C** When you are given the option to add information, determine whether the added information serves a precise role in the passage. As written, the sentence does not say anything about what little was known. Therefore, neither (A) nor (B) is the best answer. Choices (C) and (D) express similar information, but (C) is more concise, so it is the best answer.

27. **C** Notice the question: it is asking for *specific information* about Rodgers's illness. Choices (A), (B), and (D) are vague. None of them name a specific illness. Only (C) names a specific illness, so it is the best answer.

28. **C** Make sure that the phrase has some precise and definable role within the sentence or passage. It serves no role in the current sentence because the clause is about the number of copies the record sold, not where it sold. Eliminate (A). It also serves no role when placed after *In October of that year* because that piece of introductory information has nothing to do with place, only time. Therefore, eliminate (B). When placed after *after Rodgers chased his dream*, the underlined portion does serve a purpose: it explains where Rodgers chased his dream. Keep (C). When placed after *which sold half a million copies*, the underlined portion does not add relevant information. The purpose of the clause is to explain how many copies the record sold. Eliminate (D). Choice (C) is the best answer.

29. **A** Look at the answers to see that comma usage is being tested. A comma can come after introductory information, as it does in the underlined portion, so keep (A). Later in the sentence, a comma plus FANBOYS is used, so the first idea must be complete. Because *when* and *as* make the first idea incomplete, (B) and (C) are incorrect. Because a colon can follow only a complete idea, (D) is incorrect. Choice (A) is the correct answer.

30. **B** On proposition questions, make sure the phrase has some precise and definable role within the sentence or passage. The relevant information is that both Howlin' Wolf and Elvis Presley cited Rodgers as an early influence. As it is written, the underlined portion says that Howlin' Wolf also cited Elvis Presley as an early influence. This is incorrect, so eliminate (A). Choices (C) and (D) also indicate that Howlin' Wolf cited Presley as an early influence, so eliminate those choices as well. Choice (B) is the best answer.

31. **A** The word *however* indicates that the sentence is contrasting the downside of *his inability to work* with an unexpected upside for his *great passion—music*. Therefore, the word must mean something like "good luck." *Fortuitous* means "a fortunate accident," so keep (A). *Chancy* means "risky," so eliminate (B). *Blessed* means "holy," so eliminate (C). *Charmed* means "privileged," so eliminate (D). The correct answer is (A).

32. **A** Because there is a semicolon in the answer choices, use the Vertical Line Test to see if the STOP punctuation is separating two complete ideas. *Once Jimmie could no longer work the rails* is not a complete idea, so (C) should be eliminated. The remaining answer choices indicate that comma usage is being tested. Check to see if *however* is necessary or unnecessary information. If removed from the sentence, it would still make sense, so it's unnecessary information; eliminate (B) and (D). Commas should always be placed around unnecessary information, so (A) is the best answer.

33. **D** The fifth paragraph begins by mentioning Rodgers's illness, and it ends by discussing the beginning of his recording career. Therefore, it should not be where it is now, but between a paragraph that discusses his illness and a paragraph that discusses his music career. Therefore, (A) is incorrect. Because the paragraph should come between two other paragraphs, (B) is incorrect. Because paragraph 1 does not mention his illness, (C) is incorrect. Because paragraph 2 mentions his illness and paragraph 3 mentions his music career, the proper place for paragraph 5 is between those two paragraphs. Choice (D) is the best answer.

34. **D** Look at the answer choices to see that noun agreement is being tested. Because the sentence is about males and females, the corresponding noun should be plural. Eliminate (A), (B), and (C) because each uses a singular noun. Choice (D) uses a plural noun. Therefore, (D) is the best answer.

35. **A** The question asks for accurate data based on the graph, so check each answer and use POE to eliminate anything that is not consistent with the graph. Choice (A) states that only a handful of animals has a post-reproductive life span and gives the black-tailed prairie dog as an example. According to the graph, it is true that the black-tailed prairie dog does have a post-reproductive life span, and only half of the species represented on the graph do as well. Both assertions in (A) are consistent with the graph. Choice (B) states that most animals have some post-reproductive life span, such as humans. Neither of these assertions is consistent with the graph, as only half of the species have some post-reproductive life span, and humans are not represented on the graph. Eliminate (B). Choice (C) is not consistent with the graph because the common bottlenose dolphin has the longest, not the shortest, pre-reproductive life span compared to the only species on the graphic. Choice (D) is also not consistent with the graph because both of the rodent species listed do have substantial post-reproductive life spans. Both (C) and (D) can be eliminated as well, leaving (A) as the only consistent answer.

36. **D** The underlined portion of this sentence is a pronoun, so make sure it is consistent with the non-underlined portion by finding the other pronouns and nouns. The partner noun could be *humans, short-finned pilot whales, killer whales,* or *females.* Therefore, the pronoun is ambiguous, and (A) is

not the best answer. Choice (C) is incorrect because it uses the wrong case (a subject pronoun is needed). Compare (B) and (D). Choice (B) contains pronouns, whereas (D) is more specific. Because it offers the most clarity to the sentence, (D) is the best answer.

37. **A** The previous paragraph ends by discussing the surprising longevity of female whales, and the paragraph in question discusses a study that may have provided a possible explanation. Therefore, (A) is a good answer because it mentions the study and clarifies that it may provide an answer. Choices (B), (C), and (D) make no mention of the study, so eliminate them. Choice (A) is the best answer.

38. **B** Look at the answer choices. The main difference among them is word order. To determine which words should come first, look at the modifier that begins the sentence. *After watching over 750 hours of video and observing the behaviors of pods of whales* describes the scientists, so scientists should be immediately after the modifying phrase. Therefore, (B) is the best answer.

39. **A** When you are given the option to add information, determine whether the added information would serve a precise and necessary role in the passage. In this case, the information is an example of the teaching behavior mentioned in the previous sentence. Therefore, (A) is the best answer. Choice (B) is incorrect because older whales were not ignored in the study. Rather, they were the subject of the study. Choice (C) is not the best answer because there is no information that conflicts with the proposed sentence. Choice (D) is not the best answer because there is no indication elsewhere in the passage that the scientists' observations should be understood to be conclusive.

40. **D** Because there are periods and semicolons in the answer choices, this question is testing STOP punctuation. As written, the STOP punctuation comes between an incomplete idea and a complete idea, so (A) should be eliminated. Choice (B) places STOP punctuation incorrectly between two incomplete ideas and should also be eliminated. Choice (C) creates a comma splice because the comma after *knowledge* separates two complete ideas, so it should be eliminated. In (D), however, the STOP punctuation comes between two complete ideas. Therefore, (D) is the best answer.

41. **B** First, note that *longevity* means "length of a life." Therefore, the two words do not mean the same thing, so (A) is not the best answer. Because (B) indicates that the words do not have the same meaning, it is a good answer. Because (C) and (D) indicate that the words have the same meaning, both of them can be eliminated. Choice (B) is the best answer.

42. **D** The paragraph in question discusses the wider ramifications of the study's findings. Choice (A) is not the best answer because it makes a claim that is unsupported by the study's findings. Choice (B) is not the best answer because it does not make mention of the wider consequences of the study's findings. Choice (C) is not the right answer because it makes no mention of the study at all. Choice (D) is the best answer because it says that the findings have ramifications beyond the scientific community.

43. **B** The answer choices indicate that this question is testing word choice. Because the underlined word should be a possessive pronoun, (A) and (C) should be eliminated. Because each of the remaining answer choices contains a pronoun, make sure it is consistent with the non-underlined portion by

finding the other pronouns and nouns. The partner noun is *societies*, which is plural. Eliminate (D) because *its* is singular. The best answer is (B).

44. **C** Use POE to find the clearest and most concise answer. As written, the sentence is unnecessarily wordy, so it is not the best answer. Choice (B) contains the redundant phrase *long lives are long enough*, so (B) is not the best answer. Choice (C) makes no grammar errors, and is more concise than the sentence as written, so it is the best answer. Choice (D) needs a preposition to link *the accrued knowledge* to *the longer-lived people*, so it is not the correct answer. Therefore, (C) is the best answer.

Section 3—Math (No Calculator)

1. **C** There are specific points in the answers, so Plug In the Answers. Test the ordered pairs in both equations from the question and look for a pair that makes both equations true. Start by plugging (A) into the first equation to get $0 = \frac{1}{2}(3) + 3$. This becomes $0 = \frac{3}{2} + 3$. Since this cannot be true, eliminate (A). Now plug the point in (B) into the first equation to get $2 = \frac{1}{2}(-2) + 3$. This becomes $2 = -1 + 3$ or $2 = 2$. This is true, but the point must work in both equations. Plugging the point in (B) into the second equation gives $-2 = (2)^2 - 5(2) + 6$, which becomes $-2 = 4 - 10 + 6$ or $-2 = 0$. Eliminate (B). Plug the point in (C) into the first equation to get $4 = \frac{1}{2}(2) + 3$. This becomes to $4 = 1 + 3$ or $4 = 4$. This true, but test the second equation as well. This gives $2 = (4)^2 - 5(4) + 6$, which becomes $2 = 16 - 20 + 6$ or $2 = 2$. This is also true. The correct answer is (C).

2. **B** When there are variables in the answer choices and the question asks for an equivalent form of the expression, use Plugging In. Since calculator use is not allowed, use small numbers. Make $y = 1$ and $c = 2$. The expression becomes $30(1) - 12(2)(1) = 30 - 24 = 6$. Check each answer choice and look for the one that has a value of the target answer 6. Choice (A) becomes $[5 - 2(2)](1) = (5 - 4)(1) = (1)(1) = 1$. Since 1 does not equal 6, eliminate (A). Choice (B) becomes $[30 - 12(2)](1) = (30 - 24)(1) = (6)(1) = 6$. Keep (B), but check the remaining answers. Choice (C) becomes $18(2 - 2(1)) = 18(2 - 2) = 18(0) = 0$. Eliminate (C). Choice (D) becomes $18(2)(1)^2 = 36(1) = 36$. Eliminate (D). The correct answer is (B).

3. **C** The question asks to rearrange the equation in terms of acceleration, a. To isolate a, remove m from the right side of the equation by dividing both sides by m. This gives $\frac{F}{m} = \frac{ma}{m}$. Cancelling out the m terms on the right side of the equation leaves $\frac{F}{m} = a$. This matches (C). The correct answer is (C).

4. **B** The question has numbers in the answer choices and asks for a specific amount, so Plug In the Answers. The answer choices represent possible values of j. Start with (B). Plug $j = -5$ into the first equation to get $-4(-5) - 10k = 50$. Simplify to get $20 - 10k = 50$. Subtract 20 from both sides to

get $-10k = 30$ and divide by -10 to get $k = -3$. Now check if $j = -5$ will give a value of $k = -3$ in the second equation, which becomes $-5 - 3k = 4$. Add 5 to both sides to get $-3k = 9$ and divide by -3 to get $k = -3$. Since both equations gave the same value of k when $j = -5$, the correct answer is (B).

5. **D**   Label the parts of the equation to determine what they represent. In this question, y represents the weight of the giant panda and x represents the number of months after the panda was born. The equation is in $y = mx + b$ form, where m is the slope of a graph, so here the slope is 3,100. The slope of a graph is defined as the change in y over the change in x, so the slope must relate to weight over time. Eliminate (B) and (C), which simply refer to time. Plug in to determine what gives a value of 3,100. Make $m = 0$ to get the giant panda's weight after 0 months, or at birth. This becomes $weight = 3,100(0) + 105$ or $weight = 105$. Since the giant panda's weight at birth is not 3,100, eliminate (A). After one month, the giant panda will have a $weight = 3,100(1) + 105 = 3,100 + 105 = 3,205$. Therefore, in the first month, the panda gained $3,205 - 105 = 3,100$ grams in weight. The correct answer is (D).

6. **A**   There are numbers in the answer choices and the question asks for a specific amount, so Plug In the Answers. Plug each answer choice into the equation and look for the one that makes the equation true. Start with one of the middle values, such as (B). If $b = 0$, the equation becomes $3(0)^2 - 6(0) = 5 + 4(0)^2$ or $0 - 0 = 5 + 0$. This isn't true, so eliminate (B). It may be difficult to see whether a larger or smaller number is needed to make the equation true, so just pick a direction to go in. For (A), plug in $b = -5$ to get $3(-5)^2 - 6(-5) = 5 + 4(-5)^2$. Simplify this to get $3(25) - (-30) = 5 + 4(25)$. This becomes $75 + 30 = 5 + 100$ or $105 = 105$. This is true, so the correct answer is (A).

7. **A**   When given a description of a graph, make a sketch of the graph and use it to eliminate answers. This line crosses the x-axis at 4, so it contains the point $(4, 0)$ as well as the given point $(-2, 6)$. Draw the graph with these points, and then connect them like this:

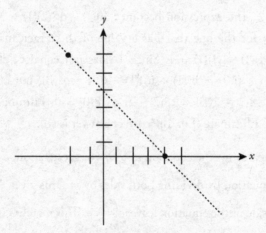

Now mark each answer as true or false. The slope and the y-intercept are easy to see, so start with those. The slope is negative, so (B) is true, and the y-intercept is positive, so (C) is true. The question asks for a statement that *cannot* be true, so eliminate (B) and (C). Choice (A) contains a point in the lower left quadrant of the graph, and (D) contains a point in the lower right quadrant. Since the line goes through only the lower right quadrant, only (D) can possibly be true. Eliminate (D). The correct answer is (A).

8. **B**   The question states that *each* of the 16 squares *must have an area of at least 340 square inches*, so the total area must be more than 340 square inches. Eliminate (D). Find the lower limit of the total area by multiplying 16 by 340 to get 5,440. Eliminate (A), which does not contain this value as the lower limit. The difference between (B) and (C) is the upper limit, so find this by multiplying 16 by 360 to get 5,760. The correct answer is (B).

9. **D**   On questions that ask for an equation, translate one bite-sized piece of information at a time and use Process of Elimination. Find parts of the choices that vary. All the choices have 51.90 and 14.90n, so ignore these parts. Choices (A) and (C) contain 1.15, while (B) and (D) contain 0.85. Determine which is correct. A discount of 15% will be applied to the purchase, so the purchase must be multiplied by $1.00 - 0.15 = 0.85$. Eliminate (A) and (C), which do not contain this value. The difference between (B) and (D) is what the 0.85 is applied to. Choice (B) applies 0.85 to x, which is the final cost. However, the final cost is the result of the 15% discount, so eliminate (B). The correct answer is (D).

10. **C**   When dealing with questions about exponents, remember the MADSPM rules. The MA part of the acronym indicates that Multiplying matching bases means to Add the exponents. The PM part of the acronym indicates that raising a base with an exponent to another Power means to Multiply the exponents. Use the order of operations to apply the exponents outside the parentheses to the bases inside by multiplying the exponents to get $\left(a^{\frac{3}{3}} b^{\frac{3}{4}} \right)\left(a^{\frac{4}{3}} b^{\frac{4}{4}} \right)$. Although it is possible to reduce some of these exponents, the next step will be to add them together, since the bases are multiplied. Leave the exponents in fractional form to make that easier, getting $a^{\frac{7}{3}} b^{\frac{7}{4}}$. This is equal to $a^{\frac{k}{3}} b^{\frac{k}{4}}$, so $k = 7$. The correct answer is (C).

11. **C**   On questions that ask for a system of inequalities, translate one bite-sized piece of information at a time and use Process of Elimination. The baker needs to buy *at least 2 containers of flour*. The phrase *at least* can be represented by the symbol ≥, and the question states that f represents the number of containers of flour. Therefore, the correct answer must contain $f \geq 2$. Eliminate (B) and (D), which do not contain this inequality. The only difference between (A) and (C) is the inequality symbol in the cost equation. The question states that the baker *has $75 with which to purchase ingredients*, which means the cost cannot exceed $75. This means it is "less than or equal to," which is represented by the symbol ≤. The correct answer is (C).

12. **A**   The question gives the equation of a parabola in factored form, which makes it easy to determine the solutions, or y-intercepts. Because parabolas are symmetrical about a central axis that runs

through the vertex, the *y*-coordinate of the vertex will be halfway between the two *y*-intercepts. If $x = 0$, then the equation becomes $0 = (y + 5)(y - 15)$. Set each binomial equal to 0 to get $y + 5 = 0$ and $y - 15 = 0$, so $y = -5$ or 15. Eliminate (C) and (D), which aren't between the intercepts at all. To find the midpoint, average the *y*-intercepts to get $y = \dfrac{15 + (-5)}{2} = \dfrac{10}{2} = 5$. The correct answer is (A).

13. **D** When given two or more triangles and information about the ratios of the sides, look for similar triangles. Sides *FJ* and *FH* are both on the smallest triangle, while *FG* and *GH* are both on the largest triangle. Redraw the two triangles side-by-side to better see the similarities. Start with triangle *FHJ*, redrawing it by itself with the same orientation it currently has, labeling the vertices. Then draw a bigger triangle next to it with the same shape as triangle *FHJ*, like this:

Since the ratio of $\dfrac{FJ}{FH}$ is equal to $\dfrac{FG}{GH}$, label the sides of this new triangle correspondingly. Make sure to keep $\angle FGH$ as the smaller angle and $\angle GFH$ as the larger one, like this:

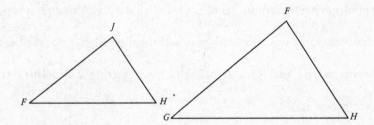

Now it is easier to check corresponding angles. Choice (A) gives the angles on the lower left of the big triangle and the lower right of the small triangle. These are not necessarily congruent, so eliminate (A). Choice (B) gives an angle that does not appear on either triangle and the angle at the top of the small triangle. These are not necessarily congruent, so eliminate (B). Choice (C) gives an angle that does not appear on either triangle and the angle on the lower left of the small triangle. These are not necessarily congruent, so eliminate (C). Choice (D) gives the angles at the tops of both triangles, so these angles are congruent. The correct answer is (D).

14. **36**   The question asks for the number of ounces of jam made on Thursday, so translate the information into an equation that can be solved for the value. Let t represent the amount of jam in ounces that Monica made on Thursday. The questions states that Monica *made half as many ounces of jam on Wednesday as she did on Thursday*, so on Wednesday she made $\frac{1}{2}t$ ounces. In total, she made *3 pounds and 6 ounces of jam on those two days*. Since the question asks for ounces, convert this total to ounces. If 1 pound has 16 ounces, then 3 pounds will have 3(16) = 48 ounces. Monica made 6 more ounces than this, so she made 48 + 6 = 54 ounces of jam. Now the full equation can be written as $\frac{1}{2}t + t = 54$. Combine like terms to get $\frac{3}{2}t = 54$. Multiply both sides by 2 to get $3t = 108$; then divide both sides by 3 to get $t = 36$. The correct answer is 36.

15. **3**   The question asks what value of z makes the equation have an infinite number of solutions. If an equation has an infinite number of solutions, it will work when any value is put in for the variable. Plug in any value for y, such as $y = 2$, and solve for z. The equation becomes $6[2(2) + z]$ = 12(2) + 18. Now solve the equation for z. Distribute to get $6(4 + z) = 24 + 18$, and then $24 + 6z = 24 + 18$. The 24s on each side cancel out, so $6z = 18$. Divide both sides by 6 to get $z = 3$. The correct answer is 3.

16. **24**   When given a quadratic in factored form, it is often necessary to use FOIL to multiply the factors out to the standard form $ax^2 + bx + c$ to solve the question. The expression becomes $6gx^4 + ghx^2y^2 - 24x^2y^2 - 4hy^2$. It might be tempting to try to figure out what the values of g and h are, given the information that they have a difference of 5. However, make sure to read the full question, which asks for the value of gh, not g or h separately. The gh appears as the coefficient of one of the x^2y^2 terms, and the question states that the coefficient on that term when *like terms are collected* is zero. This means that the middle two terms of the expression must have a sum of 0. Therefore, $gh - 24 = 0$. Add 24 to both sides to get $gh = 24$. The correct answer is 24.

17. **2**   When given a quadratic in standard form, which is $ax^2 + bx + c$, it is often necessary to factor it to solve the question. Here, the question supplies one of the factors, so use that to find the other factor. If $(2y - 3)$ is a factor, then the first part of the second factor must multiply by $2y$ to result in $8y^2$. Divide $8y^2$ by $2y$ to get $4y$ as the first term in the second factor. Similarly, the second term in the second factor must multiply by -3 to get -15. Divide -15 by -3 to get 5 as the second term of the second factor. Therefore, the second factor must be $(4y + 5)$. Now use FOIL on the two factors to both verify that these numbers give you $8y^2$ and -15 and to determine the coefficient on the y term, which will be the value of d. The expression becomes $(2y - 3)(4y + 5) = 8y^2 + 10y - 12y - 15$ or $8y^2 - 2y - 15$. Therefore, $d = 2$. The correct answer is 2.

Section 4—Math (Calculator Allowed)

1. **C**   The question asks for the profit the store makes for selling 20 pencils. Because profits increase as pencils sold increase, set up a proportion: $\frac{12 \text{ pencils}}{\$0.75} = \frac{20 \text{ pencils}}{\$x}$. Cross-multiply to get $12x = \$15$. Divide both sides by 12 to get $x = \$1.25$. The correct answer is (C).

2. **A** The question asks for the period that shows the least decrease. Ballpark to find the answer. Choice (A) has a decrease of about one interval between horizontal gridlines. Choice (B) has a decrease of about more than two full intervals. Choice (C) has a decrease of about 4 intervals. Choice (D) has a decrease of about 2 intervals. Therefore, the correct answer is (A).

3. **D** The question asks for the meaning of a constant in context. Label all the pieces. The variable A represents the remaining amount she owes, and w represents the number of weeks since she borrowed the money. Eliminate any choices that are inconsistent with this. Choice (B) describes the total amount Sydney has repaid. However, the amount will change over time, so it cannot be represented by a constant. Eliminate (B). Since (C) describes w and not 870, eliminate (C). The remaining choices both refer to amounts of money, so plug in. If $w = 1$, then $A = 870 - 30(1) = 840$, so after 1 week, $840 remains to be paid. If $w = 2$, then $A = 870 - 30(2) = 810$, so after 2 weeks, $810 remains to be paid. Therefore, between week 1 and week 2, $840 - 810 = 30$ was repaid. Therefore, $30 is repaid each week, so eliminate (A). Only one choice remains. To confirm (D), note that the original amount that Sydney owes it the amount that she owes after 0 weeks. If $w = 0$, then $A = 870 - 30(0) = 870$. The correct answer is (D).

4. **A** The question asks for the relationship between years of ownership and selling price. Look at the graph. There is clearly a downward trend in both the scatterplot and the line of best fit. Therefore, this is a negative correlation: as one variable increases, the other variable decreases. Eliminate (B), (C), and (D), which do not describe such a relationship. The correct answer is (A).

5. **B** The question asks how much more the actual selling price was compared to that predicted by the line of best fit for the car that was sold after it was owned for exactly 7 years. Find 7 on the horizontal axis and trace up to the point and the line of best fit. They lie between two gridlines on the vertical axis. Since each interval is $2,000, the difference must be less than $2,000. Eliminate (C) and (D). Since the difference makes up more than half the interval, the difference must be more than $1,000. Eliminate (A). The correct answer is (B).

6. **D** The question asks for the value of b in the equation when graphed and provides a point on the graph. Plug the point into the equation. Plug $x = 3$ and $y = -1$ into $y = 2x - b$ to get $-1 = 2(3) - b$. Simplify the right side to get $-1 = 6 - b$. Subtract 6 to both sides to get $-7 = -b$. Divide both sides by -1 to get $b = 7$. The correct answer is (D).

7. **A** The question asks for the model that best fits the data. Look at the choices. Two choices describe a linear decrease, which is a decrease by the same amount each month, and two choices describe an exponential increase, which is an increase by the same percent each month. Because linear decreases are easier to work with, first determine whether the relationship is linear with a consistent decrease. From month 0 to month 1, the decrease is $1,400 - $1,344 = $56. Eliminate (C), which indicates a decrease of $47. From month 1 to month 2, the decrease is $1,344 - $1,290 = $54.

Eliminate (D), since the decrease is not always $56. Therefore, the decrease must be exponential. To find the percent change between months, use the formula $\dfrac{difference}{original} \times 100$. From month 0 to month 1, the percent decrease is $\dfrac{\$1,400 - \$1,344}{\$1,400} \times 100 = \dfrac{\$56}{\$1,400} \times 100 = 0.04 \times 100 = 4\%$. The correct answer is (A).

8. **A** The question asks for the rate of the snail in centimeters per hour. The question states that the snail moves at a rate of 700 millimeters per second. Covert the 700 millimeters into centimeters. Since there are 10 millimeters in 1 centimeter, set up the proportion $\dfrac{10 \text{ mm}}{1 \text{ cm}} = \dfrac{700 \text{ mm}}{x \text{ cm}}$. Cross-multiply to get $10x = 700$. Divide both sides by 10 to get $x = 70$. Therefore, the snail moves at a rate of 70 centimeters per minute. Determine the number of centimeters travelled in 1 hour. Since there are 60 minutes in 1 hour, set up the proportion $\dfrac{10 \text{ cm}}{1 \text{ min}} = \dfrac{y \text{ cm}}{60 \text{ min}}$. Cross-multiply to get $y = 4,200$. Therefore, the snail moves at a rate of 4,200 centimeters per hour. The correct answer is (A).

9. **C** The question asks about the solutions to the equation. Two of the choices include numbers, and the other two are infinitely many solutions and no solutions. Plug in the easier of the choices with numbers. Plug in $y = 10$ to get $5\left(\dfrac{10}{2} + 5\right) = 2(10) + \dfrac{1}{2}(10) + 25$. The equation becomes $5(5 + 5) = 20 + 5 + 25$ or $5(10) = 50$. Since this is true, $y = 10$ is a solution. Eliminate (A), since $y = 1\dfrac{1}{2}$ cannot be the only solution, and eliminate (D), since there is at least one solution. It is still possible that there are infinitely many solutions. To test, plug in any other number. To make the math as easy as possible, plug in $y = 0$ to get $5\left(\dfrac{0}{2} + 5\right) = 2(0) + \dfrac{1}{2}(0) + 25$. The equation becomes $5(0 + 5) = 0 + 0 + 25$ or $5(5) = 25$. Therefore, $y = 0$ is also a solution. Since $y = 10$ is not the only solution, eliminate (B). The correct answer is (C).

10. **D** The question asks for the difference of polynomials, so simplify and combine like terms. Do this in Bite-Sized Pieces. Find like terms, such as $2ab^2$ in the first polynomial and $2ab^2$ in the second polynomial. Subtract to get $2ab^2 - 2ab^2 = 0$. Therefore, the correct answer must not have an ab^2 term. Eliminate (B) and (C). Now, look at the a^2 terms. Subtract $-3a^2$ from $5a^2$ to get $5a^2 - (-3a^2) = 8a^2$. Eliminate (A), which does not include this term. Only one choice remains. The correct answer is (D).

11. **B** The question asks for a percent, so translate the question into an equation. The word *what* translates to a variable. Use x. The word *percent* translates to "divide by 100." The word *of* translates to "times." Since there are 270 athletes in the school, *the athletes in the school* translates to 270. The word *are* translates to "equals." Since there are 98 right-handed varsity athletes, *right-handed varsity athletes* translates to 98. Therefore, the question translates to $\dfrac{x}{100} \times 270 = 98$. Multiply both sides by 100 to get $270x = 9,800$. Divide both sides by 270 to get $x \approx 36.296$. The question says *approximately*, so select the closest choice. The correct answer is (B).

12. **D** The question asks for the difference between the maximum weight that Helen can lift and the median, so find the median. To do so, put the maximum weights in order from least to greatest: 30, 40, 60, 70, 110, 130, 170, 230. Find the middle number by crossing out numbers in pairs starting from the outside. Cross out 30 and 230. Cross out the next least and next greatest: 40 and 170. Cross out the next least and next greatest: 60 and 130. Only 70 and 110 remain. Since there is no single middle number, find the average of the middle two to get $\frac{70+110}{2} = 90$ as the median. Find the difference between this value and the maximum weight that Helen can lift. The maximum weight that Helen can lift is 170 pounds, so the difference is $170 - 90 = 80$. The correct answer is (D).

13. **A** The question asks which statement is true, and the statements refer to mode and range. Begin with the easier statistic, which is mode. By definition, the mode of a list of numbers is the number that appears the most often. For the Physics class, 25 is the only number that appears more than once, so 25 is the mode. Similarly, for the Biology class, 32 in the only number that appears more than once, so 32 is the mode. Since the mode for Physics is less than the mode for Biology, eliminate (B) and (D). Now check the range, which is, by definition, the difference between the greatest and least number in a list. For the Physics class, the range is $31 - 23 = 8$. For the Biology class, the range is $32 - 21 = 11$. Since the range for the Physics class is less than the range for the Biology class, eliminate (C). The correct answer is (A).

14. **C** The question asks how many cars the factory can produce in 540 hours. The rate is given in minutes, so convert the 540 hours into minutes, using the proportion $\frac{60 \text{ minutes}}{1 \text{ hour}} = \frac{x \text{ minutes}}{540 \text{ hours}}$. Cross-multiply to get $x = 32{,}400$. Since the factory can produce 1 car in 1,080 minutes, set up the proportion $\frac{1{,}080 \text{ minutes}}{1 \text{ car}} = \frac{32{,}400 \text{ minutes}}{y \text{ cars}}$. Cross-multiply to get $1{,}080y = 32{,}400$. Divide both sides by 1,080 to get $y = 30$. The correct answer is (C).

15. **A** The question asks for the difference between the percentage of patients in the experimental physical therapy with a recovery time of more than 6 months and the percentage of patients in the conventional physical therapy with a recovery time of more than 6 months. Find both percentages. There was a total of $82 + 112 = 194$ patients in the experimental physical therapy, 112 of whom had a recovery time of more than 6 months. Therefore, the percentage is $\frac{112}{194} \times 100 \approx 57.731$. There was a total of $151 + 140 = 291$ patients in the conventional physical therapy, 140 of whom had a recovery time of more than 6 months. Therefore, that percentage is $\frac{140}{291} \times 100 \approx 48.11$. To find the difference, subtract to get $57.731 - 48.11 = 9.621$. The question asks for the difference rounded to the nearest percent, so the correct answer is (A).

16. **D** The question involves a ratio, so use the Ratio Box. The top row is the ratio row, so fill in 3 under One Knee and 7 under Both Knees in the top row. The bottom row is the Actual Numbers. Since there is a total of 151 + 140 = 291 patients in the conventional physical therapy, fill in 291 under Total in the bottom row.

	One Knee	Both Knees	Total
Ratio	3	7	
Multiplier			
Actual Numbers			291

Add across the top row to get 10 under the total. Multiply downward. Since 10 × 29.1 = 291, the multiplier is 29.1 Fill in 29.1 across the entire middle row. Multiply downward again to get 3 × 29.1 = 87.3 and 7 × 29.1 = 203.7.

	One Knee	Both Knees	Total
Ratio	3	7	10
Multiplier	29.1	29.1	29.1
Actual Numbers	87.3	203.7	291

The question asks for the *best approximation* of the number of patients who had both knees replaced, so round the number in the Actual Numbers row under Both Knees to 204. The correct answer is (D).

17. **C** The question asks for the probability a patient in the study selected at random will have a recovery time of more than 6 months. To find a probability, set up $\frac{\text{\# of outcomes that fit the requirement}}{\text{total \# of possible outcomes}}$. Because the question states that *a patient in the study is selected at random*, the *total # of possible outcomes* is the total number of patients in the study, which is 485. Because the question asks for the probability that the patient *will have a recovery time of more than 6 months*, the *# of outcomes that fit the requirement* is the total number of patients with a recovery time of more than 6 months. Make sure to include both those in experimental physical therapy and those in conventional physical therapy to get a total of 112 + 140 = 252. Therefore, the probability is $\frac{252}{485} \approx 0.5196$. The question says *is closest to*, so select the closest choice. The correct answer is (C).

18. **D** The question asks for the equation of a circle. The equation of a circle can be written in the form $(x - h)^2 + (y - k)^2 = r^2$, where (h, k) is the center of the circle and r is the radius of the circle. Eliminate (A) and (C), which have subtraction between the binomials instead of addition. Look at the two remaining choices. The choices differ both in the center and in the radius, so eliminate one choice using any of this information. Since the center is (-3, 5), $h = -3$ and $(x - h) = (x + 3)$. Also, since the radius is 4, $r^2 = 16$. Using either of those pieces, eliminate (B). The correct answer is (D).

19. **A** The question asks how many additional hours a performance will need to be for the piano player to charge an additional dollar. There are numbers in the choices, but because the two variables are given in terms of each other, this can be solved using Plugging In. Let $t = 2$. If $t = 2$, then $C = 100(2) + 50 = 250$. The question asks about the piano player charging an additional dollar. Since the amount charged is C, let $C = 250 + 1 = 251$. Plug $C = 251$ into the equation to get $251 = 100t + 50$. Solve for t. Subtract 50 from both sides to get $201 = 100t$. Divide both sides by 100 to get $2.01 = t$. The question asks for the *additional* hours, so subtract the two values of t to get $2.01 - 2 = 0.01$. This is equivalent to $\frac{1}{100}$, so the correct answer is (A).

20. **B** The question asks how many yards of fencing are needed to surround each area. There are numbers in the answer choices, so Plug In the Answers. Start with one of the middle choices. Try (B). If 40 yards of fencing are needed for each area, then the perimeter of each area is 40 yards. Begin with the square area. If the perimeter of a square area is 40 yards, then each side is $40 \div 4 = 10$ yards. The side of the octagon is 5 yards shorter than this, which is $10 - 5 = 5$. The perimeter of the octagon must match the perimeter of the square, so find the perimeter of the octagon, which is $8 \times 5 = 40$. Since this is equal to the perimeter of the square area, the correct answer is (B).

21. **B** The question asks for the value of k, which is the x-coordinate of one of the x-intercepts. According to the question, the graph of f is a parabola, which means it has vertical symmetry. In a parabola, the axis of symmetry goes through the vertex. Since the vertex is at $(5, -3)$, the axis of symmetry is $x = 5$. Since one of the x-intercepts is $(3, 0)$, the other must be equidistant from the axis of symmetry. Since the distance from 3 to 5 is 2, the distance from 5 to k must also be 2. Therefore, $k = 5 + 2 = 7$. The correct answer is (B).

22. **D** The question asks for an equivalent form of the function that displays values not included in the domain as constants or coefficients. Determine what is not in the domain. In a rational function, a value of x is not in the domain if it makes the denominator equal to 0. To find these values, set the denominator equal to 0 to get $3x^2 - 3x - 18 = 0$. To get the roots of the quadratic, put the quadratic in factored form. Therefore, the correct answer must have the denominator written in factored form. Factor 3 from $3x^2 - 3x - 18$ to get $3(x^2 - x - 6)$. Now factor $(x^2 - x - 6)$ to get $3(x - 3)(x + 2)$. Therefore, the denominator must be written in the form $3(x - 3)(x + 2)$. Eliminate (A), (B), and (C), which don't include this. The correct answer is (D).

23. **B** The question asks how many times the surface area of the volleyball is compared to the surface area of the tennis ball. Because the question does not ask for either surface area but only for the relationship between the two, this can be solved using Plugging In. Plug in the radius of the tennis ball as 2. If $r = 2$, then $SA = 4\pi r^2 = 4\pi(2)^2 = 16\pi$ for the tennis ball. The radius of the volleyball is three time the radius of the tennis ball, so, for the volleyball, plug in $r = 3 \times 2 = 6$. If $r = 6$, then $SA = 4\pi r^2 = 4\pi(6)^2 = 144\pi$ for the volley ball. Translate the question into an equation. The term *how many* translates to the variable. Use y. The word *times* translates to "multiplication." The term *the surface area of the tennis ball* translates to 16π. The word *is* translates to "equals." The term *the*

surface area of a volley ball translates to 144π. Solve the equation $y \times 16\pi = 144\pi$. Divide both sides by 16π to get $y = 9$. The correct answer is (B).

24. **B** The question asks for the velocity, in terms of t. Since there are variables in the choices, Plug In. According to the question, the particle accelerates from 20 to 50 meters per second in 10 seconds, so when $t = 10$, the velocity is 50. Let 50 be the target number, and plug $t = 10$ into each of the choices, eliminating any that are not equal to 50. Choice (A) is $V = -50 + 3(10) = -20$, so eliminate (A). Choice (B) is $V = 20 + 3(10) = 50$, so keep (B), but check the other answers just in case. Choice (C) is $V = -20 - 3(10) = -50$, so eliminate (C). Choice (D) is $50 - 3(10) = 20$, so eliminate (D). The correct answer is (B).

25. **C** The question asks for $h(x + 3)$. There are variables in the answer choices, so Plug In. Let $x = 2$. If $x = 2$, then $h(x + 3) = h(2 + 3) = h(5) = 2(5)^2 - 7(5) - 3 = 2(25) - 35 - 3 = 50 - 38 = 12$. Therefore, the target is 12. Plug $x = 2$ into each choice and eliminate any for which $h(5)$ is not equal to 12. In (A), $h(2 + 3) = 2(2^2) - 7(2)$, so $h(5) = 2(4) - 14 = 8 - 14 = -6$. Eliminate (A). In (B), $h(2 + 3) = 2(2^2) - 7(2) - 6$, so $h(5) = 2(4) - 14 - 6 = 8 - 20 = -12$. Eliminate (B). In (C), $h(2 + 3) = 2(2^2) + 5(2) - 6$, so $h(5) = 2(4) + 10 - 6 = 8 + 4 = 12$. Keep (C). In (D), $h(2 + 3) = 2(2^2) - 23(2) + 15$, so $h(5) = 2(4) - 46 + 15 = 8 - 31 = -23$. Eliminate (D). The correct answer is (C).

26. **A** The question asks for the intersection of two lines, which can be found as a solution to both equations. There are numbers in the choices, so Plug In the Answers. Start with the simpler equation. Plug in each choice into the second equation. For (A), $\frac{1}{4}(8) = 2$, so keep (A). For (B), $\frac{1}{4}(16) = 4$, so keep (B). For (C), $\frac{1}{4}(24) = 6$, so keep (C). For (D), $\frac{1}{4}(32) = 8$, so keep (D). Since all four choices are solutions to the second equation, plug them into the first equation. For (A), the equation becomes $10(8) - 62 = 9(2)$. This simplifies to $80 - 62 = 18$ or $18 = 18$. This is true, so keep (A). Since the coordinates in (A) work in both equations, (A) must contain the intersection of the two lines. The correct answer is (A).

27. **C** The question asks what type of decay describes the relationship between the amount of carbon-14 and time. Two of the choices describe linear decay and two describe exponential decay. Linear decay describes a relationship in which the decrease is by a constant amount. Exponential decay describes a relationship in which the decrease is by a constant factor or percent. Eliminate (A) and (D), which reverse the definitions. According to the question, the amount of carbon-14 halves every 5,730 years. This is a reduction by the same factor. To better see this, plug in. If there are 100 grams of carbon-14 to start, then in 5,730 years, there will be 50 grams. In another 5,730 years, there will be 25 grams. Since the amount of the decrease was not constant, eliminate (B). The correct answer is (C).

28. **2 or 18** The question asks for the sum of x and y and provides a system of equations. Because both equations are set equal to y, set them equal to each other to get $x + 8 = x^2 - x - 7$. Because this is a quadratic equation, get one side equal to 0. Subtract 8 from both sides to get $x = x^2 - x - 15$, and subtract x from both sides to get $0 = x^2 - 2x - 15$. Factor the right side. Find two numbers with

a product of –15 and a sum of –2. These are 3 and –5. Therefore, the equation can be written as $0 = (x + 3)(x - 5)$. Set each factor equal to 0 to get $x + 3 = 0$ and $x - 5 = 0$. The question asks for one possible sum of x and y, so it is necessary to get only one value of x. Therefore, one possible solution is to subtract 3 from both sides of $x + 3 = 0$ to get $x = -3$. Plug this value of x into the first equation to get $y = -3 + 8 = 5$. Therefore, one possible sum of x and y is $-3 + 5 = 2$. Alternatively, to get the other possible solution, add 5 to both sides to $x - 5 = 0$ to get $x = 5$. Plug this value of x into the first equation to get $y = 5 + 8 = 13$. Therefore, the other possible sum of x and y is $5 + 13 = 18$. The correct answer is either 2 or 18.

29. **20** The question asks for the least number of boxes of platinum that the jeweler can order to satisfy the requirements. Translate the requirements into inequalities. Let the number of gold boxes purchased be g and the number of platinum boxes purchases be p. Since there are two ounces of gold per box, the total weight of the gold purchased is $2g$. Since there are five ounces of platinum per box, the total weight of the platinum is $5p$. Therefore, the total weight of the metal is $2g + 5p$. The jeweler wants to purchase at least 90 ounces of metal, so $2g + 5p \geq 90$. Similarly, a box of gold costs \$2,500, so the total cost, in dollars, of the gold is $2,500g$. A box of platinum costs \$7,500, so the total cost, in dollars, of the platinum is $7,500p$. Therefore, the total cost of the metal is $2,500g + 7,500p$. This must be *at least* \$170,000, so $2,500g + 7,500p \geq 170,000$. According to the question, the jeweler already ordered 10 boxes of gold, so plug in $g = 10$ to get $2(10) + 5p \geq 90$ or $20 + 5p \geq 90$ for the first inequality and $2,500(10) + 7,500p \geq 170,000$ or $25,000 + 7,500p \geq 170,000$ for the second inequality. Solve each inequality. Subtract 20 from both sides of $20 + 5p \geq 90$ to get $5p \geq 70$. Divide both sides by 5 to get $p \geq 14$. Now look at the other inequality. Subtract 25,000 from both sides of $25,000 + 7,500p \geq 170,000$ to get $7,500p \geq 145,000$. Divide both sides by 7,500 to get $p \geq 19.\overline{3}$. The least value of p that satisfies both inequalities is $p = 20$. The correct answer is 20.

30. **160** The question asks for the value of h, which is the number of hours jogged during the month of December. The question says that the total distance jogged each of the two months was the same. Find the distance jogged in November. The question says that Robert jogged at an average pace of 8 miles per hour, and the chart says that he jogged for 140 hours. To find the total distance, multiply the rate by the time to get $8 \times 140 = 1,120$ miles. In December, the rate is 7 miles per hour and the total distance is also 1,120. To find the time, set up the equation $1,120 = 7h$. Divide both sides by 7 to get $h = 160$. The correct answer is 160.

31. **636** The question asks for the total distance jogged during June. According to the graph, Robert spent 120 hours jogging. The question says that Robert spent 70% his jogging time at the slower pace, which was 5 miles per hour. Therefore, he spent $\frac{70}{100} \times 120 = 84$ hours at 5 miles per hour. To find the distance, multiply the rate by the time to get $84 \times 5 = 420$ miles. He spent the rest of the time at the faster pace. The remaining time is $120 - 84 = 36$, so he spent 36 hours at 6 miles per hour for a distance of $36 \times 6 = 216$. Thus, the total distance traveled for the month is $420 + 216 = 636$ miles. The correct answer is 636.

RAW SCORE CONVERSION TABLE   SECTION AND TEST SCORES

Raw Score (# of correct answers)	Reading Test Score	Writing and Language Test Score	Math Section Score	Raw Score (# of correct answers)	Reading Test Score	Writing and Language Test Score	Math Section Score
0	8	8	160	25	22	26	510
1	9	8	180	26	23	26	520
2	10	9	200	27	23	27	530
3	11	9	210	28	24	28	540
4	12	10	220	29	24	28	550
5	12	10	240	30	25	29	560
6	13	11	260	31	26	29	570
7	13	11	280	32	26	30	580
8	14	12	300	33	27	30	590
9	14	13	320	34	28	31	600
10	15	14	330	35	28	32	610
11	15	15	350	36	29	33	620
12	16	15	370	37	30	33	630
13	16	16	380	38	30	34	640
14	17	17	400	39	31	34	650
15	17	17	410	40	32	35	660
16	18	18	420	41	33	36	670
17	18	19	430	42	33	37	680
18	19	20	440	43	34	37	690
19	19	21	450	44	35	38	700
20	20	22	460	45	36		710
21	20	22	470	46	37		730
22	21	23	480	47	38		740
23	21	24	490	48			760
24	22	25	500				

CONVERSION EQUATION   SECTION AND TEST SCORES

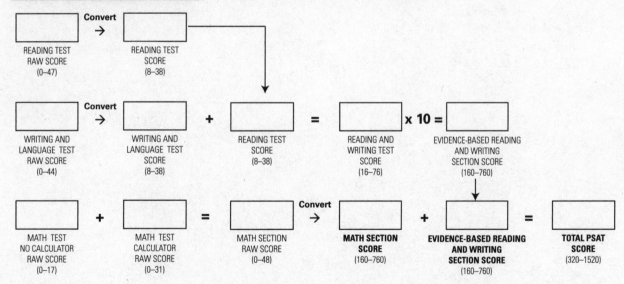

NOTES

NOTES

NOTES

NOTES

NOTES

NOTES

NOTES

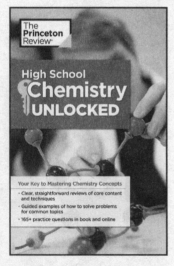